Globalisation for the Common Good: An Inter-Faith Perspective

Proceedings of the 6th Annual Conference

A Non-Violent Path to Conflict Resolution and Peacebuilding

Fatih University, Istanbul,
5–9 July 2007

Edited by

Kamran Mofid (Founder-Convener)
Alparslan Açıkgenç
Kevin J. McGinley
Şammas Salur

Fatih University Press
Istanbul

FIRST PUBLISHED IN ISTANBUL BY FATIH UNIVERSITY PRESS

Copyright © FATIH UNIVERSITY PRESS 2008

Kamran Mofid, Alparslan Açıkgenç, Kevin J. McGinley, Şammas Salur (eds), *Globalisation for the Common Good: An Inter-Faith Perspective— Proceedings of the Sixth International Conference*

ISBN
978-975-303-094-6

FSF Printing House
Telephone: +90 212 690 89 89

FATIH UNIVERSITY PRESS,
Büyükçekmece 34500, Istanbul, Turkey.
Telephone: +90 212 866 33 00
Fax: +90 212 866 33 37
Website: http://www.fatih.edu.tr

A Non-Violent Path to Conflict Resolution and Peacebuilding

What is to be done, O Moslems? For I do not recognise myself.
I am not of the East, nor of the West, nor of the land, nor of the sea;
I am not of Nature's mint, nor of the circling heaven.
I am not of earth, nor of water, nor of air, nor of fire;
I am not of the empyrean, nor of the dust, nor of existence, nor of entity.
I am not of India, nor of China, nor of Bulgaria, nor of Saqsin.
I am not of the kingdom of 'Iraqian, nor of the country of Khorasan
I am not of this world, nor of the next, nor of Paradise, nor of Hell.
I am not of Adam, nor of Eve, nor of Eden and Rizwan.
My place is the Placeless; my trace is the Traceless;
'Tis neither body nor soul, for I belong to the soul of the Beloved.
I have put duality away; I have seen that the two worlds are one;
One I seek, One I know, One I see, One I call.
He is the first, He is the last, He is the outward, He is the inward;
I am intoxicated with Love's cup, the two worlds have passed out of my ken;
If once in my life I spent a moment without thee,
From that time and from that hour I repent of my life.
If once in this world I win a moment with thee,
I will trample on both worlds; I will dance in triumph for ever.

Rumi

This book is dedicated to all those who have inspired us

CONTENTS

Foreword   i
Oğuz Borat

Our Common Good Journey   iii

Conference Attendee List   ix

Messages to the Conference   xiii

INTRODUCTION

The Role of Education in a Globalised World   xxi
Hüseyin Çelik, Ph.D., Minister of National Education
The Republic of Turkey

The Globalisation for the Common Good Initiative: xxv
An Introduction and Mission Statement
Kamran Mofid

OPENING CEREMONY

Welcome Address   1
Oğuz Borat

Introductory Address   2
Kamran Mofid

KEYNOTE LECTURES: GLOBALISATION, FAITH, AND THE COMMON GOOD

Difference is Beautiful   7
Alparslan Açıkgenç

The Quest for Justice and Peace: 13
Contributions of Islam to Peacebuilding
and Conflict Resolution

Murad Wilfried A. Hofmann
Alliance of World Religions to Promote   28
Pro-active Spirituality
Swami Agnivesh

PLENARY PAPERS: MOBILISING FOR A GLOBAL MARSHALL PLAN

Human Security and the Global Marshall Plan   39
James Bernard Quilligan

Utopian Imperative and the   62
Global Marshall Plan Initiative
Bruce Matthews

Steering Globalization into a Better Future: How to Reach   72
a Planetary Consciousness through a Global Marshall Plan
Frithjof Finkbeiner and Franz Josef Radermacher

TRANSFORMING GLOBALISATION—ENGAGING RELIGIONS

World Council of Muslims for Interfaith Relations   81
and Interreligious Engagement Project (IEP21)
Ahmad Khan

Exit the Veil, Enter Freedom and Autonomy?   86
Shamim Samani and Dora Marinova

Islamic Peace Paradigm and Islamic Peace Education: 101
Sezai Ozcelik and Ayşe Dilek Oğretir

Reconciliation, Tolerance, Coexistence: 119
The Islamic Perspective
Mohamad Iwhida Ahmed

PEACE EDUCATION AND SPIRITUALITY TRANSFORMING GLOBALISATION

Conflict Resolution through Scholarly Exchange: 131
The Role of the American Institute of Iranian Studies
Erica Ehrenberg

A Holistic, Evolving View of Peace   141
with Implications for Development
Linda Groff

Globalization and a Mathematical Journey   159
Eiko Tyler

Emphasis on Teaching Ethics in Business Schools: 176
The Recent Experience in US Higher Education
Jamshid Damooe

WAGING PEACE: RELIGION-BASED PEACEMAKING

Religion in Public Life   185
Alan Race

A *Dharmic Perspective*: Compassionate Understanding   196
and "Globalisation for the Common Good" Discourse
Andrew Wicking

The Power of Ahimsā (Nonviolence):   203
Gandhi's Gift to a Violent World
Ruwan Palapathwala

PLENARY PAPERS: MASS MEDIA, GLOBAL COMMUNICATION, AND PEACEMAKING

Mass Media, Globalisation and Information Gap   211
Yahya Kahmalipour

Globalization and Glocalization: Leveraging   215
Technological Tools to Serve the Common Good
Christopher Kosovich

Mass Media as an Instrument in   223
Counter-Terrorism Programs
Irena Chiru

PLENARY PAPERS: RELIGIONS, DIALOGUE, PEACE, AND CONFLICT RESOLUTION

Inter-Civilisational Dialogue: A Path   237
To Conflict Transformation
Joseph A. Camilleri

Global Multiculturalism versus   255
"The War of Cultures"
Ada Aharoni

In Vain: Violence in God's Name   272
Jim Kenney

Three Faiths Forum: A Path to Peace Building   281
Sidney L. Shipton

SECURITY AND PEACE: SOCIO-POLITICAL, ECONOMIC, AND CULTURAL PERSPECTIVES

The Arrow that Pierced Duality: From Dualism to   287
Holism–Cultivating a Culture of Peace in the "First World"
Mayumi Futamura

The United Nations Peace Force in Cyprus as   303
the Psychiatrist of Global Governmentality on the
"Dangerous" Cypriot Population
Nejdan Yildiz

Education for Security in Romania: 322
A Survey of Young People
Ella Magdalena Ciuperca

INTER-FAITH DIALOGUE, INTERNATIONAL MEDIATION AND CONFLICT

A False Dawn?: The Oslo Peace Accord as a Case Study   337
of International Mediation, Conflict Management
and Religious Fundamentalism
Orna Almog

Happiness and the Eye of the Beholder: The Deeper   344
Implications of GNH for a Morally Distracted World
Ross McDonald

BUSINESS, PHILOSOPHY AND LAW IN THE AGE OF GLOBALISATION

The Dilemma of Hudud and International Human Rights: 357
Proposing a Benevolent Mechanism
Shahrul Mizan Ismail

A Sustainability Agenda for Intellectual Property   376
and Indigenous Knowledge
Dora Marinova

PHILOSOPHICAL, SPIRITUAL AND PSYCHOLOGICAL ASPECTS OF PEACE AND JUSTICE

Rediscovering the Sense and Role of Common Good   395
in the Globalized Society
M. Lorenz Moisés J. Festín

From Rawls to a Worldwide Welfare System: 405
A Philosophical Draft of Arithmetical
Justice in Redistribution
Frank Tillmann

The Psychological Aspects of Peace   415
Bahman Dadgostar and Ann Hallock

THE ISTANBUL DECLARATION   433

FOREWORD

The annual conference of the Globalisation for the Common Good Initiative had ranged far across the world before 2006, through England, Russia, Dubai, Kenya, and Hawaii. The GCG conference created and continues to create an ever-widening international community of scholars, forging links and establishing dialogues across national, cultural, and religious boundaries and putting into practice the movement's core philosophy: that globalisation need not be defined merely in terms of impersonal market forces, but can be a power for good, building spiritual bonds that can unite humanity and bring different cultures and faiths closer together.

Istanbul was the perfect location for the Sixth Conference on Globalisation for the Common Good. Straddling two continents and with an astoundingly rich cultural history which has been shaped by Islam, Catholic and Orthodox Christianity, and Judaism, as well as by far-reaching and long-standing links to Europe, the Middle and Far East, Africa, and Russia and the Caucasus, the city is a living image of human life enriched by the inter-faith dialogue and cross-cultural fertilisation that the GCG initiative seeks to foster across the globe. As a living bridge between East and West, Istanbul was the perfect site to explore the means to achieve conflict resolution and peace-building through non-violent means.

Fatih University was honoured to host this conference, seeing it as fully in harmony with the university's goal of promoting education as a means of integrating local cultural perspectives within a global framework. For five wonderful days, we at Fatih University savoured a lively and enriching dialogue that flowed smoothly across the borders of cultural, national, and religious difference. This book, wide ranging and illuminating as the essays it contains are, can give only a taste of the positive and fruitful diversity which made the conference so memorable. Scholars, diplomats, peace workers, journalists, and students freely mingled and disciplinary boundaries dissolved as scientists, theologians, artists, and social scientists constructively exchanged views on religion, faith, and peace. Bonds of understanding and friendship were formed that will last well into the future and which bode well for the goals of the Globalisation for the Common Good movement. We at Fatih University are proud to have been host to such an enlightening set of multi-cultural inter-faith encounters and look forward to seeing the many relationships and dialogues established here continuing and being built on in future GCG conferences, in Melbourne, Chicago and beyond.

Oğuz Borat, President of Fatih University

i

OUR COMMON GOOD JOURNEY[1]

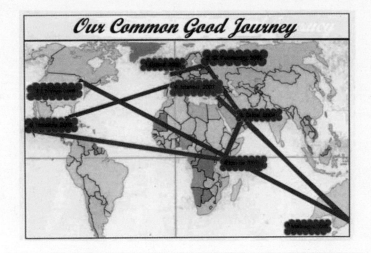

---

[1] Many thanks to Mr Peter Townend, Coventry, UK, for preparing the journey map.

Oxford, UK, 2002

St Petersburg, Russia, 2003

Dubai, UAE, 2004

Kericho, Kenya, 2005

Honolulu, Hawaii, 2006

Istanbul, Turkey, 2007

From the Middle East to Asia Pacific:
Arc of Conflict or Dialogue of Cultures and Religions?
7th Annual Conference
Globalisation for the Common Good—An Interfaith perspective
30 June - 4 July 2008
Trinity College, University of Melbourne

Famously multicultural and multi-faith, Melbourne extends a warm welcome to the participants of the 7th Annual International meeting of the Globalisation for the Common Good Conference, 2008. Melbourne in its turn is proud to contribute to the ongoing success and increasing vitality of the Common Good initiative and to the spirit of friendship and constructive encounter that has followed this visionary conference series in its transit across the globe.

Importantly, the Melbourne conference is the first in the series to be held with a clear Asia-Pacific focus. It seeks to explore the far-reaching ramifications of conflict in the Middle East for the religious, cultural, and political landscape of the Asia-Pacific region, especially after September 11. This program is designed to achieve three objectives: to explore the far-reaching ramifications of conflict in the Middle East (broadly defined) for the religious, cultural and political landscape of the Asia-Pacific region; bring together in fruitful interaction the insights of several disciplinary traditions (in particular religious studies, cultural studies, international relations, history, sociology and law); and to illuminate and strengthen the connections between the Middle East and the geographic regions which constitute

Asia Pacific, in particular West Asia, South Asia, Northeast Asia, Southeast Asia and the South Pacific.

In developing this year's program it has been the firm intention of the Planning Committee for Melbourne 2008 to build on the fruitful interaction and high standard of scholarship exhibited at the Istanbul conference and exemplified in this publication. Moreover, with keynote contributions by a list of prominent international scholars and practitioners, strong postgraduate participation, and with the inclusion a number of significant public events, we, the Planning Committee for Melbourne 2008, look forward to a conference of enriching dialogue and significant impact for all involved.

Globalization: the Challenge to America
Eighth Annual Conference
Globalization for the Common Good: An Interfaith Perspective
May 31–June 4, 2009
Loyola University • Chicago, Illinois, USA

Loyola University, Chicago's Jesuit University, is delighted to announce that it will host the eighth annual conference of *Globalization for the Common Good.*

The Event will be a featured part of Loyola University's 2009 celebration of 100 years as a university.

The conference will also be the eighth in the annual international series, Globalization for the Common Good—An Interfaith Perspective (founded by Dr Kamran Mofid).

This major global conference is being convened by the Interreligious Engagement Project (IEP21), the Center for Global Studies at Purdue University Calumet, and Globalization for the Common Good (GCG).

It is jointly chaired by Dr William French (Loyola University), Mr Jim Kenney (IEP21), Dr Yahya Kamalipour (Purdue University Calumet), and Dr Kamran Mofid (GCG).

Previous conferences have been held in Oxford (2002), St Petersburg (2003), Dubai (2004), Kericho, Kenya (2005), Honolulu (2006), Istanbul (2007), and Melbourne (2008).

Conference Themes

The Conference will focus primarily on the status of the United States in the current dynamic of world affairs and the special role that America must play if globalization is to be guided toward the common good, both within the US and in the larger world.

Other thematic areas will also be addressed. They include (but are not limited to) the following:

- Globalization, Civilizational Dialogue, and the Role of the Global Interfaith Movement;
- The Global Environment: Climate, Habitat, Water, Energy, and All Life;
- The Struggle for Social and Economic Justice and Universal Human Rights.

A Call for Papers will be announced in May 2008.

For background information on the initiative and details of previous conferences, visit: http://www.globalisationforthecommongood.info/. To access the online Journal of Globalization for the Common Good, visit http://www.commongoodjournal.com. For information on the 2008 Conference in Melbourne, Australia (June 30–July 4), visit: http://www.globalisationforthecommongood.info/conferences/australia-conference-2008/.

CONFERENCE ATTENDEE LIST

Dr Alparslan Açıkgenç, Vice-Rector and Dean, Faculty of Arts and Sciences, Fatih University, Istanbul, Turkey

Mr Swami Agnivesh, Member, International Peace Council (2003-), Chairperson, UN Trust Fund on Contemporary Form of Slavery (1994-2004), amongst others, India

Prof. Ada Aharoni, Founder, International President, IFLAC, Pave Peace, amongst others, Haifa, Israel

Mr Mohamad Iwhida Ahmed, PhD candidate, Department of Comparative Study of Religions, Charles University, Czech Republic

Dr Orna Almog, Faculty of Arts and Social Science, Kingston University, Surrey, UK

Mr Mustafa Akyol, Writer, Columnist (The WhitePath.com); Referans and Hurriyet Daily, Istanbul, Turkey

Prof. Dr Mahmut Aydin, Faculty of Divinity, Science of Philosophy and Theology, Sakarya University, Istanbul

Dr Margaret Brabant, Director, Centre for Citizenship and Community, Butler University, Indianapolis, USA

Prof. Dr Oğuz Borat, Rector, Fatih University, Istanbul, Turkey

Prof. Dr Omer Caha, Dean, Faculty of Economics and Administrative Sciences, Fatih University, Istanbul, Turkey

Prof. Joseph A. Camilleri, Director, Centre for Dialogue, La Trobe University, Melbourne, Australia

Mrs Rita Camilleri, Melbourne, Australia

Zuhal Unalp Cepel, Research Assistant, Department of International Relations, Dokuz Eylul University, Buca-Izmir, Turkey

Dr Irena Chiru, National Intelligence Academy, Bucharest, Romania

Dr Ella Ciuperca, National Intelligence Academy, Bucharest, Romania

Assist. Prof. Dr Abdulkadir Civan, Department of Economics, Fatih University, Istanbul, Turkey

Mrs Donna Corse, USA

Dr Bahman Dadgostar, Licensed Clinical Psychologist, Pain Management and Behavioral Medicine, California, USA

Prof. Jamshid Damooei, Co-Director, Centre for Leadership and Values, California Lutheran University, USA

Ms Ruhsen Dizdaroglu, Insieme tours, Istanbul, Turkey

Dr Erica Ehrenberg, Executive Director, American Institute of Iranian Studies, USA

Rev. Fr. Dr M. Lorenz Moises J Festin, San Carlos Seminary, Makati City, Philippines

Frithjof Finkbeiner, Global Marshall Plan Initiative Coordinator, Hamburg, Germany

Mr Yoav Frankel, Research Associate, Interfaith-Encounter Association, Israel

Ms Marjorie Frey, Common Ground Global Initiative, Chicago, USA

Ms Mayumi Futamura, Rotary World Peace Fellow, Rotary Centre for Peace, University of Queensland, St. Lucia, Australia

Mr Richard Garrett, USA

Mr Metin Gorgec, Insieme tours, Istanbul, Turkey

Prof. Linda Groff, California State University, Carson, USA

Prof. Dr Sinasi Gunduz, Faculty of Divinity, Istanbul University, Turkey

Prof. Dr Kenan Gursoy, Faculty of Arts and Science, Galatasaray University, Turkey

Mr Gordon Hayles, Coventry, UK

Mrs Jackie Hayles, Coventry, UK

Prof. Dr Omer Faruk Harman, the Councillor/ Presidency of Religious Affairs, the Republic of Turkey in France

Dr Murad Wilfried A. Hofmann, Counsellor, Central Council of Muslims in Germany (ZMD), German Diplomat and author, Director of Information for NATO at Brussels (1983-1987), German Ambassador to Algeria (1987-1990) and Ambassador to Morocco (1990-1994), Germany

Mr Shahrul Mizan Ismail, Public Law Department, International Islamic University of Malaysia, Kuala Lumpur, Malaysia

Prof. Yahya R. Kamalipour, Head, Department of Communication, Purdue University Calumet, USA

Mrs Mah Kamalipour, USA

Ms Niki Kamalipour, USA

Ms Shirin Kamalipour, USA

Ms Lauri Kamm, Administrator, Common Ground, Chicago, USA

Prof. Dr Bekir Karliga, Faculty of Divinity, Marmara University, Istanbul, Turkey

Mr Jim Kenney, Executive Director, Interreligious Engagement Project [IEP21], Chicago, USA

Mrs Cetta Kenney, IEP21, Photo Editor, *Interreligious Insight*, Chicago, USA

Dr Irfan Ahmad Khan, President, World Council of Muslims for Interfaith Relations, Chicago, USA

Prof. Dr Mahmut Erol Kilic, Faculty of Divinity, Marmara University, Turkey

Mr Zekihan Kiziloglu, Insieme tours, Istanbul, Turkey

Assoc. Prof. Dr Havva Kok, Department of International Relations, Hacettepe University, Ankara, Turkey

Christopher Kosovich, Postgraduate candidate, Purdue University Calumet, USA

Prof. Esmail Koushanpour, Common Ground Global Initiative, Chicago, USA

Jenny Koushanpour, Common Ground Global Initiative, Chicago, USA

Rev. Dr Kevin Long, Rector, St. Thomas More College, University of Western Australia, Crawley, Australia

Mr Todd Lorentz, Information Coordinator, Centre for Global Negotiations (USA), Edmonton, Canada

Assoc. Prof. Dora Marinova, Head, Institute for Sustainability and Technology Policy, Murdoch University, Murdoch, Australia

Dr Bruce Matthews, Bard College, New York, USA

Dr Ross McDonald, Co-ordinator, Business, Society and Culture Programme, University of Auckland Business School, Auckland, New Zealand

Dr Kamran Mofid (Founder-Convenor), Founder, Globalisation for the Common Good Initiative, Coventry, UK

Mrs Anne Mofid, Coventry, UK

Prof. Hassan Nejad, Antioch College, Yellow Springs, OH, USA

Mrs Behrokh Nejad, Yellow Springs, OH, USA

Ms Nancy Nielsen, San Francisco, USA

Dr Ayşe Dilek Ogretir, Vocational Education Faculty, Gazi University, Turkey

Dr Sezai Ozcelik, Institute for Conflict Analysis and Resolution, George Mason University, USA

Assoc. Prof. Dr Ibrahim Ozdemir, Director of Foreign Affairs, Ministry of Education, Turkey

Dr Ruwan Palapathwala, Melbourne College of Divinity, Trinity College, University of Melbourne, Australia

Mr James B. Quilligan, Managing Director, Centre for Global Negotiations, Philadelphia, USA

Rev. Dr Alan Race, Editor-in-Chief, *Interreligious Insight*; IEP21, Leicester, UK

Marshalee Ray, Chair, Common Ground Global Initiative, Chicago, USA

Ms Farahnaz Rezaei, Member of the Women Cultural ·Social Society-WCSS, State of Kuwait

Nora Rowley, M.D., Interreligious Engagement Project, Chicago, USA

Dr Sammas Salur (Co-convenor 2007), Department of Public Administration, Fatih University, Istanbul, Turkey

Dr Raviv Schwartz, Research Fellow, Harold Hartog School of Government and Policy, Tel Aviv University, Israel

Ms Shamin Samani, PhD candidate, Institute for Sustainability and Technology Policy, Murdoch University, Murdoch, Australia

Mr Sidney L. Shipton OBE KFO, Co-ordinator, The Three Faiths Forum, London, UK

Mrs Judith Shipton, London, UK

Dr Keyvan Tabari, Attorney-at-Law, USA

Mr Frank Tillmann, PhD candidate, Faculty of Philosophy, Martin Luther University, Halle-Wittenberg, Germany

Mr Peter Townend, Coventry, UK

Mrs Kate Townend, Coventry, UK

Prof. Eiko Tyler, Chaminade University, Honolulu, USA

Mr William A. Tyler, Honolulu, USA

Ms Erica Tyler, PhD candidate, Department of Anthropology, The Ohio State University, Columbus, USA

Mr Cemal Usak, Secretary General, Intercultural Dialogue Platform, Istanbul, Turkey

Mr Erol User, Istanbul, Turkey

Mr Andrew Wicking, PhD candidate, Melbourne College of Divinity, Trinity College, University of Melbourne, Australia

Mr Nejdan Yildiz, Final year student, International Relations Programme, Istanbul Bilgi University, Istanbul, Turkey

A SELECTION OF MESSAGES TO THE CONFERENCE FROM FRIENDS WHO COULD NOT BE WITH US IN ISTANBUL

"I am writing to congratulate Dr Mofid and all his colleagues for organizing a very important conference on a timely issue at a critical juncture in the life of our global community. I wish I could be present at the meeting and had the opportunity to engage in the important dialogue that will be undertaking at the event. The global scene is increasingly uglier with respect to a more just human living condition. However, efforts of colleagues like you give us hope that things could change for better, and for that I am grateful".

Hooshang Amirahmadi, Professor and Director, Center for Middle Eastern Studies, Rutgers University, NJ, USA

....

"As the twentieth century closed and the new world reality emerged post-1989, globalization became the new buzzword. On entering the 21st century, we are already increasingly aware that in our fragile interdependent world, including every human being in development and taking environmental sustainability seriously are imperative. The global and local are increasingly enmeshed: the global is local, and vice-versa, in our complex world. A new focus on rediscovering and supporting the "Common Good" is not before time. While I sincerely regret not being present, may I wish the conference well and may the participants' deliberations bear practical fruit."

Rt. Hon. John Battle MP (Leeds West, UK); Minister of State, Department of Trade and Industry, 1997; Minister of State, Foreign Office, 1999-2001; Advisor to Prime Minister Tony Blair on Inter-faith matters, 2001-2007

....

"May I send my very best wishes to all participants in the Conference on 'Globalisation for the Common Good' to be held in Istanbul in July. I am sorry not to be with you, but, sadly the dates clash with teaching and other commitments. The programme looks fascinating and highly significant. Istanbul is a good place to meet as Turkey has a vital contribution to make to the international and to the interfaith community. The visit to Konya, as I know from my own visit there, will be inspiring. May all that you do

affirm the words of Rumi that 'The religion of love is apart from all religions. For lovers the only religion and creed is God.'"

Rev Dr Marcus Braybrooke,
President of the World Congress of Faiths

....

"It is with great pleasure that I am sending these greetings and salutations to the participants of the Istanbul Conference on the theme "Globalization for the Common Good". Unfortunately other commitments prevent me from joining you. In my view, this is a highly significant event. Globalization today has many meanings, and not all of them are salutary. We have a globalization of the market, a globalization of weapons and "terror wars," and a globalization of hatred and ill will. But we have very little in terms of a globalization for the "common good". Here a major effort is needed to save humanity from disaster. All the great world religions and all the great classical teachings of the past exhort us to work for the "common good" based on shared ethical standards and a common sense of justice. I applaud the organizers, and especially Dr Kamran Mofid, for their initiative, and I wish all participants a successful meeting and an enriching cross-cultural experience".

Professor Fred DALLMAYR, University of Notre Dame (USA), Member of the International Coordinating Committee of the "World Public Forum—"Dialogue of Civilizations," Member of the Scientific Committee of "RESET—Dialogue on Civilizations" Past President of the Society for Asian and Comparative Philosophy (SACP)

....

"On this occasion of the 6th Annual International Conference on an Inter-faith Perspective on Globalisation for the Common Good, the Asia-Europe Foundation extends its warm congratulations and sincere encouragement to the organisers. The topic of 'A Non-violent Path to Conflict resolution and Peacebuilding' is one that is crucial to all segments of society, including policymakers, NGO leaders, youth and religious leaders. We are confident that this conference will be a tremendous experience for all involved, bringing a new level of engagement between the stakeholders of this very important dialogue."

Bertrand Fort,
Deputy Executive Director,
Asia-Europe Foundation (ASEF), Singapore

"I send my greetings to all the participants at the Globalisation for the Common Good conference in Istanbul. It is now many years since I was there, and I wish that I could have been there with you now. I hope your conference, held in such a place, may forward a little the prospects of Turkey in due course joining the EU, and forming a bridge between Islam and Christianity. As the Persian poet-mystic Rumi wrote concerning the religions, 'The lamps are different, but the Light is the same: it comes from Beyond'. Have a good conference".

Prof. John Hick, Emeritus Prof, Birmingham University (UK), and the Claremont Graduate University, California; Vice-President, the British Society for the Philosophy of Religion and of the World Congress of Faiths

....

"Globalization for the Common Good is a tremendously important initiative—it should become the leading Motto in development strategies the world over! The individual consciousness, which is at the heart of all actions, needs to be at the basis of globalization, so that the universal principles of existence (the common good) become the guiding line in international relations. The spirit in man, the power of vision, the ideal of love are all elements that are essential if we want to see a real flowering of humanity, the real fulfilment of the possibilities of human life. We have to find a harmonious blend of the individual and collective life so that individuals and nations can develop successfully side by side. What is needed in this crucial juncture of time when clouds are sometimes covering the sun at the horizon, are leaders like Kamran Mofid and his team who tirelessly and selflessly work to guide the changes in the right directions. Thank you and keep up the great spirit!"

Michael S. Karlen, Secretary General, Comprehensive Dialogue among Civilizations (CDAC), Geneva, Switzerland

....

"Congratulations on the Conference on Globalization for the Common Good. Kamran Mofid has once again assembled an outstanding group of intellectuals who are paving the way toward a peaceful future. There is no more important task facing our globe today than spreading the idea that our own well-being (in whatever culture or nation or religion we are in) depends on the well-being of everyone else on the planet. We must replace the old ways of thinking about security as achievable through domination of the other, and move toward a new strategy for security that comes from

generosity and caring for the other. We in the Network of Spiritual Progressives are leading a movement in the US that seeks to encourage our country to publicly apologize for the terrible crimes committed by engaging in a war and occupation of Iraq. And after that apology to withdraw our armed forces, help fund an international force that can help rebuild Iraq, and launch a Global Marshall Plan to once and for all end global poverty, homelessness, hunger, inadequate education, inadequate health care, and to repair the global environment. As a Jew, I also support those movements that seek to end the Occupation of the West Bank and to create a peace that allows for Israel and Palestine to live together as two separate states cooperating politically and economically, and to achieve mutual reconciliation and genuine caring for each other. These projects may seem utopian to some, but a correct analysis of the global situation leads us to conclude that they are the survival necessities for the human race in the 21st century. It is precisely because this new spirit of mutual caring and generosity is at the heart of what is needed for our planet that I wish to bless your important work in Istanbul this summer of 2007. Your thinking is so very important and your ideas can provide guidance to the millions of people who wish to build a different kind of world".

**Rabbi Michael Lerner, Editor, Tikkun Magazine, www.tikkun.org
Chair, The Network of Spiritual Progressives
Author of 11 books, most recently:** *The Left Hand of God: Healing America's Political and Spiritual Crisis*
....

"It is my honor to send this message of support and appreciation for the Globalisation for the Common Good conference taking place in Istanbul. The aspiration of this conference and its related endeavors is nothing less than the vision of the ancient prophets of Israel—a world that shares universal moral values while maintaining the beauty of diverse identities and cultures. In the words of the prophet Isaiah 'and many <u>nations</u> shall go forth and say let us go up to the mountain of the Lord, and he will teach us of His ways and we will walk in His paths.... and they shall turn their swords into ploughshares and their spears into pruning hooks, <u>nation</u> shall not lift up sword against <u>nation</u> and they shall learn war no more.' (2v.3, 4). Indeed a universal morality that is not constructed through respect for diversity and cultural particularity is unsustainable and even dangerous. May your deliberations enhance a sense of appreciation of the particular characteristics of different cultures and societies together with a growing

consciousness of the unity of humankind and our intertwined and inextricable responsibility for one another."

Chief Rabbi David Rosen, KCSG, President, the International Jewish Committee for Interreligious Consultations (IJCIC), International Director of Interreligious Affairs, American Jewish Committee (AJC)

....

"I wish I could be with you for the Istanbul conference of Globalisation for the Common good. This series of conferences is extremely important in providing dialoguing and sharing of experience and knowledge for developing badly needed alternatives to currently extremely harmful neoliberal globalization. Now that the policies of the World Bank, the International Monetary Fund and the International Trade Organization, along with neoliberal economic and trade policies of many governments, are under heavy criticism for their damaging economic, social and political impacts, particularly by vast popular movements in Latin America, it is most timely to undertake productive discussions of how best to transform globalization for the benefit of all people around the world. Unless we rapidly create balanced and equitable international development that emphasizes human development, with respect for the cultures and needs of all peoples, violence and terror will increase significantly, compounding the ills of much of current international economic policy. Istanbul offers a major opportunity for greatly needed advances in creating a globalization that truly is for the common good".

Prof. Stephen Sachs, Coordinating Editor, *Nonviolent Change*, USA

....

"As Co-founder of the Three Faiths Forum, Muslim-Christian-Jewish trialogue, I am pleased to send this message of good will on the occasion of the 6th Annual International conference 'Globalisation for the Common Good, A Non-violent Path to Conflict Resolution and Peacebuilding' being held in Istanbul: The City of Understanding and Reconciliation between East and West on the 5th to the 9th July 2007.

I had the pleasure of attending the first "Globalisation for the Common Good" conference held in Oxford, together with Sidney Shipton, Co-ordinator of the Three Faiths Forum, who also attended the conference in St Petersburg, and will be making a Presentation in Istanbul.

The Three Faiths Forum stands for conflict resolution and peacebuilding between people of faith and indeed of no faith and the conferences which you have organised bringing together so many faith leaders world wide can only be for the benefit of humanity in this troubled world of ours. I and all my colleagues and the Advisory Board of the Three Faiths Forum send you our good wishes for a successful and practical conference."

SIR SIGMUND STERNBERG, Co-Founder, Three Faiths Forum, London, UK

INTRODUCTION

THE ROLE OF EDUCATION
IN A GLOBALIZED WORLD

Hüseyin Çelik, Ph.D.
Minister of National Education
The Republic of Turkey

No army can withstand the strength of an idea whose time has come.

Victor Hugo[1]

The moral development of a civilization is measured by the breadth of its sense of community.

Anatol Rapoport[2]

The Sixth Annual International Conference of the Globalisation for the Common Good initiative on "A Non-Violent Path to Conflict Resolution and Peacebuilding," which was held in beautiful Istanbul, once more underlined the role of education in a globalised world and our mutual commitments and responsibilities as a "human community" to overcome the challenges of the twenty-first century.

The phenomenon of globalisation which has resulted from the worldwide integration of economic and financial sectors is considered as one of the most widespread trends our time has ever witnessed. Therefore, I usually use the term globalisation not only as a challenge but also as an opportunity for mobilization of fresh ideas. I believe that the central role of education in responding to the challenges of globalisation for less-developed and developing countries and communities is enormous. In fact, education is the only tool for understanding the full implications of globalisation and responding to it. Although there are "confused and often conflicting definitions and conceptions" of globalisation,[3] here we will focus on one definition for our purpose. The main characteristic of

---

[1] Victor Hugo, *Histoire d'un Crime*, 4 vols (Paris: Sampson Low, 1877–78), Vol. 1, part 5, section 10.

[2] Anatol Rapaport, *Certainties and Doubts: A Philosophy of Life* (Montreal: Black Rose, 2000), pp. 295–96.

[3] Derrick L. Cogburn, "Globalization and the State in the Information Age: Thoughts on Requirements for Education and Learning, in *INFOethics'98, Ethical Legal and Societal Challenges of Cyberspace, Second International Congress, Congress Centre, Monte-Carlo, Principality of Monaco, October 1–3, 1998, Final Report and Proceedings* (Paris: UNESCO, 2000), pp. 260–75 (p. 263).
http://unesdoc.unesco.org/images/0012/001204/120452M.pdf

globalisation is "capitalist globalisation," that is "the globalisation of capital, which is at the core of all the economic, social, political and cultural trends that have been associated with conventional (and more superficial) notions of 'globalisation'."[4]

Therefore, we have to rethink the role of education as a mechanism to respond to the challenges of globalisation and to co-exist and live in peace and prosperity in a globalised world. If we dream of creating a better future for ourselves and for coming generations through "non-violent conflict resolution" and the "building of cultures of peace around the world" the key and major instrument is education. Therefore, I sincerely support and appreciate the finding of the conference that "education is the key that unlocks the door to globalisation for the common good."[5]

If one expects education to foster and nurture "inter-religious and inter-cultural understanding, awareness of interdependence, moral values, and global citizenship" (ibid.), we have to re-think our educational policies, especially our curricula, which are shaped according to the aspirations of nation-states in the first quarter of the twentieth century.

As we know, each nation-state has developed a system of education that fits into its political system and social fabric. So, the Republic of Turkey, which is *statist*, retaining for central government the dominant role in social and economic planning and policy, and strictly centralized through a sophisticated bureaucracy, designed an educational system according to the spirit of the early twentieth century. Now, in the twenty-first century and in a globalized world—a time during which religious and other cultural divisions are tearing apart the fabric of social life in many parts of the world—we have to re-affirm and underline the importance of a more democratic and humanistic education and the role that it can play in healing and challenging such conflicts and creating a better future. Moreover, such a democratic education can teach our children how to live in a multi-cultural society and global world, without being victims and preys of marginal and extremist groups.

Let me remind you that the Turkish public administration system, like other nation-states, was based upon a strict centralization through the highly centralized decision making body in the capital city of Ankara, with a division of responsibility among a number of ministries. The Turkish Education system, for example, is also over-centralized. Almost all decisions are taken by the Ministry of National Education.

---

[4] Glenn Rikowski, "Globalisation and Education: A Paper Prepared for the House of Commons Select Committee on Economic Affairs Inquiry into the Global Economy, January 22, 2002," firgoa.usc.es/drupal/?q=filestore2/download/4280, p. 1

[5] "Istanbul Declaration," see below, pp. 433.

Therefore, for the first time in the history of our country, the present government has been trying to decentralize the system and share power with local administrations. We believe that we must dedicate ourselves to the reform of our educational system for the "common good" and benefit of all—old and young alike, affluent and poor, majority and minority. We expect to fill the gap between different sectors of the society. In fact, the present government has been striving to develop a free, democratic, and tolerant society that can be a useful model for the rest of the Muslim world and region. However, like any reform movement in the history, we have been facing a lot of resistance from the establishment.

As you know, in totalitarian and strictly centralized systems, schools educate students to be obedient to the establishment. They try to create one-dimensional citizens. In any democratic political systems, however, children in school learn how to make decisions autonomously, how to lead, how to tolerate different opinions, to collaborate with and respect the rights of others—these are some of the most important values and attitudes promoted by democratic societies.

When we look at the core values of the curricula of nation-states, it is not surprising to observe that they are not only based on nation-states' values, but also have this one-dimensional mentality and spirit, which requires students to memorize and internalize what is believed to be true and correct, without a critical mind. This was understandable in the formation years of nation-states. However, in the age of globalisation we need to broaden our perspectives and foster a spirit of empathy for others in order to sustain the multicultural societies of twenty-first century. Therefore, we have to start to re-shape our educational systems if we want to respond to the major challenges of the twenty-first century, which are summarized and underlined as follows:

- Global poverty, hunger, disease, and unmet human life needs;
- International militarization and obscene levels of military spending;
- Unsustainable economic, political, cultural, and ecological structures of power;
- Social and economic injustice and the systematic violation of universal human rights;
- Worldwide gender inequity in the social, economic, political, legal, and religious spheres;
- Coercive violence against women and children, including the horror of children forced into combat;
- Rampant ecological degradation and disregard for the sacredness of all life;

- Intercultural and inter-religious ignorance, mistrust, fear, and hatred.

Education can play a central role in responding to these challenges and can open up new horizons for us and next generations. Therefore, I agree with Bertrand Russell, when he defines the goal of education as "to give a sense of the value of things other than domination, to help create wise citizens of a free community, to encourage a combination of citizenship with liberty, individual creativity, which means that we regard a child as a gardener regards a young tree, as something with an intrinsic nature which will develop into an admirable form given proper soil and air and light."[6]

So, education should provide the opportunity for one to know oneself, to get acquainted with culture, the arts, nature and the environment, society, religion, technology, and the universe through an integrated approach.

Education should enable one to gain experience and utilize it, to promote cognition, the asking of questions and finding of answers; it should teach one how to learn and to assess information. As Yunus Emre, a thirteenth century dervish from Anatolia who played an outstanding role in Turkish culture, literature, and philosophy, says,

Wisdom comes from knowing wisdom,
Wisdom means knowing oneself.
If you do not know yourself,
What is the point of reading books?[7]

Therefore, the spirit of a democratic education should not teach "gaining wealth, forgetting all but self." In a globalised world, we should develop a sense of togetherness: I agree with the environmentalists' motto which asserts that "we are all on the same boat." Otherwise, brutal competition and the lust for money can destroy our sense of community.

In short, Turkey with the recent reforms in its education system, its emphasis on education in democratic values for all, and its life-long education programs, seeks to be a good example in the region. If we are successful, it will be the success of the whole region. I wish success to and wholeheartedly support the efforts of the Common Good Initiative.

---

[6] Bertrand Russell, *Power* (New York: Routledge, 1939), p. 251.
[7] Yusuf Emre, *The Drop that Became the Sea*, trans. Kabir Helminski and Refik Algan (Shambhala: Boston MA, 1989).

THE GLOBALISATION FOR THE COMMON GOOD INITIATIVE: AN INTRODUCTION AND MISSION STATEMENT

Kamran Mofid

In 2002, the Globalisation for the Common Good Initiative began at Oxford. After six years and with six global conferences, books, and many articles, as well as its own web site and the Journal of Globalization for the Common Good to its credit, the movement has become known to and respected by many around the world. We have developed a successful track record of bringing together a diverse collection of scholars, researchers, NGO leaders, policymakers, young people, religious and spiritual leaders from around the world for intense discussions on a spiritual and value-centred vision of globalisation and the common good. Indeed, we have now moved from research and discussion to articulating position papers and an active agenda for change in the international community and its economic and development policies.

Today, many people from all walks of life and different parts of the world are questioning many aspects of the moral and spiritual free-zone of life and existence. Are there sources from which we can draw meaning and wholeness to our lives? Are there resources of spirituality that would nourish and sustain our lives in this complex, pluralistic, and ever changing world? Why, when we humans have such a great capacity for caring, sharing, consciousness, wisdom, and creativity, has our world seen so much of cruelty, wars, insensitivity, injustice, and destruction?

These questions and many more are being raised in our day not only by those traditionally identified with religious traditions; they are the questions of scientists, politicians, economists, educators, psychologists, people in the business world, working people, and all who experience an emptiness and a lack of purpose and orientation to human life. Young people in particular call for an alternate vision that is centred on values that give meaning to human existence.

What matters most today, more than ever before, it seems, are money and economics, the "loadsamoney" culture and mentality. This philosophy of materialism and consumerism has brought us a bitter harvest. Indeed, the ecological degradation and environmental vandalism that we are witnessing in the interest of profit maximisation and the highest return to the shareholders has prompted many respectable scholars to ask if life as we know it can continue under present conditions. For example, Lord Rees, Prof. of Cosmology and Astrophysics, and Master of Trinity College,

Cambridge, in his recent book *Our Final Century*, gives present human civilisation no more than a fifty percent chance of surviving the current century. Are we closer to the beginning of history or to its end?

There is no doubt in my mind that we need a new direction, a new economic system, a new path: a globalisation of kindness, compassion, and justice. We need a globalisation that understands that sustainability demands that efficiency and equity should go hand-in-hand. We know there must be a convergence of these values, rather than a competition between them.

We need to understand that in this inextricably interconnected world none of us has a secure future so long as abject poverty, hunger, and violence continue unabated. We must admit that the present economic system is despoiling and depleting our beautiful Earth. We must acknowledge that there is something drastically and fundamentally wrong with the current economic rules and practices that fail to adequately value the most essential human work: the work of service, caring for ourselves, others, and our Mother Earth.

As has been noted by many saints and sages throughout history, fostering peace by overcoming evil with good requires careful reflection on the *common good* and on its social and political implications. When the common good is encouraged at every level, the conditions for peace are promoted. Can an individual find complete fulfilment without taking account of his/her social nature, that is, our being "with" and "for" others? The common good closely concerns us. It closely concerns every expression of our social nature: the family, groups, associations, cities, regions, states, the community of peoples and nations.

Each person, in some way, is called to work for the common good, constantly looking out for the good of others. This responsibility belongs in a particular way to political authorities at every level, since they are called to create that sum of social conditions which permits and fosters in human beings the integral development of their person. The common good therefore demands respect for and the integral promotion of the person and his/her fundamental rights, as well as respect for and the promotion of the rights of nations on the universal plane.

Moreover, as many have reminded us, a just economy for the common good should adhere to the following values:

1) The economy is for people; 2) The economy is for being, not having; 3) The economic system ought to be needs-based; 4) The economy is an act of stewardship; 5) The economy must be a participatory society; 5) There must be fair sharing; 7) The system

must permit self reliance; 8) The economy must be ecologically sustainable; 9) The economy must be productive.

Globalisation is fast evolving and rapidly changing the world and this symposium reveals the urgency of focusing on crucial questions. Clearly, it is an opportunity to reflect on how the common good can constitute an international platform capable of reacting to globalisation and its consequences.

As noted above, globalisation is most often thought of within economic and technological structures as a way to denote the massive and dynamic global integration of national economies and markets. Because these economic and technological forces are central to the current and future well-being of the global human family, it is essential that they be discussed within the more general framework of human moral and spiritual experience. It is only within these frameworks that we can fully explore the values and relationships that form our human communities. Central to this discussion are religious institutions and communities which have developed time-honored wisdom arising from the deep encounter of the human person with the mystery of the sacred. The diversity represented by these communities images the profound truth of the transcendent mystery in which we participate.

As has been observed by many throughout history, religion has been both a source of blessing and curse. Religion has been, and is, a major factor in many conflicts and wars around the world. It has also been, and is now, a presence calling people out of their own selfishness, challenging cultures of waste and death. Various religious communities cry out against political/economic injustice, human rights abuses, poverty, hatred, fear, ignorance, consumerism, war as an instrument of imperial policy, and the failure to respect international legal or ethical principles, even as they challenge their own communities to choose paths that nurture peace and justice instead of contributing to new conflicts, intolerance, and even anarchy around the world.

Committed to spirituality, compassion, and respect for others, truly religious people must not allow their religion to be hijacked and abused by exclusivist ideologues. We must make a stand together for peace, understanding, mutual respect, dialogue, and justice. We must welcome religious diversity and concede that no single religion can claim a monopoly of Truth. Indeed, at this time in our history and journey—facing globalisation, global warming, AIDS, and more—we need each other far more than in the past. The future of our world demands that we teach to our students, parishioners, and communities the value and benefits of dialogue, co-operation, and interdependence.

In order to provide a better understanding of the role of religions in the age of globalisation, in 2002, *Globalisation for the Common Good* came into being at Oxford. This movement is for "Rekindling the Human Spirit and Compassion in Globalisation." We articulated an alternative to the current dominant models of economic/free trade globalisation, aiming to make globalisation good for all. Our movement found many dedicated and committed friends around the world. From Oxford we went to St. Petersburg, Russia, then to Dubai. In 2005, we were in Kenya. In 2006, Chaminade University of Honolulu, in Hawaii hosted the conference, while 2007 found us at Fatih University in Istanbul. In 2008, our common good journey will take us to Mebourne, Australia. Future conferences are currently under consideration.

The mission of *Globalisation for the Common Good* is to promote an ethical, moral, and spiritual vision of globalisation and encourage adoption of public policy at all levels that builds the common good of our global community. In this way we nurture personal virtue in our relationships with each other and the planetary environment, while investing our understanding of economics, commerce, trade, and international relations with values centered on the universal common good. We will advance understanding and action on major global issues by civil society, private enterprise, the public sector, governments, and national and international institutions. We will promote collaborative policy solutions to the challenges posed by globalisation. We are committed to the idea that the marketplace is not just an economic sphere, "it is a region of the human spirit." Reflecting on the Divine dimension of life can not be divorced from consideration of economic questions and issues. Economics can not be effectively practiced without an understanding of the world of heart and spirit. Therefore we view the problem and challenge of globalisation not only from an economic point of view, but also from ethical, spiritual, and theological perspectives.

We affirm our conviction that genuine inter-faith dialogue and co-operation is a significant way of bringing the world together, supporting the creation of a harmonious environment needed to build a world of peace, justice, and prosperity for all. The call for Globalisation for the Common Good is an appeal to our essential humanity to deal with some of the most pressing concerns of peoples the world over. Business and wealth creation, when they contribute to the common good of the global community, are blessed and vital for human survival. Bringing religions and business together for the common good will empower us with humanity, spirituality, and love. It will raise us above pessimism to an ultimate optimism; turning from darkness to light; from night to day; from winter to spring. This spiritual ground for hope at this time of wanton destruction of our world, can help us recognise the ultimate purpose of life and of our journey in this world.

The Essential Dimensions of Globalisation for the Common Good:

1. To champion the highest cultural evolutionary values and aspirations of the early twenty-first century, in full awareness of their strategic interdependence:

- Respect for belief in God, Ultimate Reality, or the One, and the right of each person to religious freedom and practice;
- The investment of spiritual capital;
- The practice of selfless love;
- Deep Inter-religious and intercultural dialogue and engagement for the common good;
- Cultures of peace and non-violent conflict resolution;
- Economic justice, social justice, solidarity, and universal human rights;
- Ecological sustainability, stewardship, and commitment to an interspecies ethic;
- Global empowerment of women;
- The rights of the child;
- The elimination of global hunger, thirst, preventable disease, and poverty;
- Cosmopolitanism: the harmony of local, national, and global citizenship.

2. To seek solutions to the great challenges facing the planetary community:

- The estrangement of global North and South;
- The urgent need for a restructured global economy;
- The increasing necessity of global public governance;
- The elucidation of a global ethic identifying the rights and the responsibilities of Earth's people;
- The elimination of the scourges of actual and virtual slavery and torture;
- The creation of sustainable energy policies;
- The realization of planetary sovereignty by the peoples of the Earth;
- Cherishing and protection of the global commons;
- Commitment to service.

3. To contribute to the creation of a global interdisciplinary agenda for the common good.

The Aims of Globalisation for the Common Good are:

- GCG commits itself to a wide range of activities that are all aimed at promoting and teaching, through cutting-edge scholarly activities, research and education on Globalisation for the Common Good. Our emphasis is on providing progressive perspectives that are increasingly hard to find because of the reliance on and promotion of neo-liberalism as the sole philosophy behind the current globalisation process.
- GCG, therefore, rather than espousing and defending a single discipline or paradigm, seeks to engage a broad, pluralistic range of viewpoints and models to be represented, compared, and ultimately synthesised into a richer understanding of the inherently complex systems it deals with.
- GCG nurtures a commitment among academics and practitioners to learn from each other, to explore new patterns of thinking together, and to facilitate the derivation and implementation of effective policies for the realisation of Globalisation for the Common Good.
- GCG is committed to the idea of global cooperation and dialogue between scholars, business leaders, policy makers, opinion leaders and leading NGOs. Our aim is that such co-operation will lead to a more informed and balanced understanding of the behaviours, motivations, and objectives of the various forces, agents, and policy makers that form the globalisation process.

Among research topics carried out by GCG in fulfilment of its mission are:

- Ethics, Philosophy, Theology and Globalisation;
- Eastern and Western spirituality in Dialogue for the Common Good;
- Global Governance, Business, Economics and Globalisation;
- Ethics and Spirituality in Higher Education;
- Global Consciousness and Spirituality;
- Faith and Action in the age of Globalisation;
- The Virtuous Economy—Business as a Calling: Doing Well by Doing Good;
- Environment, Ecology, and Globalisation;

- Psychology and Globalisation;
- Politics, International Relations, and Globalisation;
- Non-violent Conflict Resolution and Peace building;
- Civilisation, Culture, and Globalisation;
- Media, Global reporting, and Globalisation;
- Global Activism for the Common Good;
- Enabling, Envisioning and Empowering: Young People Leadership Programme in Common Good;
- Regions and Globalisation for the Common Good.

Globalisation for the Common Good, by addressing the crises that face us all, empowers us with humanity, spirituality and love. It engages people of different races, cultures, and languages, from a wide variety of backgrounds, all of them committed to bringing about a world in which there is more solidarity and greater harmony. This spiritual ground for hope, arising at this time of wanton destruction of our world, can help us to recall the ultimate purpose of life and of our journey in this world.

OPENING CEREMONY

WELCOME ADDRESS

Dear guests, colleagues and friends,

Greetings and Welcome to Istanbul and Fatih University. It is a great pleasure for us to welcome you and see you at the conference. We also welcome you to this lovely city. We meet here where the continents meet. This, on the one hand is a city between continents; on the other, a city of people from all continents. Here we see the human side of geography. This conference is especially important from this point of view: İstanbul is a metaphor of coming together. Here, you feel yourself at home, as you do whenever you are abroad and see something or someone very familiar to you. Everyone can find something here that belongs to himself/herself or someone who is a sister or brother. The quintessence of our conference is to be found in this warm atmosphere.

Globalisation as a phenomenon is as old as humanity. Today, however, I suppose it is moving faster than ever before. As result of globalisation we live in a "borderless world." This does not only refer to the very permeable borders of states and regions, but also implies the togetherness of peoples once isolated by space and time. In fact, the conference itself offers proof of this. However, globalisation itself does not say much to help us solve the problems which it brings. So, we are here to talk.

The conference programme presents a rich variety of flavours. Our distinguished guests bring them from every corner of the world. Together, here, we will discuss the pros and cons of globalisation with respect to justice, peace and harmony. We will also focus on its negative sides: injustice and inhumanity.

I am grateful to all the conference participants who are attending from all over the world. I thank our Organizing Committee. They worked tirelessly and with a good sense of humour. I am, however, particularly grateful to Kamran Mofid, founder of the Globalisation for the Common Good Initiative, Alpaslan Açıkgenç, vice-president of Fatih University and head of the local committee of the conference, Cemal Uşak, President of KADİP, and Şammas Salur, co-convenor of the conference. I would also like to thank Mustafa Duran, who designed the conference website and Yıldırım Erbaş, who generously spent his time on so many matters.

In conclusion, we are here aiming at contributing to peace, giving a chance to humanity, seeking justice, resolving conflicts peacefully, seeing miracles of tolerance and respect, and sharing life.

Oğuz Borat, President of Fatih University

1

INTRODUCTORY ADDRESS

Kamran Mofid

Greetings, colleagues and friends,

It is my pleasure and honour to welcome you to our Sixth International Conference on Globalisation for the Common Good, taking place this year at Fatih University in beautiful and inspirational Istanbul, the city of understanding and dialogue between East and West. No other city in the world straddles two continents (Europe and Asia) and has been capital of two great empires (Byzantine and Ottoman). I am sure being in Turkey (Confluence of Civilisations) and in Istanbul will greatly enhance our debate and discussions on the timely theme and topic of our conference.

In these global and too often troubled times, we need new perspectives and models so that we can find humane answers to the challenge of globalisation, based on a profound respect for the diversity of cultures and religions in our world community. As global events demonstrate, there is a desperate need to reintroduce spirituality, ethics, morality, faith and common sense into the debate on globalisation.

Looking at the conference programme, without doubt and hesitation, we can see that our accomplished speakers have risen well to this challenge. The conference is truly privileged to have speakers of the highest calibre, sharing your views with us all. Without you there would have been no conference, but with you, we hope we can travel together to heal the troubled and torn cultures of our time and pave the way to global justice, peace, prosperity and harmony for all.

I wish to express the conference's respect and sincere gratitude to each of our presenters for their extraordinary commitment in being a part of this vital effort. Each one of you brings a missing and essential piece that completes the process, leading to a better understanding of what globalisation is all about. Hopefully, together we can clearly argue for and insist on social and economic alternatives that address the roots of global injustice and inhumanity, leading to Globalisation for the Common Good.

I am also grateful to and thank all the conference delegates who have come from near and far to be with us. It is wonderful for academics and non-academics to get involved and engaged with one another, so that we can all share each other's varied experiences.

I am grateful to and thank the Local Organising Committee (LOC) in Istanbul. Space alone has kept me from naming all of them. They have given their time, expertise and know-how as volunteers to *Globalisation for the Common Good*. I thank them all most sincerely.

I am however, particularly grateful to my co-convenor for this year Conference, Dr Şammas Salur. Şammas has been a tower of support in organising the conference. Thank you Sammas for all you have done.

I wish also to thank my friend and comrade for the common good, Cemal Usak. Cemal has been an instrumental force in bringing the conference to Istanbul, and his organisation, the Intercultural Dialogue Platform, has greatly assisted the conference.

I wish to extend my sincere thanks to Fatih University for hosting the 2007 conference and for all their generous support, sponsorship, and encouragements In particular I would like to thank Prof. Dr Oğuz Borat, the Rector, and Dr Alparslan Açıkgenç, the Vice-Rector and Dean of the Faculty of Arts and Sciences. In production of this book, I am grateful to and extend a very warm appreciation to Dr Kevin J. McGinley of the Department of English Language and Literature at Fatih University for his excellent work and personal support in preparing the manuscript for publication

I would also wish to thank Insieme tours, and in particular, Zekihan Kiziloğlu, for all their hard work in looking after us.

In 2006, during our conference in Hawaii, our own journal, *Journal of Globalization for the Common Good* was launched. This, I believe, has been a great achievement for our movement. I wish to give a special thanks to the Co-Founder/Editor, Prof. Yahya Kamalipour, Head, Department of Communication, Purdue University, Calumet, USA. Through this, as well as other journals that Yahya has founded, many people around the world are gaining access to educational materials that they would have been denied otherwise.

In September 2006, the www.globalisationforthecommongood.info web site was put online. This is our window to the outside world, a place of dialogue, communication, and information. This could not have been possible with the assistance of Yahya Kamalipour and his technical team at Purdue, especially Christopher Kosovich. Chris is a special young man, truly dedicated to the common good, a man of service and volunteerism. Without expecting or demanding anything in return, he developed a most wonderful web site for me. I very much thank him.

I wish also to thank my good friend, Jim Kenney, Executive Director, Interreligious Engagement Project, Chicago, USA, for his support, encouragement and inspiration.

Finally, this week, all of us, experienced and newcomers, young and old, students and teachers together will form a community, committed to exploring and debating visions and ideas for celebrating diversity,

3

appreciating uniqueness, enabling us to transform disagreements into understanding and mutual respect.

In addition to plenary sessions and workshops, there will be opportunities for informal spontaneous meetings and dialogue between participants all through the week. This, we sincerely hope, will result in invaluable collaborative learning experiences and networking as well as rich personal interactions. Please try to participate also in the cultural and social activities to cement further the newly formed friendships. I hope you will take full advantage of all these activities.

In conclusion, we invite you to share a common belief in the potential of each one of us to become self-directed, empowered, and active in defining this time in the world as an opportunity for positive change and healing and for the true formation of a culture of peace by giving thanks, spreading joy, sharing love, seeing miracles, discovering goodness, embracing kindness, practicing patience, teaching tolerance, encouraging laughter, celebrating diversity, showing compassion, turning from hatred, practicing forgiveness, peacefully resolving conflicts, communicating non-violently, choosing happiness and enjoying life.

KEYNOTE LECTURES

GLOBALISATION, FAITH, AND THE COMMON GOOD

DIFFERENCE IS BEAUTIFUL:
A PHILOSOPHICAL EVALUATION

Alparslan Açıkgenç

The title of my paper may sound romantic; but it is not intended to be so. The romantic title is used to draw attention to a human phenomenon which needs a rigorous philosophical analysis. The definition of man as a "rational animal" persisted throughout the history of philosophy. This definition brings to the fore two main aspects of human beings: animality and rationality. However, it neglects another significant aspect which can be represented by his emotionality. This means that a "human is an animal, and an emotional and rational being." By this definition we are claiming that the animality of humans is different from the animality of animals, just as both their emotionality and rationality are different from the emotionality and rationality of animals. It is because of this difference that humans can transcend their physical being and rise to the level of spirituality which is not possible for other species of lower rank. As a result, we need to modify our definition by including a fourth aspect in the classical definitions of man; spirituality which is the characteristic of angels. The first three aspects, namely animality, emotionality, and rationality, belong to man as his own nature, whereas the fourth one, namely spirituality, is given to him as a potentiality which he may or may not develop. Each of these aspects is endowed with certain potentialities and capacities that are given to humans for certain purposes. When they are used outside the limits of these purposes then problems arise. Accordingly, a meticulous analysis of these aspects of human beings must be carried out in order to avoid these problems.

The animal aspect, being endowed with life, has two basic characteristics: one is doing whatever is necessary to preserve life, such as nutrition, reproduction and defense; the other is to hold these activities within the humanly sphere, which is the link between animality and emotionality. This is the difference between human animality and animal animality. The link is found in the fact that humans are weak animals; they do not have the physical power or other defensive mechanism found in other animals. Therefore, at the level of animality they need "togetherness" in order to survive. Even if this characteristic is found in other animals still it is the main characteristic of human animality because it leads to emotionality. That is why we add an emotional aspect to "being together" and thus rise to the level of emotions.

The emotional aspect of human beings represents all human emotions as a whole. When we say that we add an emotional aspect to "being together" and thus rise to the level of emotions we do not mean that this aspect arises as a result of the animal aspect. All human aspects are already given and in this sense they form a unity. What we mean is that each aspect can be analyzed at their lower levels but cannot be distinguished at their higher levels. The basic characteristic of the emotional aspect is to give breath to all human activities whether animal or rational or spiritual. If the animal aspect is able to perceive our biological and physical needs then the emotional aspect is able to perceive our non-physical needs. Since the spiritual aspect is totally non-physical this aspect is the closest to our spirituality.

The rational aspect includes the human characteristic which according to Aristotle defines man's real nature because this is the aspect of conceptual thinking which no other animal has. The rational aspect analyzes and evaluates all the data that it receives from the lower aspects, namely the animal and emotional. It is, as such, the seat of scientific knowledge.

All of these aspects have faculties appropriate for performing their functions. The faculties of animality are the five senses at the lower level and concupiscence in general (which means it is not taken merely in the sexual connotation) at the higher level which represents the passage from animality to emotionality. The lower faculty of emotions is the heart as the seat of emotions and at the higher level it is conscience which is the moral faculty that provides the first step into intellectual thinking. But since this thinking is supposed to be conceptual we need a faculty in the rational aspect that converts all these data into the raw material that is convenient for our mind to digest. That faculty which provides this conceptual conversion is imagination, which is the lower faculty of our rational aspect with intuition being the higher faculty of our rational aspect which also provides the first step into spirituality. I am not saying that these are the only faculties belonging to human nature. The ones mentioned here are important for our purpose to evaluate the ground of human differences. Although the nature with three biological aspects and a spiritual aspect is one and the same in all humans with varying degrees of intensity, the outcome of these aspects are many. Let us try to see how those differences arise.

What I have outlined here provides a rich inner world for a human being. At the animal level, for example, a piece of land is perceived as mere "territory" which provides livelihood for us. The land is defended only for this purpose and is seen as precious as long as it provides livelihood. But at the emotional level a human being is passionately attached to the land. As such he may write poems and sing love songs for the land where he lives.

At the rational level a human being will try to conceptualize the land and call it his "country" or "homeland." Moreover, he may intellectually idealize the land where he is living. The same approach by the three human aspects can be applied to everything he encounters in this world: his belongings, his friends, his family, his relationships, his actions and so on. Everything human will have the same aspects, namely an animal aspect, an emotional, and a rational aspect according to how a human being looks at things. As a result a human being will have a rich inner world. It is this inner world that is reflected outside. That reflection may have a variety of modalities. For example as a mode of action, it is her/his behaviour; what s/he does to others and in fact to herself/himself. But as a mode of new being it is an achievement, which could be an art work, or a product. When it is in the conceptual mode it is knowledge, which is perhaps the highest achievement for a human being.

All these achievements are reflections and manifestations of the inner world of a human being. These manifestations occur in a social context called "culture." With such a diversified nature man turns in a sense inside out within a social context and turning its entire inner world into what we call "culture." Now here the system that turns an inner world into a culture is one; but that which is turned inside-out is not one but many. This in a sense resembles a system of production that is one in its structure but diversified in its output. Let us consider only two systems that belong to our nature: the digestive system and the knowledge system, by which I mean the human epistemology. Our digestive system is the same, having a mouth, tongue, teeth, stomach, and the rest of the organs. We know from anatomy the way they all work is the same and that is why when there is a problem a Turk does not have to go to a Turkish doctor but can go to any human doctor. On the other hand, quite contrary to the unity of our digestive system our culinary culture is immensely diversified. In the same way, our knowledge system also is one, having one logic and epistemology with all similar faculties. Yet the knowledge generated from that system is not one but multiple. This shows the great cultural diversity. We may ask here why only one human being but diversified output?

Let us pass from here to another human dimension which may enable us to evaluate what we referred to above as the spiritual aspect. As we have seen, the need to be together with other fellow human beings is grounded in our animal aspect. It is therefore in our inner nature to form groups to live together. But this *togetherness* is only a primitive collection of human beings. When the emotional aspect is added, the togetherness gradually turns into a community. In a community, bonds are established with strong feelings because they are evaluated emotionally and hence emotional stories of relationships are created. As a result of this, the community may be

9

organized on the basis of a "feeling relationship." There may be an elderly group that is respected and obeyed. There will also be other groups that are defined on the basis of feelings which in turn they also contribute to the organization of the community. But with the addition of the rational aspect, the organization is maintained with reason. Therefore, a political system is developed, according to which the community is governed. Now the community is a society in the true sense and the rational organization of the community is given a name, such as a state or government. In such an organization, man is able to exhibit and develop all his potentialities. He can find everything in the society. By using his reason he is also able to find the reason for existence and the cause of the universe. But he is utterly unable to reach to an all-comprehensive concept which can provide meaning to all the aspects he reflects. Moreover he finds some potentialities in himself which he is not able to develop. At this juncture he finds "Revelation" defined as religion. Upon an investigation of religion he finds that he is now able to develop some of his potentialities which he could not even imagine. This aspect which is based upon the development of these potentialities with the help of religion we call the "spiritual aspect" of human beings.

Religion is in fact the Divine Guidance for humanity. Therefore, religion is God-given. There is no seat or ground in human nature to provide a foundation for the rise of religion. There are only, if my phrase is clear enough, "receptive points" which I have called "potentialities" in human nature that may receive religion but cannot make or unmake religion. Human beings may invent religion by imitating the true religion that has been revealed. But that is a different case. I believe that man is not given the authority to invent religion because those inventions will not find the receptive points in human nature and as a result will be dangerous to humanity. There are such instances in human history. Therefore, by definition human beings do not have the authority to establish religion. Although religion is a Divine Guidance for humanity, it is not the kind of guidance that gives us an exhaustive list of how we should behave in any given situation. If this were done by religion we would have had to act as robots according to that list, in which case there would be no room for human intellectual creativity in any field, including sciences. In that case, religion as a Divine Guidance bestows upon us two fundamental states of mind: one is the consciousness of the Divine Presence in all; the other is the moral sensitivity in our behaviors. Both states of mind are expressed in general principles by religion. We therefore feel the need to interpret these principles in order to apply them to certain situations in our life. This need for interpretation gradually gives rise to a systematic exposition of religion as a system of guidance. In that case, this second intellectual understanding is also defined as religion. We thus need to distinguish between these two phenomena: Religion as Divine Guidance and Religion as the interpretation of this Divine Guidance: the former is Pure Religion and the latter is the religion within a certain cultural context. I believe that there is no harm in interpreting Pure Religion in a certain cultural context. On the contrary, it is inevitable and indeed required by God; a requirement that is clear in the fact that He does not send His Guidance as a complete set of rules readily available to be applied to human life. It is as a result of this that we develop our spiritual potentialities.

When we consider these aspects of human nature we realize that humans have a very rich inner world. When this inner world, as we have seen, is projected within a social context then it gives rise to human culture. In this sense the human being is depicted in Islamic thought as the *microcosm* because s/he includes in its being representations of all the worlds in the universe. In this sense a human being can be called a "mini universe." It is therefore natural for him to reflect all these diverse universes in the mirror of society. That is why we have so many diversified cultures and civilizations. It is this aspect of man that is taken as the locus of revelation by religion which means it is also a God-given right for humans to have diverse cultures, societies, and communities. This diversified nature of man makes him a valuable creature as the *Qu'ran* also points out:

> We have honored the children of Adam, provided them transport on land and sea and given them for sustenance good and pure food and conferred upon them special favor above many of our creation. (17/Al-Isra', 70)

Therefore, the abundance of different cultures makes life enjoyable and breaks the monotonous flow of events in history. But the beauty of diverse cultures has another aspect: it lays the burden of bearing differences. This is because each aspect of human nature is left free without any boundaries. Therefore, if they are not controlled there will arise injustice and violations. That is why each aspect of human nature must be kept under control. I think this can be done by taming the lower aspect with the good use of its next higher aspect. In that case, the animal aspect is controlled by the good use of the emotional aspect and the emotional aspect is controlled by the good use of the rational aspect; and in turn the rational aspect is controlled by the spiritual aspect which is nourished by divine revelation. If the final phase is the greatest good then religion as the divine revelation is the greatest good, providing tolerance for differences. Therefore, if different cultures arise within a civilization of religion then we can tell that the religion is fulfilling its function as intended by divine will. But human beings must also act accordingly to tolerate different cultures, or rather differences in general.

We may then briefly express our point: human nature is diversified, giving humans a rich inner world to be realized within a social context. When it is realized it leads to rich cultures which may eventually turn into a significant civilization. But since the realization of the inner world would be manifested at different planes in different communities there will necessarily be differences which open a challenge for humanity to face. Today the world is moving towards globalization which poses a greater challenge for the diversity of cultures. In the past people knew of different cultures but today we face and live with different cultures. That presents a challenge every day in every place. This puts on us a greater moral responsibility to tolerate cultures and differences within even the same culture. It is this diverse goodness in our nature that is reflected into our social contexts with the formidable challenge that I have tried to present here as the beauty of difference. I believe that human destiny depends on our realization of this beauty to face it with the challenge to accept and tolerate cultural variety. That is why I would like to express this with a romantic motto with its philosophical connotation: difference is beautiful.

THE QUEST FOR JUSTICE AND PEACE: CONTRIBUTIONS OF ISLAM TO PEACE-BUILDING AND CONFLICT RESOLUTION

Murad Wilfried A. Hofmann

Introduction

Peace and justice obviously go together. Where there is no peace there can hardly be any justice. And where there is no justice, peace remains elusive. It only takes a short glance at the situation in Palestine under Israeli occupation to illustrate these truisms. Therefore both peace and justice in Islamic jurisprudence belong to the so-called *maqasid*, i.e. overriding principles which must be obeyed even in cases where positive law remains silent.

All world religions except Islam are called after personalities (Buddha, Zoroaster, Christ) or regions (Judaism; Hinduism). Only Islam identifies itself with peace. "Islam," the word being a derivative of *as-salam*, is the religion that promotes peace and brings peace to its sincere adherents.

Justice between individuals as well as between rulers and the ruled is indeed a central notion in the Shari'ah as it is in any successful society. This is so because without justice the equality of all people under the law would be jeopardized. Muslims underscore the centrality of justice by listing *al-'adl*—justice—among the ninety-nine most beautiful names/attributes of God/Allah.

PEACE AND JUSTICE IN THE *QU'RAN*

Peace:
The *Qu'ran*[1] immensely treasures peace, describing paradise as "the abode of peace" (19: 62). There the normal greeting is indeed "Peace be with you !" or just "Peace !" (13:24; 14:23; 15:46, 52; 16:32; 25:75; 33:44; 36:58; 39:73; 50:34; 56:26, 91). In particular the *Qu'ran* describes how greetings of peace were extended by the angels to Abraham (11:69; 19:47; 37:109), John the Baptist (19:15), Jesus (19:33), Noah (37:79), Moses and Aaron (37:120) as well as to Elias (37:130). No wonder that the Night of Destiny (Lailat all-Qadr) is graphically described as a particular night whose peacefulness is assured until dawn (97:5).

---

[1] Abdalhaqq Bewley and Aisha Bewley, *The Noble Qu'ran: A New Rendering of its Meaning in English* (Bookwork: Norwich, 1999).

Muslims are instructed to salute others with greetings of peace (27:59; 28:55; 43:89), never to put such greetings into doubt, regardless of from whom they have been received (4:94), and in war to accept offers of peace as a matter of principle (8:61). Consequently Muslims can be recognized as such by their way of greeting (25:63). They know indeed that peace is bestowed on all those who lead modest lives and react to provocations and ignorance by saying "Peace!" (25:47).

The *Qu'ran* demands peacefulness towards all those who offer peace (4:90; 8:61) and rewards peace-creating forgiveness (42:40). On the whole, the Islamic acceptance and endorsement of religious pluralism (2:256; 5:48; 10:99; 109) helps to safeguard peace.

As shown, if Islam nowadays is rarely perceived as a religion of peace it is certainly not due to its core teachings but to people who, while claiming to act Islamically, disregard the profound Qur'anic commitment to peace.

Justice

The notion of justice is ever so present in the *Qu'ran*. Allah Himself declares that He will always decide, and that his word will be realized, "in truth and justice" (6:115; 34:26; 40:28, 78: 45:22), stressing that He loves those who do justice and shies away from injustice (60:8). Allah assures us that all of His messengers acted and act in accordance with justice (10:47; 57:25), justice having been expressly commanded by Him (7:29; 16:90).

To this effect the *Qu'ran* contains a general appeal to all of mankind: "Do justice!" (49:9) This is backed up by specific admonitions to do justice to one's *spouses* (4:129) and to *orphans* (4:127; 6:152). *Witnesses* in court are urged to serve justice under all circumstances (4:135; 5:8, 108), and *salesmen* in the marketplace to use just measuring (11:85; 55:9). In fact, Allah frequently when addressing justice uses the image of the weight-scale (21:47; 42:17; 57:25). Not for nothing, *judges* considered prone to corruption are specially reminded of their duty to decide in justice (4:58; 5:42, 45; 10:54; 38:26; 42:15). It therefore makes good sense when the Muslim *Ummah* is defined in the *Qu'ran* as the community which practices justice (7:181).

PEACE AND JUSTICE IN THE SUNNAH

Given the overwhelming evidence for the Qur'anic endorsement of peace and justice there is no need to prove from *hadith* literature that the Prophet of Islam in his speaking, acting, and non-acting also supported and followed these particular guidelines of the *Qu'ran*.

The Sunnah, at any rate, on the whole is much too concrete for dealing with concepts as abstract as peace and justice. In hadith collections like Imam Malik's *al-Muwatta* it is easier to find out "what to do if [in prayer] one raises one's head before the imam" (no. 3.15.61)[2] than anything on peace or justice. In fact, these two concepts do not even appear in the index of this major collection.[3]

Typical, rather, are prophetic traditions which condemn, e.g., *injustice* in general and fraud in particular.[4] Let it suffice, therefore, to refer to a famous Hadith Qudsi, related by Abu Dharr, according to which Allah *ta'ala* said that "I have ruled out injustice for myself."[5] One might add that it is "Sunnah" that "nobody really believes as long as he does not wish for his brother what he wishes for himself,"[6] this being an indirect way of highlighting the virtue of justice. The same is true for the very great reward in the *au-delà* promised to just rulers who resist abusing their power.[7]

EARLIEST MUSLIM HISTORY

The history of the foundation of Islam and of the *Khulafah ar-Rashidun* was not only religious *sira* but down-to-earth political, economic, and social interaction. Nevertheless, the Prophet's biography, at any rate, provides enough evidence of the pursuit of peace and justice.

(1) **Peace-keeping:** a) This idea, rather than resisting suppression and persecution by force, explains the need for *emigrations* of Makkan Muslims to Abyssinia and to al-Yathrib (al-hijra), the former one comprising seventy-five men and nine women from Makkah plus twenty-five Muslim clients, altogether one hundred and nine people. Emigration signalled that the Muslims would rather leave than put up resistance.

---

[2] Malik ibn Anas, *Muwatta*, trans. A'isha 'Abdarahman at-Tarjumana and Ya'qub Johnson (Diwan Press: Norwich 1982).
http://www.usc.edu/dept/MSA/fundamentals/hadithsunnah/muwatta/003.mmt.html
[3] Ibid. http://www.usc.edu/dept/MSA/fundamentals/hadithsunnah/muwatta/
[4] *Vielfach überlieferte Prophetenworte (As-Sujuti, Al-ahadith al-mutawatira)*, trans. Ahmad von Denffer (Muslime helfen, e.V.: Garching 2000), Hadiths No. 75 (p. 66), 73 (p. 65).
[5] *Al-Nawawi: Vierzig Hadite*, trans. Ahmad von Denffer (Islamisches Zentrum: Munich, 1987), Hadith 17, p. 68.
[6] Ibid., Hadith 13 [translation the author's] (Hadith related by Malik ibn Anas as reported by al-Bukhari und Muslim).
[7] *Salih Muslim*, trans. Abdul Hamid Siddiqi, Vol. III (Lahore: S. Muhammad Ashraf, 1980), Hadiths no. 4493, related by 'Abdullah ibn' Umar (p. 1016), no. 4542, related by Abu Hureira, p. 1024.

Permission to resist by force the Makkan strategic aggression against al-Madinah was given only in the 2nd year of the Hijra, after the 2nd Pledge of 'Aqaba. Only now Abu 'Ubayda's detachment was provided with a flag. Only at this point was the first Muslim arrow shot (by Sa'd Abu Waqqas)[8] in what turned out to be the first of altogether seventy-two Muslims raids against the Mak-kans.

b) Peace through justice was also the unformulated guideline behind the *Constitution* of al-Ma-dinah, dictated by the Prophet in the first year A.H., rightly called by Muhammad Hamidul-lah "the first written constitution of the world."[9] In article 25, for instance, it provided for conflict resolution via consultation, arbitration, and reconciliation. As it turned out, this basic law could not prevent hostilities between the Muslim and the Jewish tribes of Madinah. However, a remarkable peace-keeping effort had been made.

c) The *armistice* for 10 years of al-Hudaybiyyah was followed one year later by the so-called *conquest* of Makkah (8 A.H.) as well as the (only) "farewell" pilgrimage of the Prophet Muhammad (s.) (10 A.H.). There were three further incidents which helped to put the fundamentally peaceful disposition of Islam into focus. After Hudaybiyyah the Muslims felt that war had been abolished.[10] In the process the Muslims learned that to lay down arms might profit Islam much more than fighting for it. Given that the Muslim army surrounding Makkah was 10,000 warriors strong, and given the bloody persecution Muslims had suffered at the hands of the Makkans led by Abu Jahl and Abu Sufyan, it was expected as natural that there would be a massacre.

To the relief of the citizens of Makkah, Muhammad (s.) had only singled out ten people, among them four women, for punishment. Three of them had been apostates who treacherously had fought Islam actively. Others as poets or singers had made fun of Islam in a repulsive manner. In the end, only five people were put to death. The others had been allowed to escape or, including even Abu Sufyan's wife Hind, had been pardoned by the Prophet. Even though she led a life of shameless debauchery and had engineered the death of Hamza, she was treated with clemency. Such leniency was unheard of, and still is. (For instance, after the recent fall of Baghdad several hundred Baathists were executed.)

---

[8] Ibn Ishaq, *The Life of Muhammad: A Translation of Ibn Ishaq's* Sirat rasul Allah, trans. A. Guillaume (Oxford: Oxford University Press, 1955; repr. 2003), pp. 281, 283.

[9] Muhammad Hamidullah, *The First Written Constitution in the World* (Lahore: Sh. Muhammad Ashraf, 1975).

[10] Ibn Ishaq, p. 507.

d) Even before his peaceful entry into Makkah, Muhammad (s.) had shown himself as a statesman of rank and vision by addressing conciliatory letters to eight rulers in his vicinity, including the emperors of Byzantium, Heraclius, and Persia, Parviz Khosrau, the king (Negus) of Abyssinia, the amirs or governors of Bahrain, 'Uman, and Syria, and Archbishop Maukakis of Alexandria. In his messages the Prophet (s.) did not threaten them or pose any ultimatum. He simply invited them to accept Islam. In case of refusal, in consonance with the Qur'an, the Prophet (s.) was content with having delivered the message.[11]

(2) **Justice:** This, too, was a basic value underlying these early happenings.

a) Justice had even been formally introduced into the Constitution of al-Madinah. One point in its article 37 reads: "Verily, help shall be given in favor of the oppressed." On this basis, Islam sought to create a classless society.

b) It has indeed been recorded that the Makkan nobility hated this *egalitarian* impulse of Islam, seeing—to their disgust—that it was the "wretched of the earth" who were among the first to have inherited the (Islamic) kingdom, among them many freedmen or "clients" (mawali). Indeed early Islam provided excellent chances for upward *social mobility*. In fact, among Muhammad's earliest disciples quite a few former slaves were to be found, next to Bilal, including 'Amir ibn Fuhayrah, 'Ammar, Khab-bab, Yasir and, of course, Zayd ibn Harithah.

In this vein, Zayd b. Harithah, a former slave, could even become governor of al-Madinahand, another freedman, Anas b. Malik, one of the most valued narrators of *ahadith*. Abu 'Ubayda b. al-Jarrah, a grave digger, and Amr b. al-'As, a butcher, both moved up to become celebrated Muslim army commanders.

c) The Islamic value of justice and equality proved particularly incompatible with the customary Arab law of marriage (al-kafa'ah) which, e.g., had outlawed marriages between Arab women and non-Arab men, requiring equality of nobility and wealth, as a minimum. The criteria of compatibility between spouses included lineage (nasab), honor (hasab), family (bayt), property (mal), liberty (hurriyah), and profession (hirfah).

In marked contrast to this code of social rigidity in early Islamic society marriages took place between Muslims of different social standing; even marriages between non-Arabs and Arab women took place for the first time. Thus Bilal ibn Rabah, a negro, married Halal bint 'Awf, sister of the

---

[11] According to at-Tabari, the Prophet's attitude was, "Eh bien, moi je t'ai fait parvenir ce message." Mohammed at-Tabari, *Sceau des prophètes*, 2nd edn. (Paris: Sindbad, 1980), p.250.

famous Qura'ish military leader and Muslim hero 'Abd ar-Rahman b. 'Awf. Muslims proved then, as they do now, that *blood is thinner than faith*.

d) At the same time, Islam did not require poverty. There were some rich Muslims, to be sure, including the later *khulafa* 'Uthman and Abu Bakr. The latter bought and released not only Bilal but as many slaves as he could get. But the well-to-do Muslims had lost their class consciousness and thus provided support for the underprivileged without looking down on them in charity fashion.[12]

e) The early Muslims upheld justice even in cases so repugnant that it went against their grain. Thus they stuck to the agreement of Hudaybiyyah obliging them to return male Muslim asylum-seekers.[13] It was as revolting to them when Muhammad's uncle Ibn Abbas gave protection to the arch enemy of Islam, Abu Sufyan, and even carried him to the Prophet on horseback.[14] Yet, they did honor the code of hospitality.

f) When the Prophet accorded amnesty to Hind, he made her subscribe to a number of rules for her to abide by. These included a remarkable rule: "Not to refuse obedience in what is just,"[15] implying that resistance against unjust orders is permitted. Many believe that this principle—which cost the lives of many German officers after their failed plot against Hitler on 20 July 1944—was a modern achievement. As proven here it dates back 1400 years.

ISLAMIC HISTORY THROUGH THE AGES

It would be both anachronistic and overly partisan to claim that Islamic history through all the ages—the Umayyad, Abbasid, Mameluk and Osman dynasties—had been characterized by peace and justice. These dynasties indeed pursued *dynastic* interests first of all. Politics, social, and economic problems, after all, look for immediate solutions, whether or not sanctified by high moral principles. Ismaili (7er Shi'i) Islam in the twelfth century with the Assassins even produced the first cult of suicidal terrorism, directed against fellow Muslims. That is why people even today often refuse to engage in politics in order not to sully their hands.

Therefore, while justice never was entirely absent during Muslim history, this value became dominant only sporadically, in certain Muslim

---

[12] Tarik Jan, *The Life and Times of Muhammad Rasul Allah*, 2nd rev. edn. (Islamabad: Institute of Policy Studies, 1999), p. 131.
[13] Ibn Ishaq, p. 504.
[14] At-Tabari, p. 278.
[15] Ibid., p. 286.

personalities and in certain regions and institutions. On the whole, however, Muslim societies socially became as closed, rigid, and static, as they had been in pre-Islamic days. With very few exceptions, including Abu Hanifa and Abu Yusuf, the Abbasid society allowed no longer even *professional* mobility.

Crafts like dyers, peasant, sweepers, tanners, and weavers even became hereditary now as the old Arab restrictions on marriage (al-kafa'ah) infiltrated Muslim law. Alas, all of the Islamic Schools of Law (madhahib) sanctioned and enshrined inequality between Muslims.

So much more important it is to signal positive exceptions to a generally negative trend.

Personalities:

The first that comes to mind is *Salah ad-Din al-Ayubi*, the famous liberator of Jerusalem (and Palestine) from the Crusaders. His fairness, sense of justice, and chivalry were so unusual that as "Saladin" he became a moral hero even in the West. Never since 'Umar, the 2nd Khalif, was Islam so well blended into a public personality.

Similarly, the Osman Padishah, *Süleyman Kanuni* ("the Law-Giver"; 1494-1566), enjoyed the prestige of being a model "Muslim on the throne," impressing his contemporaries by refusing polygamy, his sole and only wife being Hürrem Sultan. But his image has been marred by the wanton execution, in 1553, of his son Mustafa, the crown-prince.

Other Muslims devoted to peace and justice mainly were to be found among sufis, even though some of them, especially in the Maghrib, were militant, engaging in military *jihad* against both Portuguese and Spaniards. *Muhy ad-Din Ibn al-'Arabi* (d. 1240 in Damascus) and *Jalal ud-Din Rumi* (d. in 1273 in Konya) are prototypes of non-militant, otherworldly mystics. However, a Muslim Mahatma Gandhi we seek in vain, if only because fighting in defence of peace and justice is a Muslim's religious duty.

Regions

There is at least one community which practises Islam in such a puritan and total fashion that its looks like a utopia come true: The M'Zab region in Southern Algeria, with seven small cities in barren surroundings, including Ghardaia, Melika, and Beni Izguen.

The Mozabites in each community, men and women alike and all of them, go to their (single) mosque for each of the five daily prayers. They do not maintain any hotels: Visitors stay with families as their guests. Neither are there shops. Rather, all marketable items are sold by public auction. In the central square, representatives sitting in the round, each family has a place.

All common tasks (like taking care of dams and watering the palm trees) are fulfilled by *elected* officials. During wedding ceremonies both spouses wear traditional costumes provided by the community (so as to prevent wasteful competitive consumption). Before Mozabite merchants and craftsmen leave the region, for a limited number of years only, they get married, leaving their wives behind.

During the Algerian war of independence (1954-1962) the Mozabites at very high personal risk hid Front de Libération Nationale activists operating in the Sahara region. But after the war they refused all the medals and other honors offered to them by the first FLN government.

This secessionist Kharijite brand of Islam may not appeal to everybody. But it is an example of a Muslim community totally devoted to assuring peace and justice among themselves.

Institutions

(i) *Islamic law* (fiqh) on the basis of *Qu'ran* and Sunnah was developed by Muslim lawyers employing, and honoring, methods like analogy (al-qiyas) and consensus (al-ijma). Historically Islamic jurisprudence produced seven schools of law (al-madhahib), the Ma-likite, Hanafite, Shafi'ite, Hanbalite, Jafarite, Zayidite and (extinct) Zahirite schools of law. They, and not rulers or parliaments, create law in the Muslim world. In fact, law is not *created* at all, from a Muslim perspective; it is *found* (in the divinely revealed sources).

Against this background, in Islam jurisprudence is of supreme importance. This explains why it tolerated, and still does, the existence of competing bodies of law, allowing Muslims to choose between them as they wish, and to change their choice at will. Different interpretations could be so diverse that one and the same case might be considered a major crime by one school and entirely legal by another.

No other law system in the world has ever tolerated divergent legal codices in similar fashion. I therefore submit that the unique Muslim legal scene gives evidence of institutionalized tolerance designed to assure intra-Islamic peace and justice.

(ii) *Pilgrimage* (al-hajj) is another case in point. There are no parallels to the peaceful conduct of the Pilgrimage to Makkah. Two and a half million people assemble and fulfil their religious duties in the same place without ever clashing. This corresponds to the religious command of total peacefulness according to which pilgrims are not even allowed to step on cockroaches or to pick leaves from a tree.

Obviously, the peacefulness of *al-hajj* defies each and every sociological "law" concerning mass behavior. Violence hardly ever absent in large soccer stadiums is absent among millions of pilgrims.

THE CONTEMPORARY SCENE

In today's world, few non-Muslim people would be inclined to associate Islam with peace and justice. Rather, there is an almost general conviction that Islam stands for almost structural violence against women and for terrorism against non-Muslims. These are the lessons learned from al-Qa'ida attacks as on September 11, 2001, in New York and Washington, and later on in Madrid, London, Delhi, Bali, 'Amman, Istanbul, Dar al-Beida (Casablanca), and many other places.

"Islamic" terrorism, even if carried out by certified Muslims like 'Usama bin Laden, cannot be justified Islamically because the Shari'ah allows the use of force only in two cases: *defence* against illegal attacks (2: 191, 4th Verse, 192; 4:90 ff.; 9:13; 22:39), and *resistance* against unbearable tyranny (8:39; 42:39, 42). Nor does it allow *suicide* under any circumstances (4:29).[16] Nor does it tolerate warfare against innocent civilians or against women, children, and natural resources (2:191, 3rd Verse; 22:40).

Western people perusing the *Qu'ran* without sufficient overview frequently arrive at the wrong conclusion that the *Qu'ran* supports an attitude of general aggressive hostility against non-Muslims, as if Muslims were crawling around clenching a knife in their mouth on the look-out for victims. This wrong view is reinforced by the equally wrong conviction that Muslims continue to divide the world in two with their long since obsolete medieval concepts of *dar al-harb* and dar *al-Islam*.

In this context much harm is done by the confusion of verses dealing with *ius in bello* with verses dealing with *ius ad bellum* . To be precise: The *Qu'ran* contains verses dealing with the legal conditions permitting, or not permitting, the opening of armed hostilities (*ius ad bellum*). And it contains verses dealing with the proper conduct of armed hostilities (*ius in bello*). The latter rules today form part of the humanitarian law of war.

Now, the two kinds of rules are not neatly separated in the *Qu'ran* but follow and precede each other unsystematically. This can create havoc, and it does. For instance, in 2:191 it says, "Fight[17] them wherever you come across them." If this is read as *ius ad bellum* it turns Islam into a war-mongering religion. In reality, however, 2:191 is fully in accord with

---

[16] It is erroneous to equate suicide in combat with martyrdom in the sense of 2:154; 3:157 ff., 169; 47:4 ff. It is one thing to risk one's life in combat without a realistic chance of survival and another thing to dispose of one's life, no matter for which purpose.

[17] Fighting (al-qital) and killing (al-qatl) have the same root in Arabic and are often used interchangeably.

international law that allows warfare without any territorial limits once war had been legitimately declared. Thus, 2:191 and similar verses of the *Qu'ran* in no way contradict the doctrinal Islamic commitment to peace.

b) While terrorism committed by Muslims cannot be justified, to some extent it can be explained. One must be aware of the fact that the Muslim world was enormously wronged during the era of colonization which for it began in the eighteenth century with the landing of Napoleon I in Egypt. Soon, except for Turkey and parts of Arabia, the entire Muslim world was colonized and divided among the British, French, Dutch, Portuguese, Russians, and Spanish. All of them, although with different methods, tried to eradicate Islam and to prevent the technical and scientific development of their Muslim subjects.

The Catholic cathedrals in Casablanca, Rabat, Tangier, Oran, Algiers, Bône, Constantine, and Tunis—the one in Algiers ironically called "Notre Dâme d'Afrique" (Our Lady of Africa)—infamously give witness to the excesses of Western imperialism in the Muslim world.

Decolonization in most cases did not come peacefully. Muslims had to fight for it in India, Central Asia, the Caucasus region, and in North Africa. The most prominent cases in point are Muhammad ibn 'Abd al-Wahhab (Arabia), al-Mahdi (Sudan), Abd al-Krim (Morocco), 'Abd al-Qadir al-Jazai'ri (Algeria), 'Umar al-Mukhtar (Libya), and Sayyid Qutb (Egypt). And they still have to fight against the colonization of Palestine and Chechnya.

Decolonization did not signal the end of Muslim woes. On the contrary, in many cases the Western powers left behind Westernized regimes who, to this day, maintain despotic un-Islamic governments. Worse, Zionism and neo-colonialism in the guise of globalization threw many Muslims back into their earlier bunker mentality.

In short, during the two last centuries to be a good Muslim increasingly meant to be a freedom *fighter*. As a result, Muslims during this time had to engage disproportionately often in violent resistance—to such a point that Islam came to be associated with violence.

MUSLIM CONFLICT RESOLUTION TODAY

In searching the bases for peace and justice in Islam our *parcours* has taken us from the *Qu'ran* and Sunna via Muslim history to the present time. Against this background the question now is, what does Islam have to offer for a peaceful and just resolution of conflicts *today*? The answer, again, has a theoretical and a practical angle:

1. Religious Pluralism: The best Islamic doctrine has to offer for conflict resolution is the unique Islamic endorsement of religious pluralism enshrined in Verse 48 of the 5th Sura al-Ma'ida. As from its 4th sentence this verse reads as follows:

> For every one of you We have appointed a different law and way of life.
> And if Allah had so willed, He could surely have made one single community of you.
> But He wished to test you by what He has given you.
> Compete, then, with one another in doing good works! To Allah you must all return; and then He will make you truly understand all that on which you used to differ [...].

This is a sublime manifesto for the peaceful co-existence of religious groups everywhere around the world, based on mutual respect. At the same time it is a clear-cut rejection of any attempt to claim religious superiority.

Verse 5:48, in fact, is entirely incompatible with doctrines like *"extra ecclesiam nulla salus"* (no salvation outside of the Church), until recently held valid by Catholics. Nor is it compatible with the Medieval Catholic doctrine, *"cuius regio eius religio,"* meaning that all subjects have to adopt the religion of their ruler.

What the Islamic doctrine of religious pluralism boils down to is this: Islam, while not being accepted as a revealed religion by Jews and Christians, accepts both Judaism and Christianity as authentic and legitimate faiths. But the Islamic tolerance at least in theory is not yet fully reciprocated by the two other monotheistic creeds.

To be sure, 5:48 is not the only Qur'anic passage proclaiming religious tolerance. The same follows from 2:256, *No compulsion in religion*. This formulation not only forbids conversion by force but recognizes that proselytising by force is utterly useless because the *forum internum* of people simply is beyond outside control. Therefore the very attempt of converting people at gun-point makes no sense.

The 109th Surah (al-Kafirun), too, stresses the merit of religious tolerance:

> Say: O disbelievers!
> I do not worship that which you worship.
> Nor do you worship that which I worship.
> Nor will you worship that which I worship.
> To you your religion and to me my religion.

Could any religious wars have been fought if people on all sides had abided by this concept of religious pluralism? Is this Islamic doctrine not a major, a decisive contribution to peace building and conflict *defusion* in our world, a world characterized by the imposition—called *globalization*—on the "rest" of the world of one single ideology, technology, and market?

2. Protection of religious Minorities: If Islamic doctrine from the beginning was pluralistic, so was the Islamic practice of religious pluralism, all through the ages.

a) According to the Islamic law for the *protection of religious minorities—as-siyar*—non-Muslims in an Islamic State have the right to practice their religion openly. They can apply their own family law, law of inheritance, and even penal law, to be administered by themselves and their minority courts. They are allowed to produce, consume, and trade with alcohol and pork.

The *minority community* (dhimma) was priviliged as well by being exempt from military service. The members of minority religions, so-called *dhimmi*, had to pay a special tax (al-jiz-ya) to the Muslim authorities; but this tax normally was not higher than the *zakat*—tax paid by the Muslim majority.

One can still verify the large scope of Muslim tolerance versus other faiths when visiting Muslim cities. In Istanbul, in quarters like Taksim and Beyoğlu, while one will hardly find any mosque one is bound to run into Catholic, Protestant, and Orthodox churches. The same is true for Cairo if from downtown one drives towards the airport. Coptic churches, not mosques, dominate in that area. In 'Amman (Jordan) the main mosque and the main cathedral face each other. In Damascus the crosses on church steeples are neon-lit at night.

b) Today, Muslim minorities in the West in theory are relatively well protected, much better so than in the past, not only by human rights articles inserted into individual Western constitutions but also by human rights declarations and covenants adopted by the United Nations,[18] the Council of Europe,[19] and the European Union.[20] Accordingly the Occident is

---

[18] *The General Declaration of Human Rights* adopted by the United Nations on 10 December 1948 is merely declaratory, i.e. without the force of international law.

[19] Council of Europe, *European Convention for the Protection of Human Rights and Fundamental Freedoms*.
http://conventions.coe.int/Treaty/en/Treaties/Html/005.htm

[20] *International Covenant on Civil and Political Rights* and *International Covenant on Economic, Social and Cultural Rights*, both dated 19 December 1966. http://www.unhchr.ch/html/menu3/b/a_ccpr.htm and http://www.unhchr.ch/html/menu3/b/a_cescr.htm

committed to safeguarding religious freedom for all (equally and in justice).

However, putting theory into practice, living up to one's legal obligations is a different story. As currently shown in Turkey, atheist-materialist reaction against the progress of religion in society can be as "fundamentalist" and violent as any religious fanaticism. The British Baroness Rabbi Julia Neuberger therefore was right when formulating that reaction against religion can be just as extreme as religious extremism. It's clear that while humans might be dangerous, religions aren't.[21]

The Western statutes of religious non-discrimination are a welcome step in the right direction. But they fall short of the minority rights accorded by Islamic law. This is due to the Western obsession with national sovereignty, hardly diminished during the slow process of European unification. Thus, in negative contrast to the Islamic rules for religious minorities, Muslims in the West are not allowed to administer among themselves their Islamic family law and law of inheritance. In Germany, members of noble families are, however, permitted to adhere to their own laws governing inheritance and titles of nobility.

Nevertheless, Muslims with their readiness to accept legal diversification show the way towards a truly multi-religious community of nations.

3. Racial Equality: What is true for multi-religious tolerance is also true for the potential Muslim contribution to peaceful multi-ethnic relations.

a) Any time, anywhere, the coexistence between ethnically different people was troublesome. Human history shows all too many examples of racial clashes. Black people were equally enslaved by Muslim, Jewish, and Christian dealers. Jews were persecuted everywhere in the Christian world until anti-Semitism culminated in the German Holocaust.

b) In spite of that Muslim history, has been *relatively* free of racist crimes, freer than any other civilization. Until the creation of Israel, Muslims never were anti-Semitic. In fact, they still are not since anti-Zionism cannot be equated with anti-Semitism. (After all, the Arabs are semites themselves.)

Symbolic of the irrelevance for Muslims of skin color was the appointment of Bilal as the first *muadhdhin* ever. True, there is some evidence of Persians looking down on Arabs, and of Arabs on Blacks, just

---

[21] Interview with Julia Neuberger, *Emel, the Muslim Lifestyle Magazine*, 31 (May 2007), p. 31.

as *Hijazis* and *Najdis* may look down on each other, and the "noble" people of al-Madinah on their "commercial" brothers in Makkah. But much of that is entirely normal since—important for their survival—human beings cannot but think and feel sociologically in terms of *in-groups* and *out-groups*.

What counts is the positive trend found in the Ummah to downplay ethnical differences in favor of a touchable brotherhood based on Islam. This is what makes the Ummah a reality that scares many a ruler in the Muslim world. And this is what unites Arabs, Albanians, Americans, Bosnians, Englishmen, Frenchmen, Germans, Indians, Indonesians, Iranians, Malaysians, Nigerians, Pakistanis, Senegalese, Somalis, and Turks in Occidental mosques. The British historian A.J. Toynbee put this well saying that "the extinction of race consciousness as between Muslims is one of the outstanding achievements of Islam, and in the contemporary world there is, as it happens, a crying need for the propagation of this Islamic virtue."[22]

The Ummah is indeed the closest the world has ever come to human brotherhood. Neither Communists (supposedly uniting all proletarians) nor Christians (supposedly loving their neighbours like themselves) have ever come to their ideals closer than the Muslims have.

These might indeed be the most crucial contributions Islam can make to peace building and conflict resolution world-wide.

CONCLUSION

Today's world is characterized by a dichotomy between a strong trend towards globalization and a countervailing flight into parochialism. The unitarian trend is being opposed by a cosy "small is beautiful" ideology. We all are caught in between these currents, pulling us to and fro.

Clearly, the existential problems faced by mankind these days and years to come—over-population and oversized threats to the ecology, spelling disaster—are compounded by unending armed conflicts between rich and poor, migrants and sedentary people, young and old, black and white, and between believers of divergent faiths. In such turmoil, people are bound to see the world around them as colored in black and white, in a confrontational manner. If this vicious tendency is not checked the world is heading for a catastrophe.

In this explosive situation, existing and potential, all people of faith must see each other as allies in the over-arching struggle between a sheer

---

[22] Cited in ibid., p. 12, n. 18.

materialistic world view and an opposing one defending the transcendental links to the world's Creator. Under the given circumstances all religious people from whatever denomination cannot but co-operate.

Indeed, the situation is so critical that God-fearing people must seek to profit from the special insights and spirituality of each and every religion. In that context, Islam is called upon to contribute what it can do best in terms of social interaction: to promote peace and justice through (i) religious pluralism (ii) the protection of religious minorities, and (iii) the practice of racial equality.

ALLIANCE OF WORLD RELIGIONS TO PROMOTE PRO-ACTIVE SOCIAL SPIRITUALITY

Swami Agnivesh

India is the only country which is the storehouse of ancient knowledge provided by godly saints, rishis, and maharishis. This knowledge, if shared among all the peoples of this World, would promote universal peace, brotherhood, amity, and cordiality in the age of globalisation.

The four Vedas, known as the first books in the world, promote global spirituality without discriminating humanity on the basis of caste, colour, or creed. While most of the religions divide humanity between believers and non-believers, the Vedas proclaim "Vasudhaev Kutumbhkam" (The Whole World is One) and every human being, good or bad, is the excellent creation of God.

Every person is a walking book. We may not learn substantially from books but from people around us. Every person has some qualities worth imbibing. Let's not ignore any one on face value. Let us talk. Let us interact. We will discover that we can learn something from every body. If you are more well-read or well-travelled or have interacted with the maximum number of people, you are the lamp post to guide others.

The demand of this millennium is that we have to co-exist despite our difference of opinions. We must celebrate our differences. Let everybody have the privilege to differ but without losing temper. If we respect dissension, we become democratic, tolerant, give recognition to people, and promote diversity which brings unity in society automatically. Reciprocity from the other side will be matching even if delayed. Indian society is a fine example of this diversity and multi-cultural society.

India never believed in mono-culture. Those who promote mono-culture based on religion or culture believe in their (religion's) superiority over other faiths, resort to religious conversion, thus creating tension in society. Christianity and Islam believe in institutional proselytising. The jihads and (counter) crusades have a bloody history in the past. If there is regimentation in one religious camp, it will produce automatic regimentation in the other camp, shutting out the communication channels and thus creating misunderstanding and suspicion between each other.

Religious fundamentalism, empowered by money, power-lust, and overzealousness, has given rise to terrorism. Partly to blame for the rise of terrorism is the arrogance of western imperialism and non-reconciliation between Islam and Christianity. After 9/11, Islam has come under greater scrutiny by intellectuals. Debate among non-Muslims on the need for reforms in Islam is noteworthy. Let the liberals in Muslim world take initiative on this issue of reinterpreting Islam to project it as relevant to modern times and removing obscurantism.

On the other hand, in the western context, and particularly since the dawn of modernity, the understanding and propagation of the biblical faith has been radically corrupted by the domination of power, resulting in the rejection of love as the shaping paradigm of western culture. This summary rejection of biblical culture was overlooked in the glare of power, control, and wealth; and the Way of Jesus Christ ceased to be the Way of the Cross.

Biblical texts were deployed to cover up the nakedness of western triumphalism and religious expansionism, resulting in the coinage of laughable slogans like "The Globe for Christ by 2000 AD," "India for Christ by 2000 AD" and so on. Ironically, these expansionist slogans began to emerge proportionately as the western world ceased to be Christian. Midway through the nineteenth Century, the European religious constituency was stung by Soren Kierkegaard, the foremost Christian philosopher of the times, who lamented, "Throughout Christendom, there is not a single Christian!" The more Europe ceased to be Christian, the more Europeans wanted the rest of the world to be Christian.

The continuous trend of religious conversion has been controversial in India and has resulted in demographic threats that are posing a grave social tension. We must consider banning both conversion and re-conversion. Let's not bring constitutional aspects of freedom of propagation of faith into this matter. The culture of proselytisation cuts into the roots of other religions. Mono-cultural societies have more social tension, including ethnic violence, despite belonging to the same religion. This calls for the establishment of multi-cultural societies by migration of people from different nationalities and religions or promoting inter-religious and inter-caste marriages.

Lack of proper education, parents' neglect, and degradation of traditional values lead to insecurity and fear among individuals. It has been proved wrong that money and power would give security and stability to individuals. To be spiritual, one has to have faith in God, mind one's own *karma* (deeds) and vow to behave responsibly in every act and every day. Just see whether your action is going to harm anybody. If it's so, rethink your decision. Blame yourself or your karmas for the wrong things happening to you. Non-spiritual people always find fault in others and blame others for their misery. Belief in God and vowing to perform good karmas will remove the fear among people.

No religion is safe from this inner decay. And the pathology of religion can be seen both by what it does and by what it fails to do. Religion holds considerable spiritual resources for transforming individuals and societies.

The goal of spirituality, in the Vedic tradition, is the ennoblement of all human beings. This calls for the creation of social, economic, political, and cultural conditions conducive to such a goal. The Vedas offer a comprehensive, universal vision for humanity. Unfortunately, the ascendancy of Brahmanical vested interests distorted the pure light of the Vedas, misinterpreted and degraded it into an apology for caste domination.

The greater need is to evolve Global spirituality, drawing good things from all the religions and drawing up a global school/college syllabus to promote inter-religious goodwill so that every child in every part of the world is connected with the world. The hallmark of spirituality is responsiveness to the given context. This is what distinguishes spirituality from religion in its common practice. As a matter of fact, religion in itself is meant to be a source of empowerment for human beings in their effort to make sense of and cope with, their life-world. This has four major spheres of search, struggle, and growth.

(a) First, every individual needs to relate to the divine, and live by the discipline that goes with it. Questions pertaining to the nature and being of God belong to this order of human preoccupation.

(b) Second, there is a need to understand oneself, where questions like who we are, what is the meaning and purpose of life, what is the scope of human destiny, what are the means for human fulfilment become important.

(c) Third, we need to relate wholesomely to the given social context where the dynamics of living together with others assume profound spiritual significance. It is in this context that the dynamism of our spirituality finds practical expression. The spiritually enlightened person cannot remain indifferent to the problems and sufferings of others. Justice becomes the most authentic expression of spirituality in the social context. This entails a sense of responsibility for the kind of society we create and the human predicament that prevails in it.

(d) Fourthly, every human being needs to maintain a healthy relationship with the material world, the order of creation all around him. He needs to practice justice in the way he relates to the total order of creation, taking care of the world around him, respecting the integrity of creation as an important aspect of our human vocation. When this is forgotten and creation is exploited in violation of its sanctity and sustainability, we precipitate the environmental crisis.

THE POLARIZATION BETWEEN RELIGION AND SPIRITUALITY

Spirituality needs to be distinguished in the light of these observations from the practice of religion, though spirituality is subsumed in religion. Over a period of time, as religion gets institutionalized, there comes about a gap between the two, which thereafter tends to widen. This polarization between religion and spirituality results from the degradation of religion and further contributes to it. In the end a stage is reached in which religion becomes a contradiction of spirituality. So it happens that religious rituals and sacraments become an escape route from the challenges and responsibilities of the world around us. It even happens that religious concepts are employed in justifying and perpetuating the practice of injustice.

From this perspective, our Vedic heritage presents two contrasting faces. On the one hand, we have a rich and commendable religious and philosophical tradition, unrivaled in its sophistication and subtlety. No other religious culture has scaled the heights and depths of subjective spirituality (the subtle understanding of the self) as we have done. On the other hand, the Indian religious outlook has progressively tended to close its eyes to social realities where gross aberrations continued to thrive.

Consider the idea of Dharma in the Vedic tradition. Understood properly, Dharma is essentially a spiritual concept that pertains to the foundation and sustenance of the created order in its natural, social, and political dimensions. Dharma is that which undergirds the wholeness of creation and social life. It is possible to understand this principle either in a "status quo-ist" or in a dynamic way. Seen only from a status quo-ist perspective, Dharma is that which rationalizes and preserves the existing order with all its strengths and weaknesses, beauties and blemishes, intact. Dharma in other words is a preservative. But in its dynamic paradigm, Dharma becomes a principle of transformation. It aims not only at supporting the existing scheme of things, but also to bring out the ideal potentials in the order of creation, which is not yet revealed in all its scope.

From such a dynamic perspective, two categories of spiritual task become clear. First, there is a need to reinforce what is good and righteous in the given context. Second, there is a need also to resist and reduce the aberrations and distortions in the given socio-economic order. It is because of this that Swami Dayanand Saraswati emphasized that a sense of mission is basic to the practice of religion when it is healthy and dynamic. But when the spiritual fire within a religion dies out, the first casualty will be this sense of mission, which embodies the dynamism of that religion.

The problem with us today is that we have too much of religion but little of spirituality. And our religions seem to be vying with each other in justifying Karl Marx's indictment of religion that it is the opium of the people. (The sense in which Marx used this expression is, incidentally, different from what is popularly derived from it. But that is another matter.) It is important to take cognizance of the alarming signs of religious decay in our times. Our religiosity is not imbued with a passion to resist the forces of evil. It is not ablaze with compassion for our fellow human beings and for the rest of creation. We watch mutely the shameless abuse of religion for political profits, using it as a blanket in this process for all sorts of atrocities and frauds. If this lamentable trend is not arrested, religion will be seen by the coming generation only as a liability, reinforcing the current secular prejudice.

Those who subscribe to the Vedic World View, as I do, have a lot to answer for themselves vis-à-vis the institutionalization of injustice and systemic oppression in the name of Hinduism. In one sense, our society has been a peaceful one. Different religious communities have been living, at least till recently, in remarkable amity and harmony with each other. But in another sense we are one of the most violent societies in the world.

No other society has kept as many millions for as many centuries in a state of subhuman subjugation and exploitation as the low caste people in all religious communities have been in this country. Even today, fifty years after the attainment of freedom, millions continue to suffer under the yoke of caste oppression and bonded labour. Millions exist like living ghosts under the epidemic of poverty and avoidable diseases. Forty-six percent of our people today are illiterate. They outnumber the total population of India at the time of our Independence.

The tragic thing is that what makes suffering, enslavement, and exploitation so endemic in our context is also our basic strength: our resilience as a people. Ironically we have been weakened by our strength. People put up with a lot in this country. They have the patience of mountains. They endure mutely on the edges of extinction. For far too long we have romanticized this slow suicide only because it served the interests of the status quo, of those who had everything and did not want to share the available resources with their neighbours. All religions have done it. Christianity turned the fierce biblical ethics into a tame and toothless thing, understandably castigated by Nietzsche as too mild and humane to be useful. The Church has had no use for the Jesus who exploded with indignation at the site of exploitation and overturned the tables of vested interests in the Temple premises. Instead, all through, the Church has been preaching self-denial while practising tyranny and opulence.

The point in making this reference is to emphasize the need to radically revalue our orthodox ethical dogmas and assumptions. To do this meaningfully, we need to strike a balance between our habitual otherworldliness and the need for dynamic this-worldliness. The dishonest practice of selling hope for a better birth or heaven in lieu of minimum human dignity and personal fulfillment in this world needs to be questioned. Those who cannot extend a helping hand to those who suffer and wither in this world have no moral right to insult them with the mockery of "a pie in the sky when you die." This needs to be seen as the bottom line for evolving the contours of social spirituality.

Fundamental to the question of social spirituality is the distortion of ethics affected by the religious establishment. As the religious establishment gets stronger and stronger and as vested interests of class or caste supersede the spiritual ideals of a religious tradition, we find the revolutionary aspects of religious ethics being diluted. Ethical principles begin to be re-oriented in the direction of preserving and propagating the status quo. Ironically, it is the establishment, both religious and secular, that is keen to preach ethics. The willingness to practice ethics in this connection is inversely proportionate to the eagerness to preach it.

A few illustrative cases here:

This pro status quo nature that is imparted to religion is incompatible with its true vocation, which is to transform individuals and societies. Transformation is not just any change. It is, instead, change directed towards the maximum fulfilment of human beings as human beings. Fulfilment in the human context, in other words, is a great deal more than mere material possession, indulgence, or consumption of pleasure. In its social context, transformation acquires a revolutionary character. It implies the "spiritual" duty to engage and reform institutions, systems, and practices that are subversive of our humanity. This is the essence of righteousness in its dynamic sense. Dharma is not merely a state of having some nice sentiments. It is an active orientation that refuses to compromise with forces of evil. It excludes indifference to the suffering of one's fellow human beings.

At this point we need to reckon with a basic aspect of spirituality. The spiritual is different from the material in this respect: that to be authentic the spiritual needs to be embodied. The material object is there whether or not it is used or invoked. A man who has a million rupees in the bank balance is rich, even if he maintains the lifestyle of a pauper. Not so in the case of things spiritual. If someone says he has love in his heart, but never cares to express it in his life time, he is a liar. It is hence integral to the logic of spirituality that it needs to be embodied in the given context. In that sense, we do not have to say "social spirituality," for spirituality is also "social" by definition.

Rather than recognize and develop the transformative dimension of religion—that is, the spiritual dynamism of religion—the priestly class in all religions prefers to promote its escapist aspects. Religious obscurantism is born out of this outlook. Obscurantism, as the word implies, involves disengagement with the world of realities. It obscures the element of human responsibility and the need to respond in practical terms. Rather than take the policy decision, for example, to wipe out illiteracy from India and pursue it vigorously through administrative action, we could go on chanting Saraswati Vandana. We could go on worshiping the goddess of wealth, and yet not develop a healthy work culture or sense of disciplined management of our material resources. Instead, we could improvise all sorts of rituals and practices by which the gods could be coaxed and cajoled to overlook our lapses and continue to bless us in spite of ourselves.

It is because of this that we face an embarrassing contradiction today. India is a land of profound spirituality. It is also a land of extreme inequality, injustice, and dehumanization. The sublime philosophical reach of the Indic soul has not found its social expressions. Social realities have gone almost in the opposite direction from the flight of this Indic soul. The Indian religious traditions, more than the Semitic religions, recognized the spiritual value of the female principle. But the plight of our women, especially of the widows, has continued to be lamentable all through. Hospitality has been a great value with us, but the dalits have never found a place in the architecture of our social outlook. It is here that the seed of our all-round poverty lies.

There are at least three major reasons why we need to develop social dimensions of our spirituality.

(1) Our country stands in need of social empowerment. A country in which millions are socially enslaved and disabled cannot hope to progress and attain its fulfillment. In this context, issues like endemic illiteracy, poverty, disease, and inequality need to be seen as spiritual challenges. The caste system is a patent violation of social spirituality. Dismantling this oppressive, inhuman practice is a pre-condition for the fulfillment of our destiny as a nation.

(2) We need to create a rationale for our unity and oneness as a people. Disunity and social tensions are unavoidable when social justice is overlooked. The true index of the healthy status of a society is its commitment to social justice. Unity and dynamism are its by-products. Today we are a lamentably fragmented society, wherein ironically divisive manoeuvers are being made to promote artificial unity. That is why some seek to unite the Hindu fold using various hate objects, improvised from time to time.

(3) We need to build a participatory culture of development within which the total human energies and resources available to us are deployed in nation building. The extent to which the 400 million illiterate people in this country can participate in or contribute to nation building is minimal. From the point of view of active participation or resource sharing the population of India must be reckoned in terms of a few millions. This in itself is a massive indictment of the levels of social injustice prevalent today in our context.

The need to create a dynamic social order has become all the more compelling in the context of globalism. Egalitarianism and people's participation have been major factors in the socio-economic dynamism of the developed societies. Today they are in a position to derive the best out of the emerging global order. The Market is not a place of sentimentality, compassion or charity. We have to deliver the goods to be taken seriously. Gimmicks like exploding nuclear devices will not cover the nakedness of our social underdevelopment, by which we shall continue to be judged and condemned.

Those who claim to be spiritually enlightened cannot any longer shut their eyes on the weeping wounds of our society. The situation today is such that we have to launch a new "Liberation Movement" in India. For vast segments in our country, the attainment of political freedom has not meant much. Millions wait to be liberated from bonded labour, child labour, illiteracy, poverty, ill-health, exploitation, and conspiratorial neglect at the hands of the State. Millions more need to be liberated from superstition, religious obscurantism, and fundamentalism. Above all our society needs to be liberated from the prison house of communal hatred and hostilities and the inevitable dissipation of energies and resources this involves. The rise of religious fundamentalism is made possible only by the dilution of our commitment to social justice.

One of the foremost needs in the Indian context today is to reform the very idea of religion. Our tragedy is that we have too much of religion and little of spirituality. Religion without spirituality, especially in its social dimension, tends to be a system of oppression and exploitation. It was against Christianity without a commitment to social justice that Karl Marx issued his informed indictment. Human history, including the Church, has been the richer for that.

It is time that a similar spiritual ferment took place in our context too. But that will not happen as long as this is left in the hands of professional clergy and the hangers-on of the religious establishment. People whose hearts are set ablaze with compassion and truth need to devote themselves to the task of impacting our society from a spiritual perspective and produce the fruits of the resultant transformation so that the religious establishment is forced to take note of it. While religion can be the exclusive preserve of the religious, spirituality is under nobody's monopoly. He who gives a glass of water to quench the thirst of another is spiritually more evolved than those who chant their scriptures with their eyes closed to the giant agony of our world.

PLENARY PAPERS

MOBILISING FOR A GLOBAL MARSHALL PLAN: A PATH TO CONFLICT RESOLUTION, PEACEBUILDING AND HUMAN SECURITY

HUMAN SECURITY AND THE
GLOBAL MARSHALL PLAN

James Bernard Quilligan

NEW MARSHALL PLAN

The idea of a "New Marshall Plan" to benefit developing nations has been inspiring people around the world since United States Secretary of State George C. Marshall spearheaded a major American relief and reconstruction program for Europe following the Second World War. The goal then was the emergency stabilization and reconstruction of sixteen nations in Western Europe, which were ravaged by poverty, disease, hunger, unemployment, and political chaos in the aftermath of combat. The US was motivated to assist them for humanitarian reasons, as well as to reestablish the region as a strong trading partner and a buffer against the expansion of Soviet Communism. From 1947 to 1951, the US extended as much as 2% of its annual GDP in material and financial assistance in this unprecedented development relief effort. Some people at the time also began to envision the possibility of a similar program in developing nations. Looking beyond Europe, President Harry Truman promised a new dispensation of American foreign assistance for the poor countries of Africa, Asia, and Central and South America, "a bold new program for making the benefits of our scientific advances and industrial progress available for the improvement and growth of underdeveloped areas."[1] The concept also became popular in several European nations (Germany, France, Luxembourg, Belgium, the Netherlands, and Great Britain, in particular) which were especially grateful for America's largesse and realized the logic of doing something similar to fight poverty in the world's poorest nations. A global action plan to fight poverty had long been a symbol of hope for those living in the crowded slums of poor townships and the tiny dirt farms of the world's remote and impoverished places, far from the hulking urban centers. This dream took on greater currency when the Brandt Commission's 1980 report on global development, *North-South: A Program for Survival* was hailed in the international community and the press as a new "Global Marshall Plan."[2] Since then, the theory of a global plan to benefit impoverished nations has been deconstructed, reformulated,

---

[1] Harry S. Truman, "Inaugural Address," January 20, 1949.
http://www.bartleby.com/124/pres53.html
[2] Willy Brandt, North-South: A Project for Survival (London: Pan, 1980).

and endlessly discussed by academics, policy analysts, parliamentarians, development specialists, environmentalists, and more than a few global leaders.

Over the past fifty years, the phrase has become a metaphor used in many different contexts and with a variety of meanings. Usually it refers to *an intensive development program involving financial support and technical assistance on a large scale for a specific impoverished geographical region or a complex global problem.* Most often, the goal of a proposed "Marshall Plan" is to fight poverty and underdevelopment through a massive infusion of aid and resources. The assumption is that helping local people meet their basic needs and build capacity will produce a transformational stimulus, producing self-generated and independent economic development; in turn, economic growth in developing nations would increase trade, create new jobs, and boost the economies of developed nations. But the scope of new Marshall Plan proposals has also been broadened to include many other areas related to poverty, such as finance and the environment. A deep search of the term in the Google listings shows at least sixty different proposals calling for a Global Marshall Plan (GMP). There are probably dozens more. Some of these are mere announcements, declarations of good intentions, and wish lists, while others are formal detailed proposals. We may classify them into four different types. Most uses of the term GMP refer to particular development goals for *specific issues*. Some GMPs are *region-specific* proposals, targeted for a particular geographic area. A third type—*interdependent* proposals—focus on linkages among various issues pertaining to developing nations as a class (rather than a specific issue or region). A final type of GMP includes *structural* proposals, which address systemic changes in the international economic system to promote long-term development.

While there is not sufficient space here to review all of these plans, we may offer a few observations. What is common to most GMPs is an implicit recognition that nation-state structures are inadequate in meeting systemic international problems; that increased global interdependence requires that global issues be linked together strategically and discussed by a broad array of international representatives at a new level of international political discussion; that these representatives should launch an immediate global action program commensurate with the dimensions of the issue or problem designated; and that substantial amounts of money must be raised to meet these goals. From an intra-cultural perspective, the very existence of all these different GMPs is evidence of a profound plea for global order surfacing from every corner of the Earth. The variety and persistence of proposals for a GMP are symptomatic of a planet singularly becoming conscious of its problems and contradictions, as experts from countless fields of inquiry and service call for a new framework of economic governance. Whether the particular focus is on poverty, development, environment, human security, social equity, cultural diversity, or human rights, virtually all of these GMPs suggest a need for global economic justice and a committed long-range effort to end poverty, ensure sustainable development, establish global governance, and create enduring prosperity. And this, in turn, implies a restructuring of the global economic and political order, which cannot be achieved within the scope of current Bretton Woods, World Trade Organization, and United Nations rules, policies, and institutions. This paper synthesizes the most important structural proposals for a Global Marshall Plan with an emphasis on personal security—the protection of people from external threats of all forms.

SECURITY WITHOUT BORDERS

Since the start of the multilateral era following World War II we have tended to view security and development as two distinct areas—a political realm of peace and security, and a socio-economic realm of development This bifurcated approach to security has become part of the unconscious fabric of modern government in virtually every nation. As the international flow of goods, services, money, information and people across the planet intensifies, the result is not a borderless world of personal security but a militant increase in state power and a submissive decline in individual liberty. Since the end of the Cold War in the early 1990s, progressive analysts have been formulating a new paradigm: that true security for human beings stems from sustainable development—not the sovereign defense of states. As many people are now keenly aware, while we are all globally connected by virtue of our common humanity and shared values of personal dignity and worth, globalization is not being managed according to the intrinsic rights and responsibilities we hold as a human family. We need to create a regulatory framework based on the universal norms of generosity and equitability that flow from human civilization as a functioning whole—an inclusive institutional design that establishes formal links between peace, security, development, and the environment, allowing people to live free from fear and want, with the opportunity to develop their full personal and social potentials in a healthy and supporting environment.

The safest way to build a bridge from the old world to the emerging one—applying our democratic norms of diversity, equality, and cooperation to the global system that is now evolving—is through a Global Marshall Plan. The major challenge before us today is to re-examine our traditional sources of political legitimacy and power and open a new context for global interdependence and cooperation. Because sovereignty is ultimately an individual expression of the inherent unity of humankind and does not truly depend on national boundaries or ideologies, we recognize that personal security must be generated primarily within—not between— nation-states. Indeed, the way to create lasting peace and justice in the world is through honoring the needs and sacred presence of the other person—an inner reality which the world's governmental bureaucracies studiously avoid and sometimes malign. But many people are already following this path of "security without borders" as an ethical imperative. Through our vast subjective interconnectedness, we realize that only inward security can truly lead to outer security, and it is our task to acknowledge the common interests of all nations and cultures for peaceful security and to bring this understanding into the national and international political process. Through a GMP based on human security and generosity we shall embark on a new era of global structural change, ensuring that this present transitional period of globalization leads to international equity and cooperative governance. Synthesizing the various proposals for a Global Marshall Plan that have been put forward, we see five essential points for action: (1) Fulfil the Millennium Development Goals+; (2) Establish and Meet Global Environmental Targets; (3) Create New Sources of Finance and Allocation of Resources; (4) Restructure Global Economic Rules and Institutions; and (5) Internationalize the Dialogue for Global Action.

FULFIL THE MILLENNIUM DEVELOPMENT GOALS

In the 1940s, after a devastating period of economic depression and war, our multilateral era was launched with great hope for the future, promising international peace, security, freedom, social progress, equal rights, and development for all people. Those ideals were enshrined in the 1945 United Nations Charter and the 1948 United Nations Universal Declaration of Human Rights. But global politics quickly intruded and the military defense of nation-states became the overriding theme of the post-war era. Measures for human and social development were widely identified and discussed during the Cold War period but rarely placed in the context of human security and never formally quantified at the international level. Finally, in 2000, the international community established the United Nations Millennium Development Goals—measurable targets to fight poverty and raise living standards in the world's poorest areas. These practical goals, set for 2015, include eradication of extreme poverty and hunger; achievement of universal primary education; promotion of gender equality and empowerment of women; reduction of child mortality;

improvement of maternal health; combat against HIV/AIDS, malaria and other diseases; ensuring environmental sustainability; and creation of a global partnership for development.

In 2007, midway to their target date, funding and implementation for the MDGs is woefully behind schedule. Sixty nations remain in desperate conditions of poverty and another forty are below the international poverty line, yet rich governments are not ramping up their aid budgets for 2008-2011 nearly as rapidly as they have pledged. It has also become clear that while the MDGs are a very significant start, they are just the beginning of what is truly needed to end extreme poverty and achieve inclusive development. Even if the MDGs were met by 2015, they are not likely to ensure human security and social development for the long term for several reasons. (1) The MDGs are not the minimum requirements for empowering poor nations to improve their standards of living and foster an ethic of local self-sufficiency. Additional reforms—which some in the development community call "MDGs+"—must be initiated to supplement the MDGs, including clean water, sanitation, habitat, local infrastructure, and opportunities for employment. (2) Even the MDGs+ must be enhanced by other global goals for capacity-building so that the root causes of economic, political and social instability are also addressed. The MDGs and MDGs+ cannot thrive without adequate support from local governments in developing nations to ensure self-sufficiency and self-determination. This means the complete legalization of women's rights, strong social, political and economic institutions, the rule of law and courts, moral and political freedom, full equality, property rights, a reliable civil service, community-building, public safety, stable banks, public finance, public utilities, public education, and social welfare—areas which the MDGs and MDGs+ do not address in any depth. (3) The international community also needs to look beyond 2015. Even if nations were to achieve their goals to eliminate poverty, ensure development, and encourage the creation of stable institutions in poor nations for the medium-term, the MDGs+ cannot be sustained unless they are supported by major reforms in international trade, finance, monetary and energy policy. This means that our commitment to multilateralism must be total and that sustainable development must become the collective responsibility of the international community. It must be recognized, therefore, that the philosophy underlying the MDGs—that each country should finance its own development and what it cannot undertake will be financed by investments from transnational corporations and overseas aid from individual states—is still part of the world's bilateral orthodoxy, not a formula for lasting transformation. Over the long-term, national development projects such as the GMP must be managed by a central multilateral development agency, such as the UN Development Program or a reformulated UN Economic Council.

ESTABLISH AND MEET GLOBAL ENVIRONMENTAL TARGETS

The Stern Review (2006),[3] the reports of the Intergovernmental Panel on Climate Change (2007),[4] and many other recent studies have provided convincing evidence of the reality of climate change, predicting that the average global temperature could increase from 2°–5° F over the next century. Rising temperatures and extreme climate patterns are already having an enormous impact on human security. We already know that global warming leads to loss of species, decline of ecosystem services and habitats, environmental hazards and natural disasters, all of which threaten human life and community. But the direct impact of global warming on personal security is also clear. Increased production of greenhouse gases from the use of fossil fuels, chlorofluorocarbons, and methane gas from landfills leads to higher ocean temperatures, melting glaciers, rising sea levels and acidified oceans, which results in intensified levels of rainfall, storms, flooding, loss of wetlands, heat waves, and droughts. As a consequence, many people—especially the poor in some of the world's most crowded and marginally productive areas—are affected by a lack of water for drinking and irrigation, increased resource scarcity, a decline in agricultural production, loss of supportive wildlife, widespread disease from mosquitoes and other pests, declining health, economic losses caused by volatile hurricanes and tornadoes (exacerbated by warmer rising seas), volatility in economic output and trade, and increasing poverty. In turn, the harmful impact of climate extremes on human livelihoods and living conditions, combined with the resource exploitation of poor nations by rich interests, has triggered violence, armed conflict, social and cultural disruptions, mass migration of refuges, and a widening disparity between developed and developing nations. We are currently witnessing many signs of this kind of temperature-driven civil strife in parts of Central Asia, the Middle East, Africa, and Latin America.

---

[3] *Economics of Climate Change: The Stern Review* (Cambridge: Cambridge University Press, 2006).
http://www.hm-treasury.gov.uk/independent_reviews/stern_review_economics_climate_change/stern_review_report.cfm
[4] *Climate Change 2007: Synthesis Report* (Geneva: IPCC, 2007); *Climate Change 2007: The Physical Science Basis* (Geneva: IPCC, 2007); *Climate Change 2007: Impacts, Adaptation and Vulnerability* (Geneva: IPCC, 2007); *Climate Change 2007: Mitigation of Climate Change* (Geneva: IPCC, 2007).

Although the sustainable development movement has been pressing for mandatory rules to curb global warming for more than twenty years, firm targets have not been universally adopted. Thirty-five countries have ratified the 1997 Kyoto Protocol, which set restrictions on greenhouse gas emissions for 2012, but developing nations were exempted from these binding carbon limits to protect their economic growth. Kyoto rests on the idea of capping the quantity of emissions at an agreed level and allowing companies to trade carbon credits for extra reductions (costing in the range of $20–$100 per ton of CO2 emitted). This shifting of financial burdens through the sale and trade of surplus emissions permits—creating, in effect, a global pollution market in which companies can obtain the right to produce more emissions than they otherwise would—is not the kind of deep restructuring of global trade, finance and monetary policy that will change the energy base of global society. Kyoto has already lost legitimacy since the US refused to join, and also because several other rapidly industrializing nations which were originally exempted—India, China, Indonesia, and Brazil—need to be brought under emissions caps now as well. The 1987 Montreal Protocol, which applies equally to developed and developing nations, has been very successful in cutting back global emissions of ozone-depleting gases. Ultimately, all nations need to enter into a similar universal system for the reduction of carbon dioxide and other heat-trapping gases. It is not too soon to begin formulating a more inclusive framework for stabilizing greenhouse gas emissions after the Kyoto Protocol expires, setting carbon reduction targets, and developing new international mechanisms to ensure their enforcement beyond 2012. China and the United States—the world's largest producers of carbon dioxide—must soon become active participants in global negotiations for mandatory emissions controls, particularly now that climate change is widely recognized as a major threat to international peace and security.

The international community needs to set high standards for environmental security by ending its fossil fuel dependency and wasteful use of resources that result in global warming. To do this, we need to find new ways of diversifying our energy sources through solar, hydro, wind, tide, geothermal, and biomass fuels, lower the costs of these renewable energies so they can compete with fossil fuels, and increase conservation through increased efficiency. The world's poorest nations are presently unable to absorb the cost of emissions reduction which would allow them to adapt to climate change. Developed nations must therefore give special attention to reducing the climate and coastal threats to these vulnerable regions and help them adapt to the devastating results of global warming by financing carbon reduction projects, ensuring that impoverished nations get increasing amounts of clean energy. Because sustainable development is a vital component of human security for all nations, rich and poor, we need to create a United Nations Environmental Organization to coordinate global action on ecological degradation and climate change.

CREATE NEW SOURCES OF FINANCE AND ALLOCATION OF RESOURCES

Since the Second World War, the Korean War, and the Vietnam War, many peace activists have championed the idea of channelling government funds from the production of arms and weapons directly into spending on human and social development. Under the present system, however, "economic conversion" is not an easy legislative matter of replacing one budget with another, since it involves a fundamental change in political and economic infrastructure, society, and culture—requiring a new quality and degree of public consciousness. To embark on this transformation, we must expose the illusory economic incentives that drive the "permanent war economy." As many social critics have observed, the socioeconomic infrastructure embedded in our national security state exaggerates global cultural differences in order to maintain domestic control. The objectification of foreign nations and races as enemies creates a cohesive emotional identity within our group based on fear and hatred of the Other. This enables the State to deploy a standing army which is sanctioned by the government, financed by taxpayers, supplied by the oil industry and defense contractors, tested with the latest devices by technology companies, and rationalized by the popular media—all of which generates research and development, production, consumer demand, and new spending. Demonizing the Other also takes our attention away from the political control and enormous profits that result from institutionalized war and financial exploitation, producing social regimentation and conformity, unquestioning acceptance of the political orthodoxy, collective dissociation and personal disempowerment. It is important now to educate the public on the extent to which the military-government-oil-industrial-technology-media complex stimulates the domestic economy by fostering a climate of militarism and mass anxiety over regional emergencies and national security, persuading us that the protection of our borders is more important than the human and social welfare and environmental conditions within those borders.

Despite this perennial fear of foreign invading armies, the fact is that far more people today die from poverty, disease, human rights abuses, and ecological degradation than from war. Natural disasters alone cause six times as many deaths as war. To transform the traditional meaning of security from military defense of the state against external attack to the humane protection of individuals and the community from all forms of political and economic violence, we must demonstrate the feasibility of allocating national resources based on generosity and sharing. We must show that devoting multilateral resources to the improvement of human conditions and the guarantee of freedom from danger and injury will powerfully offset the need for national defense expenditures and war profiteering, break down cultural barriers, reduce social fears, and create new demand for personal security and sustainable development, resulting in a peaceful economic stimulus. After all, it is far less risky and less costly for a nation to devote itself to mutual cooperation and peaceful change than to unending war and domination. In proposing new multilateral means for the financing and distribution of funds for social development and environmental reform, several challenges require progressive understanding and action.

First, we must be clear about what generosity means in the context of international development. The liberal and neo-liberal orthodoxy preaches that more economic growth and more foreign aid are the solution to reversing global poverty and environmental destruction—when in fact growth-driven production and consumption and aid-driven corruption have contributed significantly to global poverty and environmental destruction. So it is not simply a matter of generating more money; it also is a matter of creating new international mechanisms that level the playing field and stop draining the poor of their resources, livelihoods, and incomes so that the compassionate generosity of the wealthy may actually have a chance to be effective. Under the present scheme of bilateral foreign assistance, there are just too many opportunities for the skimming of financial flows and the manipulative use of aid for geostrategic objectives by donor nations, as well as poor planning and lack of coordination by aid agencies and widespread hoarding and corruption on the part of many recipient governments. We need to embark on a system of multilateral financing that will end the damaging double standard of country-to-country aid which turns resource distribution into a zero-sum game in which aid donors benefit and aid recipients lose. Worldwide aid distribution must be entirely reconceived. The responsibility for global resource distribution needs to be shared between creditors and recipients through a new multilateral institution. For starters, the huge inefficiencies in the present system of food aid distribution (including shipping, transportation, logistical and administrative costs) could be greatly reduced by growing and storing food nearer to the impoverished areas where it is needed and encouraging the local populace to actively participate in all decisions that directly affect their social and economic development.

Second, current estimates of the additional money that is needed for international development are short of the mark. The official development aid standard of 0.7% global GDP per year, first proposed in the 1960s, is an arbitrary figure but has been repeated so often that development policy makers feel obliged to maintain this standard as an ideal, even through most nations don't come close to meeting that level of foreign aid. Based on the 0.7% GDP figure, development economists have called for an additional $100 billion a year (above the roughly $100 billion currently being given in annual global foreign assistance) to meet the MDGs. In fact, far more needs to be raised to meet the MDGs and the MDGs+ to ensure sustainable development. Many economists believe that a mid-term burst of at least $400 billion now needs to be raised annually for the next twenty years to fully integrate policies and programs for sustainable development into the global economic system. The immediate target should be 1.5% global GDP a year, eventually reaching 2% annual global GDP or more.

Third, we need to look beyond foreign aid. It is time to explore a whole new area of global financing—innovative approaches to ensure the multilateral distribution of resources on an independent basis. Through incremental fees on "global commons transactions"—that is, taxes on global common goods—the international community could generate funds for the kinds of multilateral programs and institutions that governments and markets are unable to finance. There is much discussion currently about a global carbon tax—a small fee on international carbon emissions through which the world's heavy polluters would pay their proportionate share for adding to our global environmental problems. We should also consider the possibility of raising funds through a currency transaction tax—a small assessment on every international financial transaction, which would also help to regulate the volume of foreign exchange. France and Great Britain have recently proposed similar global commons fees for international airline tickets. Many other sources of multilateral funding are also possible, such as small transaction fees on international jet fuel, maritime freight, ocean fishing, seabed mining, offshore oil and gas, satellite orbital parking spaces, electromagnetic spectrum usage, non-sustainable resources, and energy consumption. The international community has an obligation to protect human security for the common good, especially the global commons, and these transaction fees would certainly reflect the mutual interests of all people, not simply individual nations or particular businesses, which have no sovereign or legal jurisdiction over the global commons. These fees would raise substantial funds for social development and the environment, providing a new basis for international regulation and global governance. The administration of these taxes should be undertaken by a democratically-run UN organization which is overseen by civil society groups in their new identity as global commons organizations. Another source of global financing exists but is underutilized. Special Drawing

Rights, created by the IMF in 1968, are a line of permanent credit through which national central banks, treasuries, and the Bank for International Settlements obtain foreign currencies to clear and settle outstanding balances. SDRs should be expanded to help increase international financing for development. Enlarging global liquidity through an increase in SDRs would be of real benefit to impoverished nations, where the adjustment burden is the highest and the need for credit expansion the greatest.

Fourth, as these multilateral sources of financing are developed, multilateral mechanisms for the distribution of resources must also be created. Instead of the current bilateral system in which aid flows are subject to the competing political and economic interests of donor nations, we should deliver aid through a single multilateral channel, based on the needs of each nation. To do this, the United Nations Charter should be amended to break up the UN Economic and Social Council of the General Assembly into two separate units—an Economic Council and a Social Council. Rather than bilateral flows of foreign aid, the allocation of resources would take place through a Global Development and Environment Fund of the UN Economic Council. The account of the Global Marshall Plan could be administered through this fund. The UN Economic Council would also administer global transaction fees and create new oversight of the World Trade Organization, the International Monetary Fund, and the World Bank.

Fifth, we must be more realistic about debt cancellation. Since the 1990s, debt cancellation has become a significant social and political issue through the efforts of a large coalition of NGOs and church-related groups, particularly in the US, Great Britain, and Europe. Much progress has been made in putting the topic on the international agenda at several G-8 Summits and IMF and World Bank meetings. The idea is to end the dependency of indebted nations on the IMF and World Bank and use the money that is saved through the cancellation of debt to fight poverty, enabling poor nations to make a fresh start in social and economic development. Although establishing a formal link between debt cancellation and poverty eradication is of crucial importance, some advocates of debt cancellation expect that slowing or stopping the increase of debt will lead directly to the end of poverty and increased living standards in developing nations. There are several problems with this assumption. (a) For one thing, the major plans thus far developed for debt relief do not place the savings directly into the hands of the poor. The 1999 Heavily Indebted Poor Countries Initiative of the World Bank and IMF includes conditionalities which require borrowing nations to reduce social programs, divest themselves of public utilities, increase the role of the private sector, and adjust the value of their domestic currency. Under this arrangement, the poor receive no dividend from debt relief. The Multilateral Debt Relief Initiative agreed to at the 2005 G-8 Summit, which is only addressed to a small number of qualifying nations, offers a comprehensive debt relief package that uses taxpayer-funded aid monies to pay off the international creditors, so that the money saved from debt relief never reaches the people of the borrowing nations. For debt relief to work, it must be tied to specific development projects that actually help to reduce poverty, instead of flowing directly from aid donors (Western taxpayers) to debt creditors (the IMF and international banks), bypassing the indebted nations altogether. Thus far, debt cancellation advocates seem to have no viable solution for redirecting these savings to the poor. (b) In addition, the current arrangement for debt cancellation actually encourage some nations to engage in further borrowing and overspending, since recipient governments know that their debts will eventually be forgiven. In this scheme, there is nothing to prevent the new credit from being invested by recipient governments back into the rich nations, further preventing the monies from reaching the poor. (c) Lastly, debt cancellation ignores the structural flaws in the global financial and monetary system which gave rise to debt in the first place. Even with absolute debt cancellation today for the poorest countries, the clock on interest rates would start ticking again on new loans tomorrow and in another 50 years debt levels would be back to where they are now. The system of international credit adjustment needs to be changed. Comprehensive debt cancellation will work only if it is supported by alternative sources of development finance and structural changes in global trade and finance. This transformation must include an accountable and equitable mechanism for access to global credit—a major change in the way that international credit is now allocated. In addition, the world community needs to create a formal process for independent and impartial arbitration of sovereign default on debt—fair and transparent procedures involving international bankruptcy laws and insolvency courts.

RESTRUCTURE GLOBAL ECONOMIC RULES AND INSTITUTIONS

During the past thirty years, a unique partnership has grown between the environmental and development movements, both of which are deeply committed to ecological harmony and social justice. We now recognize that sustainable development alone will not produce a just economic order, for even if development and environmental reforms are enacted, people must still be protected from the macroeconomic currents of trade conflict, financial disruption, monetary volatility, and energy insecurity caused by the structural imbalances and asymmetries of the global economic system. To address the challenges of economic globalization and bring about sustainable development with equity, we need an integrated design for the international economy. To attain true socioeconomic inclusion, we must democratize our existing international rules and institutions by increasing the political influence and participation of developing nations and creating a mutually agreeable framework for global policy-making through greater pluralism, transparency, and accountability. We need a multilateral order based on generosity, cooperation, equality, rule of law, economic self-determination, freedom from economic exploitation and abuse, and the inclusion of ethical and spiritual values in the global decision-making process. For nations to collaborate at a globally inclusive level and guarantee sustainable development and human security for the common good, we need effective new institutions and policies in four major areas:

- fair trade
- financial regulation
- stable monetary values
- energy security

Fair Trade: Since the new era of labor-capital cooperation in the 1930s and 40s, protectionism has become one of the strongest leverage points available to those involved in labor negotiations, which is why labor parties have often supported government intervention in the marketplace through tariffs to protect corporate pricing, jobs, wages, and benefits, as well as government subsidies to keep our farmers competitive in global markets. The offshoring of jobs, particularly those in communications technology, is producing major employment disruptions in many developed nations. Yet when we focus primarily on protectionist means to shield workers and farmers and their families from the loss of jobs and income, we are further empowering the competitive multilateral system without addressing the larger need for major changes in the practice of trade liberalization and the regulation of global market forces.

Many of us recognize that international corporations often pose a threat to human security. We believe that multinational corporations must be held accountable to national and international laws and follow a responsible code of conduct for treating workers fairly and helping to improve conditions in the community, society, and environment in which they operate. We also recognize that fair trade is a dynamic way of reversing extreme poverty and building human security. This is why the World Trade Organization needs to be thoroughly reformed by altering its decision-making processes, voting procedures, and polices on international development. The Development Round of the World Trade Organization, launched in 2001 in Doha, Qatar, has the objective of equalizing trade between developed and developing nations, especially by encouraging developed nations to open their markets to the labor-intensive manufactured goods and agricultural products of poor nations. However, because rich nations have been demanding tit-for-tat reciprocity rather than genuine equity in trade negotiations, these talks are now at an impasse. This creates the temptation for nations to retreat into bilateral or narrowly regional trade patterns, which is likely to cause widespread confusion and animosity (reminiscent of the 1930s).

If the Doha Development Agenda fails, a new international trade system must be formed which guarantees that developing nations have equal or better terms of trade with developed nations to ensure more proportionate representation in trade discussions, broader access to global markets for their products, protective rules for the most vulnerable economies, and a more equitable settlement process in trade disputes. Immediate progress must be made on the reduction of trade-distorting agricultural subsidies, as well as the elimination of export subsidies for farm goods in rich nations which drive farmers in poor nations out of business, robbing communities of the ability to grow their own food and undermining the essential basis of self-sufficiency, human security, and social development. We need to adopt a Global Ethics Policy to ensure consistent labor laws, the security of workers, the end of discriminatory policies, the transparency of corporations, and technology sharing agreements between rich and poor nations. Decent jobs, higher wages, and more balanced trade policies to protect the rights of workers are also needed in both developed and developing nations. Above all, we need a world trade system that is not ideologically committed to "free trade" and "open markets"—the philosophy of trade liberalization which encourages rich nations to dismantle multilateral regulations and conventions for development, environment, and personal security that are in the public interest in order to privatize those domains.

Regulated Finance: Many progressives today are calling for corporate social responsibility, debt relief for the world's sixty poorest nations, empowerment of the capital-starved poor through small amounts of micro-credit loans, and the elimination of corruption in the governments of both developed and developing nations. Growing numbers of people are also calling for comprehensive changes in the international financial system, including the speculative framework for international investment and the decision-making and voting structures of the International Monetary Fund and World Bank. The need for more equitable representation, transparency, and accountability of the governing board, management, and staff of both the IMF and World Bank is evident. At the same time, the draconian policies of these twin institutions, which clearly represent the interests of the world's creditor nations, need to be radically altered. The structural adjustment policies of the IMF and World Bank, which are imposed on indebted nations as a condition for receiving new loans, often lead to the elimination of trade barriers and capital controls on foreign investment, the privatization of state-owned enterprises, the reduction of government spending and subsidies for social programs, and the destruction of the domestic market and local earnings, all of which result in state instability, depressed commodity prices, increased debt, and currency crises.

The world's present financial arrangement is a mixed blessing for developing nations. On one hand, the deregulation of global financial flows has dramatically increased the amount of foreign direct investment in developing nations, giving business and consumers better terms for borrowing and lending. On the other hand, when there are sudden changes in interest rates or market conditions and global investors suddenly withdraw their funds from a local economy, the result is exchange rate volatility, a sharp drop in asset values, and a meltdown of the domestic banking system, which leads to recession and shatters all prospects of human security and social development. $6 trillion in financial investments flows around the world each day, entirely unsupervised. New international legal and economic measures are needed to regulate foreign investment and eliminate corruption. A new international financial regime must also ensure greater equity and security by improving wages, working conditions, and environmental standards in developing nations.

Stable Monetary Values: Since 1944, the American dollar has been the world's virtual currency—the money that most nations use to trade, pay their international debts, and hold in their Central Banks to protect their own domestic currencies from inflation or devaluation. Dollar hegemony gives the US the ability to control the international money supply to its advantage. By issuing the world's primary currency reserve and trading in the same currency, America can borrow heavily at minimal interest from other nations to settle its current-account (the trade imbalance combined with other foreign payments). This means that America does not have to balance its budget while it continues to increase its spending. But Americans are also discouraged from saving because our domestic credit, production, consumption, and investment capacities are financed mainly through foreign savings and investments. As a consequence, the US is now importing twice as many goods as it exports and, for the first time in a century, paying more to foreign creditors than it receives from its investments abroad. Dollar hegemony and credit-based affluence have provided great strategic advantages to the US, but this will last only as long as foreign investors continue to finance America's deficit spending. At some point foreigners (particularly China, Japan, and the OPEC nations)

53

will withdraw their funds and the United States will be forced to (1) reduce its massive current-account deficit (its trade flows and other international payments) through a fall in the value of the dollar; and (2) increase its savings either through a huge decline in consumer and corporate spending or by slashing its federal budget deficit drastically. These two fiscal adjustments will send shockwaves across the world, creating volatility in exchange rates and a disruption in global capital flows, access to credit, and currency value stability, necessitating a complete overhaul of the global monetary system.

We know from history that no monetary regime lasts forever. As the US loses its grip on dollar hegemony and we are forced to create a new US monetary system along with a new global monetary system, we need a good understanding of the major stakes involved when the power to issue currency and determine its value is not in the hands of the people. As we recall from the Great Depression, every aspect of personal security and social development is vitally affected by monetary stability. Currency was a major populist issue until a century ago—it should become a new popular cause today. We must insist that representatives from civil society are present at a conference which reorganizes the international monetary system, leading to the establishment of a global trade currency and a monetary union administered by a Global Central Bank. In particular, we must develop a new self-adjusting global balance of payments mechanism, allowing nations to cooperate through a system of fair trade exchange, equitable financial reciprocity, and the impartial distribution of global resources.

Energy Security: Many people regard energy security as little more than a consumer issue. For most of us, energy security means having access to sufficient supplies of energy at affordable prices for our families and communities. But the degree to which energy security is related to stable monetary values is seldom realized. From 1944-1971, America used its gold as a reserve base for the international money supply. Since the US took the world off the gold standard in 1971, no precious resource has been backing the dollar—or so it is said. Officially, the US dollar is a fiat currency, printed at will and based simply on faith in the sovereignty of the US government. As monetary experts recognize, however, all major currencies in history have been based on one or more precious resources. It takes only a moment's reflection to realize that, because oil is priced primarily in dollars across the world and has more direct influence on the value of currency than any other factor, the US dollar is fundamentally linked to global crude oil as its *de facto* reserve base. So when it sets interest rates the Federal Reserve is actually reacting to relative price stability—inflation or deflation—caused by the global reserve and flow of petroleum as it affects US and global economic output and growth. Thus, it is the oil-driven engine of productivity in relation to the global oil reserve that the Federal Reserve uses to determine the value of our currency and, by virtue of US dollar hegemony, the world's currencies.

This has broad implications. Many people are now acknowledging the need to internalize the external costs of environmental degradation and climate change into the market system by setting a real price on carbon emissions, encouraging market-driven innovation, efficient use of energy, clean technology, pollution cleanup, and the production and consumption of alternative energies to displace our production and consumption of oil. The idea is that, as consumers and businesses are forced to adjust their practices and lifestyles by reducing their oil consumption and businesses find that investing in efficiency or alternative energy is cost-effective, they will absorb most of the new environmental costs through higher prices. But an intensive transformation of the global industrial base through consumer demand and business innovation will take many decades to accomplish. As we begin to curb our appetite for oil, develop alternative fuels, and achieve energy efficiency through technological advances, petroleum will remain the most important ingredient of economic growth, and the profit and wage incentives in these "green" businesses will still be denominated in dollar values that are linked directly to oil. There is already growing anxiety about whether there is enough oil to meet the world's future energy requirements. Even the most optimistic estimates suggest that the flow of oil will reach its peak by mid-century, if not before. As a reserve asset, oil is a highly insecure resource, tightly controlled by a relatively small number of nations, many of which are part of a single cartel (OPEC) and many of which are becoming increasingly autocratic. Oil is also affected by rising demand and price volatility, and subject to many types of supply disruptions (such as natural disasters, oil spills, competition for supplies, geopolitical rivalries, political turmoil, armed conflict, terrorist attacks, and vulnerabilities to pipelines and naval chokepoints). Oil is hardly the most secure reserve asset possible for the global monetary system.

The "triple bottom line" strategy made popular by a large coalition of environmentalists, politicians, and business leaders (simplified by the slogan, "people, profit, planet") proposes that tackling our social, ecological and energy problems will create a massive stimulus for business and jobs. Although this arrangement is sometimes put forward as a neo-Hegelian or evolutionary dynamic—a tripartite arrangement that will transform the deep structure of the global economy—it is really just a neo-Keynesian program of government intervention to subsidize research, loan guarantees, and the creation of new standards, taxes, and incentives for the creation of alternative energies and technologies by the private sector.

While this formula gives primacy to the economic signals of the marketplace, it completely ignores the independent monetary driver of energy reserves, currency values, and interest rates. Any major shift by governments to price carbon emissions in market terms will result in a dramatic increase in oil prices, creating widespread inflation, a significant increase in interest rates, large fluctuations of exchange rates, upheavals in global capital markets, disruptions in access to credit, and monetary depreciation. In reducing carbon emissions on a global basis, we must be prepared not only for much higher energy costs, slower economic growth, and fewer jobs in many industries, but volatility in the US dollar and international currencies tightly linked to the dollar, resulting in monetary disorder.

Greening all of the world's businesses through the economic signals of the marketplace will not change the energy base of civilization from fossil fuel to solar or other renewable energies as long as the reserve standard of the dominant global currency remains tied to fossil fuels. Ultimately, the external costs of global poverty, the environment, and geopolitical security must be adjusted not only through global market prices and alternative sources of finance (global commons taxes and an expansion of the Special Drawing Rights of the IMF), but also through an adjustment of the world reserve currency system. One solution would be to create a new international trade currency based upon a basket of global resources (including a broad proportion of renewable resources, gold, and other non-renewable resources), in which the value of currencies would rise when the reserves in this basket are scarce and fall when those reserves are more plentiful. Global currency value would thus be determined by the priority and sustainability of global energy resources as monetary reserves—not by their price in the marketplace based on economic productivity and growth.

Thus, it is a grave illusion to see energy security in terms of national energy independence or the regional military protection of energy reserves. The idea of energy independence is virtually meaningless since the global energy market directly affects local energy costs: an energy disruption or vulnerability in one area of the world has an immediate impact on prices and energy security in other areas. But consider that national governments today own and manage more than 75% of the world's oil. The national security dangers arising from foreign oil dependence, combined with aggressive competition for strategic reserves of fossil fuels, can only lead to further degradation of natural resources and continued global warming, contributing to rising sea levels, declining food production, resource scarcity, widespread migration, political conflict over non-renewable resources, and major economic instability, particularly in the world's most vulnerable regions—which is likely to inflame further extremism and

56

terrorism. Instead of conceiving of energy independence as a national security issue, it is vital that we think in terms of global energy interdependence as a basis of human security, ensuring that everyone on earth has stable and reliable access to energy supplies from multiple sources. With the steady growth of global population, the need for increased amounts of energy production and pricing, and the diminishing supply of fossil fuels, the energy security system—the entire energy supply chain and its infrastructure—must be integrated, managed, and protected on a global basis. The International Energy Agency, or another new organization, must have the authority to oversee prices and the crude oil business cycle to prevent energy crises that could lead to social and political unrest or international conflict over scarce resources. There must be a new level of international cooperation on energy security to diffuse the evident global dangers of diminishing oil resources, climate change, and energy nationalism. A new or transformed International Energy Agency must begin an ongoing dialogue with energy producers, energy distributors, and consumers to ensure the availability of sufficient flows of energy to stimulate economic growth at reasonable prices. We need a comprehensive global energy policy to smooth the transition from a fossil fuel economy to a sustainable energy economy through the diversification of energy supplies and equitable energy redistribution. Creating a multilateral energy cooperative and providing consumers with a variety of clean energy sources that are affordable and reliable are essential components of human security.

INTERNATIONALIZE THE DIALOGUE FOR GLOBAL ACTION

After many harrowing years of economic depression and world war, the United Nations and post-war multilateral institutions were set up to create a freer and more equitable world. Yet these international agencies, which emphasize the prevention of external aggression through the sovereign defense of borders, have brought only a modest amount of peace and security to the world, while new threats to human security—such as infectious disease, environmental pollution, economic deprivation, and terrorism—increasingly transcend national boundaries. Increasingly, people across the planet are recognizing that human security, social development, and environmental safeguards must no longer involve the fictitious claims of state sovereignty and the usurpation by a government of power and legitimacy from its people based on the defense and security of national borders. Human security knows no borders.

But how do we establish our sovereign equality in the new context of interdependence? How do we shift the present hierarchy of values, which rests on territoriality and national self-interest, to the claims of the global community for a more just and humane system based on the indivisibility of the world's people? Who speaks for the global commons? There is no representative multilateral organization yet giving voice to the common interests and aspirations of humanity and the legitimate needs of future generations that lie beyond the decision-making province of multinational corporations, international banks, single nations, and groups of nations. There is no global democratic organization or network today with the legitimacy and power to enforce minimum standards for human security, sustainable development, and global governance across the world's cultures and civilizations. But human consciousness is not contained by political boundaries. A transformative political constituency could develop quickly if an existing organization such as the UN, or a new organization, were to acquire this legitimacy and power through popular international demand and collective action, giving the global commons its own representative voice. The masses of the world have never before had the ability to organize effectively, but an international political referendum is now a distinct possibility because of advanced communication technology, new levels of networking, and greater international understanding on global issues, providing citizens of the world an opportunity to choose representatives to the world's decision-making bodies for the first time through direct global elections.

For this to happen, civil society organizations and all people who recognize themselves as sovereign citizens of the planet must first change the negative, disempowering view of themselves as "non-governmental organizations," and redefine their roles as Global Commons Organizations (GCOs). (Better to identify yourself in terms of what you are for, than by what you are not.) On the basis of this new collective identity, GCOs can launch a worldwide socioecological movement with a transnational political party and create a World Parliament or People's Assembly—a third house at the United Nations—which will allow the public, civil society, labor, cultural, and spiritual organizations, and other interested groups, far greater participation in global decision-making and consensus-driven governance. We could create a new UN agency for women to achieve gender equality. We could force operational changes in the institutional and voting structures of the UN, particularly in reducing the role of the Security Council and increasing the power of the General Assembly and the Economic and Social Council. We could also create a World Commons Council for oversight of global rules and institutions. When this is organized, GCOs can help to implement and provide oversight of global commons transactions—new sources of finance for meeting global development and environmental targets. These monies, along with foreign aid, could ensure that the Global Marshall Plan is adequately funded and its results are sustainable.

We already see the beginnings of this global democratic assembly. It is comprised of the growing international networks and alliances among the global anti-war movement, the international environmental movement, the international development movement, the world's social justice movement, the anti-globalization movement, the international women's movement, the indigenous people's movement, the international trade unions, and the social solidarity networks across developing nations. This new overarching social and political force is increasingly following the moral teachings of the world's major religions and interfaith communities, the norms of international law, the evolving standards of human rights and inclusive development, and the ideals of freedom and democracy held by progressive people of all nations and cultures.

To engage the support of citizens around the world, we need a common action plan for personal security and sustainable development that is based on universally shared values and addresses world problems in a globally integrative way. In recent years, many prominent individuals have made proposals calling for a Global Marshall Plan. Various groups from Austria, Germany, the Netherlands, France, the United Kingdom, Canada, the United States, Brazil, Venezuela, and other countries have issued similar ideas or discussed elements pertaining to such a plan. However, the various issues have not been effectively linked together, these groups have not met to consolidate their proposals, nor has a fully representative international panel endorsed their recommendations in order for significant action to take place. The creation of a GMP should not be left to the G-8 nations or to the world's 29 OECD nations, which would only continue the statist policies of geo-hierarchical division, strategic exclusion, national domination, structural underdevelopment, and mass dissociation. A global plan based on personal security must involve direct transnational participation, inclusive of all member countries, economic sectors, cultures, regions, and groups. It must also be seen as a tentative step toward geo-political realignment and global financial adjustment, leading to a greater degree of international unity and the creation of inclusive global governance.

Many of us are now becoming aware of these global concerns, not through the ideological filters of government, political parties, the popular media and celebrities, but through a personal realization of generosity and care which appeals directly to our hearts as well as our heads, empowering us to take action for greater unity. We are calling for a new international dialogue on these topics. We are inviting government leaders, parliamentarians, international agencies, the various Global Marshall Plan sponsors, civil society organizations, and the public to discuss the global economic issues that will lead to a comprehensive GMP. We propose an "International Conference for a Global Marshall Plan" to

- develop a common action plan to present to heads of state and the United Nations;
- generate a global network of individuals and organizations to support and follow through on that plan;
- launch an integrative program for international development relief and reconstruction and global environmental reform.

The adjustment from a world of competitive nation-states to a framework of equitable multilateral cooperation will be difficult, possibly chaotic. Many critical problems must be addressed over the next few decades to meet the escalating crises of economic globalization, social inequality, and environmental degradation. Resolving these issues will be a monumental undertaking. It will require the coordinated effort of many individuals, organizations, and governments to address these challenges. This agenda cannot be undertaken without the understanding and involvement of people of faith and progressive vision, contributing a transcendent global ethic for political diplomacy and nonviolence, intercultural dialogue and understanding, international peace and solidarity, social justice and human rights. Global change can only arise from an awareness of our inherent unity and indivisibility as a people, expressed on the individual level through our recognition of the dignity and worth of the Other, including other persons and the natural environment. We must lead the way by demonstrating to the world that domination and force must be replaced with collaborative dialogue, shared responsibility, mutual reconciliation, global generosity, and intergenerational security. Perhaps the greatest lesson we have learned since World War II is that freedom does not lead to personal security, social justice, and sustainable development; rather, it is the realization of these goals that leads to freedom. Just as the American Marshall Plan succeeded sixty years ago because the US recognized that it needed Europe as a partner, the Global Marshall Plan will now succeed because the people of the world realize that sovereignty must no longer be predicated upon foreign defense between states, but on our collective unity as global citizens, which calls for a global operating system focused on personal security, social justice, sustainable development, and peaceful change in which all nations are equal partners.

This is where we are. Will you stand with us? Join the network for a Global Marshall Plan and help us to:

- Meet the Millennium Development Goals+;
- Establish and Meet Global Environmental Targets;
- Create New Sources of Finance and Allocation of Resources;
- Restructure Global Economic Rules and Institutions;
- Internationalize the Dialogue for Global Action.

UTOPIAN IMPERATIVE AND THE GLOBAL MARSHALL PLAN INITIATIVE

Bruce Matthews

A map of the world that does not include
Utopia is not even worth glancing at.

Oscar Wilde[1]

I. REALITY

Self-interest is no longer a viable principle to guide us. It has led to our current state of affairs: a consumerist society based on a "universe of me" that engages in wars to plunder resources and whose over-consumption results in the waste that is sickening us and our planet. We need a new point of orientation to guide us out of our current crisis, and I would like to share with you a very brief sketch of such an alternative point of orientation offered up to us by what I would like to call the *utopian imperative*.

Calling to mind the thought of Immanuel Kant, such an imperative shows us the way beyond the idolatry of self-interest. Repulsed and disturbed by our unceasing habit of repeatedly engaging in the mass murder of each other in wars, Kant's 1795 essay "Perpetual Peace" argued for the creation of a global confederation of nations that would use the rule of law to replace the rule of the sword, thereby elevating the shared interests of the common good above the competing self-interests of individual nation states. Like the concept of inalienable human rights, it took around one hundred and fifty years for us to even attempt to realize Kant's vision, first in the League of Nations and then in the United Nations.

To expose the dangers of self-interest, Kant examined Thomas Hobbes' social contract theory of the state, resting as it does in the "state of nature" and its eternal curse of a perpetual war of all against all—a terrifying idea that perhaps informs the choice of words made by the United States administration to characterize the "long war" against "terrorism" which it is currently pursuing. According to Hobbes, such a state of perpetual war was the result of our instinctual drive for self-preservation; an instinct so strong that only the fear of a Leviathan-like absolute power—which could imprison, torture, or kill us at will—only such a monstrosity could, in Hobbes' view, control our innate drive of self-interest.

---

[1] Oscar Wilde, *The Soul of Man under Socialism* (Boston: J.W. Luce and Company, 1910), p. 27.

Kant objected to this, pointing out that since in the Hobbesian world "the head of state has no contractual obligations towards the people, he can do no injustice to a citizen, but may act towards them as he pleases," a maxim of action whose results in the political realm Kant found "quite terrifying," since it inevitably leads to despotism domestically and perpetual war externally.[2] Moreover, such Machiavellian "political moralist[s]," who "fashion" their morality "to suit [their] own advantage as [...] Statesm[e]n," remove the possibility of international cooperation, since cooperation requires the surrender of self-interest to the realization of shared activity.[3] And for the political moralist, any commitment to work with others will be broken as soon as such shared activity is no longer in their self-interest.

And with this we come to the heart of the matter: a politics of self-interest, at the most basic level, removes the possibility of any form of cooperative engagement. Yet such cooperation is the condition of any form of peaceful and sustainable coexistence. As an alternative, what is required is a politics that exceeds self-interest, becoming instead a politics of principle, which necessitates a redirection of interest away from self and towards what is bigger than, and thus transcends, the immediate empirical desires of self. While this redirection of interest does not *ignore* the desires of the empirical self, it does *subordinate* them to that which transcends them, which for Kant is the moral law. For according to Kant it is only through a reorientation of the self, whereby it sacrifices self-interest to the obligations of the moral law, that humans will find the possibility of realizing the project of perpetual peace.

And it is here that today we are all too weak and feeble. Kofi Annan, former United Nations General Secretary, has said regarding the effectiveness of the UN's member states, "We don't need any more promises. We need to start keeping the promises we already made."[4]

To keep a promise demands obligation to the moral law and the categorical power of the verb *ought* expresses this imperative. As a demand, this "ought" not only implies that we have not yet lived up to the moral law, it also speaks to the reverence and awe that the moral law generates. Together these emotions supply this demand of duty with the binding power that calls us to live up to our obligations. This is an essential point for Kant: the moral law provides this binding power only through the reverence and awe we have for it, since it is only through reverence and awe that the moral

---

[2] Immanuel Kant, *Political Writings*, trans. H.B. Nisbet (Cambridge: Cambridge University Press, 1991), p. 84.

[3] Ibid., p. 118.

[4] Koffi Annan, *Secretary-General's Message for New Year*, 2004. http://www.un.org/News/Press/docs/2003/sgsm9095.doc.htm

law is capable of compelling action without coercing it, thereby preserving our autonomy. This freely chosen compulsion is the feeling of obligation and duty to the unconditioned demand of the "ought" of the moral law; a feeling of obligation and duty which according to Kant is the necessary condition for all moral acts.

To better understand this distinction between moral acts of obligation and less-than-moral acts of self-interest, Kant suggests we distinguish between the empirical will driven by material desire and the rational and spiritual will that is potentially free from such material desires.

For Kant, obligation to a promise is not conditioned by the empirical will, which, as heteronomous, is driven by the *consequences* of its decisions, and thus obeys only fear and coercion, since only fear is stronger than desire for sensual pleasures. The rational will on the contrary, is autonomous, since it can freely determine itself to act in accordance with the moral law and not the consequences of an action. What motivates the rational will is not fear, but rather reverence, attraction, respect, even love of justice and the good, viz. the moral law. It is not the possible consequences of action that determines the rational will, but rather the allegiance and reverence it has to the moral law.

Thus only those nations who have such a reverence for the moral law would be capable of keeping the promises of which Kofi Annan so eloquently speaks. Such nations would be guided by leaders who are capable of transcending their self-interest. Unlike the *political moralists* who, in good Machiavellian fashion, understand "the principles of political prudence" according to their own self-interest, Kant called those statesmen "moral politician[s]" who interpret and apply the principles of political prudence so "they can be coherent with morality,"[5] a deeply difficult and almost otherworldly task that forces us to move to consider the *utopian dimension* in Kant's project.

II. UTOPIA

As we have seen, Kant argued that the moral law which directs us beyond the interests of the self is sacred and should therefore be revered. Why? Because for Kant, only by obligating our life to be guided by the moral law can we realize the *telos* and purpose of our existence, which is none other than to be worthy of happiness, where happiness is understood in the Aristotelian sense of *Eudaimonia*, or human flourishing. In order to be

---

[5] Kant, *Political Writings*, p. 128.

worthy of becoming fully human, we must obligate our life to be guided by the moral law.

For this to work, Kant acknowledges that we must have reason to *hope* that this is possible. And for this we require what I call a *utopian vision*, for as Kant argues, to have the hope of this possibility of becoming worthy of happiness, we must see our empirical world as if it were a moral world, which he describes "as a *corpus mysticum* of the rational beings in it"; a world which he further defines as a world in which "the free will of each being is, under moral laws, in complete systematic unity with itself and with the freedom of every other."[6]

This idea of a moral world—of a *corpus mysticum*—applies only to the world of our imagination and thoughts, since it is a "mere idea" whose function is to help us bring the real world "as far as may be possible, into conformity with the idea."[7] And it is only to the extent that this idea helps us achieve this that this idea has objective reality.

This practical idea of reason provides the metaphysical infrastructure for the rational order and co-operative unity that is the necessary condition for the type of reciprocal political rights and freedoms which, externalized into the world of global affairs, provide the conditions for a moral world of international right and perpetual peace.

In brief, political rights externalize the moral law as a political law requiring duties to others. Here laws are given and enforced by others, they are designed to guide and judge actions, and demand mandatory participation. Consequently, legal systems and social sanctions must be used to make the demands of political law real. Power must be used, but only in accordance with law. This application of power is not a moral problem (of internal self-determination), but rather a political problem (of external determination). Our rights can only be guaranteed by our agreeing to submit to external guidance through laws.

Extrapolating to the global level of international relations, in the same way that an individual freely submits to live by the just laws of a nation, Kant's idea of political rights demands nations to freely agree to submit to the binding force of a similar external code, namely that of international law. If the autonomous individual ought freely to submit their self-interest to the dictates of the moral law, then so too the nation state ought to freely submit to the requirements of international law. And please note that just as voluntary participation in the laws of a nation is unworkable, so too is the

---

[6] Immanuel Kant, *Critique of Pure Reason*, trans. N. K. Smith (London: Macmillan, 1964), B 836.
[7] Ibid.

voluntary participation of nations in international law: there must be some form of law enforcement, viz. global organization, to enforce its dictates.

And it is here that Kant's longing for a truly human and humane civilization, in which justice holds sway over brute force and destruction, joins harmony with a longing as old as our species.

Among the many such works we can look to are Dante's *De Monarchia* (1313), where he called on a benevolent king to wisely enforce peace among nations; or Francis Bacon's *Nova Atlantis* (1627), and Leibniz' *Corpus Juris Pentium* (1693). More directly related to our theme, we must not forget the first plan for an international court and league of states, outlined by Abbé de Saint Pierre in his *Projet de Paix Perpétuelle* (1713)— a work that was closely studied and imitated by none other than Rousseau, in his own essay entitled *The Plan for Perpetual Peace (*1761).

All of these writings dared to advance imaginative renderings of possible future societies and states, based on principles clearly at odds with the power principles that ruled the real world of historical peoples and lands. Yet with the American and French revolutions the possibility of a new and concrete form of government, determined and guided by the rational principles of the moral law, presented itself to the world; a possible form of government and society which, given reason's universality and necessity, must be capable of extending its reach and influence to all nations. And it is this possibility of making real what had heretofore always been merely political fantasies of ideal republics that leads us to the idea of the utopian per se.

The term *utopia* was coined by Thomas Moore as a key element in the title to his work of 1516, *On the Best Kind of State and the New Island Utopia*—a work otherwise referred to today simply as Thomas Moore's *Utopia*.

Moore was ingenious in crafting this term, since his Latin transliteration of the Greek renders its etymological roots perfectly ambiguous: while the *topos* of place is clear, the prefix can be read positively as *eu*, meaning good, and thus "good place," or it can be read negatively as *ou*, meaning no, and thus "no place." But in either sense, it remains clear that utopia speaks to an ideal world so far removed from our real world that no one knows precisely how to transition from the latter to the former.

Accordingly, Moore's *Utopia*—and others of the genre—are not a political guide detailing the tactical steps required to create such an ideal society, but rather only a strategic vision of what such a society might look like. Such a utopian vision generates a surplus of meaning that goes beyond itself and is thus capable of attracting and sustaining the interest of others in that it provides hope that we might be capable of making real what is offered in a utopia, but is absent in our existence.

In doing this, utopia confronts us with a vision of life and the world that is far more robust and pregnant with meaning than the sober and boring reality of the everyday. Indeed, its relation to this reality of the everyday is that of fulfilment to longing. It tests human possibilities and sustains our demand for happiness and beauty. Utopia's point of reference is a future that doesn't yet exist; its power is that of the imagination to critically reject an inhibiting reality in favor of a vision of what could become a reality. And indeed it is precisely this dimension of irreality in the utopian vision that has a subversive and *emancipatory power* and it is precisely this anticipatory illumination of a reality not yet made real that is a fundamental category of what I call utopian philosophizing.[8]

The denigration of the utopian vision in our own society illustrates the values of our ruling order, which embraces the concrete and positivistic restrictions of the empirically real and politically powerful. In contrast to this, I would like to suggest that the utopian imperative is the demand of reason to cultivate the "utopian conscience" that realizes the value and necessity of imagination and, yes, even *illusion*, in creating a future different than our past.[9]

As such, this utopian imperative serves a purpose parallel to that served by *hope* in Kant, which, like the utopian imperative, is the opposite of certainty and naive optimism, since it entails risk and possible disenchantment: hope must be capable of disappointment for it to be hope.

Thus do we demand the idea of a moral world that does not yet exist, for it is only through the belief in the possibility of such a morally perfect world that we can have the "hope" required for us to fulfil our duty to the moral law; a law which demands we believe the human race can make progress towards making "the moral end of its existence" a reality.[10] "I base my argument," Kant writes, "upon my inborn duty of influencing posterity in such a way that it will make constant progress (and I must assume that progress is possible), and that this duty may be rightfully handed down from one member of the series to the next" (ibid.).

Following the contours of the categorical imperative, we can say that the utopian imperative is the duty to envision a more perfect world and act in such a way as to make such a vision real. It is the imperative to refuse to live in world where, as Andre Breton put it, the imagination has been reduced "to a state of slavery," for to do so, as he wrote in the first

---

[8] Ernst Bloch, *The Utopian Function of Art and Literature*, trans. Jack Zipes and Frank Mecklenburg (Cambridge: MIT Press, 1993), p. xxxv.
[9] Ibid., p. 14.
[10] Kant, *Political Writings*, p. 128.

Manifesto of Surrealism, "is to betray all sense of absolute justice within oneself. Imagination alone offers me some intimation of what *can be.*"[11]

III. BRIDGING THE DIVIDE

And with this I would like to move to a very brief sketch of the utopian imperative as it applies to the Global Marshall Plan Initiative, for here the utopian imperative manifests itself as a prophetic call for a transformation of consciousness, whereby interest of the self is directed toward that which transcends its own empirical short-term interests. As with the evolution of human rights, we stand at the beginning of an age when self is guided not by tribe, ethnicity, identity, creed, or nationality, but by an obligation and commitment to the principles that animate and focus the Global Marshall Plan. To push this process forward requires a new way of thinking about both ourselves as individuals and as citizens of a world community; a transformation of consciousness that will result in a new player and force in the political arena, namely that of civil society. This new political force will be the result of interconnected associations of citizens who know no limitations such as national identity, religious creed, or ethnic identity. As such, civil society will become a political force on a par with the established powers of business and government, but will refuse to be guided by the self-interests of profit and power, choosing instead to act in accordance with the dictates of the moral law. Only the conviction and action of civil society can displace the interests of business and governments, by providing a utopian vision for a world ordered according to moral principles, and not by profit or the power interests of individual nations.

This brings us to the first central task of the Global Marshall Plan: to internationalize the dialogue for global action by cultivating and engaging a global network of citizen organizations. Today, at this conference, this is happening right now. And this is the most crucial component of the Initiative: all the elements called for in this initiative are either already in place—either in part or as voluntary programs—or we have feasible plans for realizing them. What is lacking is the collective will—the transformation of consciousness and redirection of self-interest—to begin making this utopian vision real. And this can only be done by us working to grow our organizations. Concretely, here we call for the establishment of a World Parliament that would serve as the third legislative body of the UN,

---

[11] André Breton, *Manifesto of Surrealism*, in *Manifestoes of Surrealism*, trans. Richard Seaver and Helen R. Lane (Ann Arbor: Michigan University Press, 1969), pp. 1–48 (p. 5).

thereby allowing citizens—regardless of nationality—to articulate the concerns of civil society.

And now on to the more nuts and bolts elements of the Initiative. The Global Marshall Plan Initiative—and here I am speaking specifically about the European version—seeks to create a Worldwide Eco-Social Market Economy. (1) The first step in doing this is realizing the UN's Millennium Development Goals, outlined in the flyers for the Global Marshall Plan. (2) The second step is to establish and meet Global Environmental Targets. A possible model here is the World Bank's Equator Principles, currently followed—voluntarily—by 80% of private bank lending for all development projects. Here too the World Bank's Inspection Panel provides a paradigm for a global judicial body to hear *individual citizens'* complaints, investigate and issue rulings. And some have even suggested that if the World Trade Organization's jurisdiction were expanded, we would then also have a mechanism to begin enforcing this Court's rulings.[12] (3) The third step is to restructure global economic rules and institutions to provide both fairer trading conditions, as well as generating the funds required to execute the development projects of the Global Marshall Plan. Ultimately this will require the retooling of existing institutions so that they can be integrated into a global coherent system capable of—leading to our fourth step. (4) This is creating new sources of finance and allocation of resources. Here the goal is to raise at least $100 billion dollars a year beyond current foreign aid levels to fund the actual development projects of a Global Marshall Plan. And again here we have real solutions such as:

a) Expanding the International Monetary Fund's "Special Drawing Rights" to include all countries. As outlined by George Soros, poor countries pay into the "currency basket" using their undervalued currency, and withdraw in stronger currencies of the "basket" (euro, dollar, yen, etc.) according to a quota determined by how much they donated. George Soros' plan of the expansion of Special Drawing Rights forecasts net benefit for developing lands at 30–40 billion per year.[13]

---

[12] Franz Josef Rademacher, *Global Marshall Plan: A Planetary Contract* (Hamburg: GMPI Imprint, 2004), p. 135.

[13] George Soros, *On Globalization* (New York: Public Affairs, 2002). See also his "Special Drawing Rights for the Provision of Public Goods on a Global Scale" (Remarks at the Roundtable on "New Proposals on Financing for Development," Institute for International Economics, February 2002). http://www.iie.com/publications/papers/paper.cfm?ResearchID=447

b) Utilizing the World Trade Organization to institute and administer a Terra Tax on the $8.5 trillion dollar market of global trade. Such a terra tax would support fair trade as well as raising $30–40 billion based on a tax rate of 0.35–0.5%.[14]

c) The World Trade Organization could also be used to administer a Tobin Tax, which would consist of a 0.01% tax on transactions in international capital markets. Based on the current annual figure of a $480 trillion market, a Tobin Tax would generate $30 billion a year towards the $100 billion goal.

Finally, the last step called for by the Global Marshall Plan is 5) the creation of international mechanisms to support and demand good government through the review, investigation, and enforcement of standards of transparency and accountability in government.

In closing, a UN evaluation of the Millennium Program has shown that while some significant progress has been achieved, we have fallen far short in reaching the majority of the program's goals. Indeed, in some cases things have gotten worse, demonstrated by the increase in the number of people in many parts of the world surviving on less than a dollar a day.[15] The problem is not that we do not have solutions for the challenges that face our globe; the problem is that, as pointed out by Kofi Annan, the nations of the world have morally failed, at the very least, in not living up to their promises and commitments of assistance.[16]

The European Global Marshall Plan Initiative hopes to gain support from the German Presidency of both the European Union and the G-8. But regardless of how effective Germany may be in leading the governments of these organizations to embrace the Initiative, the ultimate success of realizing the utopian vision of the Global Marshall Plan will depend on the number of we citizens of the world who are capable of reorienting our selves, effecting an inversion of perspectives as dramatic and revolutionary as Copernicus effected in moving us from a geocentric to heliocentric

---

[14] A concrete and specific account of what a Terra Tax entails is difficult to find. Following Rademacher's account, such a tax would be strategically devised to a) help realize the goals of Fair Trade, while also b) raise funds for development projects. See Rademacher, pp. 135–142.

[15] Human Development Report 2003: Millennium Development Goals, United Nations Development Programme (New York: Oxford University Press) 2003.

[16] Case in point: whereas the OECD nations pledged 0.7 per cent of GDP to realize the goals of the Millennium Project, only a handful of Scandinavian countries have fulfilled their pledged amount of development assistance.

universe. And just as the radically different view of the natural universe initiated by Kepler, Galileo, and Copernicus helped birth the emergence of a new social and political order, a similar inversion of the self, whereby it sacrifices self-interest to the obligations of the moral law, will reveal a new spiritual order, where we become capable of realizing our utopian hopes, becoming capable of meeting our obligation not only to the moral law, but to each other and to creation

STEERING GLOBALIZATION INTO A BETTER FUTURE: HOW TO REACH A PLANETARY CONSCIOUSNESS THROUGH A GLOBAL MARSHALL PLAN

Frithjof Finkbeiner and Franz Josef Radermacher

GLOBAL ISSUES: SCENARIOS AND THEIR CONSEQUENCES

At the beginning of the new century, the world is in an extremely difficult situation. The economic globalization is inadequately regulated by worldwide frameworks. It has unleashed the global economic system and brought down national constraints, a process that is accelerating. Concomitantly, the primacy of politics is lost as the core political structures remain national or continental, but not global. New technologies can substitute more and more manpower and, together with the growing integration of parts of the labour potential of poorer countries into the world market, threaten the jobs of less qualified workers in rich countries. These feel like losers of globalization and with reason. In its current form, the globalization process does provide certain chances for development, but it runs contrary to the goal of sustainability because international standards and means of regulation are lacking. The current development is undermining the social and cultural balance as well as the ecological stability of the world. This situation is aggravated by the fast growth of the world's population toward ten billion people and the push of hundreds of millions more into resource-intensive lifestyles.

Any sustainable solution must deal in a global perspective with the central issue of limiting the consumption of non-renewable resources and ecological damage. Technological progress can reduce environmental stress per unit produced (dematerialization, eco-efficiency). In total, however, the burden on our ecological systems grows rather than lessens, due to the so-called *boomerang* effect. Yet every call for limitations, i.e. of carbon dioxide emissions, is predoomed by the global issue of distribution that remains unresolved to this day.

There are two approaches to distribution: a "grandfather" option that ultimately seeks to maintain the status quo (refusing the poor countries the same right to pollution that allowed for the standard of living in industrialized states), or "equal allocation per capita" of pollution rights and their trade.

In a global perspective that includes the next fifty years, the current situation holds three possible scenarios for the future (in terms of attractors).

Two of these are extremely threatening and incompatible with sustainability. Central to the scenarios is the question of whether two big postulates of global importance can be attained: (1) protection of our natural environment and resources, and (2) respect for the dignity of all people. If (1) fails, if we continue as hitherto, the *collapse* is inevitable. If (1) succeeds, the question is "How?" Through power, to the benefit of few and the detriment of many? We would end up with so-called *brazilianization*: massive impoverishment of large parts of the population in rich countries; a process that has already started. Only consensus can lead to a model with perspective: an *Eco-Social Market Economy*; the global establishment of the European market system.

ECO-SOCIAL MARKET ECONOMY

The solution is to advance on a global economical level the basically ordoliberal approach of eco-social, regulated markets that is typical for Europe (social market economy) and some Asian economies (network economies). One current model for this is a *Global Marshall Plan* that links the establishment of adequate structures and the enforcement of standards with co-financing of development.

The efficiency of such an approach is evident from the successful enlargement processes of the European Union. On a regional level, these processes benefit new members as well as the old ones, and Germany and Austria in particular. Following the same logic, the Montreal Protocol proves the success of the model on the international level.

In this view, the European model seems to be the only promising option for peace and a sustainable development. It contrasts sharply with the market-radical model of an unleashed economy (turbo capitalism) that imposes neither environmental nor social responsibility. However, the market-fundamentalist view is deeply engrained in many heads through media manipulation, a fact that encumbers any counter strategy. Forced to operate under false preconditions, double strategies are necessary:

1. We must develop a sensible design for the global economy (active shaping of globalization).

2. As long as an acceptable global framework is lacking, we must focus on organizing intelligent distribution processes in Germany and Europe.

A Global Marshall Plan/Planetary Contract represents an intermediate step towards a worldwide Eco-Social Market Economy. According to authoritative sources, 980 Billion US Dollars will be needed on top of the current international development aid until 2015. Moreover, the usage of these funds must follow different mechanisms than currently applied, and in close interaction with the world's civil society. Some countries have already made pledges, which reduces the amount of money needed additionally to about 860 Billion US Dollars from 2006. Under an adequate regime, and focusing on developing countries that are willing to meet the requirements, this sum could be raised from 2008 through instruments such as Special Drawing Rights of the International Monetary Fund, a worldwide levy on financial transactions (Tobin tax), a worldwide levy on trade (Terra tax), a worldwide levy on kerosene, a reasonable trade system for CO_2 emission rights, adequate debt relief measures for the poorest countries, and, finally insolvency laws for states.

NEW FORMS OF IMPLEMENTATION

As important as raising the funds are new forms of implementing the goals: in particular, financing the implementation of the UN Millennium Development Goals on a *project basis*. The effective allocation of funds for *self-directed ways of development* is maybe the most difficult aspect of a Global Marshall Plan. The responsible bodies for the implementation could be the World Bank and the United Nations Development Program (UNDP) as well as other UN organizations, such as the UNEP environmental programmes, UNESCO or the United Nations Population Fund (UNFPA). On their part, these organizations should rely more on local initiatives and NGOs than they do today, and support adapted technologies, measures to increase local welfare and private initiatives for development. The latter should compete for co-financing funds, allocated in selection procedures controlled by an independent jury. Besides satisfying basic needs, financial aid should be aimed at empowerment, capacity building and ownership. Practical experience shows that self-directed, self-assured and responsible development is best achieved by promoting participation, education, and enforcing the role of women. Guiding principles for the allocation of funds are subsidiarity (bottom-up), transparency, and control of financial fluxes to reduce corruption. Concrete examples for accordant fund allocation are *micro financing and micro credit* or the *partnership-helper model* (help for self-help).

Also, there is then pressure towards good governance within countries, making sure all people will have a decent education, some kind of health care and so on. All this will significantly increase the power of people to help themselves. This will also be supported with the significantly increased level of co-financing of about $100 billion a year. In the concept of the

Global Marshall Plan this money not just goes to governments, but to a great extent goes into small and medium-sized enterprises, into micro-credits, into regional projects, and it goes into improving the ownership situation of poor people. And all use of such funds will fall under strict compliance rules. So, all in all, the Global Marshall Plan will significantly and permanently improve the situation of the poorest.

THE CHALLENGE BEHIND THE CHALLENGES: THE ETHICAL QUESTION

The Eco-Social Market Economy model and the Global Marshall Plan approach are both based on a clear ethical foundation. This is the world ethos position, common to all great religions, to humanism, and also present in the UN Earth Charter. Two principles are basic, which can both be deduced from the golden rule, namely the principle (1) to care for the environment and keep it intact and (2) to take care of the dignity of all humans. These principles immediately translate into corresponding requirements concerning the governance of companies, which are today reflected in concepts such as ethics for business or corporate social responsibility. However, voluntary business codes, as important as they are, are usually not sufficient to address global needs. Internationally agreed-upon rules, transparency, and compliance mechanisms are the key. This is where an eco-social market approach and business ethics meet. Because, under suitable frameworks, markets will reward what is ethically desirable. We have to work harder to achieve this situation.

WHAT DO WE HOPE FOR?

Similar to Europe's economic miracle after World War II, the eco-social reasoning behind a Global Marshall Plan/Planetary Contract will create a gigantic global departure in the right direction, analogous to the EU enlargement processes: economic development, environmental protection, social balance, and cultural balance are all promoted simultaneously.

The developing part of the globe closes the gap and positive growth effects show everywhere. The future formula, $10\sim>4:34$, indicates that within the next fifty to one hundred years, a ten-fold increase of the global gross national product is achievable, at the same time taking care for efficient environmental protection and the realization of a sustainable development. The effect of a worldwide investment program in the scope required would, in a relative perspective, be comparable to the effect of constructing the transcontinental railway system in the US at its time, and would release unimagined powers for a development in the right direction. While growth rates in the rich world may average between 1 and 2% per annum for about fifty years, they will reach 6 to 7% in the poorer parts of the world. The rich North and the poor South will profit equally from the resulting boom. At the same time, the imposed social and ecological standards will contain the current polarization within both the rich and the poorer countries. Thus, *more global balance is compatible with environmental protection and does not entail less social balance within states.*

THE GLOBAL MARSHALL PLAN: A STEP IN THE RIGHT DIRECTION

The Global Marshall Plan is a concept for a world in balance. It consists of five strategic cornerstones that are interconnected:

(1) The speedy implementation of the United Nation's Millennium Development Goals, as agreed upon worldwide, as an intermediate step toward a just world order and sustainable development.

(2) To raise an average of US$ 100 billion per annum in the period of 2008 to 2015 for development cooperation. This figure is based on the level of development aid and spending power of the year 2004. If the development goals and with them the goal of global common welfare are to be realized, this is the minimum sum that needs to be added and spent exclusively for this purpose.

(3) To implement fair mechanisms to raise the funds needed. The Global Marshall Plan Initiative supports the goal of spending 0.7 per cent of the national budgets on development cooperation. However, these means will amount to considerably less than the sum needed to reach the Millennium Development Goals, even if the most optimistic scenario came true. Therefore, and for reasons of regulatory policy, a large part of the funds required shall be raised via taxes on global transactions and on consumption of global common goods.

(4) The stepwise implementation of a worldwide Eco-Social Market Economy and the replacement of global market-fundamentalism with a better regulatory framework for the global economy. A just world contract is needed. The existing global frameworks and institutions for the economy, environment, social welfare, and culture must be reformed and combined (for example, those pertaining to the UN, WTO, IMF, World Bank, ILO, UNDP, UNEP, and UNESCO).

(5) A fair cooperation in the spirit of partnership on all levels and an adequate flow of funds are preconditions for the establishment of a sensible regulatory framework. Key elements of a self-directed development are the promotion of good governance, measures to combat corruption and an allocation of funds that aim at the grass-roots level.

The Global Marshall Plan provides us with a concept for a future in balance. The growing support from politics, the economy, and non-governmental organizations gives us hope, but the road before us is long and troublesome and success far from certain.

The Global Marshall Plan Initiative focuses on a combined strategy of "bottom up" and "top down"; i.e. of raising awareness and reaching a *Planetary Consciousness* on a grass-roots level and among decision makers. People are informed about the goals of the Global Marshall Plan through lectures, information events, and publications, which generate political will for change in the middle of our societies. At the same time, decision makers at national, European, and international levels are directly approached to gain their support.

WHAT ARE THE NEXT STEPS?

A new Marshall Plan must be the result of an *international consensus*. There are currently many groups and individuals around the world that have made proposals for a Global Marshall Plan. Although their plans have much in common, there are many differences among the groups based on differing depths of research, emphasis on specific issues, political influences, and cultural interpretations. Nor have these groups been actively cooperating to develop a universal consensus to accomplish these goals. There are, of course, many other organizations addressing similar issues, although not under the title "Global Marshall Plan," and they too have been unable to reach a unified level of international dialogue and agreement. This lack of international discussion reflects the fact that the global economic system since 1944 has developed an asymmetrical internationalism in which the richer nations control the decision-making process on major global socio-economic and environmental issues, which has an adverse impact on poor nations. This has also affected organizations and individuals attempting to address the interdependence of global issues, including those working to end poverty, achieve social development, solve global environmental problems, and restructure the international economy in support of sustainable development. There is little opportunity for the various international groups and individuals interested in a Global Marshall Plan and similar concerns to meet and discuss their mutual interests because there is no existing forum for international dialogue representing all of the interrelated issues and all of the interested parties.

What is needed is an inclusive format or nexus for discussing the issues of global development, environment, and economics that involves diverse representation from business, government, civil society, academia, and media from both developed and developing countries and is fully committed to a convergent multilateralism, both in spirit and in practice. Like the American Marshall Plan, which involved a new kind of participatory framework between donors and recipients for development relief and reconstruction, an International Conference for a Global Marshall Plan must be created in which the widest possible group of international stakeholders can convene and reach international agreement on the terms of a Global Marshall Plan. Although this conference has no international authority or power to implement a multilateral program for social development, environmental, and economic reform, its purpose is to create a global democratic referendum for a Global Marshall Plan that is universally supported by business, government, civil society organizations, and other relevant groups. With a broad consensus of international representatives involved in identifying the agenda, the timeline, and the agencies required to implement a Global Marshall Plan, the conference will acquire an unprecedented level of global recognition and popular legitimacy. International public demand and political pressure will grow until the designated agencies are authorized by governments and the United Nations to launch a Global Marshall Plan. The creation of this conference will involve several steps:

1. Developing an Agenda through International Consultations

2. Consulting with International Organizations and Experts: January–December 2008

3. Mobilizing Broad Networks of Partner Organizations: January–September 2009

4. Creating Public Communications and Outreach Campaign: September 2009–April 2010

5. Generating Follow-Up Activities: May 2010–September 2012

TRANSFORMING GLOBALISATION—
ENGAGING RELIGIONS

WORLD COUNCIL OF MUSLIMS FOR INTERFAITH RELATIONS AND INTERRELIGIOUS ENGAGEMENT PROJECT (IEP21)

Ahmad Khan

PART I

I do not think there is war between the East and the West or between the "Muslim" World and the Non-Muslim World. Nor does there exist, in the real world, such an issue as a "Clash between Two Civilizations" i.e. between Islam and the West, as is some time very ignorantly proclaimed. Rather, the ideals and the higher values in Islam and the ideals and the higher values in the West are *very much the same*. It is so because Islam stands for the Divine Guidance revealed to Abraham, Moses, Jesus, Muhammad, and other messengers of God, while "the West" expresses the yearning, in modern times, of the human mind and spirit toward very similar higher concerns. The West as such is a movement which was initiated as an awakening in the geographical west, at a time when the followers of these messengers were failing in their duty to liberate humans from their mutual slaveries and to lead the world toward peace, prosperity and progress.

Perhaps, there *is* a war between two groups: one of these, in spite of huge opposition by conscientious people of the West, claims to be a custodian and representative of the "Western Civilization" without practicing the higher values for which the West stands. The other group, some of whose members are not ashamed of committing a most heinous crime i.e. creating terror through murder of innocent civilians, which according to the *Qu'ran* (25: 68–70), would bring to its doers (unless they repent and correct themselves) eternal punishment of Hell, still considers itself a defender of Islam and Muslims. However, the rest of humankind agrees that they have done the greatest disservice to Islam.

The emergence of such a group within the community which, believes that the *Qu'ran* is its most basic source of guidance, became possible because the present generation of believers has lost its direct and fresh touch with their book. The contemporary believers, instead of deriving in their own situation and with their own minds any fresh inspiration from the Divine Words, have in-authentically inherited an understanding of the Book from their various "pious" forefathers. One wonders that it is the case in spite of serious Qur'anic criticism of those who blindly follow their leaders, just as a herd of sheep would follow their shepherd. The *Qu'ran* calls these

81

blind followers "disbelievers" *or* "*kafirs*" (2:170–71). The believers, on the other hand, reflect upon signs of God or *ayat*—Allah. They ponder over the signs/verses of the Divine Book. So they continue discovering meanings in the phenomena of nature and human history. Everywhere they see the Hand of God, The Wise and The All-Knowing, working all the time. They believe that they have to answer to God for the use of their own intellectual faculties. Only hypocrites do not reflect; their hearts/minds are locked (46: 24).*

PART II

Thus, inauthenticity is the mother of pseudo-religiosity. But what is pseudo-religiosity? While true religiosity is concerned with human life, pseudo-religiosity makes people forgetful of their social obligations and their duty to the Earth and its inhabitants. These pseudo-believers would display great irresponsibility during their manipulation of Earth's physical, botanical, and zoological resources. False religiosity is showy, as indicated in the Quranic Surah Al Ma'un (107) which explains that pseudo-religiosity is the real enemy of Religion. Pseudo-worship is merely a social function. It acts like a cover to hide people's greed for power, wealth, and lust.

Pseudo-religiosity sometimes pretends to be other-worldly. The purpose is to make the worshippers neglectful of their duties assigned from God, for which they are accountable to God as well as to their fellow humans. They even do not see that Divine promises of reward in the Hereafter are only for those believers who are seriously engaged here on earth in creating a better future for humankind. The love of the Hereafter helps the virtuous in their striving for peace and justice, in the presence of all kind of hardship and in spite of persecution by the unjust powers. They continue their struggle even when there is no hope for success.

The *Qu'ran* reports the presence of a group of activists who falsely claim to be believers. They are further aggravating the situation for the remedy of which the Quranic Movement was initiated. Due to their inability to see the corruption which these pseudo-believers have been creating, they say "we are only setting things right" (2:11–12). In spite of all the injustice they commit, they say they are fighting for justice. Today's pseudo-believers also manifest similar traits.

The other cover under which these pseudo-believers hide themselves is that of tradition. They are unable to look forward toward a bright future; so they always look backward and feel proud of a past which they see as their Golden Age. Pseudo-religiosity fails to be progressive.

PART III

True religiosity is both authentic and progressive (14:24–25). It is firmly rooted in the Revealed Guidance and it meets the challenges of the existing human situation with wisdom, courage, and patience. It is like an ever-growing, evergreen tree, which is firmly rooted in the ground and all the time keeps bearing fresh fruits. In this light, Islam is the continuing process of understanding and living the Revealed Guidance. See the Model of Sunnah which is itself a process of twenty three years of understanding and living the Text by the first generations of believers under the guidance of the Prophet. The Global Muslim Community keeps this Model before its eyes and continues its striving as reader of the Book, in changing human situations and with its growing abilities to understand, i.e. with progress in science, technology, philosophy, law, art, and literature. Through advancement in human knowledge, God is preparing their minds to develop a better understanding of Divine Words. Likewise, a religiously plural world is another opportunity to learn through interaction with those who carry different religious traditions.

The believing community does need good teachers. However, after the Prophet, no scholar or imam is above criticism eitehr from within or from without the community. And every follower of the Prophet is duty-bound to reflect over the signs (ayat) of the Book, building direct relationship with Divine Words, understanding afresh their meanings and practical implications from the perspective of one's own experience, but always welcoming all genuine criticism.

Very much akin to progress in the field of science, progress in Islamic thought is necessarily the outcome of the Ummah's collective effort to authenticate its understanding of the Divine Text. The Global Muslim Community does not alienate itself from the rest of humankind. It fully shares all of its intellectual endeavors.

True religiosity has a tradition of thinking with open minds. Consider Abraham, Moses, Jesus, Muhammad, and the first generation of their believers as witnesses. That is really our Golden Age. Pseudo-believers alone are people with closed minds.

PART IV

In our plural world of degenerated faith communities, the West also conducts itself like an umbrella faith community. The above is not a picture of our real world. I am, of course, addressing only the ideal world. The world, we want to create. What we want to be. Now, therefore, I return my focus to the real world. And I open this phase of the discussion with the thesis I presented in 1997 in Granada, Spain in a seminar organized by UNESCO, on "Education for the Culture of Peace." I presented the idea that faith communities, like those which follow Judaism, Christianity, and Islam, are, in fact, peace missions, initiated by great messengers of God. Today these missions are in a state of degeneration. For their regeneration they need movements on an intra-faith as well as interfaith level. Our interfaith work and intra-faith work will enlighten and empower each other. It will give us both authenticity and progress and thus help in the development of true religiosity. Together, we shall work for a world where there is peace, justice, prosperity, freedom, and progress.

Work is already initiated on both levels so we do not have to start from scratch.

It was due to the impact of West that so many revivalist movements arose in various faith communities in the twentieth century and in the same century, the present progress of interfaith movements became possible. By the end of the twentieth century, we developed a clear understanding that we have to liberate ourselves from both, pseudo-science as well as pseudo-religion. We realized humanity is not better off after ousting Religion from human life and limiting the role of Religion to places of worship. However, there should be no more fighting in the name of Religion. Rather, people of various faiths should develop a better understanding among themselves and work together for common objectives.

God is making all this happen, the way God has been leading progress in science, technology, art, literature, and philosophy, and the way God sent prophets and messengers throughout the world, according to a systematic plan.

However, if God has been doing all this, people of good intention should also come forward to work together. This is the call of true religiosity. If we respond to this call, we qualify for more of Divine Help. The world is going the wrong way because pseudo-religiosity has taken hold of worldly affairs. But pseudo-religiosity does not have any solid ground to stand upon.

WHEN THE REALITY ARRIVES, THE FALSEHOOD WILL FADE AWAY (17:81)

I strongly hold that if truly religious people will work together, pseudo-religiosity will wither away. The Contemporary Interfaith Movement has to be a striving toward true religiosity; as such it should focus on the real problems of humanity. The most central of these is wealth's being accumulated in fewer and fewer hands. Hunger, poverty, and other related issues are only by-products of increasing economic disparity. Those who are well-off have a duty towards those who are economically broken and they are accountable in this to humankind as well to the Lord of humanity. Charity and relief are not sufficient: systematic-change is required. The next in line is social injustice and discrimination, due to differences in sex, race, etc.

However the other problem which has produced a state of emergency throughout the Globe has been created by pseudo-religiosity itself perhaps, to divert our attention from the above real issue. It is "The Terror-War" problem, which calls for our first attention.

Through the First and Second Great Wars, the West changed the meaning and concept of war. Now "war" necessarily involves killing of innocent civilians—something totally unacceptable to human conscience. The situation became worse after the invention and use of nuclear weapons on August 6 and 9, 1945 also by some power of the geographical west, in spite of the opposition of all conscientious people of the East and West.

Those who have the ability to think in human terms, who have a real concern with such issues and who can rise above their own sectarian/nationalistic considerations, are, according to my definition, truly religious people—even if pseudo-religiosity has turned them into secularists. This Dialogue is an invitation to all conscientious people to share their concerns, to take a clear stand concerning these issues and to work out a plan for future collective action.

EXIT THE VEIL, ENTER FREEDOM AND AUTONOMY?

Shamim Samani and Dora Marinova

INTRODUCTION

The focus on the Muslim woman's dress-code and in particular the headgear popularly known as the veil has been intense since the "war on terror." The discourse of the veil and calls for regulating it stem from the wider depiction and discussion of Muslim presence in western societies, a presence that now fervently invokes deliberations over pluralism and citizenship in light of conflicting religious and liberal values. Contested and challenged in the rhetoric of democratic-liberal values, the veil becomes framed as a deterrent to gender equality and in the eyes of the feminist critic defies and disparages efforts for equality rights. Our premise is that the depiction of Muslims and by extension the position of the Muslim woman needs to be analyzed and understood in the context of the broader discourse of its framing.

Following the discussion on Muslims in Australia, in this paper we examine firstly how the homily about the veil is influenced by the early perceptions about Muslims in Australia. The historical border containment to maintain an Anglo-Celtic society resulted in very small numbers of Muslims (as well as other groups) in early Australian settlement. With little contact and interaction with Muslims, conjectures were based on the dominant voices in political and media commentary. Secondly, we look at how the current discourse is highly influenced by the way political commentary and media representation use a culture critique to conjure the Muslim image; and thirdly, we argue that this stereotyping has far-reaching negative consequences on Muslim women whose own stance on the issue remains largely obscured in the debate.

METHODOLOGICAL APPROACH

We employ frame analysis to deconstruct public perception of the ontology of both Muslim women and Muslims generally in Australia (as we believe one is the consequence of the other). As a methodology, frame analysis examines the effects of what have been called frame elements in understanding phenomena. These elements or tropes are words, phrases, expressions, or images used in figurative ways to have a desired effect by triggering cognitive, interpretive responses based on existing knowledge and norms of the society. The concept of framing is generally attributed to Erving Goffman's influential work, *Frame Analysis*, in which he sought to identify some of the basic frameworks of understanding to make "sense out of events" and placed the study in the general analysis of representation and connotation.[1]

In her comprehensive review of "locating frames," Kimberley Fisher, examining the writings of key contributors to the discourse who have applied the theory in different fields, finds little consensus over "basic questions" like "what frames are" or "how individuals and cultures make use of them."[2] However, she is decided that "a study of framing informs the study of how societies process information to generate meaning" (ibid). By using major cognitive schemata through which people interpret the world around them, frames enable users "to locate, perceive, identify and label" events (Goffman, *Frame Analysis*, quoted in Fisher, para. 2.3). One aspect of Goffman's work is linked to a dramaturgical framework of social analysis where audience segregation is essential so that members of the audience for one role cannot see other performances not intended for them.[3] The media and political representation of Muslim women has actively aimed at achieving this social segregation; we employ the methodology to deconstruct the perception of the "other" so as to understand the aversion to Islam and its adherents in this context.

Since 9/11 the language and imagery used in media and public commentary have impacted negatively on Muslims in general and Muslim women in particular through their visibility in dressing. Using frame analysis the study seeks to uncover the underlying issues that contribute to these perceptions. Studies and media documents have provided the observed evidence of negative portrayal and various research reports have been consulted to provide verification of experiential evidence to illustrate the corollary concerns of attributed images.

FROM PRIVATE TO PUBLIC ISLAM IN AUSTRALIA

As perceptions cannot be isolated from historical processes, in the interpretation and understanding of the current processes of representation a brief historical setting as a starting point is deemed necessary. The

---

[1] Erving Goffman, *Frame Analysis: An Essay on the Organisation of Experience* (Middlesex, Victoria and Auckland: Penguin Books, 1974).
[2] Kimberley Fisher, "Locating Frames in the Discursive Universe," *Sociological Research Online*, 2:3 (1997), para 1.5. http://www.socresonline.org.uk/2/3/4.html
[3] Erving Goffman, *The Presentation of Self in Everyday Life* (New York: Anchor Books, 1959).

development of assumptions about Muslims and their lifestyle can be viewed as primarily situated in the historical presence of Muslims in Australia. In keeping with the early immigration policies, interaction of Australian mainstream society with Muslims was largely restricted and limited; therefore the experience of "knowing" Muslims or their diasporic cultures through personal contact has been narrow in Australian society and mostly dictated by political inclinations.

Even though early Muslim existence in Australia dates back to the seventeenth century with the presence of fishers from the east Indonesian archipelago to the northern coast of the country, the transient, work-related presences left little social influences. Writing about the later more enduring presence of the early Afghan cameleers, the first Muslim settlers in Australia, Stevens notes that these were largely all-male communities since no Afghan women accompanied them.[4] Many of these unaccompanied men married aboriginal women and mostly kept to themselves; their strict adherence to Islamic codes reinforcing their alienation from the wider society. The racial and religious intolerance of early Muslims (as well as other migrants and aboriginal peoples) was an element of the official resolve for racial purity that was legislated in the White Australia policy of the early 1900s. Tropes of the "traitorously disposed," "enemy aliens," and "disloyalty" in reference to Muslims were characteristic of the First World War era, with fears of Muslim loyalty to the Sultan of Turkey when war broke out.[5] The resulting hostility saw a decline of Muslim presence; a dispersed community living on the fringes of the society. The racial hierarchies of the time severely limited contact and the bare minimum of insight into the life of the Muslim was informed by public commentary.

Although the post-Second-World-War increase in economic and international interdependence rendered difficulties in maintaining an Anglo-Celtic Australian society, a quota system with a one-to-ten ratio of non-British to British migrants ensured the preservation of an Anglo-Celtic national identity. With no institutional and organizational support for their specialist needs in areas such as burial rites, marriage celebration, or diet, as well as an acceptance of their dress code in the public, maintaining an Islamic lifestyle was difficult for many Muslims until well after the 1970s. It was largely individual and family efforts and determination that sustained an Islamic tradition and existence (ibid.). With the large influx of Turkish

---

[4] Christine Stevens, "Afghan Camel Drivers Founders of Islam," in *An Australian Pilgrimage: Muslims in Australia from the Seventeenth Century to the Present*, ed. M.L. Jones et al. (Melbourne: The Law Printer, 1993), pp. 49–62.

[5] Mary Lucille Jones, "The Years of Decline: Australian Muslims 1900–40," in Jones *et al*, *An Australian Pilgrimage*, pp. 63–86 (p. 64).

and Lebanese migrants in the 1970s, a stronger Islamic distinctiveness developed. Today the major groupings of Muslims are from varied ethnic and dissimilar cultural backgrounds; from Lebanon, Turkey, and Bosnia to the new emerging communities from places like Sudan and Somalia. They are a disparate group, whose diversity has been little understood in the mainstream Australian community as they still remain a very small proportion of the Australian population with 1.5% officially affiliating with Islam in the 2001 census.[6]

THE DISCOURSE OF CONFLICTING BELIEFS, VALUES AND PRACTICES

Expressing their religious and cultural affinity in various observations, Muslims have found affirmations of their freedom to practice their faith contained in the Australian multicultural policy as well as in the lexis of leaders. Marking the twenty-fifth anniversary of multiculturalism in Australia in 2003, Gary Hardgrave (then Minister for Citizenship and Multicultural Affairs) vocalized his support of multiculturalism: "People in this country are free to practice their traditions, speak their old languages, adhere to their religions and wear whatever they like within the law." However since Gary Hardgrave's speech in 2003, the shift in public discourse demands a weighting of cultures in favour of western secular traditions. In 2005, for example, two female members of the Federal Parliament proposed that Muslim girls be forbidden to wear the veil if attending public schools. Although this proposal was quickly rejected, the MPs were expressing existing attitudes within the Australian society

Viewed through a lens of modernization and secularization, Muslim traditions and practices appear at variance with the mainstream culture. As the significant "other," Muslims living in western societies are often critiqued by the ideals and practices of the dominant culture, the mores of which are derived from the age of European Enlightenment that advocated rationality, the pursuit of happiness, individualism, progress, and freedom.[7] In this climate, communities found to resist the dominant culture are seen as being backward and in the debate on multiculturalism as challenging acculturation processes. Exploring how Muslims in Australia have been attributed an "otherness," Saniotis, inferring from several anthropology works, explains the anxiety about Muslim "fittingness" in western society in

---

[6] Australian Bureau of Statistics (ABS), *2007 Year Book Australia*, ABS Catalogue No. 1301.0 (Canberra: Australian Bureau of Statistics, 2007).
[7] David Kelly. *The Party of Modernity: Cato Policy Report* XXV/3 (2003). http://www.cato.org/research/articles/kelley-0306.html

terms of "order in lifeworlds" where matters out of place invoke an anxiety over a "perceived threat" or a "violation of conceptual order."[8] In the same vein, Humphrey explains this "unfittingness" in terms of faith practices: "Islamic religious values, beliefs and practices are viewed as being in conflict with the organizations and rhythms of public life in the cities of the West. Muslim practices of prayer, fasting and veiling appear to challenge the conformity of secular public space and its values (often attributed than owned) with respect to gender equality in social relationships and individual rights."[9]

This thematic conflict of cultures resonates with the rhetoric of a "clash of civilizations" of many western leaders in the "war on terror." As one of the violations of order, the issue of Muslim women's emancipation and consequently the disposal of the veil take central stage.

GENDERING THE DISCOURSE IN THE MEDIA

In looking at the construction of the image of the Muslim woman, this section draws from the broader global media discourse to help determine the role of mass communication in the characterization of Muslims:

> Whenever Islam is attacked we find that Muslim woman is used as a way of showing that Islam is an oppressive religion. And so a lot of the stereotypical images about Islam often use Muslim women as a target to attack Islam."[10]

Edward Said's critique of "orientalism" as a pattern of western thinking about the east in its typecasting retains currency in the present assumptions about the perception of the "eastern other." In his famed and influential work *Orientalism* he writes, "My whole point about this system is not that it is a misrepresentation of some Oriental essence [...] but that it operates as representations usually do, for a purpose, according to a tendency, in a

---

[8] Arthur Saniotis, "Embodying Ambivalence: Muslim Australians as 'Other,'" *Journal of Australian Studies,* 82 (2004), 49–58.
http://www.ap1-network.com/main/index.php?apply=&webpage=default&cID=4&PHPSESSID=&menuID=56

[9] Michael Humphrey, "An Australian Islam? Religion in the Multicultural City," in *Muslim Communities in Australia,* ed. A. Saeed and S. Akbarzadeh (Sydney: University of New South Wales Press, 2001), pp. 33–52 (p.34).

[10] Nada Roude, Media Spokesperson for the Islamic Council of NSW, Australian Broadcasting Corporation (ABC), *Compass, Sunday Nights on ABCTV, Transcript of Encounters with Islam,* April 21, 2002.
http://www.abc.net.au/compass/s538946.htm

specific economic setting."[11] Although Said's focus is on the broader context of the image of the east in the western mind, in its proposition of the dominance of power position in the ability to define and establish conventional understandings of representation it is significant in this discussion. The reinforcement of the image of the Muslim women's inferior position can be attributed to the visual and rhetorical frames in the political and media iconic imagery, both sites of influence on society's standpoint, and major contributors to the relationship between the minorities and majority in the context of a plural society.

Inheritance laws, female genital mutilation, honour killings, forced marriages, polygyny practice, a domesticated role for women, and of course the dress code are the principal frames that enlighten the public about Muslim women and feed notions of inequality in their minds. In the absence of any other models, extrapolations from accounts of practices in oppressive or "traditionalist" (where classical Islamic law is enforced) Muslim societies inform the status of Muslim women in Australia. Saeed explains the oppressed image of the Muslim woman in the west as being in part due to the selective footage in media reporting. He writes: "Images of how Muslim women have been treated in countries such as Afghanistan (under the rule of the Taliban) have been shown on television around the world, especially after September 11, 2001."[12] A journalism academic, Tanja Dreher, quoted in an ADB report, also remarks about the framing of the veil in media discourse: "If you go back through the newspaper coverage and also television footage, the image of the veiled woman occurs again and again and again, both in Bankstown, then in terms of the Tampa and the refugee story more generally, and again in terms of the war in Afghanistan."[13]

In addition the disproportionate focus on certain issues in analysis, reporting, and reasoning while downplaying others helps position audiences in their understanding. Through an implicit conveyance of desirable or undesirable values, media tools such as commentary, images, and polls

---

[11] Edward W. Said, *Orientalism* (London: Penguin Books, 1985), p. 273.

[12] Abdullah Saeed, *Muslim Australians: Their Beliefs, Practices and Institutions* (Canberra: Commonwealth of Australia, Department of Immigration and Multicultural and Indigenous Affairs and Australian Multicultural Foundation in association with The University of Melbourne, 2004), p. 35.
http://www.amf.net.au/PDF/religionCulturalDiversity/Resource_Manual.pdf

[13] Anti-Discrimination Board of New South Wales (ADB), *Race for the Headlines: Racism and Media Discourse* (Sydney: State of New South Wales through the Attorney General's Department of NSW, 2003), p. 75.
http://pandora.nla.gov.au/tep/39681

shape the attitudes and understandings of groups. The Anti-Discrimination Board of New South Wales' (ADB) report on racism and media discourse examined and analysed the story of a Muslim women's gym as played out in both print and talkback media. Quoting an article that detailed criticism of the gym in *The Daily Telegraph* (August 13, 2002), in regard to dispensation of discrimination from the Anti-Discrimination Board, the ADB found implications drawing on preceding contestations about the "special treatment" for minorities and the symbolic juxtaposition of the article about Muslim special diet needs on the same page (ibid., p 64). The reactive response that reflects a conflation of global and local phenomena in perception of the target group is evident in a quote from a letter to the editor: "Are adherents to [Islam] going to integrate themselves into our pluralistic freedom-loving society? No way. This has been graphically shown by recent events such as the gang rapes, the apartheid-like requirements of the Muslim women's gym and the celebrations of the murderous attacks on the USA last September." Contained in this rancorous attack are three mutually exclusive events that are merged to respond to what is made out to be an intolerable request by Muslim women. In its message, all three are linked to the Muslim lack of integration and "hostility" to freedoms available in the pluralistic society.

POLITICAL GAIN IN THE MUSLIM INTEGRATION DEBATE

In its analysis of the impact of discourse on the public perception, the ADB found an imbalance in the role of political leaders in promoting an environment of minority safety and security that is echoed in the words of Randa Kattan, the Australian Arabic Communities Council, quoted in the ADB report: "On the one hand we heard the calls for tolerance […]. Yet on the other, we heard how asylum seekers threw their children overboard, a blatant lie. We heard the half-hearted inconsistent and loaded message. […] Sadly, the opportunities to get political mileage out of moral outrage and the fear that had been whipped up against the Arabs, Muslims, people of Middle Eastern appearance, and refugees were not missed by many." (p 77)

The momentous events of 9/11 came at a very susceptible time in terms of race relations in the country. Prior to the event, a series of gang rapes committed by fourteen young Lebanese Muslim Australians got blanket coverage as racially motivated crimes and created a correlation between crime and ethnicity in their reporting. And just a month before the New York incident, Australia refused to accept about four hundred mostly Muslim refugees rescued by a Norwegian vessel from an Indonesian boat. Denying the Tampa permission to land in Australian waters, the government took a hard-line against what it called "queue jumpers" and described as "illegal refugees." The then Defense Minister, Peter Reith described the asylum seekers as possible terrorists.[14] The themes of lack of integration and hostility to freedom have since been the subject of much of the anti-Islamic political commentary in post 9/11 Australia, with the Prime Minister's comments on Muslim resistance to integration supported by others.[15]

The rhetoric of resistance is expressed in the persuasion of the endorsement of "Australian" values, learning English and mostly treating women equally, an issue enthusiastically taken up by feminists like Bronwyn Bishop (Liberal Member of Parliament) who convey that somehow, the removal of the scarf bestows freedom and autonomy onto Muslim women. In responding to a Muslim woman who told her about feeling free in the headscarf, Bishop replied, "I would simply say that in Nazi Germany, Nazis felt free and comfortable. That is not the sort of definition of freedom that I want for my country."[16] How a Muslim woman's freedom in today's world is comparable to Nazis in Nazi Germany is anyone's guess. However the choice of simile is allegorical of a fascist regime.

Without much examination and discussion an ambiguous lack of equality and autonomy is attributed to Muslim women largely in their dress code. Does the removal of the veil or the hijab confer any special liberties and opportunities for empowerment for Muslim women or award them equality? If democratic liberal laws favour freedom of choice then don't such demands also constrain the choices of those that wear the hijab out of preference? Gender equality as defined by a World Bank report is "equality under the law, equality of opportunity (including equality in terms of rewards for work and equality in access to human capital and other productive resources that enable opportunity) and equality of voice (the ability to influence and contribute to the development process)."[17] Yet these are the very processes that have not been addressed in these debates.

---

[14] Peter Manning, "Is Australia an Intelligence and Media Colony?" *On Line Opinion: Australia's E-Journal of Social and Political Debate* (2004). http://www.onlineopinion.com.au/view.asp?article=2641

[15] Australian Broadcasting Corporation (ABC). (2006). "Lateline: Transcript of Broadcast—PM Unrepentant over Muslim Remarks," September 1, 2006. http://www.abc.net.au/lateline/content/2006/s1731276.htm

[16] Terry Lane, interview with Bronwyn Bishop, *The National Interest*, Sunday, August 28, 2005. http://www.abc.net.au/rn/talks/natint/stories/s1447773.htm

[17] Cited in Anju Malhotra, Sudney R. Schuler, and Carol Boender, *Measuring Women's Empowerment as a Variable in International Development* (2002), p. 7. http://www.aed.org/LeadershipandDemocracy/upload/MeasuringWomen.pdf

EXCLUSION IN THE PUBLIC SPACE

The politicizing of Muslim cultural values and integration distracts attention from some of the challenging issues of prejudice, lack of opportunity, and mostly security issues that have received token attention. Studies on the needs and concerns of Muslim women, for example, identify some central issues concerned with their empowerment and opportunities that need addressing. Besides economic needs of education, health, employment, housing, in her research on the settlement needs of Muslim women in Perth, Yasmeen found women ranking social requirements such as safety, recognition, and acceptance in their principal cluster of requirements. Yasmeen found, "recognition" from other Australians and safety both important personal issues for the women linked to their Islamic identity. The majority of the women experienced hostility and found it hard to be accepted within the general community. Concerns over safety included experiences of "harassment from neighbours who used threatening and abusive language deriding their Islamic beliefs," and "criticism and ridicule for wearing the hijab in public places and [they] did not feel that the police could guarantee their safety."[18] Such hostility is also endured in employment prospects limiting participation in the workforce. In a report on the effects of visible discrimination Colic-Peisker and Tilbury, focusing on the employment of refugees, found that their data "indicates that discrimination in the labour market on the basis of racial and cultural visibility is quite common."[19]

As noted earlier, Yasmeen's study of Muslim women revealed safety, lack of recognition, and hostility to their dress code as major concerns. A more comprehensive study on Arab and Muslim discrimination called *Ismae* ("Listen" in Arabic) conducted by the Human Rights and Equal Opportunities Commission in 2003 reveals ample evidence of the same. A nation-wide consultation with Arab and Muslim Australians with 1423 participants in all the states and territories was conducted over seven months in 2003. Its findings show the ugly side of intolerant perception based on no personal knowledge of the targets—"[m]ost experiences described by participants were unprovoked, 'one-off' incidents from

---

[18] Samina Yasmeen, "Settlement Needs of Muslim Women in Perth: A Case Study," in *Muslim Communities in Australia*, ed. A. Saeed and S. Akbarzadeh (Sydney: University of New South Wales Press, 2001), pp. 73–96 (p. 83).
[19] Val Colic-Peisker and Farida Tilbury, *Refugees and Employment: The Effect of Visible Differences on Discrimination: Final Report* (Perth: Centre for Social and Community Research, Murdoch University, 2007), p. 17.
http://www.cscr.murdoch.edu.au/refugees_and_employment.pdf

strangers on the street, on public transport, in shops and shopping centres or on roads."[20] In his foreword to the report, Dr Williams Jones, the Acting Race Discrimination Commisioner writes, "'Terrorist', 'Dirty Arab', 'Murderer', 'Bloody Muslim', 'Raghead', 'Bin Laden', 'Illegal immigrant', 'Black c..t' are just some of the labels and profanities that we were told have been used against Arab and Muslims in public places," who were told "[g]o back to your own country." These tropes and slogans are significant consequences of the frame elements used in the discourse and commentary of the Muslim "difference." Little knowledge about Muslims and their way of life exists outside the frames created in public commentary that have contributed much to the prejudice shown towards Muslims.

In addressing the Muslim problem, the fixes are focused on proposals dealing with inherent issues suggestive of deficiencies within the faith community, with rhetorical commendation for successful integration. An emphatic denial of the media's role in propagating a negative campaign to influence public opinion helps absolve the media of culpability. In his address to the conference of Australian imams, Andrew Robb, the Parliamentary Secretary to the Minister for Immigration and Multicultural Affairs, put the onus for its stigmatization on the community, absolving the media of its role in mobilizing bias: "some people say that the problem of stigmatization of Muslim people is a problem caused and generated by the media; that the media seeks to portray Australians Muslims in a negative way […]. I don't subscribe to that point of view—[…] the media simply reflects its readership, its listeners or viewing audience […], the media is reflecting the very real anxiety and suspicion within the broader community […]." However, the Federal Police Commissioner Mick Keelty after yet another prolonged furore and coverage of a Muslim misdemeanour—that of a religious leader's apparent inflammatory comments over women—was of the opinion that the media was fuelling a bias against Australian Muslims.[21]

FRAMING A FAILED MULTICULTURALISM?

In the contemporary climate of "Islam against the west" the questions of immigration, cultural plurality, toleration, and diversity in society become urgently and emotively salient. Within these concerns, the profits and failures of multiculturalism have been brought to the fore to be fervently

---

[20] Human Rights and Equal Opportunities Commission (HREOC). (2004). *Ismae— Listen: National Consultation on Eliminating Prejudice against Arab and Muslim Australians* (Croydon Park, New South Wales: HREOC, 2004), p. 3.
[21] Quoted in J Roberts, "Media Blamed for Islam Bias," *The Australian,* October 27, 2006. http://www.theaustralian.news.com.au/story/0,20867,20652788-601,00.html

contested. The 9/11 events fuel the debate to the point of deliberations on a consensus of reversal. The various overseas attacks have produced outrage over Islamic fundamentalist values leading to an understanding of the attacks as a cultural conflict between Islam and the west, and in George Bush's terms "waging a struggle for freedom."[22] This cultural conflict lends credence to Muslim incompatibility with western liberal values, especially since the attacks in London and the fears of Muslim youth being influenced is coined as home-grown terror. Using these reference frames, sections of Australian society have persevered in rooting "home-grown terror" in multicultural policies. How multiculturalism plays a role in the perpetration of horrendous violent acts is, however, unexplained in the rhetoric of commentators, but policy directions in Muslim immigration and "containing the Muslim problem" are proposed.

John Stone, a former treasury secretary and National Party senator, questions the intent of multicultural policies, asking "can we any longer pretend that our official multiculturalism policies [...] are in our national interest? [...] how are we to handle our growing, self-created Muslim problem?" In his posting, Stone quotes the former High Court chief justice Harry Gibbs in a 2002 Australia Day address: "a state is entitled to prevent the immigration of persons whose culture is such that they are unlikely readily to integrate into society, or at least to ensure that persons of that kind do not enter the country in such numbers that they will be likely to form a distinct and alien section of society."[23] Are such renditions impacting on the government's position on diversity and multiculturalism in Australia? It does appear so, as Tim Johnson in his article on "Australians Debating Immigration and National Identity" notes, the "minor bureaucratic alteration" in the changing of the name of the immigration department from Department of Immigration and Multicultural Affairs to the Department of Immigration and Citizenship sends a message.[24] The implication of this, according to James Jupp, who has published widely on immigration and multiculturalism in Australia, is "that this is a liberal, democratic, English-speaking society which has been well established and it is up to people who come from other cultures to adjust their behavior accordingly" (cited in Johnson).

---

[22] FoxNews, "President Bush Addresses the Nation," September 20, 2001. http://www.foxnews.com/story/0,2933,62167,00.html

[23] John Stone, "One Nation, One Culture," *On Line Opinion: Australia's e-journal of social and political debate* (2005). http://www.onlineopinion.com.au/view.asp?article=3713.

[24] Australians Debating Immigration and National Identity," *Herald and Tribune*, January 28, 2007.

The current demand for Muslim integration is prompted by alleged threats of "home-grown" terrorism. How much of this is real or a perceived threat is open to debate, however, the progression of denigration of Australian Muslims in recent times, reported and discussed in the abundant anti-racist and anti-discrimination literature, is much more a disclosure of public space ownership and the type of engineered pluralism envisioned for Australia by the leadership. By focusing on ethnic and racial differences, the causality of social problems has been adroitly attributed to cultural and value distinctions and questions of nationalism, creating what Chaudhry calls a "normative symbol of reassurance" that seeks to assure the public that possible adversaries are being contained.[25]

The politically mediated innocuous differentiation makes a critical difference in the perception of minority groups and their value to Australian society. It averts what Hancock calls social investment and in this case the social investment of Muslim women in Australia.[26] According to Hancock, societies make investments of social and human resources that are needed for socially sustainable societies. It is increasingly recognized that economic well-being does not necessarily build the social fabric of communities, that we need to make investments in other areas of communal life. These investments that Putnam and Cox call social capital promote social justice by not only providing basic needs but also enhancing the physical, mental, and social well-being of the population.[27] Created through interactions between people in daily life, these investments are located in networks that thrive on exchanges in society. In the contemporary environment such investments are vital for the profit of both Muslim women and their contribution to the society that they are a part of. A conducive environment for access and opportunity in employment, advocacy, and agency is vital for enabling the generation of social capital or investment. In the following section, we look at the three areas of employment, advocacy, and agency in which intervention may help produce a favourable outcome in Muslim women's contribution to Australian society.

---

[25] E. Chaudhry, "The Politics of Symbols and the Symbolisation of 9/11," *American Journal of Islamic Social Sciences,* 21:1 (2004), 73–96.

[26] Trevor Hancock, *Strategic Directions for Community Sustainability* (Victoria: B.C. Roundtable on the Environment and the Economy, 1993).

[27] Robert D. Putnam and Kristin A. Goss, "Introduction" in *Democracies in Flux: The Evolution of Social Capital in Contemporary Society*, ed. R.D. Putnam (New York and, Oxford: Oxford University Press, 2002), pp. 3–20 (p. 4); Eva Cox, *A Truly Civil Society: The 1995 Boyer Lectures* (Sydney: ABC Books, 1995), p. 1.

ENABLING SOCIAL CAPITAL OR INVESTMENT

It is well-recognized that access to income impacts on the self-sufficiency of women, raising their status in the household. With increased self-reliance comes the ability to make choices that can assist in challenging subordination. However, there is little research available for workplace participation of Muslim women in Australia. Foroutan's statistical study of the impact of family formation and religious affiliation in the context of a multicultural Australian setting uses logistical regression (using full census data) as a standardization method. The impacting variables in the study are couple status, presence and age of young children, and partner's annual income; and findings from the study indicate less likelihood of workforce participation for Muslim women than for non-Muslim women.[28] However, the study by holding many significant variables constant overlooks important factors impacting on the economic behaviour of Muslim women in Australia. For example, the Northcote study recognizes that Muslim refugee women suffer an "isolation cycle" that stems from both internal features of religion, ethnic and refugee background and from the social, political and institutional processes of the host society.[29] Although this study is based on migrant refugee women, some of its findings resonate with the aforementioned studies by Yasmeen, Saeed, and Colic-Peisker and Tilbury, as well as others like Kamalkhani and Bedar, and El-Matrah.[30] More research needs to be done on the economic behaviour and workplace participation of Muslim women.

Like other minorities in Australia, Muslims have little advocacy representation in political processes. Highlighting of Muslim concerns has largely been due to the efforts of NGOs like the HREOC and policy measures have been consigned to consultations with community representatives without adequate knowledge of the diversity of the Muslim society. The overemphasis on the importance of religious leaders further

---

[28] Yaghoob Foroutan, "Family, Religion, and Multiculturalism: Challenging Implications on Women's Economic Behaviour," paper presented at the 2006 *Annual Meeting of the Population Association of America*.
http://paa2006.princeton.edu/download.aspx?submissionId=60030
[29] Jeremy Northcote, Peter Hancock, and Suzy Casimiro, "Breaking the Isolation Cycle: The Experience of Muslim Refugee Women in Australia," *Asian and Pacific Migration Journal*, 15(2), 177–199.
[30] Shahram Kamalkhani, "Recently-Arrived Muslim Refugee Women Coping with Settlement," in *Muslim Communities in Australia*, pp 97–115; Asha Bedar and Joumanah El Matrah, J. *Media Guide: Islam and Muslims in Australia* (Melbourne: Islamic Women's Welfare Council of Victoria, 2005).
http://home.vicnet.net.au/~iwwcv/IWWC_media_guide.pdf

mutes the voice of the Muslim woman in the debate as the authoritative stance on issues is attributed to religious leaders who are all male. In media representation, advocacy has largely been a responsive outcome to present views on Muslim "misdemeanors" and has been more geared towards damage control than issue discussions. Often ill-equipped persons have appeared to deliver messages in defensive mode and sounding less credible than non-Muslim "experts." These comments do little to overcome the negative portrayal of Muslim women. In this context Muslim women's representation in the ability to "cross over cultures" is important in vocalizing matters of concern.

The feminist discourse in the case for (or against) Muslim women is being carried forth by those that disregard the lived-out realties of the women that they speak on behalf. Giving credence only to secular forms of comprehension to analyse and understand the experiences of Muslim women, there is a sensationalizing of subjugation. Writes Chisti, "Feminists routinely present Islam within a 'fundamentalistic' or extremist framework, projecting religion as an obstacle to women's full equality and promoting secularism as the 'natural' space for neutral and progressive work toward the advancements of all women."[31] There are several empowered Muslim women that are able to speak on behalf of their own kind. Enabling this requires training programs in areas of enhancing leadership roles and the provision of forums to facilitate dialogue to clear the many misconceptions that exist about the lives of Muslim women.

CONCLUSION

In this paper we have identified several different frames that inform the Australian public about the ontology of Muslims and Muslim women. The historical images of Muslims in Australia influenced by racial hierarchies were shared by the many minority groups in its early settlement as well as by indigenous Australians. With the shift to a more racially inclusive policy, post Second World War, the lack of institutional support for cultural particularities lent an insignificant and benign presence to Australian Muslims in the public sphere. In more recent times, a modernist yardstick has been applied to Muslim "fittingness" in Australian society. This benchmark renders Islam a backward and archaic frame in total conflict with the rationalism associated with modern societies. With it comes a static

---

[31] Maliha Chisti, "The International Women's Movement and the Politics of Participation for Muslim Women," *American Journal of Islamic Social Sciences,* 19:4 (2002), 80–99.

understanding of the Muslim woman's repression and lack of agency in an attributed rejection of feminist values of gender equality.

In the current context, the focus on the Muslim conflict of culture has also been plagued by national and international events. With the large number of refugees coming in from the many war-torn Muslim countries (some of them in "leaky boats"), a more threatening image of a risk to the economic and social steadiness of the country appears to take hold in public perception. This has been exacerbated by the "war on terror" commentary that adds a malevolent angle to Muslim presence in the country. The media, politicians and political commentators have also attempted to segregate the Australian audience and present only a negative image for the veiled Muslim woman.

Some of the impacts of these negative frames have been identified in this paper and reveal a need for a better understanding of the inclusion of Muslim women in Australian public to avail their potential for contribution to this society. As pointed out, there are several areas of social investment that need to be studied and advanced not only to achieve a viable outcome beneficial to Muslim women but also one that promotes social sustainability in the general society. The current frames have played a role in perpetuating differences; we suggest a reframing of the Muslim woman's image to enable congruence.

The Australian society has given hope, desirability and potential to new coming migrants to succeed in many ways that very few countries around the world have been able to do. Ever since the convict settlers in the nineteenth century, it has been a personal choice for new migrants to call Australia home, and freedom and opportunity have been the main assets within the Australian value system. The Muslim woman's veil as a personal preference should also belong to the abundance of choices that Australia offers.

ISLAMIC PEACE PARADIGM AND ISLAMIC PEACE EDUCATION: THE STUDY OF ISLAMIC NONVIOLENCE IN THE POST-SEPTEMBER 11 WORLD

Sezai Ozcelik and Ayşe Dilek Oğretir

1 INTRODUCTION

Although the Western paradigm in peace studies has been based on modernization, secularization, democratization, and rational choice, we have witnessed a resurrection and revival of religious thoughts and actions in both conflict and peace studies. There have increasingly come more insights and practical lessons from religion and theological studies into peace studies and conflict resolution. Most scholars focus on the role of religion in peace-building, reconciliation, and peace-making. Also, religious aspects, insights, and praxis of the conflict have increasingly played an important role in the understanding of the conflicts in post-Cold War world. In other words, religion has been a major contributor to war, bloodshed, hatred, and intolerance. Yet, religion has provided the values of empathy, nonviolence, sanctity of life, humility, and compassion.

With the introduction of Huntington's "clash of civilizations" thesis, some scholars believe that civilizations—not individuals or states—become the most significant unit of analysis. They conclude that the international system will move towards the clash of civilizations. In this analysis, Islamic civilization emerges as a potential threat to "Western interests, values, and power" in a New World order.[1] However, it is misleading to speak of an Islamic "civilization" as a monolithic and holistic force in international relations. It is important to emphasize that Islamic thought is based on unity as well as diversity, leading to different approaches and schools in Islamic social sciences.

The contemporary resurgence of Islamic social sciences has focused our attention on the traditions of peace, war, and nonviolence in Islamic political thought and culture. Unfortunately, the Islamic contributions to peace and conflict studies are not in proportion to Islam's potential as a source of nonviolent social change and as a force that could influence the behavior of states in the international system. In this paper, I would like to

---

[1] Samuel Huntington, "The Clash of Civilizations," *Foreign Affairs*, 72 (Summer, 1993), 22–49 (p. 45).

present Islam as a nonviolent and peaceful tradition of social change in international conflict.

This paper will examine the Islamic contributions in the areas of peace, war, nonviolence, and social change. My intention is to present the range of ideas that characterize both historical and contemporary Islamic thought in terms of peace, war, and nonviolence, to show that there is a need for a reinterpretation and redefinition of the medieval Islamic theory and for the application of the Islamic concepts to contemporary events. Although Islamic political thought has been used for undermining the state's sovereignty and accomplishing violent social change by fundamentalists, the modernist school has challenged both traditionalists and fundamentalists in order to create more contemporary interpretations of the Islamic understanding of war, peace, and nonviolence.

There are a myriad of questions about war and peace in Islamic thought and philosophy. How does an Islamic perspective on life help us interpret and respond to international conflict? What is the definition of an "Islamic peace paradigm," and how is Islam related to nonviolence? What is the definition of *jihad*? Can *jihad* be explained as an act of nonviolence despite the fact that most of the Western world is convinced that *jihad* is a state of war, a holy war? Regardless of the nonviolent components, what is the place of violence in Islam? Can Islam be defined as a connecting force between the punishing God of Judaism and the turn-the-other-cheek mentality of Christianity? What are the methods that can be used in Islamic nonviolent struggle? How can the Islamic concepts such as *jihad (*sacred struggle*)*, *sabr* (patience), *adl* (justice), *umma* (community), *sulha* (reconciliation), and so on, contribute to the Islamic peace paradigm? What would be the contribution of Islam to the peace-building efforts within Muslim societies and globally?

In the first part of the paper, I will explain the Islamic peace paradigm with the emphasis on the Islamic understandings of peace, war, and nonviolence. I will first give a short history of Islam. Second, I will attempt to explain the Islamic conceptions of war, focusing on especially the idea of *jihad* (sacred struggle). In the next section, I will closely look at Islam as a religion of peace and nonviolence. I will focus on the Islamic concepts related to peace such as *sabr* (patience), *hijra* (exodus), diversity, and tolerance. The following section will examine how nonviolent action is the rule rather than the exception in the Islamic peace paradigm and what the Islamic nonviolent movements are, such as Abdul Ghaffir Khan in Afghanistan, *Intifada* in Palestine, and the Kosovo National Movement during 1990s. This paper will support the idea that the nonviolence struggle is not only the primary tool for *jihad*, but also the essence of the Islamic faith. In the conclusion of this part, I will emphasize the importance role of peace and nonviolence in Islamic ethics, tradition, and social science.

2. ISLAMIC CONCEPTIONS OF WAR AND *JIHAD* (SACRED STRUGGLE*)*

There are two essential sources for any debate about Islamic war and peace, the *Qu'ran* and the *Hadith* (the sayings and deeds of the Prophet Muhammad). Together they provide the sources for the Islamic *Shari'a* (the constitution of Islam). Basically, quotations from the *Qu'ran* serve as the point of departure for discussions of Islamic war and peace. The common foundations for all Islamic concepts of war and peace are based on the traditionalists' interpretations and discourse. All Islamic scholars believe that the *Qu'ran* and the *Hadith* are open to interpretation (*tafsir*) and re-interpretation (*ijtihad* and *qiyas*). The classical schools of Islamic thought mostly deal with the legalistic and judicial issues. In Sunni Islam, there are two principles of the Islamic traditionalists: the literal interpretation of the *Qu'ran* and determinism. In contrast to the traditionalists, the modernists and fundamentalists resort to the instruments of the earliest Muslim jurists: *ijtihad* (legal judgement based on human reasoning), *qiyas* (legal interpretation based on analogy), *ijma* (consensus of the jurists), the principles of equity and public interest (*maslaha*). Also, the modernists believe that human beings have moral responsibility for his/her own fate.

Although there is only a doctrinal division between the Sunnis and Shias, this paper will focus on the Sunni tradition of Islamic ethics for war, peace, and nonviolence. Also, it should be emphasized that the conceptualization of the Islamic concepts is just a theoretical construct and is not reflected in the actual real life situation. Many works of Islamic scholars should be studied in the context of their time and space.

The *Qu'ran* contains some general provisions on the initiation of hostilities, the grounds for war, conduct of war, the termination of war, and the general nature of treaties. These also created the foundations of Islamic international law (*siyar*).[2] According to the traditionalist scholars, the world was separated into two spheres: the land or abode of Islam (*dar al-Islam*) and the land or abode of war (*dar-al harb*). Dar-al Islam covered any territory where Islamic law was held and where the lives of Muslims were secure. It could also refer to any country ruled by a Muslim. Non-Muslims were under the protection of the Muslim state, having submitted to Islam either by conversion or by accepting the status of a religion minority

---

[2] Sohail Hashmi, "Islamic Ethics in International Society," in *International Society: Diverse Ethical Perspectives,* ed. David R. Mapel and Terry Nardin (Princeton, NJ: Princeton University Press, 1998), pp. 215–237 (p. 221).

(*dhimmi*). If they were the People of the Book (e*hl al-kitab*)—Christians, Jews, Sabeans, and Zoroastrians—they could live peacefully unless they did not accept the Muslim rule and the payment of poll tax (*jizya*). Idolaters were not tolerated in theory, but in practice they lived peacefully. *Dar-al harb* was territory not under Muslim rule. Theoretically, *dar-al Islam* and *dar-al harb* were constantly in a state of war and there was no peace between them.[3] Today, some scholars introduce another term, the land of neutrality (*dar al-sulh* or *dar al-hiyad*) where there is a secular state that is not inimical to Islam and does not persecute the Muslims. *Dar al-sulh* refers to the territories where there is no Islamic governance, but where there is a state of peace between the two domains based on treaties, alliances, and cooperation. Also, this situation is permitted when Muslim power is weak and a "temporary peace" (*hudna*) is preferred.[4]

The just war tradition in the West distinguishes between two notions: the justification of the war as a last resort (*jus in bellum*), and the limitations of the conduct of the war (*jus in bello*). The *jus in bellum* requires a right authority to initiate force, a justifying cause, and a right intention toward the enemy. The *jus in bello* set limits on who might legitimately be attacked (the idea of non-combatant immunity) and the means that could be legitimately employed (the principle of proportionality).[5]

The Western notion of the just war (*jus in bellum* and *jus in bello*) can be applied to Islamic notions of *jihad* (sacred struggle) and *qital* (fighting). The word "*jihad*" appears thirty-six times in the *Qu'ran*, whereas the term *qital* refers to the practice of warfare. There are four types of *jihad*: *jihad* with the heart (faith), the tongue (speech), the hand (good deeds), and the sword (holy war). For traditionalists, *jihad* is a sacred struggle to establish an Islamic rule by means other than self-discipline, persuasion, and example. They believe that *jihad* as a defensive military action is a collective duty of the Muslim community and *jihad* can be carried out by the *khalifah* or *imam*, the religious and political leader of the Islamic community. The *khalifah* or *imam* should decide when to initiate such fighting, when to avoid it, and when to bring it to an end (ibid, p. 62). Also,

---

[3] Ibid., p. 221; Ralph Salmi et al. *Islam and Conflict Resolution: Theory and Practice* (Lanham, MD: University Press of America, 1998), pp. 72–73.
[4] Bassam Tibi, "War and Peace in Islam," in *The Ethics of War and Peace: Religious and Secular Perspectives,* ed. Terry Nardin (Princeton University Press, Princeton: NJ, 1996), pp. 128–145 (p. 130); Muhammed A. Muqtedar Khan, "Islam as an Ethical Tradition of International Relations," *Islam and Christian-Muslim Relations,* 8:2 (1997), 173–188 (p. 182); Salmi et al, p. 74.
[5] Turner J. Johnson, *The Holy War Idea in Western and Islamic Traditions* (University Park: Pennsylvania State University Press, 1997).

some traditionalists claim that any war against unbelievers is morally justified. In the Islamic sense, when the Muslims wage a war for the dissemination of Islam, it is a just war (*futuhat*, the opening of the world through the use of force); when non-Muslims attack Muslims, it is an unjust war (*idwan*) (Tibi, p. 131).

The traditionalists distinguish four types of war. The first type is called "illegitimate war" that consist of skirmishes between rival families or neighboring tribes and the desire for plunder among "savage peoples." The legitimate wars have two types: *jihad* and wars to suppress internal rebellion. The *jihad* has two components. The first is literal war, fighting, or battle (*qital*), which is a last resort for the small *jihad* (armed *jihad*). Second, it is metaphorical: war as a permanent condition between the Muslims and non-believers. The *Qu'ran* distinguishes between defensive war (small *jihad* or *qital*), and aggressive and offensive war (*idwan*). The *Qu'ran* specifically forbids aggression, but it orders fighting against aggressors: "Fight for the sake of Allah (God) against those who fight against you but do not be violent because Allah does not love aggressors" (2:190) (ibid, p. 131).

As another classification, scholars make an effort to distinguish between wars in terms of motivations and objectives as good and bad wars. The "good" wars have the purposes of conquest called as *futuh*, "openings" (that is, God helps the believers "open" or conquer a given territory for the imposition of divine law and Islamic rule). On the other hand, the "bad" wars called "*fitan*"—"temptations" that can create instability in the Islamic community (*umma*), obscure solidarity among Muslims, and destroy the Islamic rule in a Muslim state.

In summary, the classical traditionalists are in agreement that fighting or waging war is permissible when there is a threat to the *umma*, and when the hostilities are directed against polytheists, idolaters, and the "enemies of Islam." This kind of *jihad* or *qital* is defined as "defensive struggle or *jihad*," that is, as war undertaken strictly to safeguard Muslim lives and property from external aggression. Thus, the Muslims may wage war for self-defense. On the other hand, war between the Muslim parties is classified under a separate category: *fitna*. Because intra-Muslim conflicts are viewed as internal strife, they should be resolved quickly by the ruling authorities. Therefore, Islamic arbitration (*tahkim*) has played an important role during Islamic history to solve intra- as well as inter-Muslim conflicts. But some scholars believe that the armed struggle and fighting is permissible if there are Muslims who are apostates, dissenters, rebels, and simply bandits, and so on, who deny Islamic faith and disturb the *Pax Islamica* (Johnson, p. 67).

On the other hand, some scholars believe that *jihad* is the equivalent of the just war in the West. The term *jihad* is used for the reasons of the assassination of Anwar al-Sadat, the war against Israel, the Iran-Iraq War, the Gulf War, the war in Afghanistan, the Bosnian War, and so on. For example, in the Gulf War, Iraqi Leader Saddam Hussein termed the struggle a *jihad* against the forces of the West, while the Saudi *ulama* (assembly of clergy) declared a *jihad* against Saddam. Therefore, the explanation and understanding of the Islamic concepts may be helpful to bring peace, stability, and justice to deep-rooted and protracted conflicts in the Islamic world. In short, there are four requirements for the use of force in the quest for peace in Islam[6]:

- There must be just cause;
- An invitation/declaration of Muslim intentions;
- There is a requirement of right authority;
- The war must be conducted in accordance with Islamic values.

The modernist approach basically rejects the traditionalist interpretations of the Islamic concepts about war and peace and emphasizes the reinterpretations of these concepts in terms of non-violence and peaceful resolution of conflicts. For example, Fazlur Rahman argues that the Qur'anic message should not be seen as a series of legal pronouncements, but as a moral code on which a legal system can be constructed. He rejects the idea that the *Qu'ran* is a lawbook and sees it as the religious source of the law.[7] Similarly, the Islamic revival can be observed among fundamentalist thinkers such as Sayyid Qutb, Abu al-Ala Mahdudi, and Hassan Al-Banna. They are concerned about the malaise afflicting Islamic civilization. Like the modernists, they also see *ijtihad* as a necessary instrument for rethinking Islam. However, they conclude that their reinterpretation aims not to generate a moral code or an ethical framework, but to confirm the divine law and the "authentic" message of the *Qu'ran*.

The modernists point out that the term *dar al-harb* is not mentioned in the *Qu'ran* and the categorization of the world into the two spheres has no Qur'anic basis. They believe that this theory is only the reflection of the historical circumstances in medieval times and it cannot be applied in

---

[6] John Kelsay, *Islam and War: The Gulf War and Beyond-A Study in Comparative Ethics* (Louisville, KT: John Knox Press, 1993), p. 35.
[7] Fazlur Rahman, *Major Themes of the Qu'ran* (Minneapolis: Bibliotheca Islamica, 1980).

modern times.[8] On the other hand, the fundamentalists introduce a new term: *dar al-nifaq* (the land of hypocrisy). They argue that *dar al-harb* is a state in which active oppression, corruption, and injustice are found even in a Muslim state. Because the *Shari'a* is today enforced in only a few Muslim states and Muslim rulers have allied themselves with the West, there has been a revolutionary struggle going on between the powerful and the oppressed people within the Islamic community (*umma*). Therefore, there is a need for armed *jihad* against the Muslim rulers and the West (Hashmi, p. 277).

Today there are two contrary positions on the Islamic notions of war and peace among the modernists and fundamentalists. As a representative of the modernist school, the Sunni Islamic scholars, especially al-Azhar University, produce a notion of *jihad* that discourages the use of force and emphasizes the non-violent means for conflict resolution in the realist international system. In contrast to this peaceful interpretation of Islamic war and peace, Islamic fundamentalists have focused on the armed *jihad* in the *dar al-Islam* and the *dar al-harb* environment.

According to the Al-Azhar interpretation, there are different kinds of *jihad*. They distinguish "armed *jihad*" or "low *jihad*" (*al-masallah*) from the high *jihad* that means everyday *jihad* against ignorance, *jihad* against poverty, *jihad* against illness and disease [...]. The search for knowledge is the highest level of *jihad*. Therefore, the call to Islam (*dawa*) can be pursued without fighting (*qital*). Earlier Meccan verses are quoted again and again in an effort to separate the call to Islam (*dawa*) from any notion of *qital* or armed *jihad*. In the *Qu'ran*: "Had Allah (God) wanted, all people of the earth would have believed in Him, would you then dare to force faith upon them? (10:99). The modernist scholars believe that in the modern age, communication networks offer a much better mean than armed conflicts for the pursuit of the *dawa*. Also, they support the idea of creating treaties between Muslims and non-Muslims. For example, they took the Treaty of Hudaybiya between the Prophet Muhammad and the *Quraysh* tribe as a model for contemporary issues. They conclude from this precedence that an armistice (*hudna*) can be valid for a period of no more than ten years between Muslims and non-Muslims.

Unlike the modernists, the fundamentalists are inclined to use Islamic texts in support of their view about *jihad*. For example, the leader of the Muslim Brotherhood, al-Banna concludes that the *jihad* is an "obligation of every Muslim" (Tibi, p. 137). For them, *Jihad* and *qital* both have the same meaning: "the use of force." It can be pursued against existing regimes as a

---

[8] Muhammed Talat al-Ghunaimi, *The Muslim Conception of International Law and the Western Approach* (The Hague: Martinus Nijhoff, 1968).

resistance or against unbelievers as a war. In contrast to traditionalists, who distinguish between the use of force for just cause and wars of aggression or unjust wars (*idwan*), fundamentalists apply the word *jihad* indiscriminately to any use of force, whether against unbelievers or against Muslims who use their power for the oppression and injustice. They quote verses from the *Qu'ran* such as, "Fighting is obligatory for you, much as you dislike it" (2:216), or "If you should die or be slain in the cause of Allah, his mercy will surely be better than all the riches you amass" (3:158). Similarly, another fundamentalist authority, Sayyid Qutb, indicates that war against "unbelievers" is a religious duty for Muslims. For him, modernity is a new form of *jahilliyya* (the pre-Islamic age of ignorance). Therefore, there is a battle against the enemy of believers and the international society of ignorance (ibid, p.139). It is clear that for fundamentalists, peace is possible only under the banner of Islam. Non-Muslims should be permitted to live only as members of protected minorities (*dhimmis*) under Islamic rule. In all other cases, war against unbelievers is a religious duty of Muslims. They quote the *Qu'ran*: "Fight against the unbelievers in their entirety as they fight against you in your entirety" (9:36). Although, the fundamentalists share the view of traditionalists in that they see war as a last resort for the defense of Muslim lands, they also add an offensive component to the armed *jihad*.

Jihad, like just war, is conceived as a means to outline the legitimate reasons for war in order to reach peace. However, Islam sees the peaceful inter-societal relations as established by obeying the divine law. This divine law is propagated by peaceful means if possible or by violent means if necessary. No war is *jihad* unless it is undertaken with right intent and as a last resort and declared by right authority. Most Muslims today renounce the call to Islam by force and limit *jihad* to self-defense. Even some scholars believe that nonviolent *jihad* is possible and necessary in the contemporary world.

3. ISLAMIC CONCEPTIONS OF PEACE AND NONVIOLENCE

In Islamic tradition, it is hard to point out a solid picture of the concepts of war, peace, and nonviolence. The basic controversy is between the Qur'anic "verses of peace" and "verses of the sword." In the *Qu'ran*: "If they incline toward peace, incline toward it, and trust in God; verily. He alone is all-hearing, all-knowing" (8:61). However, in other parts of the *Qu'ran* we encounter the following precepts: "And so, when the sacred months are over, slay the polytheists wherever you find them, and take them captive, and besiege them, and lie in wait for them at every conceivable place" (9:5); and

Fight against those who—despite having been given revelation before—do not believe in God nor in the last day, and do not consider forbidden that which God and His Messenger have forbidden, and do not follow the religion of truth, until they pay the *jizya* with willing hand, having been subdued. (9:29).

The *Qu'ran* emphasizes that peace is a basic Islamic value. The value of peace manifests itself in the messages of the *Qu'ran*. It treats peace as the desired way as well as a value or reward for righteousness. The *Qu'ran* describes Islam as the abode of peace: "And Allah summons to the abode of peace, and leads whom He wills to the straight path" (10:1). Indeed the world Islam, which means submission, is a derivative of the word *salaam* meaning peace. Islam is peace with God, peace with man, and peace with one's own self. Moreover, the Muslim greeting consists of the word *salaam* (peace). Muslims greet each other by wishing and/or praying for peace for each other—*Assalamu Alaykum* (May Peace be upon you). It is a practice based on the injunctions of the *Qu'ran*. The *Qu'ran* states that the greeting of those who are righteous and have been admitted to the heavens is "Peace!" (14:23)

There are other concepts in consonance with peace. For instance, the *Qu'ran* attaches great importance to patience (*sabr*). Patience implies reaction, whereas impatience implies a violent response. The word *sabr* (patience) exactly express the notion of nonviolence as it is understood in modern times. It has been pointed out that the incident of *Hijra* (exodus) is a nonviolent act which avoids conflict. The *Hijra* (exodus) is an example of withdrawal and non-cooperation as protest and the practice of escaping from repression. Moreover, throughout his life, the Prophet Muhammad never departed from the path of peace and nonviolent struggle except when God (Allah) ordered him to engage in war on specific occasions—*Badr*, *Uhud*, and *Hunayn*. The *Qu'ran* is a strong advocate of peace but permits Muslims to fight to protect their faith, their freedom, their lands, and their property. When means of peaceful change are pursued, violence is used as the last resort. The *Qu'ran* forbids Muslims from initiating aggression or causing *fitna* (mischief, rioting) on earth and exhorts them to make peace with their enemies if they are inclined towards peace.

Secondly, the Islamic tradition connects peace with justice so that peace should help the mankind to create justice in the world. Peace, therefore, becomes a means to create a just social order. In this sense, justice is the goal of life and peace is the form of justice. The personal and the collective struggle to build justice on earth is the essence of *jihad*. The objective of war, therefore, is neither to propagate Islam, nor is it to gain territory for the Islamic state. Rather, the war aims to establish and assure justice and to

109

annihilate oppression and tyranny. Peace in Islam does not mean the absence of war, but the absence of oppression and tyranny. Islam considers that perpetual peace can only be attained when justice prevails. Islam, therefore, allows war against regimes that prevent people from choosing their ideals and practicing their beliefs.[9]

Islam also stresses the importance of positive peace (the absence of structural violence). It is the responsibility of individuals as well as the state to provide distributive justice and social welfare. This principle has created one of the five "pillars of faith" in Islam. It is the duty of the Muslims to pay a tax on surplus wealth (*zakat*) to the society and the state for the improvement of the conditions of the poorest members in the society.

Of his twenty-three years of prophethood, the Prophet spent the initial thirteen years in Mecca. The Prophet fully adopted the way of active pacifism or nonviolence during this time. There were many issues in Mecca at that time which could have developed into confrontation and violence. But, the Prophet Muhammad strictly limited his sphere to peaceful propagation of the word of God. This resulted in the call to Islam (*dawa*) that is performed by peaceful means. Even when in Mecca the *Quraysh* tribe leaders were set to wage war against the Prophet, the Prophet consciously selected the *Hijra* (exodus) to Medina instead of reaction and retaliation. *Hijra* (Migration) was a clear example of nonviolent activism. After the migration, when his antagonists again took the unilateral decision to wage war against him, God ordered him to armed *jihad* and there were four bloody wars in Arabian Peninsula. After the wars, the Prophet still preferred peace over war and he signed a ten-year peace treaty known as *Sulh al-Hudaybiya*, and accepted all the conditions of his opponents.[10]

Following the *Hijra* (exodus) of the Islamic Prophet and his supporters in 622, the first Islamic community (*umma*) was established in Medina. The relations between this first Islamic state and the surrounding tribes have to be defined in terms of gradual nonviolence to violence. All Qur'anic verses revealed between 622 and 632 (the Medinan period) are the expression of the non-violent and/or violent struggle against the surrounding enemies. Thus, there are important differences in teachings on violence and nonviolence between the Meccan and Medinan parts of the *Qu'ran* and Islamic history.

---

[9] Lounay M. Safi, "Islam and Peace," *Islamic Horizons,* September/October 1996, pp. 42–43.

[10] Khan Wahiddudin, "Islam and Nonviolence," A Round-Table Workshop Held February 14, 1997 at the American University, Washington D.C., Nonviolence International. Gender: New Perspectives. Washington, DC: World Bank. http://www.aed.org/LeadershipandDemocracy/upload/MeasuringWomen.pdf, p.3.

The Meccan period was totally based on nonviolent resistance and the virtues of patience (*sabr*) and steadfastness. In the Medinan period, Muslims established the first Islamic state and community (*umma*) and *jihad* moved from nonviolent resistance to an armed struggle. During the Meccan period, the *Qu'ran* has mostly dealt with spiritual issues and ordered *jihad* with the heart and the mouth. Also, during this period, the Prophet showed no inclination toward the use of force in any form, even for self-defense. He followed a policy described as nonviolent resistance in spite of escalating physical attacks directed at his followers and at him personally. The Prophet insisted that the use of force was a last resort. He even ordered the most vulnerable Muslims to seek refuge in Abyssinia (Ethiopia). In the Meccan period, the Prophet's practices are defined as active nonviolent resistance and open defiance of pagan persecution (Hashmi, p. 153). In Medina, the *Qu'ran*—rooted in its historical context—provided the precepts to *jihad* in the narrow meaning of *qital* as military fighting. Clearly, *jihad* in the thirteen years period of the Prophet's life meant nonviolent resistance and there are many lessons to be learned from the Prophet's decisions during these years.

One of these lessons is about conducting a war. This guidance on how Muslims are to conduct themselves in war is similar to the Western concept, *jus in bello*. Because the goal of *jihad* is the call to Islam, not territorial conquest or plunder, the *Qu'ran* and the Prophet provide the basis for *jus in bello*. Jihad, like just war, lists strict limitations on the conduct of war and demands that proportionality and discrimination are two main principles in Islamic conceptions of war. The principle of proportionality implies that inhumane weapons in the battlefield are restricted. The principle of discrimination suggests that the parties in a conflict should discriminate between combatants and non-combatants. To quote the *Qu'ran*, "And fight God's cause against those who wage war against you, but do not transgress limits, for God loves not the transgressors" (2:190). Also, the first caliph, the successor of the Prophet, Abu Bakr, enumerated the "ten commands" about the conduct of war:

> Do not act treacherously; do not act disloyally; do not act neglectfully. Do not mutilate, do not kill little children or old men, or women; do not cut off the heads of the palm-trees or burn them; do not cut down the fruit trees; do not slaughter a sheep or a cow or a camel, except for food. You will pass by people who devote their lives in cloisters; leave them and their devotion alone. You will come upon people who bring you platters in which are various sort of food; if you eat any of it, mention the name of God over it.
> (Quoted from Hashmi, p. 161.)

The early traditionalist and juristic literature contains several examples of commands against killing women, children, and other non-combatants; similarly it hinders attacks on the enemy without first inviting them to embrace Islam and denounces unintended effects and deaths against non-combatants (the modern term of collateral damage). Islam does not tolerate indiscriminate methods such as terrorism and the use of weapons of mass destruction. Nor it allows the destruction of God's creations—human lives, trees, animals, and the environment. For example, the use of napalm is unacceptable, as are explosions in department stores, hijacking, killing hostages in any means of transportation and bombing civilian targets.[11]

One of the Islamic ideas about peace is related to Islamic universalism and Muslim solidarity. Because the Muslims constitute a political community (*umma*), modernist thinkers suggest that there is some degree of transnational cooperation among Muslims. Although they accept the idea that there may be territorial states in the international system, it is still possible to create a "Muslim League of Nations" that would be helpful to establish a peaceful co-existence between Islamic states. The existence of the Organization of the Islamic Conference (OIC) that consist of fifty states and other multinational Islamic organizations is an example of Islamic universality and solidarity.

Another idea in Islamic tradition about peace is tolerance and diversity. Although Islam emphasizes the importance of the order, similarities, and solidarity within the Muslims, it also advocates diversity and tolerance. In the earlier Meccan verses the question of faith was decided by the right of free choice: "To you your religion and to me mine." (109). Even though Muhammad failed to convert pagan Meccans, Jews, and Christians to Islam, the following verses were sent: "If it had been your Lord's will, they would have all believed, all who are on earth. Will you then compel mankind against their will to believe?" (10:99). However, this attitude shifted towards more of an intolerant and exclusivist discourse in the Medina period where the *Qu'ran* gave permission to fight against non-Muslims and even ordered not to take Jews and Christians (5:51) as allies or protectors. Some scholars argue that the *Qu'ran* emphasizes the separate character of the Muslim community and distinguishes pagan Meccans, Jews, and Christians in both the Meccan and Medinan periods. But the Medinan chapters also contain verses about toleration: "Let there be no compulsion in religion; truth stands out clear from error" (2:256). Also, the Prophet

---

[11] Chaiwat Satha-Anand, "The Nonviolent Crescent: Eight Theses on Muslim Nonviolent Action," in *Arab Nonviolent Political Struggle in the Middle East*, ed. Ralph E. Crow et al. (Boulder, CO: Lynne Rienner Publishers, 1990), pp. 25–41 (p.31).

himself worked to sow the seeds of tolerance between Muslims and non-Muslims. In one instance, the Prophet Muhammad found some scrolls of the Torah among the things that the Muslims brought to him and he ordered that they should be returned to the Jews. In another instance, the Prophet was sitting when a Jewish funeral passed by. He stood up and his companions followed his example. He said: "Is it not a human soul? If you ever see a funeral, stand up."[12]

4. NONVIOLENCE AND ISLAM

Throughout human history, violence has been seen as the only effective means of action in deep-rooted and protracted conflict situations. However, there is another unwritten side in human history and that is nonviolent techniques of struggle. In his outstanding book, Gene Sharp indicates the basis of nonviolence: "It is the belief that the exercise of power depends on the consent of ruled who, by withdrawing the consent, can control and even destroy the power of their opponent. In other words, nonviolent action is a technique used to control, combat and destroy the opponent's power by nonviolent means of wielding power."[13] Non-violence should never be confused with inaction or passivity. It is not inaction. It is action that is nonviolent. Non-violence is action in full sense of the word. It is a forceful action that does not use violence. It is a fact that non-violent activism is more powerful and effective than violent activism. When human beings are faced with problems, they often resort to violence in order to solve it. However, it is better to solve the problem by peaceful means, avoiding violence, and confrontation.

Nonviolent techniques of resistance include public protest and persuasion, speeches, petitions, and symbolic acts, many forms of social, political, and economic non-cooperation or withdrawal and renunciation, such as refusal to pay taxes or obey unjust laws, strikes, and boycotts to improve conditions or gain greater power, as well as intervention and the use of independent political institutions, or establishing "parallel" organs of government. These means of struggle involve protest and persuasion, challenge and repression, strategy and discipline (Sharp, pp. 117–445).

The religion of Islam seeks social change and justice through nonviolent means if possible. It is believed that nonviolence is a norm and rule and violence is an exception in the Islamic peace paradigm. Satha-Anand claims

---

[12] Muhammed Abu-Laila, "Islam and Peace," *The Islamic Quarterly*, 35:1 (1991), 55–69 (p. 66).

[13] Gene Sharp, *The Politics of Nonviolent Action,* 3 vols (Boston: Porter Sargent, 1973), p. 4.

that *jihad* is considered as the sixth pillar of Islam and it can be used against tyranny, oppression, and injustice with nonviolent means (p. 9). Wahid believes that the unity of the *umma* creates a sense of collectivity for Islamic nonviolent action and promotes solidarity against oppressors.[14] Islam also balances the unity of Islamic community with equality, common purpose, and brotherhood with the encouragement of pluralism and tolerance.

Because of Islam's commitment toward social and political justice by opposing injustice, corruption, and repression, Islam introduces active nonviolence in its institutions and practices. For example, fasting can be used for both the implementations of religious duty, and protest, boycott, and symbolic action (Crow (ed.), p. 12). Also, the Friday prayer, the idea of the *umma*, and the *jihad* can be applied for communal purification, discipline, and education in the nonviolent struggle. *Zakat* and *waqf* (charitable endowment) promote social justice and positive peace. Moreover, the concepts of reconciliation (*sulha*), forgiveness (*afw*), and patience (*sabr*) are important elements in Islamic religion and practice for the active exercise of nonviolence.[15]

However, many Muslims criticize nonviolence as a foreign concept and believe that there is a lack of theological and cultural bases of nonviolence in Islamic tradition. One Muslim scholar who has taken a bold position about non-violence in Islam is Jawdat Said. In his work about the two sons of Adam, Cain and Abel, Said shows us how God praised non-violent action. Cain, who wants to be accepted by God was rejected by Him, and resorted to a death threat against his brother, while the other son, Abel, was accepted by God and he responded to the death threat by saying, "If you stretch out you hand against me to kill me, I shall not stretch out my hand against you to kill you" (*Qu'ran*, 5:28). Then Cain killed him and lost God's grace and mercy and became remorseful. This nonviolent peaceful stand on the part of Abel is similar to the idea in Christianity about turning the other cheek. This stance announces that human beings are capable of resisting violence by nonviolence and of transforming a violent person into a remorseful one. Said points out that even self-defense is prohibited by the *Qu'ran* and when people are faced with aggressive hostility against them, they should behave like Abel, the son of Adam. The Prophet said to his companions: "Be as the Son of Adam!" Said also concludes that this nonviolent strategy is not only a doctrine of the Prophet Muhammad, but

---

[14] Abrurrahman Wahid,. 1993. "Islam, Nonviolence, and National Transformation," in Paige, ed., pp. 53–59.

[15] Sezai Ozcelik, "Islam and Peace: A Dialogue," *Frontline, Nonviolence International*, 7:1 (1998) 3–4.

also for the other Messengers. In other words, Said claims that the Prophetic paradigm—Abel's abnegation of violence in the face of Cain's murderous assault—is very important and asserts that even violence in self-defense is morally unjustifiable. (pp. 5–8).

Other scholars enumerate why non-violent *jihad* (struggle) is necessary in Islam:

- Nonviolent resistance is a weapon against the status quo;
- Nonviolent political struggle is not pacifism, but active pacifism;
- It provides more appropriate long-term solutions;
- It evokes sympathy and support for just causes;
- It is the surest way to build psychological strength;
- It is the weapon of the strong, not the weak;
- Oppressors fear nonviolent struggle more than violent resistance.[16]

The remarkable work of Abdul Ghaffar Khan (1890–1988) presents an example for Islamic nonviolence. Although the Pathans faced executions, jail, and persecution for years, they used *jihad* (sacred struggle) for peace. Abdul Ghaffar Khan was the leader of the Pathan (or Pashtun) tribe in North India (today Afghanistan) and a Muslim follower of Mahatma Gandhi. He founded the *Khudai Khidmatgars* (Servants of God or Army of God), the world's first non-violent army and led from 1929–1938.[17] He challenged existing social and economic institutions, uplifted peasants, introduced women into political action, and fuelled anti-colonial activity. Abdul Ghaffar Khan, later known as Badshah Khan, was a religious figure and was influenced by Gandhi's *satyagraha*: nonviolent civil resistance. He said: "[Nonviolence] was followed fourteen hundred years ago by the Prophet [Mohammed] all the time he was in Mecca... But we had so far forgotten it that when Gandhi placed it before us, we thought he was sponsoring a novel creed."[18] During the Indian independence movement, he and his followers followed the nonviolence strategy. Badshah Khan shows us that three common myths are not true: (1) nonviolence is the weapon of the weak; (2) it works only against "civilized" adversaries; and (3)

---

[16] Ralph Crow and Philip Grant, "Questions and Controversies about Nonviolent Struggle in the Middle East," in Crow (ed.), pp. 79–85.

[17] Timothy Flinders, "The Good Fight-Badshah Khan, the Frontier Gandhi," in *Nonviolence in Theory and Practice*, ed. Robert Holmes and Barry L. Gan (Belmont: Woolsworth Publishing, 1990), pp. 187–191 (p. 187).

[18] Eknath Easwaran, "Khan Abdul Ghaffar Khan," in *Protest, Power and Change: An Encyclopedia of Nonviolent Action from Act-up Women's Suffrage*, ed. R.S. Powers and W.B. Vogele (New York: Garland 1997), pp. 284–285 (p. 284).

nonviolence is not part of Islam (ibid, p.285). Mahatma Gandhi declared that he was able to perceive the origin of the doctrine of nonviolence and love for all living things not only in the sacred Hindu and Buddhist writings and the Bible, but also in the *Qu'ran*.[19]

Apart from this first modern nonviolent resistance example in Islam, there have been many cases in the Muslim and Arab worlds: Egypt (1919-1922), Peshawar Pathan (Pashtun) Resistance (1930), Palestine General Strike (1936), Iraq Uprising (1948), Pattani Resistance in Thailand (1975), Iran Revolution (1978-1979), Golan Druze Resistance (1981-1982), Defense of *Al-Aqsa* Mosque-Jerusalem, Sudan Insurrection (1985), Palestinian nonviolent resistance—*Intifada* or "shaking off" (1987-89), Albanian National Movement in Kosovo (1989-1994).[20] I will briefly summarize the last two of these cases: the *Intifada* and the Kosovo National Movement.

The Palestinian National Movement has a long and violent history, but it also held some non-violent struggles in the 1980s and 1990s. Up until the end of 1987, the Movement had focused on military, economic, and diplomatic means to achieve its goals by their leadership in exile, the Palestinian Liberation Organization (PLO). With the end of the Cold War, it was hard to continue an armed struggle against Israel in the Occupied Territories. As a result, the Palestinians began to struggle with the only weapons available—non-violent means and stones—in December 1987. At first, the resistance was spontaneous and included non-violent strategies such as stone-throwing children, strikes, protests, demonstrations, marching in the streets, chanting slogans, waving the illegal Palestinian flag, and so on. Afterwards, it became an official policy in the Movement, proving that non-violent struggle in the Middle East is more successful and effective than violent means. Some lessons about nonviolent struggle in the Occupied Territories are as follows (Crow and Grant, pp. 85–88):

- All unjust systems are vulnerable to nonviolent struggle;
- Nonviolent resistance can bridge the gap between oppressors and the oppressed;
- Nonviolent struggle can educate the oppressor;
- Nonviolent struggle can overcome the "chosen people" doctrine;

---

[19] James E. Dougherty and Robert L. Jr. Pfaltzgraff, *Contending Theories of International Relations: A Comprehensive Survey* (New York: Longman, 1996), p. 187.

[20] Brad Bennett, "Arab-Muslim Cases of Nonviolent Struggle," in Crow (ed.), pp. 41–59; Grant, in ibid., pp. 59–75 (p.59); Elez Biberaj, "Kosovo, Albanian National Movement," in Powers and Vogele (eds), pp. 294–96 (p. 294).

- The concept of *jihad* can mean inner struggle;
- It can develop social and economic strength and international autonomy.

There was also another non-violent political movement organized by the Muslim majority of the ethnic Albanians in Kosovo during the 1990s. The movement, led by prominent literary critic Ibrahim Rugova, emerged in response to the termination of self-government in Kosovo. The Serbian government suspended Kosovo's autonomy and launched a policy of political, economic, and cultural marginalization of ethnic Albanians such as the closing of the Albanian-language universities, TV, and newspapers. As a response to this, the non-violent resistance created a state within a state. They established a Solidarity Fund for a private educational system in the Albanian language. They also assisted people with financial needs because of political charges, and gave financial assistance to doctors and teachers from the Solidarity Fund. Rugova, the architect of the nonviolent resistance against Serbia, sees Kosovo struggle as a long-term process and stresses the importance of Albanian national institutions and self-confidence. In spite of the bloody violent resistance in 1999, he insisted that the use of nonviolent methods is necessary not to descend into the violence that has consumed Bosnia (Biberaj, p.295).

5. CONCLUSION

In conclusion, while the *Qu'ran* does not prescribe an explicit ethic of nonviolence and peace, neither does it give higher value to actions of violence. In the *Qu'ran*, there are no consistent or unequivocal general concepts for determining war, peace, and nonviolence. Each Qur'anic verse is related to some specific historical events. Thus, there are Qur'anic verses that call for non-violence, while others call for war. This is not a contradiction, but a reflection of specific historical situations. For example, where most Meccan verses focus on spiritual issues, after the *Hijra* (migration) to Medina the *Qu'ran* moved gradually—rooted in historical context—to provide precepts for "armed *jihad*," in the more narrow sense of *qital* as military fighting. On the other hand, if we take the consideration of the time-space dimension and gradual changes in Islamic tradition, it becomes clear that Islam tends to give moral precedence to non-violence. One can even conclude that the pursuit of religiously-oriented or informal struggle (*jihad*) in the modern world by the methods of non-violent action is fully consistent with Islamic scripture and tradition.

The *Qu'ran* makes references to "war" (*harb*), fighting (*qital*), and even more frequent references to "struggle or striving" (*jihad*) that sometimes

117

mean "armed struggle." In some passages, the words have symbolic meanings. The *Qur'an* has an ambivalent attitude toward violence and peace. On the one hand, oppression of the weak is condemned, and some passages state clearly that believers are to fight only in self-defense. But a number of passages seem to provide explicit justification for the use of force in the call to Islam.[21] It is hard to decide whether the *Qu'ran* promotes offensive war or just defensive war. But in modern times, many Muslim scholars believe that Islamic public interest necessitates only defensive action because of weapons of mass destruction and the Islamic ethic of war (*jus in bellum* and *jus in bello* in Islamic tradition). In the *Qu'ran*, for example, "Those who disbelieve and divert (others) from the way of God, He will lead their works astray [...]. So when you meet those who disbelieve (during a military campaign), smite the necks; so that when you have overcome them, you may set (them) in bondage. Afterwards (free them) either as a favor or for ransom until the war (*harb*) puts down its weapons" (47: 1–4). Some verses imply that war should be defensive: "And fight in God's way against those who fight you, but do not act aggressively. Indeed God does not love those who act aggressively" (2:190). But the very next verse states, "kill them wherever you overtake them, and drive them out from where they drove you out. For *fitna* (tempting people away from Islam) is worse than killing. But do not fight them at the Sacred Mosque, unless they fight you in it; but if they do fight you (in it), slay them. Such is the recompense of the unbelievers" (2:191). Therefore, many scholars accept that war and fighting are seen as valid necessary means in dealing with non-Muslims as a last resort to end oppression and injustice. But the *Qu'ran* specifically prohibits any violent acts among Muslims and urges the Islamic community to use non-violent conflict resolution tools such as arbitration (*tahkim*), mediation (*wasata*), and reconciliation (*sulha*).

Although Islam is seen as a "religion of the sword" that is guided by conversion, coercion, and war in the Western media, the majority of contemporary Muslim scholars and jurists restrict *jihad* only to a defensive act against outside attack toward Muslim nation-states and/or against internal subversion.[22]

---

[21] Fred M. Donner, "The Sources of Islamic Conceptions of War," in *Just War and Jihad: Historical and Theoretical Perspectives on War and Peace in Western and Islamic Traditions,* ed. John Kelsay and James Turner Johnson (New York: Greenwood Press, 1991), pp. 75–91 (p. 77).

[22] Richard C. Martin, "The Religious Foundations of War, Peace, and Statecraft in Islam," in Kelsay and Johnson (eds), pp. 31–71 (p. 108).

RECONCILIATION, TOLERANCE, COEXISTENCE: THE ISLAMIC PERSPECTIVE

Mohamad Iwhida Ahmed

INTRODUCTION

Modern interpretations of Islamic teachings vary enormously, as current developments show. Some groups believe that Islamic law requires the most repressive and cruel actions for some issues, while on the other hand there are Muslim human rights activists who see human rights as a natural outflowing of the teachings of the *Qu'ran* and who support human rights as complementary to their Islamic faith.

The Prophet Muhammad established the first Islamic community, which was actually a Jewish-Muslim federation that extended to religious minorities the rights that are guaranteed to them in the *Qu'ran*. Muhammad's community was based on a covenant, a real and actual social contract agreed upon by Muslims, Jews, and others and which treated them as equal citizens. They enjoyed the freedom to choose the legal system they wished to live under. Jews could live under Islamic law, Jewish law, or pre-Islamic tribal traditions. There was no compulsion in religion even though it was an Islamic community.[1]

The difference between Muhammad's community and some Islamic communities nowadays is profound. The situation of Muhammad's community was based on a real social contract that applied divine law but only in consultation and with consent of all citizens regardless of their faith. Some groups of Muslims are actually in direct opposition to the spirit and letter of the *Qu'ran*. The *Qu'ran* is very explicit when it says there is no compulsion in religion. The *Qu'ran* exhorts Jews to live by the laws revealed to them in the Torah. The *Qu'ran* also orders Christians to live by their faith. From these examples it is clear that Islam advocates religious pluralism.

Nowadays there are Muslims with new perspectives contributing to the understanding of Islam. New dimensions of the Islamic heritage are being highlighted, many of which point to compatibility between Islamic law and human rights.

---

[1] Kamel Al-sharif, "Human Rights in the Medina Charter," (In Arabic), *Scientific Conference Human Rights between "Shari'a" and Written Law* (Riyadh: [n.p.], 2001), p.56.

THE VALUE OF LIFE AS A MAIN PRINCIPLE IN ISLAM "RECONCILIATION"

Life is the highest asset for Islam. This is why the *Qu'ran* demands absolute protection regardless of ethnic background, religious confession, ideology, material or intellectual property. "If anyone killed a person not in retaliation for murder, or (and) spread mischief in the land—it would be as if he killed all mankind, and if anyone saved a life, it would be as if he saved the life of all mankind" (5:32).

In this context we must keep in mind that there are four important principles when talking about reconciliation, tolerance, and coexistence in Islam:

1. Rights are given by God: rights in Islam are not just human conventions, they are God's orders.[2] They should be considered permanent values, universal standards. They should not be given only to those who shout most or who lobby most, but they should be given even to those who are not yet empowered to speak for themselves or who are not even aware due to social circumstances of what rights they should have. The rights are rights even when no one asks for them.

2. There are rights and there are duties. Muslim scholars have debated whether the rights come first or the duties come first. Some have emphasized duties and some have emphasized rights. However, both of them are important. It is not possible to have rights without duties. There is mutuality between rights and duties. Someone's right is another person's duty and someone's duty is another person's right. In Islam the Human person has absolute value.[3]

3. Islam has a detailed scheme in its priorities. All people have rights but no one has a right above God's rights. Among the people there are rights of parents, rights of spouses, rights of children, rights of other relatives. There are rights of neighbors. There are rights of employers and employees. There are rights of Muslims and there are rights of other human beings. There are rights of animals. Sometimes there are conflicts between one right and another right and so the question comes: what is the first duty? It is for this reason the issue of rights becomes very complex and difficult. The most important thing is to have the fear of God in all relations.

---

[2] i Faroua Al-Dousok, *The Human Being as Agent on Earth* (in Arabic) (Beirut: Islamic Office [n.d.]), p. 21.

[3] Robert Traer, "Muslim Support for Human Rights," *Religion and Human Rights,* (Conference on Human Rights) (Khartoum, May 1992), p.58.

4. Muslims scholars have mentioned five basic objectives of the Shari'a, which it came to preserve:

- Religion;
  Life;
  Progeny;
  Intellect;
  Wealth.

Within the Shari'a there are some rules that are called necessities, some that are called needs, and some that are called comforts. Preservation of religion is at the top. Life is the second most important thing and so on and so forth. Similarly there are things that are obligatory, there are things that are recommended and there are those that permissible. The same is true in modern interpretations of rights where there are certain rights that are on the top and then other rights that come after them.[4]

ISLAM AND TOLERANCE

In the Bible, the human being is made "In God's image" (*Genesis* 1:27) and since love is the most outstanding aspect of God, The Bible reveals God as "The God of love" (*Corinthians* 13:11). Also the Bible sums up a human being's obligation in these words: "'You must love your God with your whole heart and with your whole soul and with your whole mind.' This is the greatest and first commandment. The second, like it, is this, 'You must love your neighbour as your self.' On these two commandments the whole Law hangs" (Matthew 22:37–40). And besides loving God and your neighbour, love one another. In this context—which amounts to the same idea—Muslims believe that human beings were created by a transcendental God who doesn't favour one human over another except in terms of piety and good conduct. In a bid to defend Islam or to promote it, several contemporary Islamic scholars and thinkers have sought to show that Islam has from the outset laid the foundations for human rights by asserting the supremacy of the value of justice and of the principle of human dignity.

Tolerance comes from recognition of:

1. The dignity of human beings.
2. The basic equality of all human beings.
3. Fundamental freedom of thought, conscience and belief.

---

[4] Al-Shatiby, "Almowafakat" 2/17-18 (In Arabic), revision by M. A. Draz, 1st edn, (Cairo: [n.p.] [n.d.]).

The *Qu'ran* speaks about the basic dignity of all human beings. The Prophet Muhammad spoke about the equality of all human beings, regardless of their race, color, language. or ethnic background. Shari'a recognizes the rights of all people to life, property, family, honor, and conscience.

Islam emphasizes the establishment of equality and justice, neither of which can be established without some degree of tolerance. Islam has recognized from the very beginning the principle of freedom of belief or freedom of religion. It states very clearly that coercion is not allowed in matters of faith and belief.[5]

If in the matters of religion, coercion is not permissible, then by implication one can say that in matters of cultures and other worldly practices it is also not acceptable.

The *Qu'ran* says to the Prophet Muhammad, "But if they turn away, We have not sent you as a *Hafiz* (watcher, protector) over them (i.e. to take care of their needs and to recompense them). Your duty is but to convey (the Message)" (42:48). In another place the *Qu'ran* says, "Invite (mankind) to the Way of your Lord with wisdom and fair preaching; and argue with them in the way that is better." (16:125) The *Qu'ran* also says "Say: Obey Allah, and obey the Messenger: but if you turn away, he is only responsible for the duty placed on him and you for that placed on you. If you obey him, you shall be guided rightly. The Messenger's duty is only to convey in a clear way (i.e. to preach a plain way)" (24:54)

All these verses give note that Muslims do not coerce people: they must present the message to them in the most cogent and clear way, invite them to the truth, and do their best in presenting and conveying the message of God to humanity, and it is up to people to accept or not to accept. The *Qu'ran* says "And say: The truth is from your Lord, then whosoever wills, let him believe; and whosoever wills, let him disbelieve." (18:29)

We can say that there are many levels of tolerance in many angles, between family members, between husband and wife, between parents and children, and between siblings. There is also tolerance between the members of the community, tolerance of views and opinions, tolerance between the juristic schools, and tolerance between Muslims and the people of other faiths within interfaith relations, dialogue, and cooperation.

Muslims have been generally a very tolerant people. Scholars and educated Muslims must emphasize this virtue among Muslim communities and in the world today. Tolerance is needed in Muslim communities: Muslims must foster tolerance through deliberate policies and efforts. Islamic institutions should be multi-ethnic and should teach respect for each

---

[5] Mohamad Allal Sinceur, "Islamic Traditions and Human Rights," in *Philosophical Foundations of Human Rights* (Paris: UNESCO, 1986), p. 211.

other and should not generalize about other races and cultures. Institutions should exchange opinions and meetings with each other and have dialogues and good relations with non-Muslims and should inform non-Muslims what is acceptable and what is not and why they cannot accept things which are contrary to the religion. With more knowledge, more respect and cooperation will develop.

In all respects and from all angles, it's unfair to judge according to the few who give a bad name to the many. The role of scholars, writers, and intellectuals, as well as leaders of religions and political communities, is to guide people to the right path. Those who should be speaking out about values and do not are tacitly agreeing with and encouraging extremism. Some of the actions carried out in the name of religion or ideology or philosophy are indeed against their true principles or goals. In the case of Islam, which has a population of over one billion, Muslims strive to live by Islamic teachings of love, peace, and forgiveness. Those teachings, which have become universal values, remind us that Jews, Christians, Muslims, and all others have more in common than we think.

Tolerance is a basic principle of Islam. It is a religious moral duty. Muslims are tolerant with their enemies as well as their fellow Muslims. Islam teaches tolerance on all levels, to individuals and groups. It should be a political and legal requirement. Tolerance is the mechanism that upholds human rights, pluralism (including cultural pluralism), and the rule of law.

ISLAM AND COEXISTENCE

To trace the contours of the principle of coexistence and its dimensions in the Islamic sense, nothing is more eloquent and relevant than the *Qu'ran* : "Say : 'O People of Scripture Come to a word that is just between us and you'" (3:64). The common denominator between Muslims and other People of the Book is vast. Since Islam has instilled in the hearts of Muslims the seeds of a predisposition for coexistence with the whole of humankind, it is inclined to foster coexistence among believers in God, but coexistence, from this perspective, does not mean a mandatory agreement on all matters.

Coexistence in Islam is grounded on an ideological basis, taking root in the faith. Muslims believe that the divine guidance was relayed through a long series of messages and prophecies, the last of which were Judaism, then Christianity, and finally Islam. It is therefore only natural that these three religions should be nearer to one another than to the rest of religions. The *Qu'ran* refers to the Christians and the Jews as the "People of the Book," because God had revealed The Torah to Moses and The Gospel to Jesus before the Prophet Muhammad received the integral Message giving credence to the former messages

123

One of the most salient manifestations of coexistence in the Islamic civilization throughout the ages is reflected in Islam's sustained perception of Jews and Christians as followers of God-revealed religions.

The Muslims gave substance to justice in the way most befitting the status of humans. This is clearly reflected in their treatment of those who do not believe in Islam and its principles, in their endeavor to purify society from evil, in their performance of humanitarian services, and in their close cooperation for the dissemination of virtue and righteousness. History attests that the treatment administered by Muslims to non-Muslims in conquered lands was a paradigm of tolerance unmatched in history.

There is no doubt that for centuries Muslim societies usually practiced tolerance towards believers of other religions, to a much greater extent than Europe in the Middle Ages or in the early modern period.[6]

Muslims in their prayers and when they start acts mention God's mercy many times everyday when they say, "In the Name of Allah, the Most Gracious, the Most Merciful." In this, Islam emphasizes the concept of God's mercy and at the same time inter-human mercy.

The concept of God's mercy is essential in Islam. When God is merciful, human beings must be merciful, regardless of race, religion, or color, and what is interesting is that the mercy gives the person a feeling of safety, because mercy is something which is returned when given to others, as also suggested in the Bible when Jesus Christ said: "There is more happiness in giving than in receiving" (Acts 20:35). Mercy always leads to happiness and happiness is the main factor of coexistence.

MUSLIMS IN EUROPEAN SOCIETIES

Let us focus on the position of Islam in Europe. This is an important part of a process which, in an increasingly concrete inter-Muslim discourse dealing with practical questions, should strengthen the identity of Muslims in Europe. The compatibility of the Muslim way of life with the European one needs to be made visible inside as much as outside Europe

The ten commandments of the European Union set out herewith are an entirely Euro-centric attempt to capture what currently seem to be the values and ideals of the European Union. This of course does not imply that the system of European Union values is better than others, simply that these

---

[6] Luboš Kropácek, "Islam and Human Rights," *in Islam in Contact with Rival Civilizations* (Prague: Institute of Philosophy of the Academy of Science of the Czech Republic,1998), p. 18.

values are all either explicit or implicit somewhere in the draft Constitution. The European Union considers itself to be values-based and driven.[7]

Muslims suffer increasingly from an unacceptable equation between Islam and terrorism which generates a constantly growing attitude of rejection in public opinion. Muslims are confronted with a strong pressure for justification. Within the global war against terror, the concentration on a very small and narrow segment of radicals, which is omnipresent in every debate about Islam, has led to a fatal impression.

In this situation, Muslims themselves have the responsibility, even the obligation, to provide the highest possible transparency and to bring the focus onto the overwhelming majority of Muslims who, in living up to the teachings of their religion, stand for mutual respect and understanding and reject terrorism as disdainful for human beings. Multipliers of a peace-loving and rational Islam are key players in this process.

The voices of the scholars, theologians, and intellectuals need to reach Muslims as well as non-Muslims. They are in close contact with the people and can achieve a great deal. The clear position of Islam concerning freedom and human dignity needs to become common knowledge. The best medicine against hatred and intolerance is knowledge.

Diversity is a phenomenon common to all European societies. A key to acknowledging this diversity in a useful way lies in the recognition that it is a common good, the biggest common denominator between Muslims and people of other religions or ideologies. Common goods like the above reveal the universal character of values which ensure the quality of human coexistence.

As far as Jews and Christians are concerned, Moses and Jesus are, according to the *Qu'ran*, important envoys among the five greatest prophets in world history. Prophet Muhammad followed their steps and paths. Within a universal frame, the belief of Muslims in an equal and common origin of all mankind forms the basis of the school of thought which, in the same way as the humanistic tradition, defines humanity as the central value. The sense of mutual responsibility among humans and the responsibility for the Creation can only become effective if human beings are considered equal without application of different measures.

This principle can only be translated into reality if values are not jealously claimed by single groups. The search for freedom, justice, and human dignity is what we have in common with other religions, ideologies, and world views. Opposed to this are poverty, oppression, discrimination, racism, and occupation.

---

[7] Michael Emerson, *What Values for Europe: Islam and Tolerance in Wider Europe* (Budapest: Open Society Institute, 2006), p. 9.

There are practical advantages linked to Islam's recognition in Europe, like the right to practice religion freely and openly. The moderate and open attitude towards Muslims in Europe creates a positive atmosphere of cooperation with the whole society. The culture of dialogue enables the building of bridges, taking up topics of general interest in an objective way instead of closing oneself up in ignorance and retreat. The negative consequences of isolation in some kind of parallel society are recognized by the Muslims of Europe; thus, segregation models are rejected.[8]

It can be said that Moslems in Europe, who are better educated, more affluent, and more powerful than the Moslems of other countries are also more tolerant.[9]

Let us conclude my idea with some examples:

1. Islam in Spain, which is often retrospectively idealized as a golden age of peaceful Jewish, Christian, and Muslim coexistence.
2. In the Vatican Council of 1962–1965 the Church defined its attitude towards Islam in the formula which echoed the terminology of the *Qu'ran* itself.[10]
3. Many times each day Muslims recite an important chapter of the *Qu'ran* in their prayers as well as in all their actions and if anyone understood this verse as in its simple meaning, we could reach real coexistence and tolerance: "Guide us [Our God] to the Straight Way" (1:6)
4. When Prophet Muhammad won a great victory and he returned to his homeland, Mecca, he asked the captured people, "What do you think shall I do with you?" They said, "You will treat us as a merciful brother and nephew would." He replied simply, "Go wherever, all of you are free."

According to the last two examples, from two important sources in Islam, the *Qu'ran* and Traditions of Prophet Muhammad, we can understand Islam as a religion of tolerance and coexistence. In addition, I disagree with some Muslims commentators who interpret the verse following the last verse (1:6) that the *Qu'ran* implies rejection of Jews and

---

[8] See Austrian Imam Conference, April 2005.
http://www.derislam.at/islam.php?name=Themen&pa=showpage&pid=165
[9] Laciner Sedat, "Identity in Turkey—EU relations."
http://www.usak.org.uk/junction.asp?docID=296&ln=EN]
[10] Albert Hourani, *Islam in European Thought* (Cambridge: Cambridge University Press,1991), p. 49.

Christians in stating, "The way of those on whom you have bestowed your Grace not (the way) of those who earned your Anger, nor of those who went astray" (1:7).

CONCLUDING REMARKS

There are seven concluding remarks to be made:

Islam supports the principles of pluralism. This finds its expression in the Islamic principle of the diversity of positive effect that people and cultures have on the development of civilization.

In Islam Justice and freedom represent two essential human values and it is the duty of every society, all people included, to stand up for justice anytime and anywhere so that all human beings may enjoy their rights and liberties.

Dialogue is the best instrument for the exchange of ideas between the various social groups and religions. It guarantees mutual recognition and peaceful coexistence. In order to continue and develop constant networking and effective working processes and to be able to respond in time to challenges, these dialogues and discussions between different religions, cultures, and civilizations need to take place.

We must develop strategies to fight extreme views as well as raise awareness concerning rigid and unilateral attitudes which could be harmful to Islam and Muslims, in the past or today, and build a shared commitment concerning protection against such views or thoughts. For this purpose, the argumentation builds on a detailed theological and practical approach which keeps focusing on the current challenges.

The international community has not yet agreed upon a definition of the term "terror" but points out that terror can not be associated with any one religion, nation, or civilization. Furthermore, it stresses the fact that anyone who threatens an innocent civilian with terror and murder is a terrorist whatever his affiliation may be. It is absolutely necessary for the international community to deal seriously and scientifically with the phenomenon of terrorism and support the creation of a committee of intellectuals and opinion-makers to deal intensively with this matter.

Networking and better communication between the associations and the Islamic Religious Community in Europe should accelerate the positive development of the dialogue, as well as deepening the Muslims' understanding of the significance of active participation in all areas of the society: cultural, economic, political, and social. Muslims in Europe are a vital link between Europe and the Islamic world. A closer and more trustful relationship should arise from the perception of and the esteem for their role as bridge-builders.

The Muslims of Europe are a constituent part of the European societies and the relationship between the Muslims and the European societies should build upon mutual good will and understanding. From this perspective the religious duty is peaceful coexistence with and within the society and its different ethnic and religious groups. Muslims in Europe—as much as any other citizens—have the duty to commit themselves actively to the security and peace of their country and its inhabitants.

PEACE EDUCATION AND SPIRITUALITY
TRANSFORMING GLOBALISATION

CONFLICT RESOLUTION THROUGH SCHOLARLY EXCHANGE: THE ROLE OF THE AMERICAN INSTITUTE OF IRANIAN STUDIES

Erica Ehrenberg

US SUPPORT FOR INTERNATIONAL EDUCATION

Educational exchange plays an increasingly larger role in globalization and can be a potent force underlying conflict resolution. More students than ever before are studying overseas and more countries are playing host as well as sending students abroad. Historically, young Americans who could afford to do so made a grand tour of Europe to learn about classical sources of western civilization. Today, greater numbers of American college students spend terms overseas and look to countries beyond Europe, while the US continues to welcome students from around the world. A number of American colleges and universities have increased budgets for study abroad and one, Goucher College in Maryland, now requires students to earn credits abroad.[1] While international and Area Studies became features of American higher education in response especially to the World and Cold Wars, the events of September 11, 2001, brought home on a vaster scale the dearth of American familiarity with much of the world beyond its borders and the need for individuals fluent in the languages and cultures of the wider world, if any degree of international understanding is to be achieved.

A leading role in the establishment of international educational exchange in the US was played by the Institute of International Education (IIE), founded after World War I to promote multi-national understanding. It arranged for student and faculty exchanges with European countries and petitioned the US government to create student visas that bypassed established post-war immigration quotas. In subsequent years, it took on the administration of the graduate Fulbright Program, created by Congress in 1946, which now sponsors thousands of students annually to study abroad or to come to the US for study and research (http://www.iie.org/). Last year, Fulbright began new programs to emphasize education in so-called "critical languages," less studied and less accessible to American

---

[1] S. Lipka, "Goucher College to Require Study Abroad," *Chronicle of Higher Education*, Vol. 52, Issue 38, May 26, 2006, p. A40. http://chronicle.com/weekly/v52/i38/38a04002.htm

students but of increasing importance to world security and engagement in the changing demographics and politics of the current day.[2]

The Federal role in international education was boosted in response to strategic needs created by the Cold War and the scientific and military race with the Soviet Union. The National Defense Education Act of 1958 supported, in addition to the study of sciences, foreign language and Area Studies through Title VI of the Higher Education Act.[3] Currently, there are over 100 National Resource Centers supported by Title VI at American colleges and universities, concentrating on particular world areas. Other Title VI programs include fellowships for the study of less common languages; language resource centers for language teacher training and research; programs to support language curriculum development; and the American Overseas Research Centers (AORCs) which promote the training abroad of students and faculty.[4] The AORCs are members of the Council of American Overseas Research Centers (http://www.caorc.org), which advocates on their behalf and sponsors its own fellowship programs. There are nineteen member AORCs of the Council, spread geographically from Mexico through Africa, the Mediterranean, the Middle East and India to Asia. While receiving Federal funds, the AORCs are non-governmental entities whose independent boards formulate and oversee their academic programming. The American Institute of Iranian Studies is one such AORC.

AMERICAN INSTITUTE OF IRANIAN STUDIES

Purpose

The American Institute of Iranian Studies (AIIrS), founded in 1967, is a not-for-profit, non-governmental consortium of American universities and museums (www.simorgh-aiis.org). The purpose of its founding was the establishment of an overseas research center in Iran to provide an institutional infrastructure for the support of American academic research on Iran, and to promote scholarly training, research, collaboration, and exchange. The AIIrS aims to increase academic interaction between the two countries through the facilitation of dialogue. Involvement in person-

---

[2] E. Strout, "Fulbright Steps Up Language Training," *Chronicle of Higher Education*, Vol. 53, Issue 9, October 20, 2006, p. A41.
http://chronicle.com/weekly/v53/i09/09a04101.htm; B. Bollag, "A Failure to Communicate," *Chronicle of Higher Education*, Vol. 53, Issue 34, April 27, 2007, p. A24. http://chronicle.com/weekly/v53/i34/34a02401.htm
[3] See http://www.ed.gov/about/overview/fed/role.html
[4] See http://www.ed.gov/about/offices/list/ope/iegps/index.html

to-person exchanges is the most effective way to promote mutual understanding and cement a foundation of trust over generations between American and Iranian intellectuals. The AIIrS seeks to support the advancement of the interdisciplinary study of Iranian civilization and knowledge of Iran from the earliest periods to the present. The Institute's purview comprises the historical Iranian world of Central Asia, the Middle East, and South Asia as well as the modern political state of Iran. Not only does Iran have a documented history of linguistic and cultural identity going back two and a half millennia, but Iranian culture pervades the surrounding region from Azerbaijan through Central Asia to western China, Pakistan, India and the Persian Gulf. Persian language continues to be a cultural force beyond the boundaries of modern Iran, and Classical Persian and Persianate civilization are still the key to a large area of eastern Islam in the Caucacus, South and Central Asia and a vast area of non-Arab Islam from Bosnia and Turkey to western China.

In the US, the larger objectives of the Institute are to represent American institutions of higher education and research in the field of Iranian Studies and to promote the study of Iran as a significant component of world history. The Institute works with humanists and social scientists to further Iranian Studies in the American curriculum. As one of the consequences of political and economic globalization, Iranian Studies is becoming increasingly important in the American curriculum. Persian has been taught for several decades now in all the major Middle East programs in the US, first as a classical language but since the 1970s also as a modern language. Academic attitudes toward Iranian Studies have changed as a result of the re-emergence of Iran as a major regional power in the 1960s and because of changes in academic priorities, including the rise of Area Studies and changes in the criteria for inclusion of particular languages in the curriculum. A particularly important factor is the forging of institutional relationships between the two countries; opportunities for direct intercourse will reinvigorate the academic resource base.

The Institute's central purpose is to provide an institutional infrastructure in Iran for the support of American academic research interests and for collaboration and dialogue between American and Iranian students and scholars in the interdisciplinary study of Iranian civilization. The larger objectives of the Institute are to represent American institutions of higher education and research in the field of Iranian Studies and to promote the academic field of Iranian Studies as a significant component of world history.

History and Current Programs

The AIIrS was created in response to the needs of the first generation of American researchers as the number of Iranists steadily increased in the late 1960s. Through the 1970s, the Institute maintained a center in Tehran and provided a full range of services for American scholars in Iran, including accommodations, library, processing research requests to the Iranian government, and other related assistance. Virtually every American scholar specializing in fields of Iranian Studies benefited from affiliation with the Institute. The center was obliged to suspend its activities in December 1979 following the rupture of diplomatic relations between the US and Iran. For the next two decades, the Institute devoted itself to furthering Iranian Studies in the US, by offering graduate students grants and prizes for dissertations and dissemination of their work, holding joint conferences and fostering a sense of community in the field, among other initiatives.

When former President Khatami opened up the possibility of resumption of cultural dialogue in a CNN interview in 1998, the AIIrS responded immediately and was encouraged to make specific proposals. Since that time, the AIIrS has worked closely with the ambassadors at Iran's Permanent Mission to the UN, who help to facilitate the visa process and make important connections for the programs in Iran. Language study was singled out as a priority Facilities for advanced Persian language study had not been available for American students in a Persian-speaking environment since 1979. As a result, no Americans had been trained to an advanced level in this major modern and classical language of Western and Southern Asia for two decades, and the continuity of academic programs was threatened. A language program was therefore organized and the AIIrS was invited in 1998 to resume sending doctoral students for language training at the International Center for Persian Studies/Dehkhoda Institute, at the University of Tehran. This program continues today and allows students to enrol in one of three eight-week long sessions offered each year. All selected students are doctoral candidates at the intermediate level of Persian language proficiency who require advanced training in order to pursue dissertation research.

Encouraged by the success of the language program and the support of officials in Iran, the AIIrS moved ahead with new programs. A six-month fellowship was launched to allow a scholar at the junior faculty level to reside in Iran both to pursue research and function as overseer of the pre-doctoral fellows, assisting them with logistics and practical matters, while remaining in contact with our Dehkhoda sponsors. A one-month Bibliographer grant was designed for an American scholar with a professional interest in the history of research in Iran since 1979 and the current research establishment to conduct bibliographic research in Iran. Also for American scholars, a fellowship program was created for senior scholars and faculty, designed to bring practicing professional Iranists back into active interaction and collaboration with their Iranian colleagues by means of short-term fellowships. Senior fellows from various academic fields have since travelled to Iran to pursue research, give lectures, survey archaeological sites, and attend conferences. In 2002, AIIrS instituted yet another program, this one to bring Iranian scholars to the US to pursue short-term research projects with colleagues in America. These grants last up to one semester and are hosted by American institutions, which sponsor the visa applications. This year, a new language training program has been implemented in Tajikistan to expose students to the greater Persianate world and its dialects of Persian. It is hoped that this program will be expanded in the future to include research exchanges between the US and Tajikistan.

Fellows

Fellows of the AIIrS pursue many fields within the humanities and social sciences, including language and literature, ancient and modern history, archaeology, art and architectural history, political sciences, philosophy, religion, sociology, and anthropology. Fellows also assist in composing lists of research facilities and resources in Iran that will be of use to future fellows. Examples of recent research topics undertaken by fellows, by field, include:

Political and Social Science
- Electoral processes in Iran, Egypt, Burma, and the Philippines;
- Health and aging among Afghan refugees and underprivileged Iranians;
- Rural development in Iran;
- Theoretical and ideological debates among Iran's Shi'ite thinkers;
- Comparative study of French, Russian, and Iranian revolutions;
- Cognitive psychology and poetry as therapeutic tools in clinical practice.

Religion
- Persianate Sufism;
- Women's participation in the Shi'i community of remembrance;
- History and practice of Sufism in South Asia;
- Theoretical and ideological debates among Iran's Shi'ite thinkers;

- Role of philosophy in religious education in Tehran;
- Dialogue between Islam and Christianity.

History
- History of Iranian press and media;
- Archaeology and nationalism in the Middle East, 1919–1939;
- Eighteenth-century diplomatic relations between Iran and the Ottoman Empire;
- Role of British consuls in the strategic and economic interests in Iran 1889–1921;
- History of rational processes in Muslim scholarly culture;
- Historiography and diplomatic history of the Afsharid era;
- Development of perceptions of the Battle of Karbala in Islamic history;
- Early twentieth-century political developments in Azerbaijan.

Language and Literature
- Comparative verbal system of the Baluchi language;
- Semantic approaches to compilation of a Persian language thesaurus;
- English translation of the prose of Bayhaqi;
- Translation of Borhān al-Din Mohaqqeq Termezi's Ma'āref, thirteenth-century prose text;
- Portrayals of the Bahram Gur period in literature;
- Literary dimensions in historiographic discourses of the Middle Ages;
- Akhlaq advice literature;
- Sufi poetry of Attar;
- Urban and architectural poetry of the Safavid period.

Architectural/Art History and Archaeology
- City of Tehran: past, present, and future;
- Architectural education in Iran;
- Contemporary Iranian women artists;
- Modernity, national identity, and monuments in 20th century Iran;
- Images of modernity in Iranian visual culture during the rule of Reza Shah;
- Qajar calligraphy;
- Seventeenth-century Persian painting and the Armenian community of New Julfa;
- Timurid patronage of Sufi and Shaikhly families;
- Sassanian seals and bullae in the Iran National Museum;

- Bronze and Iron Age materials in the Iran National Museum;
- Archaeology of Iranian prehistoric periods;
- Macrobotanical material recovered from excavations in Fars Province.

Ethnomusicology
- Role of music in relation to Iranian-American concepts of identity;
- Role of music in the political arena of identity in post-revolutionary Iran.

Projects
AIIrS occasionally funds non-fellowship projects, including support for conferences, symposia, and publications pertinent to the fields of Iranian Studies. Recent and upcoming projects that have received funding are:

- Translation from Japanese into English of the site reports from Sang-i Chakhmaq in north-eastern Iran, one of the earliest Neolithic sites in the eastern part of the Middle East, excavated by the Japanese in the 1970s;
- Travel of American and Iranian scholars to present papers at a 2006 symposium, "New Directions in Persian Carpet Studies," at the Textile Museum in Washington, DC;
- Photography exhibition on Bam after the earthquake, mounted at the United Nations and the Library of Congress, 2004;
- Volume of collected essays in honor of Robert H. Dyson, professor and curator emeritus at the University of Pennsylvania and director of the Hasanlu excavations;
- Conference in London on the writings of Jalal al-Din Rumi in honor of his 800th anniversary;
- Attendance of young Iranian archaeologists at a panel discussion on current archaeology in Iran, at the annual conference of the American Schools of Oriental Studies, San Diego;
- Conference in Paris on preservation of early Persian material culture, organized by the Oriental Institute of the University of Chicago;
- Hosting at the New York Academy of Art of a travelling exhibition of emerging Iranian artists;
- Travel of Iranian scholars to a symposium on the Ardabil shrine and carpets at the Los Angeles County Museum of Art;
- Conference on the Iranian economy, organized by the University of Illinois, Urbana-Champaign.

Roth Prize

The AIIrS seeks to broaden exchange of ideas between the US and Iran by emphasizing translation of written works as well as through actual citizen contact. Although the AIIrS does not have funding for its own translation program, it offers an annual translation prize through a gift from the Lois Roth Endowment. Established in the memory of Lois Roth, who was instrumental in the founding of the Institute, the prize recognizes outstanding translations of literary texts from Persian to English. Recent awardees are:

2006: Simin Behbahani, *A Cup of Sin: Selected Poems*, ed. And trans. by Farzaneh Milani and Kaveh Safa (Syracuse University Press, 1999);

2004: Jalal al-Din Rumi, *The Masnavi, Book One*, trans. Jawid Mojaddedi (Oxford: Oxford University Press, 2004);

2003: Nizami Ganjavi, *Haft Paykar*, trans. Julie Meisami (Oxford University Press, 1995);

2002: *The Sands of Oxus: Boyhood Reminiscences of Sadriddin Aini* trans. John Perry and Rachel Lehr (Costa Mesa, CA: Mazda Publications, 1998);

2001: *In the Dragon's Claws: The Story of Rostam and Esfandiyar, Ferdowsi,* trans. Jerome W. Clinton (Washington, DC: Mage Publishers, 1999);

2000: Farid al-Din Attar *The Conference of the Birds*, trans. Afkham Darbandi and Richard Davis (Harmondsworth and New York: Penguin, 1984);

1999: Iraj Pezeshkzad *My Uncle Napoleon*, trans. Richard Davis (Washington, DC: Mage Publishers, 1996).

Joint Institutional Projects

Along with its own grants program, AIIrS works collaboratively with affiliated organizations with which it undertakes joint projects.

• **Institute of International Education (IIE)**

AIIrS works with the International Institute of Education to assist in its Foreign Language Teaching Assistantship program (http://flta.fulbrightonline.org/home.html). Through this program, graduate students from around the world are invited to spend a year studying at an American university while acting as teaching assistants in language courses in their native languages. Persian speakers have recently been included in this program, and AIIrS assists to identify potential candidates in Iran.

- **Hollings Center**

The mission of the Hollings Center, operating in Istanbul, is to provide a forum for interaction between citizens of the United States and Muslim-majority countries on issues of mutual concern, in order to open and reinforce channels of communication and deepen understanding between the US and the Muslim world (http://www.caorc.org/hollings).

AIIrS has worked with the Hollings Center on its conferences on higher education in the Muslim world, inviting Iranian higher education professionals to participate. A future conference is being arranged on the topic of the state of Iranian Studies in the US, at which American and Iranian academics will present papers on the history of and trends in the various disciplines that constitute Iranian Studies; the proceedings will form the core of a planned volume on the subject.

- **Digital Library for International Research (DLIR)**

The AIIrS is cooperating with the Council of American Overseas Research Centers and its numerous members around the world to create the DLIR, a digitized catalogue of the library holdings of the various research centers and their host-country affiliates The goal is for researchers around the world to be able to view from their own computers the holdings of libraries across the globe (http://www.aiys.org/aodl/index.php). Because the AIIrS no longer has its own library, it is working to enlist other research libraries in Iran to share their catalogues with this database. Other CAORC members of relevance to the Islamic world that are participating in the project are: American Center of Oriental Research, Jordan; American Institute of Bangladesh Studies; American Institute of Indian Studies; American Institute for Maghrib Studies, Morocco and Tunisia; American Institute of Pakistan Studies; American Institute for Yemeni Studies; American Research Center in Egypt; American Research Institute in Turkey; Cyprus American Archaeological Research Institute; Center for South Asia Libraries; Palestinian American Research Center; West African Research Association, Senegal.

- **International Society for Iranian Studies (ISIS)**

AIIrS is an institutional member of ISIS, Like AIIrS, ISIS is a private, not-for-profit, non-political organization whose mission is to promote scholarship in the field and the teaching of Iranian Studies at the university level, and to facilitate exchange and collaboration among scholars. (http://www.humanities.uci.edu/iranian-studies). ISIS holds a biennial conference and AIIrS played a prominent role in this year's Sixth Biennial Conference of Iranian Studies, held in London, acting as one of the principal supporting organizations of the conference and supplying travel grants for over thirty scholars from Iran to attend and present papers. The organizers and participants at the conference considered the large numbers of Iranians scholars in attendance (especially younger academics) to be a positive development for the field and a notable success for the conference.

Future directions

For the near future, the Institute has formulated the following specific objectives: to expand the flow of American students and scholars of Iranian Studies to Iran and other Persianate countries, and to enable senior Iranian scholars to pursue research in the US, thereby developing reciprocal opportunities. On the institutional level, AIIrS aims to assist the Iranian and American research and educational communities to build ties and formulate regular exchange mechanisms for scholars and resource materials. Because so little original work is translated, much scholarship produced in the US and Iran remains unavailable to Iranians and Americans, respectively. To address this situation, AIIrS would like to shepherd the development of a translation center to support collaborative American-Iranian translations projects. And, when the political environment normalizes, AIIrS foresees the re-establishment of an actual research center to house scholars, support lecture series and symposia and provide a physical space for the meeting of the minds. It is hoped the work AIIrS now pursues will in some small way pave the path toward such a time.

A HOLISTIC, EVOLVING VIEW OF PEACE WITH IMPLICATIONS FOR DEVELOPMENT*

Linda Groff

*The model on the evolution of seven aspects of peace in Part II of this paper was developed with the late Dr Paul Smoker, a long-time Peace Researcher and past Secretary General of the International Peace Research Association, and my late husband.

> *The means are as important as the end.*
> Mahatma Gandhi

> *An eye for an eye only ends up making the whole world blind.*
> Mahatma Gandhi

> *That which is attained through violence can only be sustained with violence.*
> Mahatma Gandhi

> *If you want to change the world, change yourself.*
> Mahatma Gandhi

INTRODUCTION

After introducing different definitions and ways of looking at peace, this article presents an overview of the evolution of seven aspects of peace, which collectively lead towards a more holistic, integrative view of peace, followed by discussion of how these different aspects of peace relate to development issues facing countries around the world. In short, it is argued that there are significant ways in which working for peace and working for development overlap and are mutually reinforcing for each other, and that all of these efforts are important to creating a better future for people around the world.

This article has five parts. Part I introduces different definitions and ways of looking at peace. Part II looks at how our views of peace have evolved to include at least seven aspects. Each type of peace adds an additional dimension, leading towards a holistic, integrative view of peace. Part III summarizes how our views of peace have evolved. Part IV shows how different cultural-religious groups each contribute in different ways to different aspects of peace, illustrating how a collective vision, incorporating all of these elements, forms a stronger foundation for global peace in the

141

twenty-first century. Part V discusses implications for the development of countries of this broader, more holistic view of peace.

PART I: INTRODUCTION TO DEFINITIONS AND WAYS OF LOOKING AT PEACE

What is peace, and how have our views of peace evolved—especially since the end of World War II? It is argued that one can look at peace in at least three ways: (1) as *goals/visions* for creating a more peaceful society and world in future (the focus of this paper); (2) as the *means/processes* used to create these goals/visions (including various forms of non-violence, including conflict resolution, management, and transformation; alternative dispute resolution, including negotiation, arbitration, and mediation; dialogue instead of debate; strategic non-violence, as well as spiritually-based non-violence); and prayer and meditation; and (3) as a *feeling*, i.e., how does one feel when one is peaceful? While all these aspects of peace are important, this paper (in Parts II-V) will especially focus on (1), i.e., on how our visions and goals of what a more peaceful society and world might look like have evolved over time, especially since the end of WWII.

Several other important terms are also used in the Peace Studies field to describe different aspects of peace. These include:

a) *narrow definitions of peace* (as absence of war) vs. *broader definitions of peace* (adding additional aspects of peace to one's definition of peace). (See Parts II-IV of this article for a broader, evolving, and holistic view of peace.)

b) *peacekeeping* (moving in United Nations or other troops to keep the peace between formerly warring parties) vs. *peacemaking* (helping parties in conflict to make peace with each other, including signing a peace agreement to end the conflict) vs. *peacebuilding* (building the conditions over time for the creation of a more peaceful society and world). The focus of many people today is on peacebuilding, which takes a longer term perspective.

c) the peace movement vs. the movement for peace—a distinction made by the late Dr Kenneth Boulding. He said that the *peace movement* includes all the people who are actively working for peace in different areas in the world, while the *movement for peace* are things that indirectly lead to more interrelationships and interdependencies between people that thereby reduce the prospects of war. An example would be the old idea that no two countries that have MacDonald's Hamburgers have ever gone to war with each other.

d) the United Nations Declaration of the *Year 2000 as the Year for a Culture of Peace*, and the *Decade 2001-2010 as the Decade for a Culture of Peace and Nonviolence for the Children of the World*. The concept of a "culture of peace" began with UNESCO (United Nations Educational, Scientific, and Cultural Association) and was then adopted in the United Nations Declarations noted here.

PART II: EVOLVING VIEWS OF PEACE, LEADING TO A HOLISTIC, INTEGRATIVE VIEW OF PEACE

Since World War II, our views of what a more peaceful society and world might look like have evolved to include at least seven aspects—including six types of outer peace, as well as inner peace—covering ever more system levels. These aspects of peace can be grouped into three broad categories, as follows.

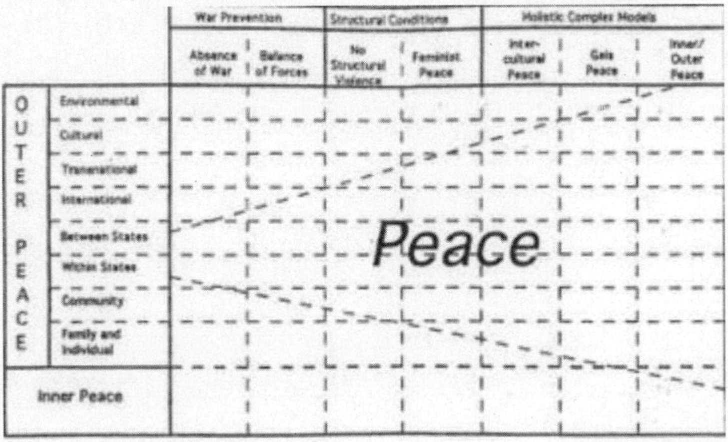

Fig. 1: Seven Concepts in the Evolution of Peace Thinking, Leading to a Holistic, Integrative View of Peace

The overall framework for looking at these seven aspects of peace thus includes the following:

(A) *War Prevention (Focusing on the Elimination of War and Physical Violence and the Maintenance of This Situation by the International System)*

143

1. Peace as Absence of War and Physical Violence (later called "Negative Peace" by Johan Galtung[1]).

2. Peace as Balance of Forces in the International System.[2]

(B) *Structural Conditions for Peace (Added to the Elimination of War and Physical Violence)*:

3. Peace as No War and No Structural Violence on Macro Levels (Galtung's "Negative Peace" and "Positive Peace," respectively).

4. Peace as No War and No Structural Violence on Micro, as well as Macro Levels (Adding Community and Family Peace, as also essential, along with National, International, and Transnational Peace; also eliminating patriarchal values and institutions on all levels) (Feminist Peace).

(C) *Holistic: Complex Systems Models and Views of Peace* (that focus on unity and diversity within systems and include positive as well as negative definitions of peace in multiple areas and on multiple system levels—from the macro to the micro, including inner peace).

5. Intercultural Peace—Between All Humans and Their Diverse Cultures, Civilizations, and Religions.

6. Holistic Gaia Peace—Between All Humans and the Earth or Gaia.

7. Holistic Inner-Outer Peace: Adding Inner Peace—From the World's Diverse Spiritual Traditions—To All the Forms of Outer Peace (above).

Each of these seven types of peace will now be examined in more detail.[3]

A. *Peace Thinking that Stresses War Prevention*

The first two types of peace both deal with war and how to prevent it, and the need to do so if any lasting peace is to be possible in the world.

---

[1] Johan Galtung, "Violence and Peace," in *A Reader in Peace Studies,* ed. Paul Smoker, Ruth Davies, and Barbara Munske (New York: Pergamon Press, 1990), pp. 9–14.

[2] Quincy Wright, *A Study of War* (Chicago: University of Chicago Press, 1941).

[3] On seven types of peace, see also Paul Smoker, and Linda Groff, "Spirituality, Religion, Culture, and Peace: Exploring the Foundations for Inner-Outer Peace in the Twenty-First Century," *International Journal of Peace Studies*, 1:1 (1996), 57–113; Groff, Linda. "Seven Concepts in the Evolution of Peace Thinking," in *Peacebuilding: Newsletter of the Peace Education Commission of the International Peace Research Association,* 3:1 (January 2001).

(1) *Peace as Absence of War (and Physical Violence) (Galtung's "Negative Peace")*

The first perspective, peace as the absence of war, focuses on avoiding violent conflict between and within states—war and civil war. This view of peace was of utmost importance to people at the end of World War II—following two devastating world wars—and is still widely held among general populations and politicians in most countries today. There are good reasons why this is so. Everyone knows the ravages of World War I and World War II, as well as those occurring during the so-called "Cold War," where superpowers often intervened in local conflicts, such as Vietnam and Afghanistan. Wars, including those of the internal or civil type, as well as those begun by outside intervention, such as the current Afghanistan and Iraq Wars, continue to rage around the globe, and the lives of millions of people are daily threatened by the spectre of war. Under these circumstances, peace is seen as the absence of war—at least until the killing stops.

All seven definitions of peace discussed here include absence of war, but only this first one defines peace as just the absence of war, which can be seen as a precondition for any of the other types of peace becoming possible. During the Cold War, some people advocated deterring nuclear war by stockpiling nuclear weapons (and building strong second strike or retaliatory capabilities) on both sides, leading to United States-Soviet arms races. In general, however, this type of peace seeks to build trust between countries and to reduce or eliminate dangers of nuclear weapons—on earth and now in space, as well as conventional weapons, chemical and biological weapons (the poor man's nuclear weapons), land mines, and any weapons endangering human life and taking resources away from other life-enhancing uses. It also seeks to reduce dangers of nuclear proliferation, nuclear terrorism, and accidental nuclear war.

Johan Galtung (a famous peace researcher) called this first type of peace "negative peace," which was also extended later to include not only eliminating war, but also eliminating physical violence. Galtung also distinguished this "negative peace" from what he called "positive peace," which was eliminating structural peace (see peace # 3).

(2) *Peace as Balance of Forces in the International System*

Quincy Wright, in his path-breaking work, *A Study of War*, stated the view that peace is a dynamic balance involving political, economic, social, cultural, and technological factors, and that war occurred when this balance broke down in the international system. The international system includes the overall pattern of relationships between states and International Governmental Organizations (IGOs) and domestic public opinion within a state—the community level of analysis. Any significant change in one of the factors involved in the peace balance would require corresponding changes in other factors to restore the balance. For example, Robert Oppenheimer, the much misunderstood "father of the atomic bomb," insisted on continuing to develop the bomb so that a global political institution, the United Nations, would have to be created to help control the new global military technology.

This is a systems view of peace in which the international system—if it can dynamically adjust to changes as they occur within the system—is the best solution for preventing war and preserving peace in the world. Because the number and types of actors in the international system—nation-states, international governmental organizations or IGOs, non-governmental organizations or NGOs, multinational corporations or MNCs, and now grassroots local communities through a movement for a U.N. People's Assembly—has greatly increased since the United Nations was formed in 1945, this type of peace also looks at proposals for reform of the international system and the United Nations itself. Much discussion has also focused on issues of global governance, as increasing issues require global cooperation in our increasingly interdependent world—if solutions are to be found. A related issue focuses on creating civil societies and democratic participation within countries as the foundation for more peaceful relations between states and more citizen participation in the international system.

B. *Peace Thinking that Stresses Eliminating Macro and/or Micro Physical and Structural Violence*

The next two types of peace each deal with and add social-structural dimensions of peace—including macro international and translational levels, and then micro community, family, and individual levels—to the efforts at eliminating physical violence and war (noted under A above).

(3) *Peace as Negative Peace (No War) and Positive Peace (No Structural Violence) on Macro Levels*

Johan Galtung expanded our concept of peace to include both "negative peace" and "positive peace"—two terms now standardized within the Peace Studies field. He defined "negative peace" as the absence of war and physical violence and "positive peace" as the absence of "structural violence," defined in terms of avoidable deaths and suffering caused by the way large scale social, economic, and political structures are organized—often in inequitable ways. Thus if people starve to death when there is food to feed them somewhere in the world or die from sickness when there is medicine to cure them (such as AIDS today), then structural violence exists since alternative structures could, in theory, prevent such deaths.

This type of peace thus deals with social and economic justice issues and with protecting basic human rights, as enumerated in the Universal Declaration of Human Rights (United Nations, 1948). Peace under this rubric involves both positive peace and negative peace being present in the global economy, which is influenced by non-state actors, such as International Non-Governmental Organizations (INGOs), and multinational corporations (MNCs). In this type of peace, the structural inequities in the international system itself are seen as major obstacles to world peace versus peace # 2, where the international system and international institutions such as the United Nations are seen as the solution for creating and preserving world peace.

(4) *Feminist Peace: Eliminating Physical and Structural Violence on Both Micro (Community, Family, and Individual) Levels and Macro Levels, and Eliminating Patriarchal Values, Attitudes and Institutions that Block People's Opportunities on All Levels*

During the 1970s and 1980s, a fourth perspective was ushered in by feminist peace researchers, who extended both negative peace and positive peace to include eliminating both physical and structural violence down to the individual level. The new definition of peace includes not only abolishing macro-level organized violence, such as war, but also eliminating micro-level unorganized violence, such as rape or domestic violence in war or in the home. The concept of structural violence includes personal/micro and macro-level structures that harm or discriminate against particular individuals, ethnic communities, races or genders, thereby denying them opportunities available to other groups. This feminist peace model came to include the elimination of all types of violence (physical and structural) on all levels, from the individual, family, and community levels on up to the transnational level, as well as the elimination of patriarchal values, attitudes, and institutions on all levels, as necessary conditions for a peaceful planet.[4]

C. *Peace Thinking that Stresses Holistic Complex Systems*

The last three types of peace all deal with holistic complex systems based on the unity and interdependence of diverse, interacting parts. Intercultural peace celebrates the diverse cultural forms human beings

---

[4] Birgit Brock-Utne, *Education for Peace: A Feminist Perspective* (New York: Pergamon Press, 1985); Birgit Brock-Utne, *Feminist Perspectives on Peace and Peace Education* (Oxford: Pergamon Press, 1989); Brock-Utne, "Feminist Perspectives on Peace," in Smoker, Davies, et al. (eds), pp. 144–49.

exhibit on this planet and Gaia peace honors the diversity of life forms and their interdependencies in the single living system Earth. These two types of holistic peace focus on the external world. The last type of peace, drawing on the world's rich spiritual traditions, adds inner peace to all the forms of outer peace, and is thus the most comprehensive view of peace.

(5) *Intercultural Peace: Peace Between Peoples and Their Diverse Cultures, Civilizations, and Religions*

The interaction between cultures (defined broadly as socially-learned behavior shared by people with common identities, values, lifestyles, and histories) has accelerated dramatically during recent centuries and decades. Too often the militarily stronger or economically more powerful culture has subordinated the militarily weaker or economically poorer one. Yet the world is becoming more interdependent each day and an honoring of the rich cultural diversity of the planet is an essential component of a future peaceful world.

While internal wars and cultural and ethnic violence have become a global phenomena and focus for social science and peace research, especially in the post Cold War period,[5] wars with outside intervention—as in Afghanistan and Iraq today, have also polarized the world and destabilized countries already suffering from internal divisions. The consequences of these wars will be with us for years.

Despite the above, relations between cultural, ethnic, racial, and religious groups can also be positive, creative experiences that enrich the lives of everyone involved. The fields of intercultural communication[6] and interreligious dialogue,[7] as well as other prejudice reduction techniques, provide people with positive tools for dealing with cultural diversity.

---

[5] See Samuel P. Huntington *The Clash of Civilizations: Remaking of World Order* (New York: Simon and Schuster, 1996); Samuel Huntington, "The Clash of Civilizations," *Foreign Affairs,* Summer, 72 (1993), 22–49; Galtung, "Violence and Peace."

[6] Fons Trompenaars and Charles Hampden-Turner, *Riding the Waves of Culture*, 2nd edn (New York: McGraw-Hill, 1998); Craig Storti, *Figuring Foreigners Out: A Practical Guide* (Yarmouth, Maine: Intercultural Press, 1999); Linda Groff, "The Challenge of Cultural and Religious Diversity and Peacebuilding in an Interdependent World," *Futures Research Quarterly*, 21:4 (Winter 2005), pp. 23–54; Linda Groff, "Insights on the Evolution of Cultures, Civilizations, and Religions: Past, Present, and Future," in *How Evolution Works (*Bellevue, WA: Foundation For the Future, 2005), pp. 139–166.

[7] Joel Beversluis (ed.) *Sourcebook of the World's Religions: An Interfaith Guide to Religion and Spirituality*, 3rd edn (Novato, CA: New World Library, 2000); Groff, "Challenge of Cultural and Religious Diversity"; Groff, "Insights."

Intercultural Peace requires that everyone realize that every culture is a different learned map or version of reality (not ultimate reality) and that every culture has particular gifts (based on their geographic and historical experiences and learning) that they bring to the table of humanity today. Intercultural peace requires the positive co-evolution of cultures at both macro and micro levels and the recognition that the whole diverse global cultural mix is a cause of strength for humanity, in the same way that the rich diversity of plants and living creatures are seen as a strength for the ecosystem.

(6) Holistic Gaia Peace: Peace with the World and the Environment

Gaia Peace is named after Gaia, the ancient Greek goddess of earth. In addition to the earlier types of peace, Holistic Gaia Peace—peace with Mother Earth and all her diverse ecosystems—also sees the Earth as a complex, self-organizing, living system or being, of which humans are a part (not separate), and places all forms of peace between people in this broader context.[8]

Gaia Peace therefore requires peace between people at all levels of analysis—from the individual and family levels to the global cultural level, while also placing a very high value on the relationship of humans to bioenvironmental systems—the environmental level of analysis. Peace with the environment, sustainable development (that does not take from nature at a faster rate than it can replenish itself) and responsible stewardship of the earth are seen as central to this type of peace. Without the food, energy, and resources provided by earth, there could be no human or other life on the planet and also no human economic systems.

Human beings are seen as one of many species inhabiting the earth, and the preservation of the planet is seen as the most important goal. The increasing extinction of other species, as the human population on earth keeps increasing and inhabiting more of the land area of earth, also cries out for humans to wake up to what we are creating. Global climate change is another warning to humanity, along with various forms of pollution. Indigenous peoples—who see themselves as part of nature for centuries and as a voice for the earth—also warn us that the earth is dying in various places today because of our human neglect and greed. Thus human rights must be expanded to acknowledge the rights of the earth—our life support system, on which all of our futures depend.

---

[8] James E. Lovelock, *Gaia: A New Look at Life on Earth,* 5th edn (Oxford: Oxford University Press, 1991); E. Joseph Lawrence *Gaia: The Growth of an Idea* (New York: St. Martin's Press, 1990); Elisabet Sahtouris, *Gaia: The Human Journey from Chaos to Cosmos* (New York: Pocket Books, 1989).

In some cases, the Gaia concept is interpreted scientifically, in terms of a complex biochemical, energy system. In other cases, the inner, spiritual aspects of Gaia are also seen as essential, and Gaia or earth is also seen as a sacred, living being or Goddess.

(7) *Holistic Inner and Outer Peace*
This last type of peace includes all of the outer aspects of peace (covered above), as well as adding inner peace as an essential component and precondition for a peaceful world. While inner peace can be just psychological, it frequently has a spiritual foundation that acknowledges some spiritual or transcendent aspect to life beyond just the physical world of our outer senses. Inner Peace then draws on the world's rich spiritual-religious traditions, including their mystical aspects—with mysticism being defined as "a direct experience of ultimate reality,"[9]—and uses different forms of prayer and meditation (including breathing techniques, chanting, and various forms of yoga) as tools to become centered within and reach deeper states of inner peace.

This approach to peace recognizes different dimensions and levels of consciousness related to inner peace, just as different aspects of outer peace have been elaborated above. For example, Eastern spiritual traditions talk about seven chakras, or energy centers, in the body that are each related to different types and levels of consciousness.[10]

This spiritual dimension is expressed in different ways, depending on one's cultural and religious background and context, and draws on centuries of experience by spiritual masters from the East, indigenous cultures, and some more ancient Western cultures, where such traditions are more developed and honored than in modern Western culture. Even in the West, however, there is now much greater interest in such topics, including a greater openness to exploring such inner dimensions of consciousness and peace. Western medicine and hospitals are also recognizing the important role of stress reduction techniques such as meditation in healing, due to an increasing recognition of the mind-body connection.

Eastern cultures and religions, such as Hinduism and Buddhism, have produced many mystics, avatars, and spiritual seers who have focused on the importance of inner peace as an essential condition for creating a more peaceful world. In this view, all aspects of outer peace, including one's perception and experience of the world, reflect one's inner state of consciousness and must therefore be based on inner peace.

---

[9] Denise Lardner Carmody and John Tully Carmody, *Mysticism: Holiness East and West* (New York: Oxford University Press, 1996).

[10] Ken Wilber, *A Brief History of Everything* (Boston: Shambhala, 1996).

PART III: SUMMARY OF THE EVOLUTION OF THE PEACE CONCEPT

As the world continues to change it is clear that our concepts of peace have also continued to evolve over time, especially since the end of World War II. While many people within the peace studies and peace education fields have focused on one or more, but not all of the above aspects of peace, it is clear that if one takes all of these different aspects of peace collectively together, a more holistic, integrative view of peace emerges, which has the following characteristics (Smoker and Groff, Groff, "Seven Concepts").

- Peace is a multi-factored process, focusing on many different substantive aspects and dimensions of peace, not just a single factor—the absence of war.
- Peace is multileveled, dealing with multiple system levels, from macro to micro levels in the external world, as well as now also inner peace.
- Seeing peace on multiple system levels also means that many more different types of actors are involved in the peacebuilding process besides just states, who are the primary actors in peace as absence of war. 9/11 is a good example illustrating the increasing importance of non-state actors in the international system—including in peace and wartime situations.
- Peace includes not only six aspects of outer peace in the world, but also inner peace as an essential component for creating a more peaceful world in the twenty-first century, with different dimensions and levels of consciousness and inner peace now also open for further exploration.
- Peace is defined not only in negative terms—what one wants to eliminate (such as physical or structural violence), but also in positive terms (focusing on what one wants to create in a positive sense). As Fred Polak said, "A society without positive images of itself is doomed."[11] If one wants to create a better future, it is not enough to just eliminate the negative; one must also clearly visualize, and commit one's life to, alternative, positive images of what one wants to create.
- Peace must honor both unity AND diversity, interdependence AND pluralism, of the world's diverse peoples, races, cultures, civilizations, ethnic groups, nations, and religions, as well as of the multiple species on earth; neither homogenized unity alone

---

[11] Fred Polak, *The Image of the Future*, trans. and abridged E. Boulding (New York: Elsevier, 1973).

nor diversity only (without seeing what also connects us) will create the conditions for a more peaceful world.
- A holistic view of peace thus explores how these multiple aspects of peace fit together into some kind of dynamic and coherent, integrated, whole systems view of peace.

In conclusion, the emergence of more holistic peace paradigms in peace research—whether intercultural, environmental, and/or spiritual—has included an increasing emphasis on positive conceptions of peace. In part, this is because of our realization that, whatever our nationality, culture, or religious tradition, we are all interconnected and interdependent. Viewed from space, planet Earth is a beautiful blue-green sphere, without national borders, but with land, water, ice caps, deserts, forests, and clouds supporting one interdependent planetary web of life based on multiple interacting ecological systems. We as individuals and groups are but a part of the planet, as the planet itself is a part of the solar system, galaxy, and universe. This whole systems mindset enables an appreciation of the interdependence of species in the global ecosystem, of particular cultural meanings in the context of the total global cultural system, and of particular faiths in the rich diversity of global spiritual and religious traditions—all contributing to the tapestry of the whole. The whole is more than the sum of the parts, and the greater the variety of the parts, the richer the expression of the global whole.

PART IV: AN ALTERNATIVE MODEL SHOWING CONTRIBUTIONS FROM DIFFERENT CULTURAL-RELIGIOUS TRADITIONS TO DIFFERENT ASPECTS OF PEACE

Part II above focuses largely on how our concepts of peace have evolved, beginning with Western Peace Research and then adding elements from global peace research. It is noteworthy that inner peace was the last aspect of peace to be added in largely Western peace research and that Gaia Peace was added not long before Inner Peace. Both of these last two aspects of peace are the particular focus and concern of different non-Western cultures and religions, who have thus most forcefully advocated the importance of adding these aspects to any overall concept of peace. Indeed, if one starts with an Eastern cultural and religious perspective, such as Hinduism or Buddhism, one always begins with inner peace as the necessary precondition for peace in the world, with inner peace affecting what type of external world one was creating and experiencing. Similarly, if one starts with the earth-based cultures and religions (including indigenous spiritual traditions and followers of the goddess), who are closely tied to Mother

Earth, who see all of nature as alive, and who see their role as caretakers for the earth, which is currently endangered by increasing human activity and occupation of the planet, one would begin with Gaia Peace as the most fundamental and important aspect of peace. Likewise, Western cultures and religions, being activists seeking progress in the world, traditionally begin with support for aspects of outer peace in the world—the focus of the first five aspects of peace.

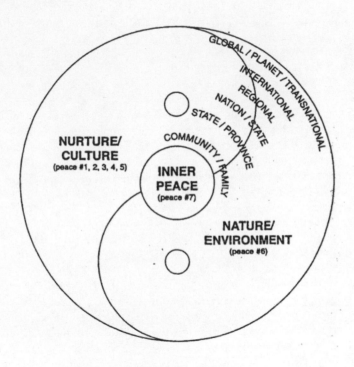

Fig. 2: Relationship Between Inner/Outer Aspects of Peace
Need Dynamic Balance Between:
* Inner Peace and Aspects of Outer Peace
* Nature/Environment & Nurture/Culture

Fig. 2 (based on an adaptation of the yin-yang symbol from Taoism) shows an alternative model of how these different aspects of peace are all dynamically interacting with each other all the time.

What is significant is that the collective vision of peace that we end up with—when we add the particular focus and concern of earth-based religions and cultures (Gaia Peace # 6), Eastern cultures and religions (Inner Peace # 7), and Western cultures and religions (Peace # 1–5, focusing on different culturally and socially-learned aspects of peace in the external world)—is a much more powerful and comprehensive vision of the foundations for a peaceful world than any of those visions would be alone. As we enter the twenty-first century in an increasingly interdependent world, it is fitting that our conceptions of peace also draw from all the major cultural and spiritual-religions traditions on the planet to create a synergistic vision that is more powerful than any of us could have created on our own. In this sense, there is much that we can all learn, and are learning, from each other about peace, and this cross fertilization of ideas can only benefit humanity and all life in future.

PART V: IMPLICATIONS FOR DEVELOPMENT OF THIS HOLISTIC VIEW OF PEACE

People do not always explore the relationship between development issues and peace issues. Nonetheless, it is clear in looking at these seven aspects of peace (above) that they each have important implications for economic, political, social, cultural, and environmental development of countries around the world. A few of these implications are outlined below.

(1) *Peace as Absence of War (and Physical Violence) (Galtung's "Negative Peace"):*

It is very clear that when countries spend large amounts of their government budgets on the military—for defensive or offensive purposes—that this takes physical and human resources away from other pressing development issues. This is even more the case in countries with pressing development concerns and limited national budgets to accomplish their development goals. In this regard, it would perhaps be significant to develop some kind of index for different countries based on the percentage of their government budget spent on military/defense issues versus on other development issues, and how this then correlates with rates of economic development for each country. Development in developed countries, such as the US, can also be greatly effected by war, such as in the current situation with the Iraq and Afghanistan Wars, where the defense budget and US overall budget deficit have ballooned, taking resources away from many other areas, leaving huge deficits for future generations to pay off, and greatly polarizing not only the world, but the US domestically.

It is interesting to note that war, and cultures and economies of war, have existed since at least ancient civilizations and empires when one civilization conquered another and made them into slaves. US President Eisenhower—a former Allied Commander in World War II—warned during his Presidency of the dangers of a "military-industrial complex" and economy, which seems to have become the major obsession and focus of the Bush-Cheney Administration. Militant Islamist views, of Bin Laden and others, are equally black and white worldviews, both being inappropriate—in this writer's view—in an increasingly interdependent world where cooperation on vital issues and tolerance for different cultures, religions, and worldviews instead of dominance is what is needed. The real challenge is how to transform this war mentality and culture into a culture of peace and non-violence, which will also free up resources for other purposes, such as social, economic, and political development of countries.

(2) *Peace as Balance of Forces in the International System:*

Given that the United Nations is the major forum today where leaders of different countries around the world can come together and agree on policies, including development policies, and that the United Nations regularly collects data from all countries to monitor their levels of development and key development issues, it is clear that the state of the United Nations is critical to the future development of countries around the world. One great example of data collected and published each year on different countries and key issues effecting their development is the *Human Development Report* (published annually by Oxford University Press). It is also clear that when conflicts between countries are not able to be resolved through the United Nations or other multilateral means then sometimes these conflicts lead to violence and wars, which again divert resources of countries away from other development issues.

Another important issue affecting the viability of the United Nations itself is whether member countries of the U.N. pay their dues on a regular basis or not. This has not always been the case, also undermining the ability of the United Nations to carry out all of its functions effectively—in development, environmental, and peacekeeping areas. When any of the five permanent members of the U.N. Security Council veto a peacekeeping operation as not in its national interest then such operations are also effectively thwarted.

Even though the ability of the United Nations to act in the world is limited and countries have not given up their sovereignty to the United Nations, issues of global governance (not global government) nonetheless remain high on the global agenda. Global governance deals with how countries can find ways to cooperate with each other and reach a consensus on a whole range of urgent policy issues confronting the world.

(3) *Peace as Negative Peace (No War) and Positive Peace (No Structural Violence) on Macro Levels: (Galtung's Negative and Positive Peace):*

This type of peace adds the goal of eliminating structural violence to the goal of eliminating physical violence and war, which affects development in the following ways. Eliminating structural violence and promoting social justice and human rights are important aspects of any society's development, which ideally needs to include not only economic but also social aspects of development, which can open up educational and employment opportunities for all the diverse citizens of a given society and country. When significant segments of a population in a country are denied opportunities for an education or jobs that will enable them to better their lives and support their families, then the contributions that these people could be making to a society's development is lost, and the development of society as a whole is lessened. Societies which ignore social justice issues also lay the foundations for future conflicts, which can divert resources from that society's development efforts until such conflicts are resolved The information age also requires an educated and skilled workforce, which is best drawn from all the diverse groups that make up any society.

(4) *Feminist Peace: Eliminating Physical and Structural Violence on Micro (Community, Family, and Individual) Levels, as well as Macro Levels, and Eliminating Patriarchal Values, Attitudes and Institutions that Block People's Opportunities on All Levels:*

It is very clear that the status of women in a society has a direct effect on the development prospects of any society. In short, when women are educated, that effects how they raise their children and helps in the education of their children, thus also increasing the opportunities their children will have to get jobs that will help in the economic and social development of their communities and country. When women become educated, they also usually voluntarily have less children, thus also increasing the opportunities for a better life for their children. Educated women also increasingly join the workforce and contribute to the social and economic development of their countries, as well as contributing as breadwinners to their own families.

(5) *Intercultural Peace: Peace between All Humans and Their Diverse Cultures and Religions (as Part of Culture):*

One of the largest sources of conflict in the world today is interethnic conflict within countries, as well as between countries since 9/11 and the onset of the Afghanistan and Iraq Wars. Interethnic conflicts increased once the Cold War ended, especially in formerly Communist Bloc countries, where people sought new identities and often went back to their ancient tribal identities, thereby exacerbating conflicts that were submerged during the Cold War days. Since 9/11/01, there has also been an increase in terrorism by non-state actors (such as Al Qaeda)—usually against governmental targets, such as the United States and Israel, as well as an increase in counter-terrorism efforts—usually by governments who have been the target of such terrorist efforts. In these cases, interethnic, intercultural, and interreligious factors are playing an important role, even though other factors are also involved in these conflicts. Iraq itself has descended into near civil war—especially between Sunnis and Shiites, making the formation of a strong national government much more difficult.

It is clear that making the world safe for cultural and religious diversity—both within and between countries and groups—remains a very high priority for the world, which will affect both the prospects for peace and for development of countries in future. As long as interethnic-type conflicts continue and are also transformed into violent conflicts, peoples and governments will continue to focus their resources on these security issues rather than on other development issues. Healthy economic, social, and political development also requires that people from diverse backgrounds learn to live together in peace and with respect for each other's traditions. It is also important that education and development opportunities are available to all the diverse racial, ethnic, and cultural groups that make up a society. As the development of a country moves beyond the agricultural and industrial ages into the information age, having educated, trained, white-collar workers—including from all the diverse cultural groups making up any given society—becomes increasingly important for the functioning of that society.

(6) *Holistic Gaia Peace: Peace between Humans and the Earth or Gaia:*

The United Nations has held various global conferences on the environment and these conferences have concluded that countries around the world all need to focus on dealing with environmental pollution issues, but that if developing countries are to be able to afford to do this then they must get financial assistance from more developed countries of the North. Without this assistance, the other development needs of developing countries will take precedence over environmental issues, given the limited governmental budgets of developing countries and their other pressing development needs. (See, for example, the U.N. Report on *Environment and Development*, also called "The Brundtland Report," named after the Prime Minister of Norway, Gro Brundtland, who headed the U.N. Commission

157

that researched and wrote this report. See also Agenda 21, the report that came out of the U.N. Environmental Summit.)

Global warming is also threatening the planet in the view of almost all scientists. Many species are also becoming extinct, due to humans taking over more and more of the planet. These can both have huge impacts on the development of countries. Growing seasons can change, coastal cities can be flooded, and ecological systems can collapse as species leave their normal environments looking for food. These can all pose huge challenges for the development of countries and are an increasingly important and urgent danger threatening the human and planetary future, if not addressed.

(7) *Holistic Inner and Outer Peace: Adding Inner Peace (From the World's Diverse Spiritual Traditions) To All the Forms of Outer Peace (above):*

The relationship of inner peace to development may not be as apparent, at first, as some of the other aspects of outer peace are to development. Nonetheless, there are some important relationships here. First, when people are not conscious of or responsible for their inner thoughts and feelings, especially their negative thoughts and feelings, these can be projected out onto other people in the form of hatred and prejudice, which increases social conflict and divisiveness in society, not aiding the development of all the people in any given society. Instead, elites and dominant groups in power are favored. Secondly, when people are spiritually-based (in contrast with religious dogmatism), part of that perspective on life includes feeling connected to all of life, including other people. Such sensitivity to other people's suffering and difficulties should hopefully be translated into public policies that help in the development efforts of all people in a given society, not just the elites or those in power.

CONCLUSIONS

In conclusion, it is clear from the above discussion that peace issues are integrally related to development issues. A few of these relationships have been explored. Undoubtedly, many more exist. It is important to explore these relationships in more depth and to educate scholars, peace researchers and activists, and development officials and community members about these relationships, thereby hopefully also influencing development policies of countries to the benefit of all the citizens of a country and thereby the world.

GLOBALIZATION AND A MATHEMATICAL JOURNEY

Eiko Tyler

INTRODUCTION

Globalization is defined by the International Monetary Fund as "the growing economic interdependence of countries worldwide through increasing volume and variety of cross-border transactions in goods and services, free international capital flows, and more rapid and widespread diffusion of technology."[1] According to this definition, cross-cultural exchanges that occurred along the Silk Road, which involved the citizens living along the routes economically, politically, technologically, and culturally is in fact an early example of globalization. The objective of this paper is to attempt to describe how exchanges between eastern and western cultures and religions along the Silk Road facilitated the development of Islamic mathematics. I will examine two important concepts that were essential for the development of mathematics: namely, the Indian numbering systems and the concept of zero, which was developed by Indian mathematicians and later introduced to Islamic mathematicians. Islamic mathematics merged the mathematics of China, India, Egypt, and Greece and, as a result, developed decimal arithmetic, plane and spherical trigonometry, algebra and geometry. One result of the dazzling development of Islamic science and mathematics was the facilitation of an early form of globalization in the Eurasian world of the thirteenth century. Exchanges of goods, ideas, etc., occurred from the Adriatic Sea in the west to the Japan Sea in the east. With this early form of globalization, the Islamic empire flourished. At its height, the Islamic empire was one of the most brilliant civilizations in history.

In this paper I will explain how Islamic mathematicians solved cubic equations by using geometry. Similar achievements and other examples of brilliant Islamic mathematical and scientific works were later introduced to Europe. During the Dark Ages in Europe, a substantial amount of the brilliant work of the Greek and other European mathematicians and scientists were lost. However, with the introduction to Europe of the work of the Islamic mathematicians and scientists, ideas that were developed by peoples who embrace different religions were merged. The mathematics and

---

[1] *World Economic Outlook, May 1997*, (Washingon D.C.: IMF, 1997), p. 45.
http://www.imf.org/external/pubs/weomay/weocon.htm

159

sciences of different civilizations are in fact dependent on each other. Ideas developed in one part of the world inevitably influence scientific thinking in other parts of the world.

This paper intends to show that the concept of zero connects Buddhism, Islam, and Christianity. The early globalization that occurred in the thirteenth century did not last long. In the twenty-first century, we have to learn from the past and realize that we are all interconnected and that we must maintain an open interfaith dialogue between and among different religions to cultivate a global culture whose aim should be the prevention of violence and advocacy of world peace.

By showing the interrelationship between various cultures and religions through mathematics, this paper will attempt to promote the cause of peace by promoting mathematics education along with hope, love, compassion, and social justice for all the people that share the planet.

Through an explanation of the concept of "sunyata," I will attempt to demonstrate how the concept of zero and other aspects of Indian mathematics influenced Islamic mathematicians who in turn influenced European mathematics. I will show this inter-relationship in the context of the history of the Silk Road.

HISTORY OF THE SILK ROAD

The Silk Road generally refers to a historical East-West trade route that connected China, Western Asia, and the Adriatic Sea region. The eastern end of the Silk Road was established in the second century BC during The Han Dynasty (BC 206–AD 220). The Silk Road established not only economic relations between Eastern and Western civilizations, but it also acted as a vehicle for cross-cultural exchanges between these regions.[2] The Silk Road consists of three routes; the Steppe route in the north (at about 50 degrees north), the Sea route in the south, and the Oasis route in central Asia, connecting scattered oases skirting the Taklamakan Desert (at around 40 degrees north). The north route crossed Kyrgyzstan and Uzbekistan between the cities of Tashkent and Samarqand.

The name Silk Road came from the fact that the silk produced in China was transported to India Western Asia, and even to Rome. A German geographer, Ferdinand von Richtofen named the route "Seidenstrasse" in 1870. Later, Swedish archeologist Sven Hedin also used the term "Silk Road." In addition to silk, other goods such as spices, metals, and fur were transported along this route.

---

[2] Kathleen Cohen, "A World of Art and Culture."
http://gallerry.sjsu.edu/silkroad/history.htm

The western end of the trade route started to develop after the Iranian empire of Persia was conquered and colonized by Alexander the Great in about 330 BC. Thus the Greek language, mythology, and arts were brought into the south of the Hindu Kush and Karakorum ranges. This region became a crossroad of Asia where the cultures of Persian, Indian and Greek merged.

In the second century BC, Emperor Wudi of the Han Dynasty sent the general Zhang Quian to recruit the Yuezhi people from the Northern borders of the Taklamakan Desert. The Yuezhi settled in Northern India after the Xiongnu tribe took their traditional homeland in the second century BC. In the first century AD the descendents of the Yuezhi people, who were Buddhists and called Kushan, moved into this crossroads area. The Kushan people generally adapted to the Greek culture that existed in the area and produced the interesting sub-culture called Gandhara. The Gandhara culture fused Greek and Buddhist art into a unique style. Before the Kushan people no one had expressed the Buddha in human form. The sculptures of Buddha, Tathagata (a person who has attained Buddhahood), and Bodhisattva (a Buddhist saint) have strong remembrances to the Greek mythological figures. By the first century BC, the Ghandhara civilization was well linked to the trading centers of Khotan where economic, cultural, and religious exchange between east and west took place. One of the ancient provinces of Khotan is called Turkistan, which was situated along the east-west passage connecting China with Kushan and Gandharai in Afghanistan and Pakistan. The Greco-Buddhist Gandharan culture was later propagated to Japan through Turkistan and Khotan.[3]

In 125 BC, Zhang Quian returned to China with information about unknown states to the west, and exciting news of seeing larger horses, which could be trained for use by the Han cavalry. In addition to many objects that Zhang Quian and his man brought back from the crossroad regions, they also brought a faith known as Buddhism. The Han people were especially appreciative of the religious artwork from Gandhara. An expedition under the leadership of Zhang Quian opened the route to the west. For this reason, Zhang Quian is often referred to as the "father of Silk Road" (Rust and Cushing).

During the Tang Dynasty (AD 618-907) the network of routes that made up the Silk Road thrived. In the tenth century, the success and influence of the *Qu'ran* began to have an effect and the once flourishing Buddhist temples were replaced by Islamic places of worship. The success of the land route known as the Silk Road began to decline as well.

---

[3] William Rust and Amy Cushing, "The Buried Silk Road Cities of Khotan," *Athena Review*, 3:1 (n.d.). http://www.athenapub.com/9khotan1.htm

From the eleventh to the twelfth century, various goods as well as aspects of culture and religion were exchanged between the East and West along the four routes which connected the Chin dynasty (AD 1115-1234) in China, the Karakitai dynasty in Western Liao, and the Khorezm kingdom in central Asia and Rome. A monetary system using silver and paper currency was established. The prosperous commerce that developed along the northern route of the Silk Road encouraged the establishment of the South Sea route that also became prosperous at about this same time.

Established about 1270, this ocean route became increasingly important. From the East, trading ships departed the port of Quanzhou, China, sailing to India via the Strait of Malacca. From the West, trading ships travelled from Basra and Hormuz to India. Within twenty years, the ocean trafficking had developed into one of worldwide scale and heavy cargo such as china was transported in mass quantity. Marco Polo visited the court of Kubili Khan in Khanbalik (Beijing). He travelled the land route of the Silk Road, passing through Turkistan in 1271. In 1292, he returned by the ocean route to Venice from Quanzhou, China (Rust and Cushing).

From the latter half of the thirteenth century to the fourteenth century, the Eurasian continent, from the Adriatic Sea in the west to the Japan Sea in the east, was recognized as one worldwide region and an exchange of cultures and institutions occurred which is unprecedented in history. Thus, world trading began to occur in the Eurasian world. Through the trade routes of the Silk Road, Islam was spread not only along the northern Silk Road from Central Asia to Western China, but also along the southern sea route to various island nations in Asia. Through this early example of globalization, Islam had contact with Christianity in the west, Hinduism in the south, and Buddhism and Confucianism in the east. As a result of this early form of globalization, the development of Islamic civilization surpassed any other civilization in the world.[4]

The Silk Road witnessed the rise and fall of nations and the progress of civilization. When the Ming Dynasty (AD 1368-1644) closed China to outsiders, it effectively ended the centuries-old Silk Road connection, which had connected Imperial China with Imperial Rome.

NUMBER

The definition of a natural number is given from Peano's Axiom (1858-1932), which contains five propositions as following[5]:

---

[4] Taichi Sakaiya: "The Prophetic Dream of Taichi Sakaiya: Not a Clash but a Merging of Civilizations" (in Japanese), *Weekly Asahi*, April 11, 2003.
[5] Hisao Yoshihara, *An Unexpected Connection Between Mathematics and Buddhism*.

Let N be a set with the following properties:

I)   N contains 1.

II)   There exists a map f from N to N.

III)   If (N) does not contain 1.

IV)   f is injective.

V)   If f is a subset N`of N has the following properties (i) and (ii),

    (ii)   N` contains 1

    (ii.)   f (N`) is a subset of N`.

then N=N`.

Then an element of N is called a natural number. The number f (n) is called a natural number successive to n.

From this definition, we can conclude "1" is a natural number by proposition I. From proposition II, f (i) is a natural number as well. If we define f (1) = 2, 2 is a natural number. By defining f (2) =3, f (3)=4, f (4)=5,....,'1', '2', '3', '4', '5'...are natural numbers.[6]
Stated in another way we can say, "A number is an abstract entity that represents a count or measurement. It is used originally to describe quantity. At least since the invention of complex numbers, this definition must be relaxed. Preserving the main ideas of 'quantity' except for the total order, one can define numbers as elements of any integral domain."[7] The symbols used to represent numbers are called numerals. For example, the base ten numeral "4" and the Roman numeral "IV" represent the number four.[8]

HINDU MATHEMATICS

In India, the oldest mathematics book called Shulba Sutra, which contains geometry for supporting astronomical work, dates back to around 800 BC.

---

[6] Syoukichi Iyanaga, *Number System* (Iwanami Shinsho: Tokyo, [n.d.]), pp. 62–80.
[7] http://wordnet.princeton.edu/perl/webwn
[8] http://en.wikipedia.org/wiki/Number

In 1500 BC, 700 years before the first "modern" mathematics book was written, the Vedic people moved to India from the region that is Iran today. Their religion was called Vedic, which means the collections of sacred texts known as the Vedas. The texts date from about the fifteenth to the fifth century BC. The Sulbasutras are appendices to the Vedas and rules for constructing altars for a ritual were described in them. A scribe wrote the Sulbasutras and they contained all the knowledge of Vedic mathematics. The Sulbasutras do not contain any proofs of the rules of the contents. One of the rules describes constructing a square of area equal to that of a given circle. The Baudhayana Sulbasutra, written about 800 BC, and the Apastamba Sulbasutra, written about 600 BC, are the two most important Sulbasutra documents. The Manava Sulbasutra and the Katyayana Sulbasutra, which are of lesser importance, were written about 750 BC and 200 BC respectively. The Baudhayana Sulbasutra gives only a special case of the Pythagoras's theorem explicitly:

> The rope, which is stretched across the diagonal of a square, produces an area double the size of the original square.

The Katyayana Sulbasutra however gives a more general version:

> The rope, which is stretched along the length of the diagonal of a rectangle, produces an area, which the vertical and horizontal sides make together. [9]

Note here that the results are stated in terms of "ropes." In fact, although sulbasutras originally meant rules governing religious rites, sutras came to mean a rope for measuring an altar. While thinking of explicit statements of Pythagoras's theorem, we should note that as it is used frequently, there are many examples of Pythagorean triples in the Sulbasutras. For example (5, 12, 13), (12, 16, 20), (8, 15, 17), (15, 20, 25), (12, 35, 37), (15, 36, 39), (5/2, 6, 13/2), and (15/2, 10, 25/2) all occur.

The Apastamba Sulbasutras contains the approximation to $\sqrt{2}$ as

$$\sqrt{2} = 1 + 1/3 + 1/(3 \times 4) - 1/(3 \times 4 \times 34) = 577/408$$

1.414215686.

A correct value is $\sqrt{2} \approx 1.414213562$ (correct to 9 decimal places). The Apastamba Sulbasutra has the answer correct to five decimal places. The

---

[9] J. J O'Connor and E. F. Robertson, "History topic: The Indian Sulbasutras." http://www-history.mcs.st-andrews.ac.uk/history/PrintHT/Indian_sulbasutras.html

Sulbasutras were basically geometry texts and in the documents we find irrational numbers, prime numbers, the rule of three and cube roots, the square root of 2 to five decimal places, the method of squaring the circle, the solutions to linear and quadratic equations, Pythagorean triples, and a statement and numerical attempt of proof of the Pythagorean Theorem.

In the fifth century BC, Panini (who is called the father of the computing machine) formulated the Sanskrit grammar rules and wrote the Astadhyayi. In his book, metarules, transformations, and recursions are discussed. The original purpose of this book was to systematize the grammar of Sanskrit. In 300 BC, The Sanskrit word "sunya" was used for referring to the concept of "void."

In 300 BC, the Brahmi numerals came into being in India. These Brahmi numerals were symbols for the numbers from 1 to 9. However, the Brahmi numeral did not include the concept of the place-value of numbers system Various symbols originating from the Brahmi numerals started to develop and in the eleventh century, the Islamic mathematician al-Birumi, who wrote twenty-seven works regarding India, wrote:

> Whilst we use letters for calculation according to their numerical value, the Indians do not use letters at all for arithmetic. And just as the shape of the letters that they use for writing is different in different regions of their country, so the numerical symbols vary.[10]

The Brahmi one, two, three and four are written as follows:

$$1 \quad 2 \quad 3 \quad 4$$

$$- \quad = \quad \equiv \quad +$$

Around 150 BC, the Jaina mathematicians in India wrote the "Sthananga Sutra," which contains theory of numbers, arithmetic operations, geometry, quadratic equations, cubic equations, and permutations and combinations.

During the third to first century BC, Pingala wrote the treatise of a prosody called "Chhandah-shasfra." It contains the first use of zero as a digit, which was indicated by a dot, the Fibonacci numbers (called maatraameru), and Pascal's triangle. The notation by dots for zero was used as follows:

---

[10] Cited, http://wwwhistory.mcs.standrews.ac.uk/history/HistTopics/India.html

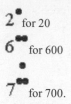

$2^{\bullet}$ for 20

$6^{\bullet\bullet}$ for 600

$7^{\bullet\bullet}_{\bullet}$ for 700.

In 500 AD, Aryabhata wrote the "Aryyabhata-Siddahanta. Aryyabhata introduced trigonometric functions and showed the methods to approximate their numerical values. He defined the concepts of sine and cosine and constructed the earliest tables of sine and cosine values in intervals of

$$3\frac{3}{4}^{\circ}$$

He also computed π as 3.1416.

Sanskrit numerals were also created around this time. Between the fourth century AD and the sixth century AD, the Gupta numerals were developed from Brahmi numerals. In 628 AD, an Indian mathematician, Brahmagupta, wrote the Brahma-Sphuta-Siddhanta wherein the concept of zero is explained. Zero was added as a tenth positional digit in his work.[11]

Around the 7th century, Gupta numerals changed into Nagari numerals, which contained zero as a number. Nagari numerals are sometimes called the Devangari numerals, which means the "writing of the gods." The Nagari numerals were then introduced to the Islamic people. The words for the Devangari numerals in Sanskrit are given as follows[12]:

sunya
eka
dva
tri
catur
pancan
sas
saptan
astan
navan

[11] http://sunsite.utk.edu/math_archives/.http/hypermail/historia/apr99/0197.html
[12] http://www.mandalar.com/DisplayJ/Bonji/index6_E.html

From the 7th century to the 11th century, Indian numerals became more advanced with operations such as plus, minus, and square root. Indian numerals started to have their modern form. The significance of the development of the positional number system is described by the French mathematician Pierre Simon Laplace (1749–1827). Laplace wrote

> The ingenious method of expressing every possible number using a set of ten symbols (each symbol having a place value and an absolute value) emerged in India. The idea seems so simple nowadays that its significance and profound importance is no longer appreciated. Its simplicity lies in the way it facilitated calculation and placed arithmetic foremost amongst useful inventions. The importance of this invention is more readily appreciated when one considers that it was beyond the two greatest men of antiquity, Archimedes and Apollonius.[13]

The positional number system we use today was developed in India. Some may wonder why this number system was not developed in the West. There are theories to explain why the establishment of a positional number system occurred in India. Among them, three of the noteworthy conjectures are as follows:

> Some historians believe that the Babylonian base 60 place-value systems were transmitted to the Indians via the Greeks. We have commented in the article on zero about Greek astronomers using the Babylonian base 60 place-value systems with a symbol o similar to our zero. The theory here is that these ideas were transmitted to the Indians who then combined this with their own base 10 number systems, which had existed in India for a very long time.
>
> A second hypothesis is that the idea for place-value in Indian number systems came from the Chinese. In particular the Chinese had pseudo-positional number rods, which, it is claimed by some, became the basis of the Indian positional system. This view is put forward by, for example, Lay Yong Lam […]. Lam argues that the Chinese system already contained what he calls the:
>
> > three essential features of our numeral notation system: (i) nine signs and the concept of zero, (ii) a place value system and (iii) a decimal base.
>
> A third hypothesis is put forward by Joseph […]. His idea is that the place-value in Indian number systems is something, which was developed entirely by the Indians. He has an interesting theory as to why the Indians might be

---

[13] Cited in http://wwwhistory.mcs.standrews.ac.uk/history/HistTopics/India.html

pushed into such an idea. The reason, Joseph believes, is due to the Indian fascination with large numbers. Freudenthal is another historian of mathematics who supports the theory that the idea came entirely from within India.[14]

Names of large numbers are found in the Buddhism sutra called Buddha-avatamsaka-nama-maha-vaipulya-sutra. In this voluminous sutra, which forces the practices of a bodhisatova, names of large numbers are mentioned in section 30 of Asamkhya (innumerable) of volume 45.[15]

大方廣佛華嚴經卷第四十五

于闐國三藏實叉難陀奉　制譯

阿僧祇品第三十

爾時心王菩薩。白佛言。世尊。諸佛如來。演說阿僧祇無量無邊無等不可數不可稱不可思不可量不可說不可說不可說。世尊云何。阿僧祇乃至不可說不可說耶。佛告心王菩薩言。善哉善哉。善男子。汝今為欲令諸世間。入佛所知數量之義。而問如來應正等覺。善男子。諦聽諦聽。善思念之。當為汝說。時心王菩薩。唯然受教。佛言。善男子。一百洛叉。為一　胝。　胝　胝。為一阿庾多。阿庾多阿庾多。為一那由他。那由他那由他。為一頻波羅。頻波羅頻波羅。為一矜羯羅。矜羯羅矜羯羅。為一阿伽羅。阿伽羅阿伽羅。為一最勝。最勝最勝。為一摩婆(上聲呼)羅。摩婆羅摩婆羅。為一阿婆(上)羅。阿婆羅阿婆羅。為一多婆(上)羅。多婆羅多婆羅。為一界分。界分界分。為一普摩。普摩普摩。為一禰摩。禰摩禰摩。為一阿婆(上)鈐。阿婆鈐阿婆鈐。為一彌伽(上)婆。彌伽婆彌伽婆。為一毘[打-丁+羅]伽。毘[打-丁+羅]伽毘[打-

丁+羅]伽。為一毘伽(上)婆。毘伽婆毘伽婆。為一僧羯邏摩。僧羯邏摩僧羯邏摩。為一毘薩羅。毘薩羅毘薩羅。為一毘贍婆。毘贍婆毘贍婆。為一毘盛(上)伽。毘盛伽毘盛伽。為一毘素陀。毘素陀毘

100 洛叉（rakusha）equals 1 俱胝（kutei）, that is

$$100 \times 10^{5} = 10^{2} \times 10^{5} = 10^{2+5} = 10^{7}$$。

---

[14] Ibid.

[15] http://www.buddhist-canon.com/SUTRA/DCX/EHuaYan/T100237b.htm

倶胝 倶胝 is equal to $\left(10^7\right)^2 = 10^{7 \times 2}$ 。

The Hindu Arabic numerals for the first 19 units and the last 7units in section 30 of Asamkhya (innumerable) of volume 45 are listed below[16]:

Large Number—Japanese Word

10^5 洛叉 （Rakusha)

10^7 倶胝 （Kutei)

$10^{7 \times 2}$ = 1014 阿[广<奥]多 （Ayuta)

$10^{7 \times 2^2}$ = 1028 那由他 （Nayuta)

$10^{7 \times 2^3}$ = 1056 頻波羅 （Binbara)

$10^{7 \times 2^4}$ = 10112 矜羯羅 （Kongara)

$10^{7 \times 2^5}$ = 10224 阿伽羅 （Akara)

$10^{7 \times 2^6}$ = 10448 最勝 （Saisyou)

$10^{7 \times 2^7}$ = 10896 摩婆羅 （Mabara)

$10^{7 \times 2^8}$ = 101792 阿婆羅 （Abara)

$10^{7 \times 2^9}$ = 103584 多婆羅 （Tabara)

$10^{7 \times 2^{10}}$ = 107168 界分 （Kaibun)

$10^{7 \times 2^{11}}$ = 1014336 普摩 （Huma)

$10^{7 \times 2^{12}}$ = 1028672 禰摩 （Nema)

---

[16] http://www.sf.airnet.ne.jp/ts/language/largenumber.html

$10^{7×2^{13}}$ = 1057344 阿婆[金今]（Abaken）

$10^{7×2^{14}}$ = 10114688 弥伽婆（Mikaba）

$10^{7×2^{15}}$ = 10229376 毘[才羅]伽（Biraka）

$10^{7×2^{16}}$ = 10458752 毘伽婆（Bikaba）

$10^{7×2^{17}}$ = 10917504 僧羯邏摩（Sougarama）

$10^{7×2^{116}}$ $= 10^{58153724815590069439541558887265 0752}$
不可思転（Hukasiten）

$10^{7×2^{117}}$ $= 10^{116307449631180138879083117774530 1504}$
不可量（Hukaryou）

$10^{7×2^{118}}$ $= 10^{232614899262360277758166235549060 3008}$
不可量転（Hukaryouten）

$10^{7×2^{119}}$ $= 10^{465229798524720555516332471098120 6016}$
不可説（Hukasetsu）

$10^{7×2^{120}}$ $= 10^{930459597049441111032664942196241 2032}$
不可説転（Hukasetsuten）

$10^{7×2^{121}}$ $= 10^{186091919409888222206532988439248 24064}$
不可説不可説(Hukasetsuhukasetsu)

$10^{7×2^{122}}$ $= 10^{372183838881977644441306597687849 648128}$
不可説不可説転（Hukasetsuhukasetsuten）

SUNYA AND SUNYATA

The concept of zero may have been facilitated by the Buddhism concept of Sunyata. Sunyata is often translated as emptiness, void, or nothingness. However the Buddhist concept of sunyata is relativity. Sunyata does not deny the concept of existence as such, but holds that all existence and the constituent elements, which make up existence, are dependent upon causation. In Hinayama, the concept of sunyata primarily indicates the impossibility of having an independent atman (self) but Mahayana goes one step further in denying the possibility of a self-existing nature within the dharma, which make up the material world. All things (dharmas) are sunyata, i.e., relative, and hence dependent. The teaching of Buddha explains sunyata as following:

> This is the concept that everything has neither substance nor permanence and is one of the fundamental points in Buddhism. Since everything is dependent upon causation, there can be no permanent ego as a substance. But, one should neither adhere to the concept that everything has substance nor that it does not. Every being, human or non-human, is in relativity. Therefore, it is foolish to hold to a certain idea or concept or ideology as the only absolute. This is the fundamental undercurrent in the Prajuna Scriptures of Mahayana Buddhism.[17]

ISLAMIC MATHEMATICS

The early contributions of Islamic mathematicians affected all branches of western mathematics. The word "algebra" first used in Arabia in the ninth century AD. Around the middle of this century, Baghdad became the center of world culture and learning under a Moslem caliphate.

Although the concept of zero was developed in India, the name "zero" derives from the Arabic word "sifr." Zero was discovered in India in the seventh century and it was used as both a placeholder and as a number between positive numbers and negative numbers. With this event, the modern place-value numeral system was fully developed. This development was recorded in the Brahma-sphuta-siddanta.

Meanwhile in the early seventh century, the beginning of the Islamic Empire was about to occur. In the Arabian Desert, Muhammad established the religion of Islam. He escaped from his hometown of Mecca to Medina in 622 AD. Later, that date became the first date of the Muslim calendar year. When he returned to Mecca after eight years of exile, the religion of Islam began to spread rapidly to the north of the Arabian Peninsula to areas such as Syria, Iraq, Egypt, to all of North Africa, to Persia, and even to the borders of India. Eventually, the religion of Islam spread to the borders of China in the east and to Spain in the west. In twenty years, Muhammad

---

[17] Bukkyo Dendo Kyokai, *The Teaching of Buddha* (Tokyo: Toppan Printing Co., 1966).

successfully achieved the conversion all of Arabia to the ideas embraced in the *Qu'ran*. Within a hundred years, the religion of Islam spread to the borders of India, to North Africa, and even to Spain. After the death of Muhammad, the Umayyad family ruled the empire. The empire from the period of Muhammad to that of the Umayyad family is called the Arabian Empire. The empire that lasted from the time of Muhammad to the end of the Abassid rule is sometimes called the Islamic Empire. Combined, the Arabian Empire and the Islamic Empire is sometimes referred to as the Sasanian empire.

In 751 AD, the military of the Tang dynasty of China and that of the Islamic empire had a battle along the River Tales. The Islamic armies achieved a victory and took many Chinese soldiers as prisoners of war. Among them were papermaking experts, who later showed their captors how to make paper. With the knowledge gained from these Chinese papermakers, papermaking was established in the Islamic empire. The first paper mill was built in Samarqand and the name "Samarqand Paper " spread and it was known even by the people of Persia and as away far as Spain. Samarqand paper was made by using a sweet bay or mulberry. By 900 AD, papermaking technology had spread to Egypt, the birthplace of papyrus scrolls. By 1040 AD, it spread to Africa and in 1100 AD papermaking technology reached Morocco. From there, papermaking technology was propagated to France in 1189. (Before the Islamic empire learned the method of papermaking, sheepskin was used as a writing medium.)

From the seventh century, books from India along with mathematics books in Greek were translated into Arabic. In 773 AD, about twenty years after the introduction of papermaking to the Islamic people, the Brahma-sphuta-siddanta, written by Brahmagupta, was brought to Baghdad. The Indian numeral system along with the table of sine was contained in the Brahma-sphuta-siddanta, which was translated into Arabic, and those new concepts were introduced to the people of Islam. By this time, the Abassid family had already replaced the Umayyad family, and the religion of Islam had spread from Spain to the borders of China. The empire ruled by the Abassid family is called the Islamic Empire. The Abassid ruled from 750 AD to 1258 AD. This period was the golden age of Islamic Sciences and mathematics. During the ninth century, Baghdad became the world center of learning. The culture of Islam expressed a great degree of tolerance toward the people who lived in the empire. Rulers promoted learning and scholarship eagerly. Noteworthy is the effort of the Caliph Al Ma'mun who began a state project of translating Greek, Syrian, Pahlavi, and Sanskrit texts into Arabic. Mohammed ibn Zakariya al-Razi (865-925) wrote,

Books on medicine, geometry, astronomy, and logic are more useful than the Bible and the *Qu'ran*. The authors of these books have found the facts and truths by their own intelligence, without the help of prophets.[18]

Even though arguments occurred against such heresies, Mohammed ibn Zakaria al-Razi lived a long life.

From 750 AD to 1450 AD, Islamic civilization produced a series of brilliant mathematicians, among whom, Al-Khwarizmi, Al-Biruni, Umar al-Khayyami, and Al-Kashi are the most well known.

Al-Kwarizmi (780-850) was the greatest Muslim mathematician in medieval Islam. His works range from arithmetic, algebram and trigonometry to astronomy. Al-Kwarizmi served Caliph al-Mamun in the House of Wisdom. He introduced the Hindu methods of arithmetic to the Islamic world through his arithmetic work, "The Book of Addition and Subtraction According to the Hindu Calculation." His other arithmetic book, "al-jabr wal-muqabala (The book of restoring and balancing) contains solutions for quadratic equations, geometric proofs, and trigonometry. The first Arabic arithmetic book translated into Latin is the one written by al-Kwarizmi and that was "al-jabr wal-muqabala." From "al-jabr," the west came to use the word "algebra." Al-Biruni (973-1048) was a central Asian scholar. He wrote a number of books. Most noteworthy among them are books called "the determination of the Coordinates of the Location" and "India." In "India," the comparisons of Islam with Hinduism are discussed. He translated Islamic mathematics into Sanskrit. Umar al-Khayyami was a Persian poet and mathematician who found a solution of a cubic equation by using a pair of intersecting conic sections. This was truly the golden age of Islamic mathematics. Ghiyath al-Din Jamshid Al-Kashi was born in Kashan. He wrote the "Aryabhatiya Bhasya," which contains works on infinite series expressions and spherical geometry.

Change began to occur in Islamic culture in the twelfth and thirteenth century AD. The Mongols started to gain power and threatened the Islamic Empire. The Muslim Seljuk Empire, which captured Constantinople in 1453, defeated the Christian Crusaders.

EUROPEAN MATHEMATICS

The first European who introduced the Hindu numeral system in Latin was Gerbert d'Aurillac (940-1003). In 1202, Leonardo Fibonacci introduced Hindu-Arabic numerals to Europeans in his book "Abacus." Through this

---

[18] Cited in Philip J. Davis, *A Brief Look at Mathematics and Theology*, p. 15. http://www2.hmc.edu/www_common/hmnj/davis2brieflook1and2.pdf

book many people in the west learned about Islamic mathematics for the first time. These ideas contributed to the development of mathematical studies in Europe. He also introduced Fibonacci numbers:

$$1, \quad 1, \quad 2, \quad 3, \quad 5, \quad 8, \quad 13, \quad 21, \quad 31,$$

$$\cdots \quad \frac{1}{\sqrt{5}}\left\{\left(\frac{1+\sqrt{5}}{2}\right)^{n} - \left(\frac{1-\sqrt{5}}{2}\right)^{n}\right\} \quad \cdots$$

In the thirteenth century, there were many great mathematicians who were are also theologians, such as Albertus Magnus, Robert Grosseteste, Thomas Aquinas (1226–1274), and Roger Bacon (1214–1294). In the 1470s, Luca Pacioli became a Franciscan friar and he was a mathematics tutor to Leonardo Da Vinci. Pacioli wrote several books on mathematics. Most noteworthy among them are the "Summa de Arithmetica, Geometrica, Proportion et Proportionalita" (written in Venice in 1494), "De Viribus Quantitatis (On the Powers of Numbers), "Geometry," and "De Divina Proportione," which contained the subject of the golden ratio and its applications.

The mathematics of medieval Islam was propagated to Europe by the commercial route, which connected Constantinople and Vienna via the Balkan nations.[19]

Conclusion

I believe that there is a strong possibility that the concept of zero was developed out of the Buddhism concept of Sunyata. Though Sunyata is often translated as emptiness, void, or nothingness, zero was understood as a number between positive numbers and negative numbers. That is the Buddhist concept of sunyata, which is relativity. When the Indian numerical system was developed after the introduction of zero, it was quickly propagated to various civilizations. The swift propagation was possible because papermaking was introduced to the Muslim world by the Chinese civilization. Muslims embraced the Indian numerical system, which has zero or sunya in Sanskrit, and in turn Christians accepted it. Muslims

---

[19] J. L. Berggren, *Episodes in the Mathematics of Medieval Islam* (New York: Springer-Verlag, 2003).

174

translated various texts from the Greeks, Indians, Persians, and other civilizations. In doing so, they preserved the important works of the past. They also advanced the works of the Indians and Greeks and helped modern mathematics to develop. Clearly, there exists an interrelationship between the mathematics of India, Islam, and Europe and those cultures and religions. As a result of the early form of globalization brought about by contacts from the Silk Road, Islamic culture prospered and the works of the scientists and mathematicians of medieval Islam influenced the cultures of the Eurasian continent. At its height, the Islamic empire was one of the most brilliant civilizations in history. It truly pursued intellectual Excellencies.

All the world religions share basic moral and spiritual values. They all affirm that all of life is sacred. By recognizing the moral and spiritual values of each religious tradition as bridges of peace and justice, and affirmations of the sacredness of life, we can work together to promote a non-violent path to conflict resolution and peace building.

ACKNOWLEDGMENTS
I am grateful to Brother Jim Faccett of the Chaminade University Marianist Community of Honolulu, Hawaii and Archbishop Ryonkan Ara of Tendai school of Buddhism in Honolulu, Hawaii for their help in the completion of this paper. I thank Brother Jim for his encouragement, help with getting books for research by giving me rides to the library, discussing many topics and giving me insight on the mission of the Marianist Community, commenting on the manuscript and buying me tortillas. I thank Ara sensei for his guidance in the understanding of the concepts of "sunya" and "ichinenn sanzen" of Mahayana Buddhism and for lending me numerous books on Buddhism.

EMPHASIS ON TEACHING ETHICS IN BUSINESS SCHOOLS: THE RECENT EXPERIENCE IN US HIGHER EDUCATION

Jamshid Damooee

THE GENERAL CONCEPT

Morality refers to the social norms and values that guide both individuals and their interaction with their fellow human beings, communities, and environment. There are important rules that are set in all such interactions. These rules and norms are created to protect these values. The rules create certain duties for the purpose of fostering these values. It is human virtues and capabilities that enable us to act accordingly. Human societies create their own moral factors that are often interwoven with religious practices and social power structures. Nonetheless, the very essence of moral behavior is the self-preservation of the human species. Ethics is often looked at as an analysis or interpretation of morality that can guide the conduct of people in a society. It is the practice of using moral judgment to arrive at a decision.

The importance of ethical behavior in various aspects of our lives is a practical question. The common tendency among many in our society is to consider it as a noble behavior that separates people with higher moral standing from those who have not yet reached the boundaries of an enlightened and ethical life. Some tend to see it as a product of adhering to religious conduct and Godly beliefs. This study tends to dispel the myth of having ethical behavior as a religious tendency or moral elitism and argues for its relevance and functionality as a practical code of conduct in a society that is capable of creating a better economic environment for more efficient business conduct and prosperous living.

If there is one characteristic which distinguishes Homo sapiens from other species on Earth, it is, according to the biologist Garrett Hardin, our ability to ask the question, "What then?" To imagine the future, and thereby predict the consequences of our own actions is indeed a unique evolutionary legacy. Regrettably, as a species we at times fail to exercise this gift and take steps without asking this question. The importance of unintended consequences of our decisions is an important principle and purposely choosing to ignore it often causes disastrous consequences.

Human societies have long debated the metaphysical distinction between the human being as an individual and as a person. This distinction is important in understanding the interaction between the common good of the economic enterprise and a common ethical ground. The challenge in most societies is to define ethical behavior in the face of injustice. Are moral codes a set of unbendable rules that have to be followed without any recourse?

These and many similar questions have engaged ethicists, religious leaders, and philosophers for decades. This paper will make an effort to use such principles to explain the unavoidable need for United States higher education to teach ethics as a core requirement in many liberal arts colleges.

A SURVEY OF THE EXISTING LITERATURE ON BUSINESS ETHICS AND ITS RECENT SURGE IN BUSINESS SCHOOL CURRICULUM IN THE USA

The debate about whether ethics is good for business or is a good business brings out an important distinction about the intention of business leaders. The question of why they choose to run their business ethically or want to appear to be ethical is to an extent a misplaced debate and unimportant. Arriving at the conclusion of running a business ethically from either of the two routes brings out the importance of recognizing its significance from a social and economic perspective. In a developed economy, reaching such recognition and "branding" comes with specific measures that companies need to take. This shows itself in all aspects of their business.

It is a common belief that running a business ethically is good for business. However, some may argue that "business ethics," if properly interpreted, means the standards of conduct of individual business people, not necessarily the standards of the business as a whole. This portrays the ethical management of a business as a choice that companies need to make. Henry Posters explains the dilemma of being an ethical company and focusing on profit in a way that has been debated for the last several decades:

> Business leaders are expected to run their business as profitably as they can. A successful and profitable business in itself can be a tremendous contributor toward the common good of society. But if business leaders or department managers spend their time worrying about "doing good" for society, they will divert attention from their real objective which is profitability and running an efficient and effective organization.[1]

The issue in the above statement is the way many have looked at the question of business profitability and a possible trade off between the two.

---

[1] Henry, Posters, *Importance of Ethics, American Society for Quality (ASQ)* (2003). http://www.asqsandiego.org/articles/ethics1.htm

The question is if this is a realistic dichotomy for the business world today and if the situation has changed over the last several decades.

Iraj Mahdavi et al. note the need for proper ethical behavior within organizations. They assert that ethical behavior has become crucial to avoid possible lawsuits.[2] The public scandals of corporate misconduct and misleading practices have affected the public perception of many organizations. The recent expansion of global business and fall of trade barriers worldwide have further underlined the interest in the topics of ethical behavior and social responsibility. Many scholars believe human rights and environmental conservation are gaining more recognition in both academic and commercial settings.

Mahdavi states

> As multinational companies expand globally and enter foreign markets, ethical conduct of the officers and employees assume added importance since the very cultural diversity associated with such expansion may undermine the much shared cultural and ethical values observable in the more homogeneous organizations.

The issue of culture and its relation to ethics is an interesting topic of discussion. Schein makes a distinction between the ethical climate and cultural differences between nations.[3] Denison believes that culture should be more associated with deeper beliefs, values, and assumptions.[4] Bartels et al. state that one can value an individual's culture by his or her actions and personal activities, and ethical climate can be observed on a larger scale; in this case, the organization.[5] Ethical climate is, in essence, the employee's perception of the norms of an organization.

The interesting picture that emerges from many examples around the world shows that organizations with a strong ethical climate experienced few serious ethical problems and were more successful coping with such problems.

---

[2] Iraj Mahdavi, Shawn Mokhtari, and Kamal Dean Parhizgar, "Ethics in international business." *The Business Review*, 6 (2006).

[3] Edgar H Schein "Organizational Culture," *American Psychologist*, 45 (1990), 109–119.

[4] Daniel R. Denison, "What is the Difference between Organizational Culture and Organizational Climate? A Native's Point of View on a Decade of Paradigm Wars," *Academy of Management Review*, 21:3 (1996), 619–54.

[5] Kynn L. Bartels, et al. "The Relationship between Ethical Climate and Ethical Problems within Human Resource Management," *Journal of Business Ethics*, 17 (1998), 799–804.

Following corporate scandals in the US and Europe and rapidly heightening concerns about climate change and corporate social responsibility, business schools are increasingly feeling the need to address these topics in the curriculum.

According to a 2007 report, a survey of 50 business schools reported "a five-fold increase in the number of stand-alone ethics courses in the past eight years, with 25 percent of the schools requiring students to take a course in business ethics. [...] In the survey, deans reported high levels of interest in these topics among students, and this was particularly strong at schools ranked in the top 10. [...] The research was based on interviews conducted with deans or MBA directors from the top 50 global business schools, as ranked by the Financial Times in 2006. Student demand was only one factor behind curricular development, says Prof Hartman [Laura Hartman, Professor of Business Ethics at De Paul University]. 'Deans are hungry for it, reflecting the hunger in the market.'"[6]

As Bradshaw notes, "One of the biggest questions in business schools has been whether these subjects should be taught in stand-alone courses or integrated with other subjects such as finance, accounting, marketing or strategy" (ibid.). There is no empirical evidence to clearly state if the trend has encouraged the schools go for stand-alone ethics courses or treat ethics as a common thread in many other business courses. There is, however, some anecdotal evidence that developing business ethics as a course has found great support in a number of schools.

Ronald Sims explains the importance of building an effective classroom learning environment that requires business ethics teachers to pay particular attention to creating a classroom environment that values the ideas others have to offer.[7] Of particular importance to successful business ethics teaching is the recognition that the introduction to talking and learning about values, beliefs, morals, virtue, integrity, and other ethically related issues often generates in students powerful emotional responses ranging from self-doubt and shame to frustration and confusion. These emotional responses, if not addressed, can result in student resistance, limited risk

---

[6] See Della Bradshaw, "Right Thinking Faculties Get to Grips with Moral Issues," *Canadian Business Ethics Research Network.*
http://www.businessethicscanada.ca/dialogue/news/itemCcxccHVnkU.html
[7] Ronald R. Sims, "Business Ethics Teaching: Using Conversational Learning to Build Effective Classroom Learning Environment," *Journal of Business Ethics*, 49:2 (2004), 201–11.

taking, failure to listen to others and mistrust in the classroom, all of which can stifle student learning in business ethics teaching efforts.[8]

Russ Skiba addresses the importance of the Social Curriculum for schools in their study. He explains there is a social curriculum that acts as a guide for student behavior throughout the school day.[9] Hosmer argues that the goal of dealing with ethical issues in the curriculum is not to change the values and beliefs of students but instead to teach systems of analysis to help students use their own values to weigh the potential benefits and harms of their actions to the organization, to society, and to individuals.[10]

Additional criticisms of teaching business ethics include the suggestion that the topics are too controversial, that they do not lend themselves to evaluation of student progress, that instructors may impose their own values on the students, and that the "invisible hand" of the market should rule the behavior of businesses.[11] Some scholars note that ethical behavior is often not the result of an individual's choices, but is influenced by the context of the interaction,[12] and our understanding of ethical dilemmas will remain flawed until we gain a better understanding of how social settings and interactions affect our perceptions.[13] As a result, current methods of teaching business ethics may not be realistic, as the bureaucratic nature of organizations militates against the type of autonomous moral reasoning which may be encouraged in the classroom.[14]

Scholars in the field agree about one issue: that education in business ethics should assist students in the formation of their personal values systems, should introduce them with a range of the existing moral problems,

---

[8] Ronald R. Sims, "Debriefing Experiential Learning Exercises in Ethics Education," *Teaching Business Ethics*, 6:2 (2002), 179–97

[9] Russ Skiba, "Teaching the Social Curriculum: School Discipline as Iinstruction," *Preventing School Failure,* 47 (2003), 66–73.

[10] LaRue Tone Hosmer, "Adding Ethics to the Business Curriculum," *Business Horizons* (July–August 1988), 9–15.

[11] Michael McDonald, "The Canadian Research Strategy for Applied Ethics: A New Opportunity for Research in Business and Professional Ethics," *Journal of Business Ethics*, 11 (1992), 569–83.

[12] Bernard J. Reilly, and. Myroslaw J Kyj, "Ethical Business and the Ethical Person," *Business Horizons* (November–December 1990), 23–27.

[13] Stephen L. Payne, and Robert A. Giacalone, "Social Psychological Approaches to the Perception of Ethical Dilemmas," *Human Relations*, 43:7 (1990), 649–665.

[14] Kerner F. Furman, "Teaching Business Ethics: Questioning the Assumptions, Seeking New Directions," *Journal of Business Ethics*, 9 (1990), 31–38.

provide them with knowledge of ethical theories, and give them an opportunity to grapple with ethical questions.[15]

Janet Adams et al. promote the idea of teaching ethics through role playing. Students are introduced to role set theory as a framework for considering ethical dilemmas. Providing students with a theory on which to base their analysis provides them with a tool which may help them to feel more secure in their analysis of an otherwise amorphous situation. They found that students are willing, even eager, to share their ethical dilemmas in class. The student-generated material removes the discussion from the arena of the instructor's values and encourages students to analyze the situation rather than assuming that the instructor has a single right answer. This is a result of the students being more expert regarding their own situations than their instructor and their being able to add clarifying details when asked by other students. Students have a more personal investment in the discussion when the person having experienced the problem is someone they can speak with directly. The authors argue that this approach shows the immediate relevance of business ethics by focusing on early-career ethical dilemmas actually faced by individuals with whom they can identify.[16]

STEPS TAKEN IN CALIFORNIA LUTHERAN UNIVERSITY TO ADDRESS TEACHING OF BUSINESS ETHICS

California Lutheran University is a comprehensive Liberal Arts College in the city of Thousand Oaks in Southern California. CLU offers undergraduate, graduate, and continuing education programs through its College of Arts and Sciences, School of Business and School of Education. The university offers thirty-six majors and twenty-eight minors, in addition to professional preparation programs in specified fields of study. Master's degree programs are offered in education, business administration, public policy and administration, computer science, and psychology. A doctoral program in educational leadership is offered through the School of Education.

In the words of its president, Dr John Sladek, the culture of CLU is based on a concurrence of faith and reason that is apparent not only in classrooms but also across the campus. CLU is a diverse, scholarly

---

[15] Ronald R. Sims, and Serberinia. J. Sims, "Increasing Applied Business Ethics Courses in Business School Curricula," *Journal of Business Ethics*, 10 (1991), 211–219.

[16] Janet S. Adams, et al. "Challenges in Teaching Business Ethics: Using Role Set Aanalysis of Early Ccareer Dilemmas," *Journal of Business Ethics,* 17 (1998), 1325–35.

community dedicated to excellence in the liberal arts and professional studies. Rooted in the Lutheran tradition of Christian faith, the University encourages critical inquiry into matters of both faith and reason. The mission of the University is to educate leaders for a global society who are strong in character and judgment, confident in their identity and vocation, and committed to service and justice. The issue of ethical behavior forms one of the core pieces of its identity as a place of higher education.

In the words of the Dean of the CLU Business School, Charles Maxey, the school strives for the following objectives:

- A quality education for a dynamic world of business;
- A faculty committed to student learning;
- Flexibility for working professionals;
- The opportunity to build a network for success;
- Innovative programs;
- Professional tracks to marketable expertise and competencies;
- A personal and values based community of learning.

Teaching as well as blending ethical judgment in our curriculum is vitally important to the school and its programs. Ethics have a special place in the philosophy of our teaching at the School of Business and the school would like to be considered as a Business School with a Conscience. This name for the school is not a mere slogan, but has encouraged the school to take various measures to live up to this slogan. One of the primary concerns of the school has been to find innovative ways of bringing ethics into the pedagogical aspects of its program. The question of whether we should have special courses or create an emphasis on bringing ethics to as many courses as possible has yet not being totally resolved. We do nonetheless have business ethics and professors are encouraged to explore ethical aspects of what they teach. But this is not mandatory, nor do many of us feel that it should be. Here are some of the measures that we have taken to bring ethics to the forefront of the school's attention:

1. We offer courses in Business Ethics for both our undergraduate and graduate studies. These courses offer information and challenge students in realizing the value of ethical business practice in our emerging global economy. The following issues and topics are covered:

- Situational dilemmas and relationships with employees;
- Unions, customers, competitors, government and society are examined from an ethical point of view;

- Students get engaged in debates over topical issues of our recent event and offer their perspectives in contrast or in support of other opinions in their projects. We use ethics games and simulation programs where students are faced with many dilemma that require ethical decision making and they have the opportunity to employ what they learn in the theoretical construct and debate about it in their classes.

2. We encourage faculty to develop courses in various disciplines that take up ethical behavior as a criterion of assessment, planning, and policy implication within the content of the subject matter. Based on what has been followed in the school we have developed the following courses in Economics and Marketing and are interested in going much further in the years to come:

- Economics of the Environment;
- Social Marketing;
- Business Round Tables and ad hoc speaking events with emphases on ethical business practices within a particular course;
- Developing the Distinguished Speakers' Series that can address Business Ethics within the Center for Leadership and Values.

We are very interested and are actively seeking other outlets and partnerships that can help us to strengthen our focus on the ethics of business from a research perspective and as an area of scholarship in the near future

WAGING PEACE:
RELIGION-BASED PEACEMAKING

RELIGION IN PUBLIC LIFE

Alan Race

Let me start with a simple parable. In the interests of promoting friendly interfaith relations my city's Christian-Muslim dialogue group last year decided to arrange a soccer match between Muslim Imams and Christian Clergy. The Imams romped home with a stunning 6-0 victory. Undeterred by defeat the clergy proposed a cricket match. Again, the Imam group was triumphant. We needed a solution to a developing crisis: how to rescue a reverse colonial take-over, a potentially religious holy war, and the politics of oppositional antagonism? A brilliant solution emerged. There was to be a further cricket match, but this time one between joint teams of clergy and Imams from two cities, Leicester and Bradford. Leicester batted to victory and celebrated its sense of multicultural pride.

My simple parable is intended to raise the issue of how, in western society, we can move from oppositional politics and oppositional intellectual life to some sense of shared hope. How to move from defining ourselves in terms of Us-Against-Them to Us-As-Them? Right now the antics of a polarised outlook shape the public space—in the media, government and academy. Take all three contexts. Recently a story was published in the British press that the teaching of the Holocaust of the Jews in the Second World War was to be discontinued in schools because some Muslim pupils objected to it. The story circulated across the globe and outrage about blackmail was boiling up. It turned out that there was one incident in one classroom in one school involving one weak teacher. No national policy hung on it. Yet the media loved the oppositional politics of it. Then, in government circles, there has begun a concerted policy move in the UK, with financial backing, for local communities to promote multicultural and multifaith community cohesion in order to derail the potential radicalising of young Muslim men. This would be fine, but at the same time the government refuses to accept the overwhelming evidence that part of that radicalising is to do with its foreign policy and particularly with the "war on terror" and the occupation of Iraq. Government and the majority of the citizens are at logger-heads. Finally, in relation to the academy, in the West we are aware of the recent industry of anti-God books, most famously that of Richard Dawkins's *God Delusion*. By common consent, Dawkins sets up a straw-man and comfortably destroys it. That's not difficult to do. Or take another author, Sam Harris, and his books

The End of Faith and *Letter to a Christian Nation*.[1] He says that Muslims and the American Christian Right are two of a kind. To the Christian Right, he says "Non-believers like myself stand beside you dumbstruck by the Muslim hordes who chant death to whole nations of the living. But we stand dumbstruck by you as well—by your denial of tangible reality, by the suffering you create in service of your religious myths and by your attachment to an imaginary God." (*Letter to a Christian Nation*, p, 91) Psychological denial, responsibility for suffering, intellectual craziness—that's quite an accusing list. And there is truth in some of it. But there is no truth in its oppositional caricature.

In the UK, as in other western countries, we have a crisis in relation to globalisation. On the one hand we have pursued the economics of liberalism and the free movement of capital and the labour market. That continues to bring benefits to the already rich. On the other hand, we are resisting other aspects of globalisation: the movement of peoples to our shores, the need to develop better models of multiculturalism, and, most significantly now, the recognition of religious plurality. If globalisation conjures up an "Us-As-Them" then we are not sure we want it. Into that uncertainty comes a polarised debate of Religion versus Secularism, Multiculturalism versus Assimilation, and Political Liberalism versus Traditionalism. It is difficult often to carve out any shared ground for sensible debate between these opposites. Each side has its foundational dogmatics for comfort, yet each knows that in a post-critical world the spectre of relativism is always threatening.

So I repeat: how to move from "Us-Against-Them" to "Us-As-Them"? Without it, what chance will there be for the common good to influence the rapid globalisation now taking place?

Actually oppositional postures do not characterise the whole of the political and intellectual landscape. There are some on the secularist left who lament the absence of any worthwhile moral direction in western political liberalism which seems, they aver, to have surrendered everything to economist interpretations of human living. For example, *Guardian* columnist Neal Lawson, self-confessed "atheist and a full-time politico," has written: "[I]n words and deeds, in the world I see around me, the positive role faith plays far outweighs the negatives. Religious leaders hold a mirror up to the injustice and immorality of our society and are prepared

---

[1] Sam Harris, *The Ends of Faith: Religion, Terror, and the Future of Reason* (New York: Norton, 2004); Sam Harris, *Letter to a Christian Nation* (New York: Knopf, 2006).

in their own small way to do something about it."[2] In other words, there is no need for the polarising of views. Then from the religious side, the Muslim academic, Mona Siddiqui, Professor of Islamic Studies and Public Understanding in the University of Glasgow, has written in support of anti-discrimination law, arguing that there should be no opt-out clause for religions on matters of discrimination. She observes that "if our Government has deemed fit to make illegal any sort of discrimination, whether it be on the grounds of race, religion or sexual orientation, it is inevitable that this eradication must be total; there can be no room for just a little bit of discrimination."[3] And again, "if we are all to be treated as equal citizens, then the ills committed in the name of our faith and culture, should be equally condemned" (ibid.).What she had in mind specifically here was the practice of forced marriages. In other words, there is no reason why the religions should pose themselves as necessarily opposed to the political liberalism of the West.

In practice too, the polarisation so beloved of the media and the academic community does not reflect every context. In Leicester—city of interreligious soccer and cricket!—there are several public dialogue groups which flourish; churches and mosques jointly raise money for justice projects around the world; faith leaders meet regularly in order to anticipate the fall-out from the next international event, and they stand robustly by their commitment that an attack on one community is an attack on all. Over a decade ago the Leicester Anglican bishop's chaplain was also employed as the Secretary for the Jain Centre of Europe one mile from my home, and the pioneering St Philip's Centre, which is run as a Christian ecumenical centre for study and engagement in a multifaith society, also employs a Muslim and a Sikh on their staff. Leicester has not always been like this. We have come a long way since the 1970s, when Idi Amin was persecuting and expelling his Asian population from Uganda and the Leicester City Council took out an advert in the Uganda Times telling people not to come to Leicester on the grounds that there was no work and nowhere to live. Today the city could not function without its Asian entrepreneurs and it trumpets itself as a successful multicultural and multifaith city. Everything is not totally well, of course. New groups are arriving from Eastern Europe and parts of Africa at a time when the "war on terror" is being used as an excuse for tightening immigration measures and creating an air of suspicion

---

[2] Neal Lawson, "If They Preach the Cause of the Poor, They're my People," *The Guardian*, January 3, 2007).
http://www.guardian.co.uk/commentisfree/story/0,,1981655,00.html
[3] Mona Siddiqi, "Eradication Must be Total. There Can be no Room for Just a Little Bit of Discrimination," *The Tablet*, February 10, 2007, p. 11, col.3.

around Muslims particularly, but also around anyone else not recognisably British, and this puts a strain inevitably on neighbourhood relationships. Moreover, the good cooperation between religious leaders does not always filter down to local levels or into people's homes. But my main point here is that, on the whole, not only in theory but also in practice, the polarising of views does not properly reflect reality.

However, we need to understand why the polarising has happened. The reasons inevitably will be complex. I cite two major ones. The first is to do with what is called religiously-motivated violence, and the second with the making of an ideological "-ism" out of a pragmatic procedure. Let me take each in turn.

Undoubtedly, 9/11 and the subsequent "war on terror" have made a massive impact. This is not breaking news, but it is persisting news. It is sometimes said that, having once been banished, religion is back in the public arena with a vengeance. Precisely how this return is experienced or received will be different in different European countries, and different again in the United States. In the UK, a country fairly robustly secular in outlook, in spite of having an established church, the picture is mixed. The spectre of religiously-motivated violence created a suspicion of Muslims which was further deepened after our own violence with the London killings on 7/7/05. The realisation that the perpetrators of the 7/7 killings were home-grown young men whose backgrounds were not defined by poverty or educational under-achievement led to pressure being put on Muslim communities to do something about those who might be vulnerable to extremism. The scene was set for collision between Islam (and by extension other communities, including even the secularised Christians) and secular liberalism, as present realities were filtered through the historical lenses of medieval history, crusades, and holy war, colonialism and occupation. So-called "otherness" was a threat. Enlightened Freedom versus Religious Dogmatism had returned. Perhaps we should not be surprised at this, for it was wars between religions and within religions which was partly instrumental in promoting the secularist outlook in the first place.

So, religiously-motivated violence has thrust religion back into the public gaze, but in a fashion which requires religion to justify itself even more than previously and after a period of unprecedented secular dominance. And religiously-motivated violence, we might agree, is a good enough reason for holding religion as such at arms length in the public square.

The second cluster of reasons why the polarisation of views has happened concerns the enormous success in western countries of political liberalism in theory combined with secular pragmatism in policy-making. But there is a feeling now that secular liberalism has not brought all of the benefits it perhaps once promised. For example, it has not had the strength to withstand the corrosive effects of globalisation. More than that, in separating off the material bases of living from spiritual needs it has no convincing answer to the basic question of what goals we should pursue as human beings in society. This was summed up in a famous sentence once uttered by our former PM, Margaret Thatcher, who said that there is no such thing as society, there are only individuals and the family. In a simple point, one commentator has observed: "The politics of recent years has been almost obsessively focussed on economics. Over the next few years, we need to turn our attention once again to the social—to what it is that makes us able to live together well."[4]

Political liberalism combined with pragmatic decision-making has brought many benefits. It brought an end to the over-weaning power of religious institutions and opened up a new sense of dignity for individuals. Yet wholesale accommodation to the processes of secularisation which accompanied political liberalism was bound to remain problematic for the religious mind. The concern is mainly with what is sometimes termed the Rawlsian contract theory of liberal democracy, from John Rawls the American political scientist. Theoretically speaking, Rawls proposed that our reasoning over public policy should be based on that which no reasonable person could reasonably reject. It is a sort of highest common factor or pragmatic approach: put simply, decisions are made according to what works and what citizens will accept.[5]

From the same point of view, the philosopher, Richard Rorty, says that when religion enters political/public debate it acts as a "conversation-stopper." When the religious person says that God commands this or that policy, what sense can be made of it by citizens outside of that particular framework? Therefore religious believers ought to keep it for themselves—privately. This is a familiar secularist argument.[6]

The difficulty for many believers is that this immediately cuts out religious doctrines as a basis for moral decision-making in relation to public policy. Religious voices want to ask questions of purpose and meaning in the making of public policy, but a government shaped by secular-pragmatic

---

[4] Alessandro Buonfino and Geoff Mulgan, "Goodbye to All That," *The Guardian*, Jan 18, 2006.
http://www.guardian.co.uk/society/2006/jan/18/communities.guardiansocietysupplement
[5] See John Rawls, *A Theory of Justice*, 2nd edn (Oxford: Oxford University Press, 1999).
[6] Richard Rorty, "Religion as a Conversation-Stopper," in *Philosophy and Social Hope* (London: Penguin, 2000), pp. 168–74.

assumptions has no mechanism for answering those questions. In law, government might maximise human liberties and even help civil society to develop the intermediate means for influencing public policy, but it simply is at a loss when it comes to policy-making from a single comprehensive point of view. In the debate between "human goods" and "human rights," the religions are likely to be on the "goods" side and the governing powers of a liberal democracy on the "rights" side. Finding a decent balance between the two seems continually precarious, to say the least.

Furthermore, there may be a contradiction at the heart of the social contract theory. If the social contract is meant to allow freedom of expression and argument for all citizens and yet cuts out the reasons a great number of citizens give for arguing the way they do, then how can the social contract facilitate proper freedom?

There is a feeling from many educated religious voices that public debate requires deepening. Where are the virtues that create human character and habits of relating based on respect and dignity? Political arrangements must surely have some connection with what human life is for. Freedom from coercion is good but there is freedom "for" as well as freedom "from." Liberal democratic governments have no answer to what our freedom is "for." So Archbishop Rowan Williams, for example, complains that secular liberalism needs to address better the issue of what view of the human is involved when it comes to legislation. Pure pragmatism, he avers, seems not up to the task when deciding on matters such as "the status of the embryo in relation to genetic research, or the legalisation of assisted dying, or the legal support given to marriage." He observes further, "While there can be no assumption that a government will or should assume that such arguments (derived from religious tradition) must be followed, there must equally be no assumption that these arguments may not be heard and weighed, that an issue has to be decided solely on arguments that can be owned by no particular group."[7]

So what is to be done? We do not want to return to the theocratic state, yet a polarised stand-off between "Religion" and "Secularism" seems equally unattractive, not least because it oversimplifies what probably really transpires. It might help to see that there is no need to imagine that secular approaches to public reasoning are necessarily a function of an ideology labelled Secular Liberalism. The American political scientist, Jeffrey Stout, reminds us that secularization arose at the beginning of the modern period because of difficulties over finding common assumptions in the

---

[7] Rowan Williams, "Secularism, Faith and Freedom," lecture delivered at the Pontifical Academy of Social Sciences, November 2006.
http://www.virtueonline.org/portal/modules/news/print.php?storyid=5073

interpretation of biblical texts, and not because of commitment to an alternative philosophical ideology based in the Enlightenment. He cites the historian Christopher Hill who has documented how the Bible passed from a position of unquestioned authority in political debate at the beginning of the seventeenth century to one where it had been effectively "dethroned" by the end of the 1650s. Different interpretations of holy writ came to prevail and this undermined any common ground on which to decide issues of difference over policy-making. It follows that theocracy cannot be sustained if there are legitimate different interpretations of the bases of polity and policy. Democracy, on the other hand, allows difference of views. So in the seventeenth-century religious arbitration in political matters began to seem unstable, but not because there was supplanting by something called secularism. Therefore in present-day debate, argues Stout, there is no reason to suppose that religious voices cannot make their points boldly from a theological perspective; they simply must understand, however, that their reasoning will not necessarily be accessible to everyone in the debate, and they will have to make their own adjustments in terminology and argumentation accordingly.[8]

Out of similar sympathies, Rowan Williams makes a distinction between "programmatic secularism" and "procedural secularism." Programmatic secularism is what prevails in the minds of those who call themselves secularists; it confines comprehensive convictions to the private sphere and considers public debate about moral direction in society to be purely instrumental. On the other hand, procedural secularism imagines a public square crowded with argument, necessarily untidy, risky in terms of ordered debate, and where religious voices take their place alongside others in open exchange. What emerges from such an open exchange will not necessarily be the outcome of a kind of free-for-all ethical slanging match but, in the best possible world, the fruit of listening and rational persuasion—rational, that is, in the desired sense of seeing the persuasive reasons for something, even if one disagreed with the comprehensive view of life lying behind them. As Williams spells it out in "Secularism, Faith and Freedom":

> Procedural secularism is the acceptance by state authority of a prior and irreducible other or others; it remains secular, because as soon as it systematically privileged one group it would ally its legitimacy with the sacred and so destroy its otherness; but it can move into and out of alliance with the perspectives of faith, depending on the varying and unpredictable outcomes of honest social argument, and can collaborate without anxiety

---

[8] Jeffrey Stout, *Democracy and Tradition* (Princeton NJ: Princeton University Press, 1994), pp. 94–100.

with communities of faith in the provision, for example, of education or social regeneration.

Williams' optimism is that public political life flourishes better, even benefits from, being engaged with what he calls "larger commitments and visions" (ibid.) derived from religious commitment. So much is commendable. However, there still remains the increasingly unsettling issue of religious plurality. This brings me to my positive proposals in trying to move beyond the stand-off between secularists and religionists.

What seems to be necessary is a model of participation in public democratic debate which allows for the particularities of religious and secular voices, seeking common ground while respecting differences, and balancing compromise where necessary with critical solidarity for the sake of the common good. Such a model must surely be dialogical at heart if the religions are to develop their democratic political relevance. Most of all, the model must involve the religions self-critically if they are both to overcome their historic mistrust of one another and to learn the values of provisionality and humility that are necessary in the context of interpreting and negotiating plurality. A report prepared by the Millennium Institute for the Third Parliament of the World's Religions in 1999 expressed the view that "the greatest single scandal in which Earth's faith traditions are now involved is their failure to practise their highest ethical ideals in their relations with one another."[9] Thankfully, this is slowly changing, partly under pressure from world events (9/11 and 7/7) and partly as a result of the permission for dialogue that has been hard-won over three decades of scholarship.

Dialogue, I take it, proceeds best on the basis of trustful acceptance, critical friendship and mutual accountability. With that in mind I suggest two principles which help to place dialogue within the matrix of globalisation: firstly, dialogue is what the world needs from the religions, and secondly, dialogue is what the religions at their best potentially offer the world. Let me a say a word about each aspect.

First, dialogue is what the world needs from the religions. Calls for dialogue have often begun with reference to crisis. The world is in desperate trouble and so we need co-operation on as many fronts as we can muster to tackle the problems. What has become interesting about this approach is that often those who would normally operate within a secular discourse are now beginning to reach out to the religions. From the pragmatic perspective of the world's leaders, analysts and institutional shapers, there is a growing

---

[9] Gerald O. Barney, Jane Blewett and Kristin R. Barney, "Global 2000 Revisited: What Shall We Do?" www.webofcreation.org/Manuals/krause/2000.html

recognition that perhaps the religions have more to offer than the violence with which they are associated in the popular mind. The resources of spirituality, transcendence, and rootedness in human community are being pitted against the dominance of purely political or economist models of human living.

For example, Richard Falk, who has been a long-time analyst of international affairs and advocate of social and spiritual values in global thinking, has written that

> Without religious identity, prospects for global humane governance are without any social or political foundation; and more importantly, they are without the spiritual character that can mobilize and motivate on a basis that is far more powerful than what the market, secular reason, and varieties of nationalism have to offer.[10]

The point seems to be simply that the values which are embedded in our varied religious visions are perennial and are a considerable part of what motivate people at the levels of community and cultural identity.

A similar point was made a number of years ago at a series of meetings, in which I participated, between Jews, Christians, and Muslims, convened to discuss democracy in relation to religious views of the state. As the discussion wore on it seemed to the only political scientist in the group that the theologians, in a bid to embrace democracy wholeheartedly, were not as critical as they should have been in relation to democracy's yoking with political liberalism and economic capitalism in the period of modernity. He thought that liberalism and capitalism, as these have developed, were often destructive of democracy's best values—values, for example, of building human community and the empowerment of people to take responsibility for their own lives in ways which were not captive to global capital and big business. He put it simply:

> The concern for universal human solidarity, the imperatives of social justice, the privileging of the poor, the oppressed and excluded which lie at the heart of the sacred texts of Islam, Judaism and Christianity point us in the right direction.

I thought the point was fairly made, and more so for being made in an interreligious dialogue context and by a political scientist.

---

[10] Richard Falk, 'The Religious Foundations of Humane Governance,' in *Toward a Global Civilization? The Contribution of Religions*, ed. Patricia M. Mische and Melissa Merkling (New York and Oxford: Peter Lang, 2001), p. 56.

My second principle is that dialogue is what the religions at their best potentially offer the world. As theologians and religious leadership are fond of saying, religions provide ethical frameworks, binding beliefs and a sense of human solidarity in community. They promote values such as justice, peace, empathy with the suffering, friendship with the stranger, and connectedness to the earth. In a dialogical setting, the question arises how to cross-pollinate the ethical resourcefulness of the traditions. This opens door to global ethic thinking.

One exercise in harnessing ethical resourcefulness was offered in the much-discussed global ethic thinking of the statement *Declaration Toward a Global Ethic*, first promulgated at the 1993 Parliament of World's Religions.[11] This is not the only example of global ethic thinking, but has received the most discussion. It is worth recalling the Four Commitments that lay at the heart of the Parliament's Global Ethic statement:

- Commitment to a culture of non-violence and respect for life.
- Commitment to a culture of solidarity and a just economic order.
- Commitment to a culture of tolerance and a life of truthfulness.
- Commitment to a culture of equal rights and partnership between men and women.

These four Commitments, it seems to me, provide sufficient substance for the religions to have themselves a dialogical field day. Moreover, they provide for a substantial critique of much of the destructive effects of human behaviour. They propel the religions and other worldviews into patterns of relationship that will transform the outlook of all of us.

But there is more. We also open ourselves up to challenges from critical reasoning and the democratic spirit. This entails that the values of equality, human rights and human responsibilities, the scientific search for truth in understanding the way the world works, looking hard at the ambivalence of religious texts and traditions towards violence—these cumulatively exact a price to be paid for signing up with a Global Ethic!

Some have said that the four Commitments of the Global Ethic represent nothing more than a liberal agenda and do not arise naturally from the religions themselves. That may be partly true. But dialogue is more than conversation; it is interested in change, and global ethic thinking is an attempt to harness religious energies towards a purposeful end. Moreover, the objection that the religions envisage different ends for the religiously-motivated life and that therefore global ethics is necessarily an oxymoron is

---

[11] *Declaration Toward a Global Ethic.*
http://www.memefest.org/2006/shared/texts/declaration_toward_a_global_ethic.pdf

not fully sustainable. For the religions themselves are not static entities but dynamic spiritualities which have adapted and changed through history and culture. Why can we not see the present as the latest setting in a series of historical challenges in which we make our own adaptations to a changing world and in the light of new encounters? If dialogue is what the religions can offer at their best then they must also be open to change themselves in the wake of the global problems facing us and the need to cooperate with others on the public square.

Of course, what these commitments entail at practical levels beyond generalisation is the point at which the interesting arguments begin. But that is not for such a model to solve. Each of the religions has its arguments and range of views about each of the themed commitments. My point is that this agenda provides sufficient material for the growing dialogue between religions for the sake of globalisation for the common good.

Dialogue is not value-free. None will be unchanged. There is a journey to undertake.

In summary, let me return to my starting point about religion in public life. What seems needed is not so much an empty public square but what we might call a dialogically filled public square. We acknowledge the history of how secular liberalism arises—there was no agreement on interpretative principles once critical reasoning had arisen—but that doesn't mean that we cannot explain to one another the reasons we have for believing the things we do and acting on them. Why can we not come to decisions based on that mutual listening and mutuality of respect? This is why I believe our interreligious dialogue is so necessary. It is not only good for our own learning from one another; it could well pose itself as a kind of model for helping us to move beyond the stand-off between "religion" and "secularism." But the religions should only be allowed their voices if they transcend their historic antagonisms and mistrust—listening to reasons we give for policies and becoming aware of the limitations of different perspectives even as we might cherish them.

The public square should not be filled with a theocratic religious voice or be left hostage to a secular liberal absence of religious reasoning, but should be occupied by a dialogical conversation that values the other even as it might disagree with them. This seems to me to be the next step in the support for liberty and democracy in a plural society. There is, however, one major problem in taking such a step. It will likely require us to suspend, if not surrender, our religious senses of absolutism. And the trouble is, as we know, the religions don't like to do that.

A *DHARMIC* PERSPECTIVE: COMPASSIONATE UNDERSTANDING AND "GLOBALISATION FOR THE COMMON GOOD" DISCOURSE

Andrew Wicking

Having written this paper a couple of months after the Sixth Annual Globalisation for the Common Good Conference held in Istanbul during July 2007, I would like to take the opportunity to fold into this particular presentation of my argument valuable feedback garnered at that meeting.

I began my Istanbul paper by stating my belief that if we are serious about making ours a truly interfaith perspective on "Globalisation for the Common Good" then we are obliged to consider and engage the *dharmic* religions—notably Buddhism and Hinduism, but also Confucianism and Taoism among others. Indeed, the paper I presented at the conference, entitled "Three Poisons: A Buddhist Perspective on Globalisation for the Common Good," was one of only a handful dealing explicitly with any of these traditions.

Admittedly, seekers after progressive social change, and even those of us engaged with the "Globalisation for the Common Good" movement, may feel uneasy at the introduction of Buddhism into the discourse of social justice, wary of being charged with emotionality, idealism, or recourse to exoticism in the face of "real issues."

It is my contention, however, that the contribution of a *dharmic* perspective could not be more important. By way of an exemplification of the "three poisons" I want to show that Buddhism offers some highly instructive and, I hope, constructive, critical themes that we might bring to our understanding of the social and economic structures that are creating and perpetuating suffering the world over.

INTRODUCTION

We often evaluate today's world of globalisation by talking about the need for "social justice" and the state's role in "distributive justice." Yet this emphasis, so important in the discourse of the Abrahamic religions, is not found in traditional Buddhism. Rather—as recently articulated by prominent Western Buddhist scholar David Loy, for example—the Buddhist path seeks to eliminate social exploitation by consciously transforming the "three poisons" of personal suffering into their positive counterparts: greed into generosity, ill-will into loving-kindness, and delusion into wisdom.[1]

On this understanding the transformation of the "three poisons" is the fundamental basis for cultivating compassionate understanding—*karuna*. Thus we might say that the Buddhist antidote to exploitative social systems is personal or individual rational awareness, ultimately manifesting unconditional kindness and compassion for all.

So, marrying the political arguments of contemporary commentators of social justice with a consideration of the "three poisons" of Buddhism, this paper seeks to demonstrate the nature and importance of *karuna* for "Globalisation for the Common Good" discourse.

COMPASSIONATE UNDERSTANDING AND THE DISCOURSE OF PROGRESSIVE SOCIAL CHANGE

Arguably, many contemporary commentators on issues of social justice are determinedly compassionate in their desire or intention to relieve suffering. Yet, the term "compassion" itself is rarely invoked, articulated or discussed, even by writers and activists prominent in this kind of discourse, such as Howard Zinn, Noam Chomsky, Ed Herman, or John Pilger, for example. In contrast, the whole thrust of Buddhism is to examine, understand, articulate and cultivate compassion consciously and maximally. It does so on a basis of profoundly rational foundations and offers a wealth of insight into the nature of greed, hatred, and delusion, on which all forms of social injustice are based. On this point David Edwards, in *The Compassionate Revolution: Radical Politics and Buddhism*, provides an apposite comment:

> In my view it is compassion that marks the difference between mainstream and dissent, between the clichés of conformity and liberating insight, between a murderous status quo and change, between despair and hope...Recognizing this great value of compassionate understanding, Buddhism takes us in all our laughable self-importance, greediness and irascibility, and declares that even we can work on ourselves to increase our compassion [...]. In the process, we are told, we will experience freedom (from greed, fear, hatred and delusions).[2]

---

[1] See David Loy *The Great Awakening: A Buddhistic Social Theory* (Boston: Wisdom Publications, 2003). www.stwr.net/content/view/1529/37/

[2] David Edwards, *The Compassionate Revolution: Radical Politics and Buddhism* (Devon: Green Books, 1998), p.11.

It is the contention of this paper that the scholarly investigation of this very perspective (involving the transformation of the "three poisons") combined with the analysis of social justice commentators, suggests a response to the everyday suffering inherent in a Western mindset rooted in violence, economically and morally. Furthermore, by bringing together an appreciation of the implications of a *dharmic* perspective with the social concerns expressed by writers such as those mentioned above, we can, I hope, usefully expand the horizon of "Globalisation for the Common Good" discourse.

In a published series of dialogues entitled *Global Civilisation: A Buddhist-Islamic Dialogue*, and within the context of discussing human rights discourse and the hubris of the Enlightenment project, Daisaku Ikeda and Majid Tehranian draw out a theme important to this contention:

Tehranian: We still need a [generation to] move the focus away from human rights onto human caring and compassion. It would mean shifting discourse from rights to responsibilities, from legal precepts to social obligations, from the letter of the law to the spirit of the law, from minds to hearts.

Ikeda: [...] I myself feel that the discourse on human rights [...] is now approaching the level of the teachings of the world's religions, including Shakyamuni's idea of compassion. Let me relate an anecdote [...].One day Shakyamuni encounters a sick person. He bathes the person's body with a cloth, washes the dirty bedding, and dries it in the sun. Shakyamuni then tells his disciples that, "Helping the sick is the same thing as serving the Buddha."

Tehranian: What the sutra is saying, then, is that compassion does not mean giving alms or doing something charitable from someone below you, but acting for that person out of a feeling of respect.

Ikeda: Because to show compassion is to venerate the Buddha, if anything it expresses a sense of doing service for someone greater than yourself. In Buddhism, therefore, an altruistic act is considered a practice that elevates oneself.

Tehranian: That makes a lot of sense. It really is a noble way of thinking [...].[3]

As the *sutra* recounted in the above dialogue represents, Buddhism is concerned first and foremost with the everyday and everyday-suffering; in

---

[3] Daisaku Ikeda and Majid Tehranian, *Global Civilisation: A Buddhist—Islamic Dialogue* (London: British Academic Press, 2000), pp. 117–118.

a world of globalizing, self-interested greed, Buddhism holds at it's foundation the conviction that "Whatever joy there is in this world / All comes from desiring others to be happy / And whatever suffering there is in this world / All comes from desiring myself to be happy."[4] This brings us to the notion of the transformation of the "three poisons" and its implications for an interfaith perspective on "Globalisation for the Common Good." .

THE TRANSFORMATION OF THE "THREE POISONS"

How might the Buddhist notion of the "three fires," popularised as the "three poisons," broaden (and perhaps deepen) the discourse of "Globalisation for the Common Good"? In pursuing this question we will be guided by the obvious interrogative of how Buddhist teachings from another time, culture, and intellectual language, taught in an age of localized social and economic interactions, might relate to the highly complex and increasingly globalised world in which we now live?

Often anglicised as "The Fire Sermon," the *Adittapariyaya Sutta* (*Samyutta Nikaya* XXXV, 28) is a discourse of the Pali Canon. In it, Gautama Buddha puts his view that born existence is on fire—inherently painful, burning, or driven by desire—but the fire is not necessary and can be cooled or ultimately quenched. This image of the "coolness" that ultimately quenches the fire is the central meaning of *nibbana* (*nirvana*, in Sanskrit) in Buddha's philosophy.

Thus, Buddha's argument is devoted to convincing us of the existence of this fire and motivating us to put it out and his method for cooling the fire took the form of a number of instructive arguments and techniques. In a generalised formulation we might summarize Gautama Buddha's "Fire Sermon" as arguing that we suffer, and cause others to suffer (*dukkha*), because of our own greed, hatred and ignorance (The "three fires" or "three poisons" are also variously translated as "desire, aversion, illusion" etc.).

Furthermore, we might say that the Buddha's teaching for overcoming this effect involves a transformation of these "three fires" or "three poisons," having first recognised their existence. This would entail, for example, transforming our greed into generosity, our hatred into loving-kindness, and our ignorance into wisdom; as is certainly the popularised interpretation. But what does such a teaching imply about the global societal situation we now find ourselves in?

---

[4] Aryasura, *The Marvellous Companion, Jatakamala: Life Stories of the Buddha*, Dharma Publishing, 1983, p. 65.

The argument of David Loy, in an article in *Tikkun* magazine entitled "The Three Poisons, Institutionalized," is that the Buddhist principle of the "three poisons" can help us to understand the connection between our collective selves and collective *dukkha*, where "our present economic system institutionalizes greed, our militarism institutionalizes ill-will, and our corporate media institutionalize delusion [...], the problem is not only that the three poisons operate collectively but that they have taken on a life of their own. Today it is crucial for us to wake up and face the implications of these three institutionalized poisons."[5] Picking up on Loy's point, we might posit that while *dharma* practice traditionally focuses on transforming the poisons in the individual, the problem today is complicated by the institutionalisation of the "poisons," equally in need of transformation.

As Stephen Batchelor writes of Buddhism: "The contemporary social engagement of dharma practice is rooted in awareness of how self-centred confusion and craving can no longer be adequately understood only as psychological drives that manifest themselves in subjective states of anguish. We find these drives embodied in the very economic, military, and political structures that influence the lives of the majority of people on earth."[6] In a related observation Noam Chomsky finds that the corporate goal "is to ensure that the human beings who [it is] interacting with, you and me, also become inhuman. You have to drive out of people's heads natural sentiments like care about others, or sympathy, or solidarity [...]. The ideal is to have individuals who are totally disassociated from one another, who don't care about anyone else [...] whose conception of themselves, their sense of value, is 'Just how many created wants can I satisfy?'"[7]

And as Vandana Shiva writes in an online article titled "Globalisation and its Fallout," "The fundamentalism of the market and the fundamentalism of ideologies of hate and intolerance are rooted in fear—fear of the other, fear of the capacity and creativity of the other, fear of the sovereignty of the other. We are witnessing the worst expressions of organized violence of humanity against humanity because we are witnessing the wiping out of philosophies of inclusion, compassion, and solidarity. This is the highest cost of globalization—it is destroying our very capacity to be human. Rediscovering our humanity is the highest

---

[5] David Loy, "The Three Poisons, Institutionalized."
http://www.tikkun.org/magazine/tik0706/frontpage/poisons
[6] Stephen Batchelor, *Buddhism Without Beliefs: A Contemporary Guide To Awakening* (London: Bloomsbury, 1997), p. 112.
[7] Quoted in Joel Bakan, *The Corporation* (London: Constable, 2004), pp. 134–135.

imperative to resist and reverse this inhuman project. The debate on globalization is not about the market or the economy. It is about remembering our common humanity and the danger of forgetting the meaning of being human."[8]

What comes through in these analyses is that today's global consumer culture nurtures the "three poisons" of greed, hatred and ignorance on both an individual and collective level. As such, the "three poisons" can be found to be to some extent present in every human being, but reflected in, and also encouraged by, our institutions and structures.

So, in search of a response to "disassociation" and the "destruction of our capacity to be human," a Buddhist perspective highlights two interrelated phenomena. Firstly, the ultimate source of the imbalance in the distribution of the world's resources and the violence to which this imbalance gives rise ("the cost of globalization") is rooted in the individual human tendency to the "three poisons" of greed, hatred and ignorance. Secondly, the "three poisons" have become institutionalised in our political, economic and media structures which now depend upon the promotion the same (in the individual) for their survival.

In this way a Buddhist perspective leads us to see that what we should respond to and how we should respond, beginning with the very acknowledgement of the existence of the "three poisons" at a personal, individual level and at an institutional and collective, societal level; hence, both aspects of the phenomena need to be tackled simultaneously.

As Pankaj Mishra in his recent book *An End to Suffering: The Buddha in the World* argues: "I began to see [...] what the Buddha had stressed to the helpless people caught in the chaos of his own time: how the mind, where desire, hatred and delusion run rampant, creating the glories and defeats of the past as well as the hopes for the future, and the possibility for endless suffering, is also the place—the only one—where human beings can have full control of their lives."[9] Again, this suggests that a Buddhist response to globalisation begins with everyone truly practicing to understand himself or herself.

The imperative of such a Buddhist response is articulated by bell hooks in an interview in the July 2006 issue of *Shambala Sun*: "Great moments for social justice have occurred [...] but these movements have also been deeply flawed, in that they could not sustain themselves." She continues, "What's needed is a Buddha-like process of self-actualizing that spreads

---

[8] Vandana Shiva, "Globalisation and its Fallout."
http://www.globenet3.org/Articles/Article_Globalization_Shiva.shtml
[9] Pankaj Mishra, *An End to Suffering: Buddhism in the World* (London: Picador, 2004), p. 402.

into the political world [...]. We know from Buddhism, if we look for the end, we will despair and not sustain our efforts. But if we see it as a continual process of awakening then we can move forward."[10] Thus only on this basis, grounded in a recognition that we are all, as individuals, part of and responsible for the collective, can we then actively work together to transform the "three poisons" at that level. Mishra writes, "ultimately this kind of deepening and ethicizing of everyday life was part of the Buddha's bold and original response to the intellectual and spiritual crisis [...] [of his] time. In much of what he said and did he addressed the suffering of human beings deprived of old consolations of faith and community— human beings adrift in the world" (p. 403).

Indeed, the nature of the response suggested here clearly involves much self-awareness and honesty and introspection, but perhaps above it all it requires the slow erosion of our naive faith in selfish living as a viable source of personal happiness—motivated by the understanding that, surely, in the last analysis, it is our own wilful ignorance, empowered by our own greed and hatred, that fuel systemic, institutional greed and hatred.

Strange though it might sound then, the Buddhist teaching of the "three poisons" leads us to see that despite or rather because of the ruthless and violent nature of the system facing us, the only realistic individual, social, and political antidote to Batchelor's "self-centred confusion," Chomksy's "created wants" or Vandana Shiva's "inhuman project," to our "collective dukkha," is the kind of personal radical awareness required to bring about a transformation of the "poisons"—in ourselves and ultimately in our structures and institutions.

Although we Westerners may find this naive or idealistic, presumably not many of us can claim to do so on the basis of personal experience. Can we honestly say that such radical personal awareness is at the heart of our own response to the manifest destructive side of globalisation?

---

[10] bell hooks, quoted in Barry Boyce, "Love Fights the Power" *Shambhala Sun*, July 2006, pp. 57, 96.
http://www.shambhalasun.com/index.php?option=com_content&task=view&id=2939&Itemid=0

THE POWER OF AHIMSĀ (NONVIOLENCE): GANDHI'S GIFT TO A VIOLENT WORLD

Ruwan Palapathwala

Gandhi once said, "in this age of the rule of brute force, it is almost impossible for anyone to believe that anyone else could possibly reject the law of the final supremacy of brute force."[1] Although it is nearly six decades or so since he pronounced these words the truth they reveal has remained unchanged to this very day. The scale of destruction we witness across the globe today and the economic and political imperialism which has engulfed the world in the form of globalisation in the twenty-first century have come to mirror and embody various aspects of this "brute force" which Gandhi called *himsā* (violence). Gandhi's teaching was that *ahimsā* (nonviolence) alone is the antidote for this violation of life. His message that *ahimsā* is a universally applicable spiritual reality and that it is the most fundamental means to self-knowledge, to social truth, justice, and happiness offers us a significant alternative to work with for the betterment of our world.

While it is the view of some that the political and economic conditions that were created by the two Great Wars contributed to the ending of British rule in India, the role that Gandhi's *satyagraha* (soul force) movement played in the process also cannot be overlooked. The optimism that the same soul force can morally and spiritually win over brute force once again led me to write this essay. Through answering five questions I will explain Gandhi's understanding of *ahimsā* and demonstrate its capacity as a powerful spiritual instrument by which we may transform the conditions of a violent world for the good of humanity and all creation.

WHAT DOES GHANDI MEAN BY "NON-VIOLENCE"?

At the outset, it can be said that Gandhi's teaching of *ahimsā* is based on the classical Indian philosophy of God-realisation and its penultimate experience of union with the Divine—the state in which one can say: *tat twam asi*, I am, Thou art. However, in developing his notion of *ahimsā* Gandhi goes beyond this Vedic and ascetic static notion of ultimate union with the Divine and reconstitutes this process of becoming or God-realisation into a moral action. Gandhi does this by firmly anchoring his

---

[1] Richard Attenborough (ed.), *Gandhi: In My Own Words* (London: Hodder and Stoughton, 2002), p. 39.

religious outlook in the classical Indic position of God-realisation while adopting, at the same time, the dynamism Buddha introduced to the static state of "being That" as a means of wayfaring towards the Divine. For Gandhi, this dynamic life process is the spiritual development of the inner truth for social good which has moral duty as its most essential perquisite. The outworking of this moral duty is what is meant by the word *ahimsā* and the breadth of its meaning can be best explained by understanding what he means by violence or *himsā*. Gandhi explains violence in three ways: as "killing," "killing by inches," and "tearing."

For Gandhi the Sanskrit word *ahimsā*—which can also be translated as "non-killing"—is too limiting if it is taken only to mean the material ending of physical life. This is so because for Gandhi killing primarily refers to the soul—the life principle. However, since the soul is imperishable, *ahimsā* cannot mean non-killing. Therefore, he defines *himsā* as injury done or suffering caused. The only exception is when it is done for the greater benefit of a society or an individual who would otherwise suffer the injury (e.g. stopping a tyrant and amputating a leg to save life). By *himsā* Gandhi also means killing for the sake of the destructible body. Such killing includes activities such as eating, breathing, walking, and occupying space. In this sense of the word physical embodiment itself can mean *himsā*.

"Killing by inches" means two things for Gandhi. Firstly, it means the interruption of the soul's natural life and growth in the body. Secondly, its means the damage caused to the body which results from the effects that have culminated by obstructing the soul's natural life. This killing, which can injure the physical, emotional, or mental make up of an individual, Gandhi calls "tearing." Terror, repression, humiliation, systematic false trade, starvation, and chronic under-nourishment are examples of such violence.

Gandhi's interpretation of *himsā* indicates clearly that the negative particle "non" in the word "nonviolence" does not mean that it is a negative force. Gandhi said that he had to coin the word "nonviolence" "to bring out the root meaning of *ahimsā*."[2] For him *ahimsā* is a spiritual force which has the *atmā*—the soul—as its source of origin. This understanding enables him to make nonviolence an absolute force and maintain that in the same way as the soul does not depend on the physical body for its existence, "similarly, nonviolence, or soul-force, does not need physical aid for its propagation or effect. It acts independently of them. It transcends time and space."[3]

---

[2] Mohandas K. Gandhi, *Non-Violence in Peace and War* (Ahmedabad: Navajivan Press, 1945), Vol.1, pp. 121–22.

[3] Mohandas K. Gandhi, *The Law of Love*, ed. Anand T. Hingorani, 2nd edn (Bombay; Bharatiya Vidya Bhavan, 1962), p. 11.

Therefore, for him, *ahimsā* is *the* "greatest and the activist force in the world" (*Non-Violence*, pp. 121–22). He believed that his activities of nonviolence—*satyagraha*—were channels for this force to come to effect. So when he describes an act of "nonviolence" what he means is that the soul-force has the effectiveness to nullify the evil in violence. Therefore, according to Gandhi, "nonviolence" is not "un-violence"; it is the restraint of expected violence resulting from the spiritual force.

WHY IS THERE VIOLENCE IN THE WORLD?

Gandhi answers this question by bringing together the views of two schools of Hindu philosophy: the schools of non-duality and duality. By taking this position he claims to be both an *advaitist* (believer in non-dual subsistent reality underlying all reality) and a *dvaitist* (believer in dualism). By holding this dual position he affirms two opposing philosophical views by maintaining that:

- there is an essential unity of humanity and all that lives.
- we experience two forces, "God and Satan," in the world which we experience at an empirical level. This empirical world for Gandhi is the world of duality where evil is real. Based on this understanding, he maintains the principle dichotomy of violence and non-violence, he equates violence with evil and believes that all analysis of the empirical world proceeds in terms of this dichotomy.

The paradox of Gandhi's position is that while he believes in the goodness of the all pervading God who is One, it is God who creates in this world what human beings imagine as evil. For Gandhi, this imaginary evil is an incentive for human beings, as moral beings, to struggle against actively. Therefore, while evil is ultimately imaginary, it is real and the moral imagination which creates it follows its own laws. According to Gandhi, human beings can sustain themselves in the world "only by assuming the existence of the imaginary dual to be real."[4] His fundamental claim here is that God creates this evil in our mental consciousness to induce the activity, virtues, and discrimination which can eventually lead us to our ultimate goal—God-realisation.

(3) WHAT IS THE PHILOSOPHICAL BASIS OF GHANDI'S *AHIMSĀ*?

---

[4] Mohandas K. Gandhi *In Search of the Supreme*, 3 vols, ed. V.B. Kher (Ahmedabad: Navajivan Press, 1961), Vol. 1, p. 226.

It is well-known that the *Bhagavat Gītā* was Gandhi's constant companion and inspiration.[5] In spite of the fact that the word *ahimsā* only appears four times in the *Bhagavat Gītā*, verses 54–72 in Chapter II of the *Gītā* were particularly important for Gandhi's development of his concept of *ahimsā*. In *Shloka* 54, Arjuna asks Krishna, "Who is the person of poise, Krishna? Who is steady in devotion? How does this person speak, rest, walk?" Krishna's answer—*sthita-prajya*, the steady minded person whose consciousness is established in the Spirit—provides Gandhi with his archetype of the nonviolent person. *Sthita-prajya* is the ideal person who subdues desires, anger, ignorance, malice, and other passions and thus cultivates restraint, selflessness, and detachment. Because this person is content in the *atman* he is above the mutual pulling and tearing of material forces and therefore causes no *himsā*. *Sthita-prajya*, therefore, is the one who discovers and cherishes the truth which transcends matter, the *atman*—the life principle—and can thus speak out of his innermost conviction that he is not this body but *atman* and that he may use the body only with a view to expressing *atman*, i.e. self-realisation. By this exercise of restraint *sthita-prajya* progressively grows in the power to express nonviolence even in his material make-up.

From this understanding of the ideal person and *sthita-prajya*'s identification with the *atman*, Gandhi proceeds to define Truth as moral authenticity and equates Truth with nonviolence. "Moral authenticity" is what *sthita-prajya* represents: his outer conduct is guided by his inner status. Espousing such action, Gandhi believes, brings into the world the moral quality of "Truth." Conversely, he believes that the Truth involved in moral authenticity leads to nonviolence. Therefore, he says: "We have to live a life of *ahimsā* in the midst of a world of *himsā* and that is possible only if we cling to Truth. That is how I deduce *ahimsā* from Truth" (*Law of Love*, pp. 4–5).

(4) WHAT GIVES THIS PHILOSOPHY ITS DYNAMISM?

My view is that Gandhi adopts the dynamism he found in Buddhism to demonstrate how *sthita-prajya*'s experience of Truth can be implemented as a progressive moral ideology. Gandhi's indebtedness to Buddhism has been noted on several occasions. One of the most revealing confessions is found in a letter which he wrote to a Burmese friend in 1919, saying, "When in 1890 or 1891 I became acquainted with the teaching of Buddha, my eyes

---

[5] *The Bhagavad Gita*, trans. P. Lal (New Delhi: Roli Books, 1994).

were opened to the limitless possibilities of nonviolence."[6] In another context Gandhi said that the Buddha was the greatest teacher of *ahimsā* and that he "taught us to defy appearances and trust in the final triumph of Truth and Love."[7] Since the word *ahimsā* does not occur frequently either in the Buddhist scriptures or the commentaries, one may wonder how Buddhism came to give the dynamism to Gandhi's idea of *ahimsā*.

Mrs Rhys Davids, the eminent Buddhist scholar, claims in her *Outlines of Buddhism*[8] that the search for the *self* inwardly which is one in nature with the Highest—the *"progressive revelation of a More in man"* in the Upanishads, the pursuit seen as the Way leading to *Brahman*, the Ultimate, was the teaching that Buddha taught and on which he expanded (pp. 8–9, 19–20). Davids also refers to that *"More in man"* as "God-in-Man," "Divine Selfhood," "Very God," and *Mahattam* (the Great Self)" (pp. 12, 13, 55). Davids highlights two aspects of the early teaching which, she says, were Buddha's original contribution to the existing teaching of the Upanishads: (i) that "the true Becoming (where there is no decay) is in every [person], the spirit the soul"; (ii) substituting the Upanishadic teaching of attaining the splendid human knowledge of "I am, Thou art" from a static state of "being That" to the dynamic: "For the rapt complacency Buddha taught the divine unrest of the inner urge we call "duty," "conscience," and which India, though not then in religious terms, called *Dharma* (that which should be "borne," in mind, in heedfulness)" (p. 21). The outcome of this transition from the static to the dynamic is, she claims, that *Dharma* in Buddhism came to take prominence over the idea of *self* in the Brahmanic teaching. According to Davids, there is a further relational aspect to the "becoming more" that is found in the idea of "Amity (*Mettā*) and its kindred sentiments […] between man and man […] as an essential way of 'becoming More in wayfaring towards the Most'" (pp. 30–31). However, she sees the gradual disappearance of the "Way of Becoming," which she says is "now universally called not becoming, but Eightfold Way (more usually Path)" (p. 22). Consequently, while the Buddhist "never lost sight of the need of 'making become' this and that in thought and conduct," she says, the Buddhist "fell away" from seeing that "the Becoming was *the Way towards becoming 'That'* [The Most or *Self*]" (p. 38).

---

[6] Quoted in Raghavan Lyer, *The Moral and Political Thought of Mahatma Gandhi* (Oxford: Oxford University Press, 1973), p. 226.
[7] Mohandas K. Gandhi, *The Collected Works of Mahatma Gandhi*, 82 vols (New Delhi: Government of India Publications. 1959), Vol. 40, p. 160.
[8] Caroline A. F. Rhys Davids, *Outlines of Buddhism*. (New Delhi: Oriental Books Reprint Corporation, Munshiram Manoharlal, 1978).

While Davids' interpretation is less acceptable to the Theravādians, I am of the opinion that she provides us with a helpful framework to interpret how Gandhi himself may have understood Buddha's message and the dynamism he had introduced to the process of becoming or God-realisation.

(5) HOW DOES NON-VIOLENCE WORK AS A MORAL PHILOSOPHY?

Because Gandhi believes that the quality of evil is a material quality which belongs to the empirical word and thus arises and resides in the psycho-physical phenomenon of the human person, he says that only a force whose origin is spiritual and whose power is greater than that of any material force can conquer violence. For this reason his actions of nonviolence and methods employed do not attempt to rearrange the material elements of the phenomenal order, but rather draw into action this spiritual force of the soul which alone, he claims, has the power to change the quality of human relations. To that extent, for Gandhi, *ahimsā* is a universally applicable force and *satyagraha* was the art of bringing the effect of this spiritual force to remedy the ills of the world. At large, what Gandhi seeks to do is to employ this soul-force to eradicate evil that manifests in society in the forms of social and political injustice. Then, for Gandhi, *ahimsā* is a means to truth—it is the path to seeking social truth and justice for all.

CONCLUSION

In spite of the seeming idealism of *ahimsā* and the impossibility of its achievement by ordinary human beings, Gandhi says, "I am not a visionary. I claim to be a practical idealist. The religion of nonviolence is not meant merely for the *rishis* and saints. It is meant for the common people as well. Nonviolence is the law of our species as violence is the law of the brute" (Attenborough, 43–44).

Ultimately, the driving force for nonviolence is based on one coming to a consciousness, a living awareness that one's soul is identical with God, and so with all humanity and all creation. In short, his position is that since the ultimate aim of humanity is the realisation of God, all our activities—social, political, and religious—have to be directed by that ultimate goal. If this is achieved, the experience of the divine will be made manifest in life. In this way, Gandhi offers his methods of nonviolence as the "sovereign" means for the realisation of Truth through this moral struggle.

In a world that is increasingly violent and seeks to resolve conflicts and establish peace by the means of war and threats of pre-emptive strikes, Gandhi's call to embrace a path of nonviolence is a beacon of hope for us. Furthermore, in a world where religious fundamentalism is on the rise in the forms of militant Islam and the Religious Right, to note that Gandhi's understanding of nonviolence is fundamentally an interfaith one is of great significance.

The forcefulness of Gandhi's teaching of *ahimsā* is that he grounds this sublime truth in the reality of our empirical world and admits that nonviolence is an unattainable ideal. However, his argument is that it is an ideal which must be constantly striven for as if achievable. Gandhi's realism aligns us with the central Vedic teaching from which he proceeds and expands on for practical application—the fundamental aim and yearning of humanity for God-realisation and attaining it through moral action. Therefore, it is this yearning—or as our Muslims brothers and sisters say, the *jihad al nafs*—the struggle for one's soul against one's own base instinct—which can give us that dynamic impulse to resist violence and work for the transformation and betterment of humanity.

PLENARY PAPERS

MASS MEDIA, GLOBAL COMMUNICATION AND PEACEMAKING

MASS MEDIA, GLOBALIZATION, AND INFORMATION GAP

Yahya Kamalipour

In our contemporary global environment, information is the key to understanding and dealing with social, political, financial, and other aspects of our lives. Most of us, regardless of geographical location, rely heavily for our daily news and information on the mass media. In fact, it would be practically impossible for us to imagine a world without the media. Unfortunately, one of the problems is that the media, in their relentless race for obtaining higher audience ratings and disseminating news in a speedy manner, often overlook the social, political, economic, and emotional implications of their coverage of epidemics.

Some of the main functions of mass media, in addition to providing news and information, include entertainment, education, commerce (making profits), persuasion (propaganda and advertising).

Collectively, the mass media are highly influential and effective in raising public awareness, increasing knowledge, informing, and changing peoples' attitudes and behavior both nationally and globally. It is through the mass media that we learn about a wide range of issues such as politics, war, natural disasters, health, crimes, achievements, sports, arts, and famine. Our dependency on the media was illustrated in a newspaper cartoon in which a child is standing in front of his father. The caption reads, "Dad, if a tree falls in the forest and the media aren't there to cover it, has the tree really fallen?"[1]

The mass media, like other institutions or businesses, have their own priorities and limitations. For instance, they (1) are a major part of the global economy, (2) are in the business of making a profit, (3) rely on advertising dollars for their survival, (4) are marketing and advertising channels for manufacturers, (5) are run by professionals who are not trained in dealing with medical and scientific issues, (6) tend to be sensational in order to attract viewers, and (7) tend to be biased in covering certain issues and events.

Globalization is a vast and multifaceted process that cannot be easily defined. In fact there are as many definitions as there are disciplines. Nonetheless, according to Tollison and Willett the following explanation

---

[1] Drawing by Robert Mankoff, *Saturday Review*, reprinted in Elisabeth Noelle-Neumann, *The Spiral of Silence: Public Opinion – Our Social Skin* (Chicago: University of Chicago Press, 1993), p. 150.

seems to capture the essence of this evolutionary process: Globalization has resulted in the *integration* of economics through increased *interdependence* among nations, *decreased* trade barriers, and the *generation* of open markets. Globalization is a process which is technologically driven and as this process continues to unfold, it leaves behind it some "winners" but many "losers."[2]

Globalization seems to benefit the advanced countries while damaging the economies of developing countries. According to the Information Society Index (ISI, 2000), "in digital terms, the rich countries are getting richer while the poor are too, but that digital divide between groups and societies will eventually grow larger and larger."

Based on the same ISI report, nations maybe divided into five groups. The variables that they used to categorize the nations were: (1) Computer infrastructure, (2) Internet Infrastructure, (3) Information Infrastructure, and (4) Social infrastructure. The categories are:

SKATERS: Advanced countries that are in a strong position (technologically, economically, socially, and politically) to benefit from the Information Revolution. Examples would be Sweden, the United States, Finland, Australia, Japan, the United Kingdom, Germany, and so on.

STRIDERS: Have the necessary infrastructure in place and are moving forward. Examples would be Belgium, Austria, France, Korea, and so on.

SPRINTERS: Nations that are shifting their priorities and at times seem to move forward by making the necessary adjustments. Example would be Poland, Chile, Argentina, Malaysia, Russia, Brazil, and so on.

STROLLERS: Moving ahead but in an inconsistent and limited manner. Examples world be Egypt, China, Indonesia, India, and so on.

STARTERS: Nations at the beginning of the road to information revolution which together constitute about 40% of the world's population.

Some of the obstacles among the Sprinters and Strollers include: Over population, lack of infrastructure, lack of resources, lack of planning and management.

---

[2] Robert D. Tollison and Thomas D. Willett, "International Integration and the Interdependence of Economic Variables," *International Organisation*, 7:2 (1973), 255–71.

Indeed, global problems require global cooperation and the global media can certainly play a crucial and decisive role in informing and educating their audiences about AIDS, poverty, health, the environment, and other contemporary matters.

Scholars adhering to the belief of globalization as a new phase of imperialism maintain that the emergence of a single global market is bringing about a "denationalization" of economies in which national governments are relegated to little more than transmission belts for global capital.[3] In Ohmae's terms, the older patterns of nation-to-nation linkage have lost their dominance in economics as in politics.[4] In other words, nation-states have already lost their role as meaningful units of participation in the global economy of today's borderless world.

According to Miyoshi, transnational corporations have replaced nation states to continue colonialism. In the current period of Third Industrial Revolution, even though the nation-state still performs certain functions such as defining citizenship, controlling currency, providing education, and maintaining security, its autonomy has been greatly compromised and thoroughly appropriated by transnational corporations.[5] In the realm of communication, Hamelink observes that today's global governance system differs from the system operated during the past one hundred years in that the old system existed to coordinate national policies that were independently shaped by sovereign governments, while the new system determines supranationally the space that national governments have for independent policy making.[6]

In fact, the information and economic gap or the digital divide between the "haves" and "have-nots" has increased dramatically. For instance, according to the World Bank, since 1997, the percentage of population living on less than One-Dollar-a-day has more than doubled. This is in view of the fact that the dominant global corporations, with governmental

---

[3] David Held, Anthony McGrew, David Goldblatt, and Jonathan Perraton, *Global Transformations: Politics, Economics and Culture* (Stanford, CA: Stanford University Press, 1999).

[4] Kenichi Ohmae, *The End of the Nation State: The Rise of Regional Economics* (New York: The Free Press, 1995).

[5] Masao Miyoshi, "A Borderless World? From Colonialism to Transnationalism and the Decline of the Nation-State," in *Global/Local: Cultural Production and the Transnational Imaginary*, ed. R. Wilson and W. Dissanayake (Durham, NC: Duke University, 1996), pp. 78–106.

[6] Cees J. Hamelink, "The Politics of Global Communication," in *Global Communication*, 2nd edn, ed. Y. R. Kamalipour (Belmont, CA: Cengage Learning, 2007), pp. 161–187.

support, continue to increase their size (through mergers), global reach, and income.

Consider the growth of a once relatively small corporation, *Times Inc.* In recent years, Times has acquired Warner Brothers, Turner Broadcasting, and America Online—through mergers—to become one of the largest media conglomerates in the world.

Other major global media players include Walt Disney, News Corp., Sony, Vivendi Universal, Viacom, and Berletsmann. These corporations have their hands in practically every mode of communication that you can imagine—movies, books, radio, television, magazines, newspapers, consumer products, and more. Today a handful of media conglomerates produce and distribute most of what we see, read, and hear through the global media around the world.

In general, people throughout the world are more alike than different but, unfortunately, we tend to focus on what sets us apart rather than what brings us together. What is missing in today's global environment is a collective effort to empower peoples and nations so that they can not only solve their internal social, political, and economic problems but benefit from the enormous wealth which is generated globally.

What is needed is a concerted effort by the mass media, transnational corporations, health organizations, governmental and non-governmental organizations to join hands and focus their resources and energies on funding research, finding remedies, saving lives, educating, and informing people in a balanced, fair, and truthful manner.

As a concerned teacher, scholar, and human being, I am quite perplexed by the complexity and immensity of the social, political, economic, communication, relational, and environmental problems that face our global community today. Hence, I consider it my duty to do whatever I can—in cooperation with other likeminded individuals, such as yourselves—to devise mechanisms and new communication channels, such as *Journal of Globalization for the Common Good* and *Global Media Journal*, that will help us to explore, discuss, share, inform, and educate as many people as possible. As the saying goes, in this Information Age, knowledge is power.

GLOBALIZATION AND GLOCALIZATION: LEVERAGING TECHNOLOGICAL TOOLS TO SERVE THE COMMON GOOD

Christopher Kosovich

PUTTING WEBSITES TO WORK

The internet is the mechanism through which one gains access to websites. The internet is increasingly making websites one of the most essential tools for non-profit and activist organizations.[1] A website can be an extremely cost effective method of making information available to a public audience. Domain names can be purchased for less than ten dollars per year with many website hosting options costing less than ten dollars per month. Some host providers even offer free website hosting services to registered non-profit organizations.[2]

The mere presence of non-profit and activist organizations on the internet has given them equality in status to corporations and these websites are levelling the playing field between large and small organizations.[3] Today a small non-profit or activist organization with few funding dollars can present an image of the organization on the computer screen that can rival a transnational corporation with a multi-million dollar budget. Regardless of the size of an organization, a computer screen has a limited amount of space for presenting information. A website can be a powerful tool to engage audiences and provide access to information. Exactly how organizations are using the limited amount of space on the computer screen is becoming increasingly important for organizing information so that audiences can use the information presented in meaningful ways.

Despite having a web presence, some non-profit and non-governmental organizations struggle to get information to the right people at the right place and time. Such low costs for web publishing have now made it possible to publish content for public consumption with fewer barriers than

---

[1] W. Timothy Coombs, "The Internet as Potential Equalizer: New Leverage for Confronting Social Irresponsibility," *Public Relations Review*, 24:3 (1998), 289–304.

[2] Dreamhost.,"Non-Profit Discount."
http://wiki.dreamhost.com/Non-profit_Discount

[3] Maureen Taylor, Michal L., Kent and William J.White, "How Activist Organizations are Using the Internet to Build Relationships," *Public Relations Review*, 27 (2001), 263–284.

in the past, but some technical and information design issues continue to persist.

With advances in technology, simply having a website presence displaying virtually the same content that may exist in an organization's paper publications and brochures is not enough to keep pace with the tools and behaviors of internet users today.

Producers of information in small and large organizations compete on a similar playing field when communicating via the internet. Regardless of the budget of the content producer, communicating effectively via the internet is heavily dependent upon a variety of factors.

Exploring Web Publishing Needs

Seeking to understand websites and internet communication from the perspective of information architecture will help to emphasize how content management systems can help non-profit organizations maximize the return on investment in their internet based communication technologies.

Information architecture is defined by Morville and Rosenfeld as

- The structured design of shared information environments;
- The combination of organization, labelling, search, and navigation systems within web sites and intranets;
- The art and science of shaping information products and experiences to support usability and findability;
- An emerging discipline and community of practice focused on bringing principles of design and architecture to the digital landscape.[4]

Information architecture is a perspective that can help one examine an existing website and begin to look at the content with a new set of eyes and begin shaping that content for maximum usability by the audience(s).

Quality information architecture design is informed by three major areas according to Morville and Rosenfeld. Understanding the business goals along with resources available for design and implementation, understanding the nature and volume of content that exists today and how this will change in the future, and understanding the information-seeking behaviors of the audience are all important factors to consider when organizing information on a website and selecting tools to aid the

---

[4] Peter Morville, and Lou Rosenfeld, *Information Architecture for the World Wide Web* (Sebastopol, CA: O'Reilly Media, 2007), p. 4.

publishing and information organization process (Morville and Rosenfeld, *passim*).

Through the lens of the information architecture perspective, one can examine a website as a container of information where information needs to be organized for the audience(s) to use the information in meaningful ways.

One of the first steps to organizing the content is identifying the type of container the content will be put inside. An increasingly common type of container for content is known as a content management system. A content management system provides the ability to impose consistency on unstructured content and enables publishers to edit and manage content without expert help.[5]

CONTENT MANAGEMENT SYSTEMS: DESIGN AND IMPLEMENTATION

Fortunately powerful "open source" software applications already exist for solving many web based communication challenges and these "open source" options are available without the associated licensing fees that are required by private or corporate owned software providers.

"Open source" software is essentially source code that has been made available for free that has been developed by computer programmers around the world.[6] These "open source" software applications also provide complete access to how the software functions and can be adapted to fit the unique needs of content producers.

There are many content management systems that have already been designed for a simple functional installation on a website. As a result of the "open source" movement, content management systems developed through this model continue to evolve into more mature and sophisticated products through the efforts of developers all over the world. Their design is evolving as the behaviors of internet users continue to evolve. It makes sense for organizations with limited funding for web development to utilize "open source" content management systems rather than designing and building custom content management system applications.

When examining resources, particularly for non-profit and non-governmental organizations, licensing issues can quickly drain budgets. Identifying "open source" options for software opens new doors for publishing content in a much more organized fashion that lets the publisher

---

[5] Rama Ramaswami, "Keep Up or Fall Behind" *Campus Technology*, 20:11 (July 2007), 40–48.

[6] Chris DiBona, Sam Ockman, and Mark Stone, *Open Sources: Voices of the Open Source Revolution* (Sebastopol, CA: O'Reilly and Associates, 1999).

focus more on the content and organization of information and less on the technical aspects of publishing a website.

It is important to note that despite the computer programming code that runs the core features of a content management system, organizations have the ability to completely brand the public view of the website to match the particular organization's style including logos, colors, and writing style. This means that websites one currently visits have a completely unique look and feel from the user experience on the public side of the website, very different from the administrative back-end of the website. The computer code that drives the website in the background is similar to other websites that are running from the same version of content management software but the graphic design can match the look and feel of the organization using the content management system to publish the website.

Two popular "open source" content management system software options are WordPress and Joomla. Choosing between these two particular brands of content management systems will depend on the volume and style of content one intends to publish but the design and implementation of each system from the perspective of a content producer are similar.

Each of these "open source" software options is available for download for free from their respective websites, www.wordpress.org and www.joomla.org. Both of these software options have hundreds of customizable modules, also available for free download, that help the content producer or publisher of the website to tailor the exact design of a website to suit the particular needs of the intended audience. Each content management system software option lists the technical website hosting requirements on their respective websites but those specific requirements are beyond the scope of this article.

It is most important to know that such software options exist. Smaller organizations with small budgets are able to leverage free "open source" software options and invest in expert technical web communication specialist support to help establish a website on a content management framework. Rather than investing development in a custom content management system, organizations can gain a head-start by building on a system that already exists and functions. It is like the familiar phrase, "no assembly required" where one is able to use a new product immediately after opening up the product box. These "open source" options listed above are ready to be used immediately after installation with the option of performing extensive further customization but often such customization isn't absolutely necessary.

After the initial installation and module customization the organization can then focus on publishing content to the website without technical expertise every time a new piece of information needs to be added to the website. Content on the website can be organized and positioned on a website through web-based interfaces that are user friendly and most often require no knowledge of web programming languages. This puts even the most novice internet user in a position to be an internet publisher. Essentially, posting a new article to the website can be as easy as posting a message on an internet messageboard or sending an e-mail to a friend.

SELECTING A CONTENT MANAGEMENT SYSTEM: VOLUME AND TYPES OF PUBLISHING

The two examples of "open source" content management systems presented in this article are WordPress and Joomla. While both of these are technically content management systems, each has unique strengths and weaknesses and understanding the volume of content publishing an organization will demand can help a content producer determine the best content management solution to select.

WordPress is a simple content management system that displays content published to the website in a chronological order on the main homepage. Samples of this system may be found at the WordPress website at www.wordpress.org. When WordPress is installed in the original default setup, the website content appears to resemble a blog or weblog with new content appearing at the top of a list of all content posted to the website in chronological order.

A publisher using WordPress to manage information on a website also has the option of making a particular information posting to a website appear out of the chronological order on the website and appear as an actual webpage. This option is available in the administrative interface of the WordPress content management system. All content management systems have a public interface where anyone with an internet connection and browser has the ability to read content. These content management systems also have an administrative interface where the publisher must login using a username and password to add new information to the website or make changes to existing information. Only users with administrative permissions to a website may post information for the public to see in a content management system.

Publishers requiring a greater level of specificity for categorizing and manipulating content on the homepage of a website might select the "open source" Joomla content management system as an alternative to WordPress. Joomla provides the publisher, through the administrative interface, with the ability to select the priority importance of items appearing on the homepage based upon each particular piece of information rather than simply based upon chronological order.

There are other distinguishing characteristics of Joomla that can be experienced by visiting the www.joomla.org website to try the demonstration system from both the public and administrative perspectives.

Content Management Systems in Action: Understanding the Audience

While content management systems assist the publisher with organizing and categorizing information, attending to the audience(s) and the information seeking behaviors they exhibit is critical for building relationships and supporting relationship building among audience members.

Fortunately, the "open source" content management systems WordPress and Joomla do more than categorize information on websites. These systems have a variety of modules that enable a non-technical publisher to upload special modules, plug-ins, and components that enhance the user experience for the visitors of the website.

For example, WordPress has a special plug-in that enables the entire website to be translated into several different languages. This requires no special technical expertise. Uploading the module to the website is as easy as attaching a document to an e-mail message. A publisher downloads the plug-in from the wordpress.org website and then uploads the plug-in to the publisher's own website and activates the plug-in through the administrative interface. Instantly the ability to translate the website into several languages exists.

The ability to offer such functionality is radically different from website publishing of just a few years ago before the more refined and mature content management systems such as WordPress and Joomla came into existence. Organizations can now leverage the collective development that has been invested into these "open source" content management software applications by thousands of computer programmers around the world. It is the collective effort of these developers in the spirit of supporting the common good of internet communication that enables organizations of all sizes to have the ability to create dynamic digital environments where people can learn and interact.

Discussion

Non-governmental, non-profit, and scholarly content producers are leveraging increasingly dynamic internet-based technological solutions to distribute content. In our society of globalization as we are now digitally linked, information is crossing borders faster than ever before.[7]

As communication technology has reduced barriers and opened access to new information, content publishers are able to build upon these new technologies and engage new audiences that were previously unattainable. Plug-in modules in content management systems that translate websites help to focus website content on a localized audience in the local language while also providing the option to also speak to a global audience.

Not long ago it would have been cost prohibitive for the budgets of some non-profit and activist organizations to translate an organization brochure into five different languages and make it available on three different continents. Now, with the aid of content management systems such as WordPress and Joomla, it is possible to translate an entire non-profit website into many different languages anywhere on the globe with internet access at a fraction of the cost. Access to information for local audiences, as well as global audiences, can be satisfied thorough the use of "open source" content management software.

Additionally, because all information in a content management system is stored in a database, new opportunities for sharing information have come to exist. As a content publisher posts new content on an organization website, the headline associated with a news article on that website is now in a position to be picked up in syndication readers inside the portals that are used by internet users. This means if a user finds a website valuable, a link to the website can be added to a personalized portal which increases the likelihood that the user will visit the website again in the future.

For example, a user may login to their personalized google.com portal by visiting google.com and clicking the "igoogle" link at the top of the page. Perhaps the user wishes to see headlines from a non-profit organization website upon every login to the personalized portal on the same screen where other services such as personal e-mail, calendar, and other favorite items exist. A user may simply type the URL or website domain name of the non-profit organization where content is stored inside a content management system and the headlines from that organization's website will appear in the users personalized portal. A user then has the opportunity to determine if there is interest in any of the headlines and, if there is a desire to learn more, upon clicking the headline within the personalized portal the user is taken directly to the content on the non-profit organization's website.

---

[7] Daya K. Thussu, *International Communication: Continuity and Change* (New York: Oxford University Press, 2000).

Prior to content management technology and the possibility of syndication, a user would have to visit a non-profit organization's website just to see if anything had changed. If no new changes have occurred on that website after a few visits, a user may likely not return again. Now a user may login to a personal portal and perform other functions such as checking e-mail, personal calendar, and viewing other news alerts, and also monitor a favorite organization website without needing to intentionally visit the organization's website. Content management systems bring consistency to unstructured content and make that content portable so that other systems and devices are able to obtain content through recognized established formats.

An understanding of how "open source" software can be used to distribute content is critical for surviving in the global society while also accommodating local interests. Content management systems help to position information so the needs of multiple audiences are addressed with the least amount of redundant work by the content publisher. This is particularly important for non-profit organizations as resources are frequently scarce and funds are not available for large technical staff to support web based communication. Content management systems enable content producers within organizations of all sizes to focus on the mission of the organization while consistently publishing important content about the organization in a manner that engages audiences based upon their information-seeking behaviors at a lower cost than traditional methods of web publishing.

MASS MEDIA AS AN INSTRUMENT IN EDUCATIONAL COUNTER-TERRORISM PROGRAMS

Irena Chiru

Motto
Bad assumptions or misunderstandings
cannot lead to good policies or programs.

At first sight, in the triangle of terrorism, mass media, and government, the media would be associated with the fight against terror, siding with the governmental forces. Still, during the past four decades the majority of the mass media studies have insisted on their role as an essential factor and a weapon for disseminating terror. Moreover, the confluence of interest between the media—that is for unique, scoop news—and the terrorist organisations—that is even for a few minutes or words in the public area of expression (television, radio, or newspapers)—has raised debates about the possible complicity of today's media in terrorist acts. The common conclusion is that terrorism reacts and uses the mass media in the same way as the media take benefit from the terrorist acts.

Considering the high number of approaches to the subject, the differences in interpretation are small. Studies on the theme began in 1970s but since then there have not been major developments. Frederick Hacker noted that "if the mass media did not exist, terrorists would have to invent them. In turn, the mass media hanker after terrorist acts because they fit into their programming needs: namely sudden acts of great excitement that are susceptible, presumably, of quick solution. So there's a mutual dependency."[1] Raymond Tanter comments on the dilemma of the relationship, stating that "since the terror is aimed at the media and not at the victim, success is defined in terms of media coverage. And there is no way in the West that you could not have media coverage because you're dealing in a free society."[2] Most commentators have similarly accepted this

---

[1] Frederick Hacker, *Crusaders, Criminals, Crazies: Terror and Terrorism in Our Time* (New York: Bantam, 1978).
[2] Cited in Cindy C. Combs, *Terrorism in the Twenty-First Century* (New Jersey: Prentice Hall, 2003), p. 138.

interdependency of the media and terrorism, differing only in the details of how that interrelationship operates.[3]

The blood, the victims, the good or bad heroes, the political crime, the exotic, the mystery, the incomprehensible, are all current ingredients of the terrorist act as it is rendered profitable and spread by the media by virtue of the impact. "The terrorists have quickly accepted a major lesson: the mass-media are of crucial importance in their campaigns, the terrorist act itself is near to nothing, while the publicity is everything. Nevertheless, media, constantly needing diversity and new prospects, are false friends. The terrorists must constantly innovate. They are somehow the super-entertainment of our times."[4]

Terrorists often behave like specialists in communication and a fundamental component of terrorist strategy is the *media strategy*—that part of the terrorist activity which deliberately orientates it to media conversion. The latter implies particular ways of action, particular targets, particular weapons, which make up as many "recognising marks" expressing not just an ideology, but also a kind of marketing of that ideology.[5]

Elaborating veritable "media" or "marketing" plans targeting certain segments of the public, the terrorist organisation relies on two types of effects (ibid., p. 166). The first is the effect of *saturation*, obtained through multiple assaults concentrated over a short period of time, in randomly chosen public places. The result is a generalised state of panic and insecurity resulting from the possibility that such an attack may occur in any place, at any time (the example of Hamas). The second effect is that of *targeting* particular symbols of the aimed-at entity or particular known personalities. The result, in this case, is decreasing the general morale, but particularly decreasing the confidence in the capacity of the attacked system to keep the terrorist menace under control (the most eloquent in this case is the Al-Qaeda strategy within the last century).

Wieviorka and Wolton identified a series of risks with respect to manipulating the press by the terrorists through the instrumentality of

---

[3] For further discussion and documentation of critical analyses of the media/terrorism relationship, see Neil Hickey, "Gaining the Media's Attention," in *Struggle against Terrorism*, ed. William P. Lineberry (New York: Wilson, 1977) 45–62; William. E. Biernatzki, "Terrorism and Mass Media," in *Communication Research and Trends*, 21:1 (2002), p. 3–42. www.escc.scu.edu

[4] Walter Laqueur, *The Age of Terrorism* (Boston: Little, Brown and Company, 1987), 305.

[5] Jean-Luc Marret, *Tehnicile Terorismului* (Bucharest: Corint, 2002), p. 165.

internal and external conditioning of the mass media institutions.[6] A first risk deriving from the journalists' prime mission—giving information—lies in the possibility that the media *invent explanations* for the terrorist acts or take them over from politically involved sources, without having the necessary leisure and information for developing an adequate idea about what happens. Moreover, the motivations of competent journalists place their writings in the subjective sphere from the very beginning.

To get near the terrorist environment, a journalist must show a certain *fascination and empathy* for the manners of thinking and action particular to this environment. The terrorists may use this curiosity as a weapon of seduction. The risk of shifting from a neutral statement to an involved one, namely interpretations and justifications, increases proportionally to the journalist's getting closer to the environment which fascinates him. The terrorists are in fact interested in blocking the communication processes. Consequently they will only give information to a journalist provided that the latter gives the public what they want to be given.

Any other position adopted by the journalist entails wasting the hard and costly work of the journalistic investigation. The reporters are consequently confronted with a choice: they either report the phenomenon from the outside, depending on official versions, unclear and incompetent, or they seek to investigate at the core of the problem which, apart from the evident risks, makes them dependent on the manipulating message of the terrorists.

From this situation, another risk results, symmetrically opposed to the preceding one: the temptation to give too much credit to the official message (political, police, special services). Manipulation occurs, in this case not in relation to the facts, but through influencing of the framework of analysis, the perspective from which facts are presented in the context in which journalists derive their information.

James Curran gives a short survey of the virtually detrimental effects of the accentuated media shifting of the terrorist act. They are as follows:

- providing a platform for expressing the extremist concepts which bring about violence and undermine state authority;
- contagion—through the presentation of spectacular terrorist acts, the probability that other groups should also adopt the same methods increases;
- undermining ongoing police operations by presenting their working methods and devices etc. thus endangering the life of the hostages and of the order forces;

---

[6] Michel Wieviorka and Dominique Wolton, *Terrorisme à la une: médias, terrorisme et démocratie* (Paris: Editions Gallimard, 1979).

- inducing a pressure over the authorities which limits the power of taking decisions;
- reinforcing the feeling of power experienced by terrorists, especially in pathologic cases, resulting in an artificial prolongation of the incidents and an increasing of the gravity of the consequences;
- misrepresentation of the spectacular, thrilling side of the events through the competitive nature of the journalistic activity, the result of which is transforming public violence into entertainment to the detriment of information;
- footage and certain practices related to it (telephone conversation with the terrorists) make the journalists direct participants to the event and puts them in positions for which they do not have the necessary competence (negotiator, law person etc.).[7]

From a different perspective, Wieviorka and Wolton (p. 8) identify, next to the role of media in propagating terrorist menace, another role, which is essential in the functioning of a democracy affected by the terrorism: the contribution to *determining the representations* of the public about the menace and the response of the society to the phenomenon:

- revealing the deficiencies of political power;
- informing about police work;
- questioning the role of the law and of the intelligence services.

The idea of a mutual relation is doubled by a special hypostasis of the media: not as much as a counter instrument but rather as a generator of the terrorist action. This does not, of course, mean that the mass media plan or deliberately suggest terrorist attacks. Nevertheless the implication of the media has frequently been analysed to decide whether the journalistic coverage of terrorism has been decisive in choosing a certain way of action (for example, direct bombing versus hostage taking).

Surveying these different opinions, *which is the most appropriate interpretation for the role of mass media in the terrorist acts?* Is the media only the responsible instrument in informing the public about the actors and the events on the international scene? Or is it "the whore" whose favours are available to anyone who has a gun (see Hickey)? Certainly, recent history and its tragic events (New York, Moscow, Madrid or London) confirmed the above thesis. But at the same time they have made the present

---

[7] James Curran, *Media and Power* (London and New York: Routledge, Taylor and Francis, 2002), p. 77.

situation an unprecedented challenge for the media. The ways these attacks are organised seem to be similar to the way media events are carefully organised and especially directed for target audiences. And the efficiency seems to be guaranteed by the theatre effect that is obtained through rapid and dramatic communication.

Media and Counteracting Terrorism

The third perspective that we propose is an inverse perspective: *how to imply the mass media in counter-terrorism?* If the twentieth century terrorists learned to use the media in their own interest, is there any chance to involve the media as a responsible actor in the fight against terror?

It is well known and generally accepted that the mass media have the capacity to provide a significant amount of information in an unforeseen situation, while radio and television have the capacity to directly keep the public in touch with the victims and their families. Equally, the mass media may provide information referring to the progress of the events and may make recommendations concerning the protection of the civil population.

Therefore the mass media must be an important part in any educational counter terrorism program: (1) as a reliable channel or interface with the citizens, *and as an agency through which the public is informed with respect to the events and the vectors interacting in the public interest arena; (2)* as a responsible actor often featuring on the scene of the terrorist act. *Of course, the success or the failure of such programs decisively depends on the professionalism of the actors and the maturity of the democratic system in which they act. That is why also informing the mass media representatives with respect to the security problems and forming a security culture to secure a balanced reaction on behalf of the press are indispensable efforts.*

Counter-terrorism communication programs have originated in understanding that a country which is confronted with the terrorist menace must, of course, prepare not only its soldiers, but also its citizens. And its mass media, we may say. It is particularly after the September 11 attacks that in most democratic countries the institutions empowered with prerogatives in the field of national security have started information campaigns which were intended to increase the alerting degree regarding terrorism (for example, the United States' initiative–*Antiterrorism Personal Protection Guide: A Self-Help Guide to Antiterrorism*). The programs aim to help the public in coping with terrorism focusing on a comprehensive explanatory/educational policy for changing the public attitude towards terrorism. They aim to diminish the level of irrational anxiety and strengthen the morale and sense of personal safety with respect to the threat. Consequently, the communication programs are based on understanding the fact that promoting and defending the national interests must be doubled by knowing, rendering valuable, and accepting the latter in public opinion, because "it is much less probable that people should come to panic if they know what happens."[9]

The main benefits of the communication programs aiming at education for security culture are reflected by the strategic goals of this education type. A carefully thought-out campaign (for different segments of the public, with different information expectances or needs) may change or improve perception of what security means and of the citizen's part in building security, thus entailing advantages for the security state itself.

Concretely, by means of these communication programs, the citizens receive information with respect to the terrorist phenomenon: danger sources, terrorist organisations, means and methods used by the latter, implications on a national or local plan, recommendations regarding people's reaction in case of a terrorist attack. Last but not least, such campaigns also offer the citizens a telephone number which they may use for reporting any unusual situations that are currently associated with a terrorist attack.

ROMANIA'S EXPERIENCE

At first sight, such counter-terrorist preparation programs for the population of Romania may seem an unjustified initiative. Nevertheless, evoking the attacks of March 11, 2004 in Madrid, September 1–3 in Beslan, and July 7 in London—which proved that September 11 was not an isolated case and that terrorist attacks can strike targets indirectly and indiscriminately—has decisively changed the perspective.

In Romania, the security culture is directly related to developing a stable democracy. It may be generated by informing and indirectly making the population responsible regarding the values, norms, and rights which can guarantee that social and individual life will be laid on a basis of liberty and democratic values. Thus, the security culture represents more than a social behaviour exercise. It is built upon a coherent legislative system, upon an efficient control of the tendencies to restrict the individual rights and

---

[9] Maxine Singer, "The Challenge to Science: How to Mobilize American Ingenuity," in *The Age of Terror: America and the World After September 11,* ed. Strobe Talbott and Nayan Chanda (New York: Basic Books, 2001).

liberties which may be adopted by the political power and the state institutions and upon a powerful civil society, active and responsible, which should shape the citizens' behaviour, with respect to promoting both national security and the citizens' interests.

Romania too, after such attacks, structured a new security attitude principle, stating that individual security is to be found within any security system based on the fundamental human rights and liberties. This principle is however completed by the necessity of explaining the position of a citizen as not only a beneficiary of state security, but also as an effective, contributive participant, since individual security is part and result of collective security, and an intelligence service can only be efficient, in full legality, if the citizens which it serves support it in its measures.

ROMANIA ON THE MAP OF TERRORISM AND THE UNITED STATES' TROOPS AT THE BLACK SEA: A COMMUNICATION PROJECT FOR APPROPRIATE REPRESENTATIONS

In May, the Romanian Parliament approved, by 257 votes in favour and one vote against, with 29 abstentions, the request of the interim president regarding the entry and stay of USA forces on Romanian territory for the entire period of applicability of the agreement between Romania and the USA signed on December 6, 2005.

The presence of American troops on Romanian territory is considered to be a decisive contribution to the extension of security and projection of stability towards the Middle East, an integral part of the global effort to fight against terrorism. By virtue of these security objectives, Romania contributes to the fight against international terrorism. According to the Romanian officials, the stationing of the American troops brings benefits to Romania: "The privileged military relations with the Washington authorities will lead to the strengthening of bilateral cooperation at all levels and will generate greater trust in the business environment. Other consequences of this decision will be the development of high level political dialogue between the governments of the two countries, and, at European level, the assertion of Romania as a leading actor with an active role in deepening trans-Atlantic relations" (Romanian Prime Minister Călin Popescu Tăriceanu).

The US Government will send its first military troops to Romania and Bulgaria starting this summer. In Romania the USA will have military bases and training centres at Mihail Kogălniceanu, Babadag, Cincu, and Smîrdan. The number of military to be employed in Romania-based units will not be over 3,000. The main purpose of the exercises to be developed is to ensure the regional stability and to maintain presence in the Caucasian and Black Sea area.

As compared with all these official arguments, the Romanian mass media proposed a different discourse. In opposition to the diplomatic dissertation, the Romanian mass media (especially the newspapers) have underlined the terrorist risk rather than the advantages that Romania may obtain. Paradoxically, the presence of the American troops would bring more insecurity that security for the Romanian people. *Romania would become a target on the terrorists' map of action simply because it directly contributes to the fight against terrorism.*

This fear was somehow emphasised by Washington's official request addressed to the Czech Republic and Poland to play key roles in the expansion of its anti-missile protection system by placing a radar station and interceptor missiles on their soil. The United States, which already has a network of early warning satellites, radars and interceptor missiles in Alaska and California, wants to extend its defence umbrella to Europe by 2011 to deal with the threat of possible rocket attacks from Iran or North Korea. According to the Czech Republic's Prime Minister, Mirek Topolanek, the deployment of the US missile shield in Central Europe would "not only reinforce the security of the Czech Republic but also its allies" and the US project is "strictly defensive," in line with NATO plans. Once again and paradoxically, the comments in the Romanian press rather underlined the dangers that come together with the "international defence umbrella" than the benefits.

Certainly, the current interpretation offered by the Romanian media has influenced people's representation about "the United States troops at the Black Sea." The more so as people cannot know such a subject directly, but mostly by means of the press, television, and radio. And in addition to influencing people in this respect, media interpretation shapes the people's representation concerning all the proximate themes (such as "security in Romania" or "the risk of terrorism," "the North-Atlantic Alliance") and generally Romanian external affairs. This brings the potential risk of generating and supplying stereotypes. This latter assumption does not need more than the already well-known arguments:

(1)   because mass media have an incontestable role in shaping representations of reality;
(2)   because selective media depictions of reality apparently provide the most salient information for people on risks, hazards and disasters, also on terrorist acts;

(3)   because most people have little real understanding of what goes on and what affects the production of news. The news is read as reality.

The implied problems may vary and be surely counterproductive for security: unjustified panic, anxiety and fear. B.P. Foreman summarised the facilitating factors for panic, and two important factors—besides people's lassitude—are relevant for the current argument. It is the lack of information considering the dangerous situation and the rumours that decisively facilitate panic (and in Foreman's interpretation, these two are separated from the starting factors—the danger itself).[10]

In this respect, our communication project is meant to counteract false representation that can lead to exaggerated reactions such as fear and panic. We are firmly convinced that

a. unless people have a good understanding of what actually happens, there is little point in trying to extrapolate from past situations to find how the citizenry and the mechanism of the social system might be used to counter terrorism;

b. bad assumptions or misunderstandings cannot lead to good policies or programs;

c. in certain situations, having an informed and prepared population may represent a defining advantage.

This communication program would mediate the relation with the public and thus assure reactions (or at least the premises of some reactions) that support security and the measures taken by the state authorities. In our opinion it should contain two levels of intervention: one for the relation with the mass media and one for the relation with the citizens.

The program would comprise:

• **A preliminary analysis** that should adequately evaluate the present situation: the media representations, and the social representations concerning the campaign theme;

• **The objectives:** to correctly inform the public, to explain in rational terms and to educate the public (attitudes and behaviours). It seems essential to explain the decision in the larger context of Romania's geopolitical interest;

---

[10] Paul B. Foreman, "Panic theory," *Sociology and Social Research*, 37 (1953), 295–304.

- **The target-public**—the mass media, the citizens;
- **The communication channels**—mainstream mass media (with high audience or specialised in news);
- **The message**—an unbiased one that should present the advantages but also the disadvantages, the opportunities and also the threats. The main and representative "voices" for the message are the experts on political and geopolitical issues, security analysts who should explain the decision in the larger context of Romania's geopolitical interest;
- **The schedule, the budget and the post program evaluation procedures.**

Concretely, such an initiative would take the form of a nationwide debate concerning the presence of American troops on Romanian's Black Sea shore. Its conclusions will offer an insight of the extent to which such a decision is accepted and also of the implications that are assigned voluntarily or not.

It must be noticed that the mass media are a target public, and maybe the most important one because they assume a high position in guaranteeing success with the other public (the citizens). Therefore, another special part of the program should be addressed particularly to the media in the form of a training campaign: a campaign that approaches broader aspects such as national security and also specific ones—directly subordinated to the main campaign theme. In our opinion there are two important ideas the media should reflect on: publish the official "side of the story" and separate official information from the journalists' opinions.

Conclusions

False representations usually lead to misunderstandings and to incorrect and harmful decisions. Moreover, when it comes to external affairs and national interest, the importance of appropriate representations needs no arguments. A theme such as "the United States' troops in Romania," together with all its implications and connected themes will certainly be included in the public debate. But without official information—conceived and transmitted in proper forms (as suited and available to public opinion)—the representations will develop along the lines of popular beliefs and stereotypes. Exaggeration of risks and accentuation of some aspects (most probably stress on the negative implications) are frequent mechanisms in social representations. And without supplementary information, the representations are considered reality. But in this case, unjustified exaggeration of the terrorist risk can bring only disadvantages.

The importance of preparing the population has been tested countless times (for example, during terrorist attacks such as hostage takings) and it is incontestable. Preparing the population must aim at the two sides of security: both the *offensive* side and the *defensive* side. In other words, the population must be informed and prepared through the communication programs to apprehend possible dysfunction or vulnerabilities which may indicate the preparation of a terrorist action, but must be simultaneously prepared to react in crisis situations caused by terrorist actions (for example, managing the panic or giving first aid). This brings a new approach to the potential conflict between "communicating" versus "keeping the secret." To illustrate, we cite a significant (contrary example) assertion of an American censor during World War II: "I shall tell them nothing until everything has finished and then I shall tell them who is the winner."[11]

In their turn, the mass media are a port-parole in the counter-terrorist preparation of the population: responsible media, of course. Journalists bear a heavy responsibility as they control a powerful instrument that, when used appropriately, provides the citizenry with the accurate, reliable information necessary for an open society. Journalists also act as a watchdog against oppression and a voice for the otherwise voiceless. Still, the media's words and images can also be an instrument of evil purposes, whether intentionally or not.

As they become media events, terrorist acts, even potential ones, need special regulations. Journalistic standards of ethics, while not universal in their content, already exist in many areas of the media. But while almost all journalistic standards include the responsibility to report truthfully and accurately, surprisingly few overtly list a responsibility to "minimise harm." Once more, a balanced mass media reaction may also counterbalance what A. P. Schmid calls "the intrinsic escalation imperative" which demands that the terrorists should commit the most bizarre and cruel acts to gain attention.[12] This is the main "perverse effect" of the media coverage of the terrorist phenomenon, among other numerous effects, roles, and functions of the media within the social system.

In an open society, it is impossible to guarantee that the antiterrorist strategies and actions will not be blocked or interrupted by certain more or less responsible journalistic practices. "As terror is directed towards the media and not towards the victims, its success is defined in terms of media

---

[11] Phillip Knightley, *Tell Them Nothing Till It's Over And Then Them Who Won: In Wartime, Government Considers Media a Menace* (2001). http://www.publicintegrity.org/
[12] Alex P. Schmid and Janny J. de Graff, *Violence as Communication: Insurgent Terrorism and the Western News Media* (Beverly Hills, CA: Sage, 1982).

related coverage. And there is no way in the West that you could not have media coverage because you're dealing in a free society" (Combs, p. 138).

Nevertheless, in systems characterised by a solid political culture and mature democratic practice, media contributions to the antiterrorist fight are significant. This statement is not an *a priori* truth, it is not a lemma of the public space, nor is it a prophecy. Where no universally valid laws and concepts exist, but only variables and abstract notions, where pluralism and the democratic game constantly establish and re-evaluate the dimensions and definitions of the latter, the only supporting point of all the involved entities is the regulatory principle. The above statement represents this regulatory principle of the system, without which no homeostasis may exist.

Therefore, a communication program concerning counter-terrorism should be supplemented with the recommendation that the mass media should avoid sensationalism and exaggeration in covering such events. Excluding mass media censorship is, beyond any ethic and legal considerations, a practical and functional necessity for a system which wants to be democratic. Otherwise the system is not functional.

Media coverage is the "terrorism oxygen," as in the well-known words of ex-Prime Minister Margaret Thatcher. There is considerable difference of opinion as to whether the measures to deprive terrorists of "the oxygen of publicity"—on which they thrive—are attacks on that legal tradition or simply reasonable precautions taken by governments faced with a crisis. As one commentator noticed, "nobody calls it censorship when Mafia spokesman are not allowed to explain, over the airwaves, why it is advisable to pay protection money" (Combs, 142).

But the same media transmission is also the oxygen of the public space and, implicitly, of democracy. Restricting the freedom of the press by means of the legal norms gives way to variants which may lead to censorship. That is why media censorship may bring to a suffocation of the terrorism, yet it brings, at the very same time, a suffocation of the liberal democracy, killing the whole body to eliminate one parasite.

As a functional alternative, particular to a democratic society, self-regulation seems to be, in specialists' opinion, the most reliable solution. This very idea is reflected by a resolution of EU Parliamentary Assembly concerning the journalistic ethic: "Besides the rights and duties stipulated by the legislation in force, the media assume, in front of the citizens and of the society, a moral responsibility which must be taken into account nowadays, when the information and communication are highly important for both developing the personality of the citizens and for the evolution of the society and of the democratic life" (Resolution no. 1003/1993 of UE Parliamentary Assembly concerning the journalistic ethic). Hence, applying the solution of self-regulation may create the premises for reconciling both the interests of the press and the national interests.

PLENARY PAPERS

RELIGIONS, DIALOGUE, PEACE, AND CONFLICT RESOLUTION

INTER-CIVILISATIONAL DIALOGUE:
A PATH TO CONFLICT TRANSFORMATION

Joseph A. Camilleri

The global condition is one of heightened vulnerability. National boundaries are increasingly porous. States are finding it harder and harder to run their economies and defend their borders. As the terrorist attacks on New York and Washington, Bali, Madrid, and London have demonstrated, wealth, power, and nuclear arsenals offer little guarantee of protection.

The word global is now a cliché. So are such terms as global village, global economy, and global culture. We are often told that we live in an era of globalisation. In the words of Roland Robertson, the world is fast becoming a "single place."[1] Others speak of an emerging global consciousness. Globalisation has become a subject of discussion among corporate managers, scholars, policy-makers, and citizens alike. Yet, there is no consensus on its meaning, its origins, or even its long-term implications.

Globalisation is in some ways as old as capitalism itself, yet it points to a new historical phase.[2] The contemporary world is one in which a number of seemingly distinct processes are occurring more or less simultaneously, and acquiring a global reach, often in highly interconnected fashion.

In a rapidly globalising world, "high consequence risks" have become integral to the functioning of society.[3] The global condition is one of heightened vulnerability as much for states as for groups and individuals. One need only think of the effects of financial crises, oil spills, ozone depletion, global warming, ethnic cleansing, genocidal policies, or terrorist attacks. If there is one characteristic that distinguishes contemporary life it is the "globalisation of insecurity."

If this reading of events is at all accurate, then a number of difficult questions suggest themselves: What challenges does the globalisation of insecurity pose for ethical and political discourse, for the way societies organise themselves, for the way people participate in society and in the decisions that vitally affect their future. What are appropriate cultural and institutional responses? And what of the role of the world's religious

---

[1] Roland Robertson, *Globalisation: Social Theory and Global Culture* (London: Sage, 1992).
[2] Richard Higgott and Anthony Payne (eds), *The New Political Economy of Globalization*, 2 vols (Aldershor: Edward Elgar, 2000).
[3] Ulrich Beck, *Risk Society: Toward a New Modernity* (London: Sage, 1992).

traditions and civilisations? Before turning to these questions, it may be useful to probe a little more deeply into the dynamic of globalisation.

GLOBALIZATION OF INSECURITY

To make sense of this current we first need to revisit the meaning of "security," since it remains a problematic and highly contested concept. It has been traditionally understood as referring to a set of objective conditions involving some form of protection from military threat. There is, however, much to be gained from conceptualising security as a state of mind and not just as a physical condition. This is precisely the nature of the terrorist threat. Its effectiveness does not normally lie in the destruction of the enemy's military capabilities. The terrorist succeeds if his actions and utterances manage to produce fear, panic, and a combination of counter measures that are at best costly, and at worst likely to prolong the current state of uncertainty. In reality, all security discourse and practice ultimately revolves around the experience of "insecurity." Security policies, whether or not they rely on the use and threat of force, derive their content and legitimacy from the way they address, or are thought to address, this generalised sense of insecurity.

The question arises: how does the insecurity/security dynamic manifest itself in the present conjuncture? What, in other words, are the specificities of this period of transition? A key part of the answer lies in the first of the three currents that we propose to examine, namely the "globalisation of insecurity." To convey something of the multi-dimensional character of this phenomenon, we focus on three distinguishing traits: the destructiveness of military technology, the rise of transnational threats to security, and the growth of international and transnational actors on the world stage.

The lethality of modern warfare has intensified over time. The ascendancy of offensive over defensive weapons systems has meant a marked decline in military protective capability. The fortress-type shells of defence characteristic of the European state system in the sixteenth to the eighteenth centuries have been rendered obsoleste by the advent of total war,[4] the potency of economic and ideological instruments of warfare, and the rise of urban and aerial piracy. These trends have combined to increase the vulnerability of all societies, including advanced industrial systems. In

---

[4] John Herz, *Politics in the Atomic Age* (New York: Columbia University Press, 1962).

the atomic age, the power to hurt has vastly outdistanced the power to defend.[5]

Nowhere is this trend more graphically exemplified than in the advent of weapons of mass destruction. The balance of terror, which underpinned the nuclear edifice of the Cold War period, was in this sense the ultimate exercise in competitive risk taking. Nuclear deterrence—the politics of reciprocal nuclear brinkmanship—was credited by some as making war unthinkable as a rational instrument of policy. Insofar as nuclear powers had to ensure that their rivalries did not degenerate into armed hostilities, nuclear deterrence, it was argued, made for a more stable system of international security. Such a conclusion, however, rested on the assumption that deterrence would continue to hold sway and that nuclear powers would continue to threaten wholesale destruction without ever having to carry out the threat. The validity of this paradoxical logic came under serious challenge during periods of heightened Soviet-American tension. The end of the Cold War has seen the reduction of the Russian and American nuclear arsenals, but not their destructiveness. The underlying logic that had driven their development and deployment continues to hold sway, namely the view that the actual use of nuclear weapons may in certain circumstances be effective, hence rational. Even with the collapse of the Berlin Wall, Germany's reunification and NATO's expansion, US strategic policy continues to entertain the possible first use of the nuclear weapon. A new generation of nuclear weapons is envisaged which could be used pre-emptively to deal with chemical or biological threats or to destroy deeply buried and hardened targets.[6]

Mirroring and reinforcing the policies of the major declared nuclear powers has been the slow but steady widening of the nuclear club. Given the prospect of a North Korean or Iranian nuclear capability, it is now entirely feasible that US counter-proliferation policy might lead to a pre-emptive nuclear strike. In so far as the nuclear weapon remains a symbol of power and prestige, proliferation tendencies are likely to intensify, with far-reaching implications for the reliability of strategic calculations and the predictability of state behaviour. Adding fuel to these uncertainties is the scale of the nuclear black market. As of December 2004, the IAEA's Illicit Trafficking Database advised that 662 incidents of illicit nuclear trafficking and other related unauthorized activities were confirmed as having occurred

---

[5] Thomas C. Schelling, *Arms and Influence* (New Haven, Conn: Yale University Press, 1996).

[6] United States, *Nuclear Posture Review* [Excerpts], submitted to Congress on 31 December 2001. http://www.globalsecurity.org/wmd/library/policy/dod/npr.htm

since January 1993.[7] The cumulative impact of these developments prompted the *Bulletin of the Atomic Scientists (BAS)* in January 2007 to move the hand of the Doomsday Clock closer to midnight—the figurative end of civilisation. In explaining their decision the BAS Board of Directors offered the following explanation:

> We stand at the brink of a Second Nuclear Age. [...] North Korea's recent test of a nuclear weapon, Iran's nuclear ambitions, a renewed emphasis on the military utility of nuclear weapons, the failure to adequately secure nuclear materials, and the continued presence of some 26,000 nuclear weapons in the United States and Russia are symptomatic of a failure to solve the problems posed by the most destructive technology on Earth.[8]

The multiple threads connecting politics, economy, and technology in the nuclear age—porous national borders, expanded commerce in potentially dangerous dual-use technologies and materials, intensifying conflicts and nuclear ambitions—point to a trend that is pervasive yet diffuse, namely the *globalisation of insecurity*.

A second and closely related feature of the phenomenon has to do with the transnationalisation of security relations.[9] While the vocabulary of international security has traditionally focused on the dangers posed by the military policies of states, increasingly communities have had to contend with the threats posed by "irregular substate units such as ethnic militias, paramilitary guerrillas, cults and religious organisations, organised crime, and terrorists."[10] It is now commonplace to refer to the proliferation of transnational threats. International debt, destabilising financial flows, transborder pollution, epidemics, nuclear proliferation, terrorism, piracy, drug trafficking, other forms of transnational crime, and large unregulated population movements have all come to be viewed as actual or at least potential sources of insecurity.[11] The trend has assumed global proportions

---

[7] IAEA, "Illicit Nuclear Trafficking Statistics: January 1993–December 2004." http://www.iaea.org/NewsCenter/Features/RadSources/Fact_Figures2004.html

[8] "'Doomsday Clock' Moves Two Minutes Closer to Midnight," *Bulletin of the Atomic Scientists*, January 18, 2007.
http://www.thebulletin.org/weekly-highlight/20070117.html

[9] Joseph A. Camilleri, "Human Rights, Cultural Diversity and Conflict Resolution: the Asia Pacific Context," *Pacifica Review: Peace, Security and Global Change*, 6 (2), 1994, 17–41.

[10] Victor D. Chad, "Globalization and the Study of International Security," *Journal of Peace Research*, 37:3 (May 2000), 391–403 (p. 394).

[11] Barry Buzan, "New Patterns of Global Security in the Twenty-First Century," *International Affairs*, 67:3 (1991), 431–51; Michael Renner, *Fighting for Survival:*

not simply in geographic terms but in the more profound sense that borders are increasingly permeable and offer diminishing protection against the diffusion of threats. The transnationalisation or, as we prefer to describe it, the globalisation of insecurity stems from the rising volume, speed and interrelatedness of flows—financial, atmospheric, viral, population, and other flows—whose impact on the experience of insecurity is compounded by the exponential growth of information flows. We are witnessing, as a direct consequence of the communications revolution, the rising consciousness of the scale and multifaceted character of global disorder.

Here a brief digression may be in order. It is not just the latest advances in communications and information technology that have propelled the transnationalisation of threats. Paradoxically, tradition has also played a part. The contemporary role of religion and culture as significant contributors to international tension offers perhaps the most graphic illustration of this trend. The large number of serious conflicts with a religious dimension to them (over half of the world total in 2001) and the steady rise in religiously motivated international terrorism are manifestations of a complex and wide-ranging phenomenon. Diverse local and regional influences are no doubt at work, but an important common factor is the widespread disillusionment with Western modernity, and in particular with the role it assigns to science, technology, and bureaucracy, and its marginalisation of religion, the sacred, or the spiritual. The increasing importance of religious beliefs, practices and discourses in personal and public life, and as a consequence in local and national politics, has spread across diverse religious traditions and regions of the world. The trend is not confined to Muslim societies, poverty-stricken countries or failed states. It has become a significant current in the life of many Western societies, where conservative and Charismatic Catholics, evangelical and Pentecostal Protestants, radical Christians, New Age spiritualists, and a growing number of converts to Islam and Buddhism have made their presence felt.[12]

Gilles Kepel's analysis is highly revealing in this regard. The religious identity movements of the last few decades, he argues, represent a response to two interlinked developments: the growth of transnational threats to security and the collapse of communism and socialism. They represent a

---

Environmental, Decline, Social Conflict and the New Age of Insecurity (New York: Norton, 1996); Peter W. Singer, "AIDS and International Security," *Survival*, 44:1 (Spring 2002), 145–158.

[12] M. Thomas Scott, *The Global Resurgence of Religion and the Transformation of International Relations: The Struggle for the Soul of the Twenty-First Century* (Basingstoke: Palgrave Macmillan, 2005), pp. 10–11, 26.

response to the perceived confusion and disorder in international relations and an attempt to revive "the vocabulary and the categories of religious thought as applied to the contemporary world." Many of them view the modern secular city as "completely lacking legitimacy" and consider that "only a fundamental transformation in the organization of society can restore the holy scriptures as the prime source of inspiration for the city of the future."[13] But beyond this agreement they have widely divergent visions of social order and are often deeply hostile to each other as well as to the wider secular society. In recent decades, the resurgence of religion has given rise to new and sharper forms of contestation in multiple local, national and international settings—a trend greatly amplified by the rapid growth of large religious diasporic communities. Put simply, the return of religion to international centre stage is one manifestation, albeit the most dramatic thus far, of the underlying tension between modernity and tradition.

The lethality of modern war and the pervasiveness of security threats that are simultaneously subnational and transnational point to another closely related trend, namely the interpenetration of the national and the international. In such diverse areas of security as terrorism, drug trafficking, money laundering, climate change, immigration, or infectious diseases the dividing line between internal and external security has become increasingly problematic. It is as if the spatial dimension of security relations has been radically altered. Traditionally, the sovereign nation-state has based its assumed monopoly over security policy on its control of physical distance. State boundaries and their protection by means of armed force were widely seen as the necessary instruments for both assessing and countering threats. However, with the transportation and communications revolutions, and the exponential growth of transnational actors and processes, national control over space has steadily dissipated. As a consequence, agency is exercised by old entities (states) in new ways, and by new or relatively new entities (subnational, transnational, supranational, and international) in ways both old and new. The telling blows inflicted on the United States by Al Qaeda and other small terrorist groups through use of the airwaves—courtesy of Al Jazeera and a wide array of western media outlets—are a case in point. Present-day terrorism may be understood as a product of the dual movement of communitarianism and transnationalism. Born of the variable geometry of communication, commerce, industry, and

---

[13] Gilles Keppel, *The Revenge of God: The Resurgence of Islam, Christianity and Judaism in the Modern World*, trans. Alan Braley (University Park, Pa: Pennsylvania State University Press, 1994).

migration, transnational flows often restructure space in ways that deepen and extend the sources of insecurity.

The net effect of the multiple trends we have briefly outlined has been to call into question traditional concepts of security and the bureaucratic mindsets that accompany them. Although national policy making elites and even the security studies community have found it difficult to break loose from the constraints of past discourse and practice,[14] there has nevertheless been a noticeable drift away from highly militarised, zero-sum definitions of security towards more inclusive conceptions which privilege or at least give added emphasis to notions of reassurance, co-operation, and interdependence.[15] The decline of Cold War tensions and the attempts to overcome the division of Europe mirrored and reinforced notions of common destiny and common security, which Gorbachev's slogan of a "European home" sought to harness and institutionalise.[16]

In contrast to the idea of collective defence, which seeks to draw a sharp dividing line between aggressive and law-abiding states, notions of common security seek to manage the problem of aggression not so much by punishing or coercing the aggressor as by influencing his motivation, by offering a mix of incentives and disincentives which predispose him to act within the constraints set by agreed norms and procedures. The concept acquired considerable currency in both academic and political discourse, especially during the 1980s and early 1990s,[17] and has since continued to surface in a great many official documents issued by both national governments and international organisations.[18] The minimalist approach to common security seeks to reconcile the competing interests of states by institutionalising co-operative behaviour, whether through confidence- and security-building measures (CSBMs) or more ambitious arms control and disarmament agreements.

---

[14] Mikkel Vedby Rasmussen, "'It Sounds Like a Riddle': Security Studies, the War on Terror and Risk," *Millennium: Journal of International Studies*, 33:2 (March 2004), 381–95.

[15] Andrew Mack, *Reassurance versus Deterrence Strategies for the Asia/Pacific Region*, Working Paper No.103 (Canberra, Australian National University Peace Research Centre, 1991).

[16] Seweryn Bialer, "'New Thinking' and Soviet Foreign Policy," *Survival* 30:4 (July–August 1988), 291–309; Joseph A. Camilleri, and Jim Falk, *The End of Sovereignty? Politics in a Shrinking and Fragmenting World* (Aldershot: Edward Elgar, 1992).

[17] Stockholm International Peace Research Institute (SIPRI), *Common Security* (London: Taylor and Francis, 1985).

[18] Organization for Security and Co-operation in Europe, *Lisbon Document 1996*. http://www.osce.org/documents/mcs/1996/12/4049_en.pdf

Equally important in the changing conception of security has been the attempt to move beyond its purely military connotations, to include not only the physical control of territory but the protection of social, political, economic, and ecological values deemed vital to material and psychological well-being. This idea has given rise to numerous formulations, including "unconventional security," "democratic security," and "alternative security."[19] But by far the two most influential formulations in a policy sense have been "comprehensive security" and "human security." In the Asia-Pacific context where the idea has gained considerable currency, comprehensive security, at least in the case of Japan, dates back to 1976. In time the Association of Southeast Asian Nations (ASEAN), the most concerted attempt at regionalism in Asia, would formally adopt comprehensive security, at first largely as a rhetorical device but increasingly as a policy framework. For ASEAN the attraction of the concept was its emphasis on threats to internal security and the wider tasks of nation building,[20] but as time went on a broader security agenda embracing such transnational issues as narcotics, money laundering, environment, and illegal migrants assumed increasing importance.[21] Comprehensive security became a major focus of regional second track diplomacy and an abiding, though uneven, preoccupation of the ASEAN Regional Forum (ARF) established in July 1994.[22]

A closely related but distinct conception of security has gained even greater prominence especially since it was formally enunciated by the UNDP Human Development Report of 1994 (UNDP 1994).[23] While human security shares with comprehensive security a concern for inclusiveness in defining the security agenda, it focuses more explicitly on human beings

---

[19] Robert E. Bedeski, "Unconventional Security Threats: An Overview," North Pacific Cooperative Security Dialogue Research Programme, Working Paper, No. 11 (Toronto: York University, 1992); Robert C. Johansen, "Real Security in Democratic Security" *Alternatives*, 16:2 (1991), 209–42; Johan Galtung, *There Are Alternatives: Four Roads to Peace and Security* (Nottingham: Spokesman, 1984).

[20] Muthiah Alagappa, "A Comprehensive Security: Interpretations in ASEAN Countries," in *Asian Security Issues: Regional and Global*, ed. R. Scalapino et al (Berkeley: Institute of Asian Studies, University of California, 1988).

[21] ASEAN, "Joint Communique of The 29th ASEAN Ministerial Meeting (AMM) Jakarta, 20–21 July 1996." http://www.aseansec.org/1824.htm

[22] Joseph A. Camilleri, *Regionalism in the New Asia-Pacific Order: The Political Economy of the Asia-Pacific Region, Volume II* (Cheltenham: Edward Elgar, 2003), pp. 306–342.

[23] United Nations Development Program, *Human Development Report 1994, New Dimensions of Human Security* (New York: Oxford University Press 1994).

rather than the state as the primary unit of analysis.[24] As a consequence, UN policy discourse has tended to describe human rights and human development as essential pillars of human security. National governments have also made use of the concept, but with notable differences of emphasis, with some, in particular Japan, putting their weight behind economic development goals and strategies, and others, notably Canada, stressing instead the protection of human rights and fundamental freedoms.[25] A further development in this conceptual shift has come with the rising incidence of humanitarian emergencies (often accompanied by varying forms of institutional failure and gross abuse of human rights), which has stimulated and justified the recourse to "humanitarian" intervention, and most recently the notion of the "responsibility to protect." This shift in security discourse is still very much at an embryonic stage. There is evidence, however, of movement towards a subtler understanding of the conditions making for insecurity, and of the structures, relationships, and agencies that may be needed to sustain a viable security system.

THE CONTRIBUTION OF THE DIALOGUE OF CIVILISATIONS

Globalisation, as we have noted, is an elusive, confusing and contradictory phenomenon. With the collapse of communism no credible alternative to global capitalism is in sight. There is as of now no international agency or political movement that can exercise effective leadership in interpreting, much less guiding, economic and political change. There is no simple or single solution to the globalisation of insecurity

In response to the uncertainties and complexities of the present conjuncture, numerous ideas and initiatives have been proposed since the end of the Cold War as an ethical and political compass for the journey ahead. Particularly useful in this regard are the various proposals to democratise the institutions and mechanisms which will make vitally important decisions about the future.[26] This is why the reform of institutions

---

[24] Woosang Kim and In-Taek Hyun, "Toward a New Concept of Security: Human Security in World Politics," in *Asia's Emerging Regional Order: Reconciling Traditional and Human Security*, ed. William T. Tow, Ramesh Thakur and In-Taek Hyun (Tokyo: United Nations University Press, 2000), p. 39.

[25] Ramesh Thakur, *The United Nations, Peace and Security: From Collective Security to the Responsibility to Protect* (Cambridge: Cambridge University Press, 2006), p. 73.

[26] Eşref Aksu and Joseph A. Camilleri (eds), *Democratizing Global Governance* (London: Palgrave, 2002); Commission on Global Governance, *Our Global Neighbourhood* (Oxford: Oxford University Press, 1995); David Held, *Democracy*

has become such a critical issue—institutions at all levels: local, provincial, national, regional, and global.[27] In this context, the rather limited achievements of the 2005 UN summit have been a source of widespread disappointment.

But if we are to develop a much more encompassing and integrated approach to the multiple sources of human insecurity and if we are to build institutions that citizens can trust and in which their voices can be heard,[28] what intellectual and cultural resources can we call upon as we approach these daunting tasks? It is here that the dialogue of civilisations may have a great deal to offer. It may in fact hold an important key to the future.

Dialogue across cultural and religious boundaries is not, of course, a new idea. It is now well over a century since the 1893 World's Parliament of Religions, held in Chicago, brought together representatives of eastern and western spiritual traditions. Today it is recognized as the occasion that formally launched inter-religious dialogue in the modern period. The Council for a Parliament of the World's Religions (CPWR), which officially dates from 1988, was established as a centennial celebration of the 1893 Parliament. The 1993 Parliament adopted *Towards a Global Ethic: An Initial Declaration*, a powerful statement of the ethical common ground shared by the world's religious and spiritual traditions.

The dialogical agenda has since gained considerable momentum with several national and international centres making civilisational dialogue a focal point of research, education and advocacy. These include the Institute for Interreligious, Intercultural Dialogue, the International Interfaith Centre (Oxford), the Global Dialogue Institute, the International Movement for a Just World (Kuala Lumpur), the International Centre for Dialogue among Civilisations (Tehran), the Centre for World Dialogue (Nicosia), and the Toda Institute for Global Policy and Peace Research (Honolulu and Tokyo). Other important institutional developments have included the establishment of the World Council of Religious Leaders and the World Conference of Religions for Peace. More recently, the UN General Assembly adopted in

---

and the Global Order: From the Modern State to Cosmopolitan Governance (Cambridge: Polity Press, 1995).

[27] Aseem Prakash and Jeffrey A. Hart (eds), *Globalisation and Governance* (London: Routledge, 1999).

[28] Will Kymlicka and Wayne Norman, "Return of the citizen: A Survey of Recent Work on Citizenship Theory," in *Theorizing Citizenship*, ed. Ronald Beiner (Albany, NY: State University of New York Press, 1995), pp. 283–322; Richard Falk, "The Making of Global Citizenship," in *The Condition of Citizenship*, ed. Bart van Steenbergen (London: Sage, 1994), pp. 127–40; John Urry, "Globalization and Citizenship," *Journal of World-Systems Research*, 5:2 (Spring 1999), 263–273.

November 1998 a resolution proclaiming the year 2001 as the Year of dialogue among Civilizations. In November of that year, the General Assembly adopted the *Global Agenda for Dialogue among Civilisations*, which has in turn given rise to a great many governmental and non-governmental initiatives. Most recently, the Spanish Prime Minister launched the idea of an "Alliance of Civilisations." The proposal launched in partnership with the Turkish Government has now been endorsed by the UN. Any such initiative is to be welcomed, to the extent that it advances the idea of dialogue.

Let me, then, develop in greater depth what I believe to be the holistic contribution of the dialogical approach, which I believe to be central to the "Globalisation for the Common Good" initiative. First what is envisaged is a prolonged and dynamic interaction between cultures, aimed at promoting an approach to world order which can grapple with the globalisation of insecurity and the divisions which it mirrors and reinforces. In such interaction all traditions, not least the Islamic, Hindu, and Confucian worlds, must be accorded full respect. They must be accepted as major poles of cultural and geopolitical dialogue. Such a project needs to appreciate the specificity of each culture, while contributing to an evolutionary process that builds on commonality but more importantly strives for synthesis.

For all their differences, these axial traditions share a sense of the dignity of human life, a sense of the transcendent, a commitment to human fulfilment, and a concern for standards of "rightness" in human conduct.[29] Common to all of them is the notion of humane and legitimate governance, although the criteria used to measure of legitimacy may vary considerably from one tradition to another. There is, one may reasonably conclude, sufficient common ground between these religious and ethical world-views to make possible an on-going conversation about human ethics in general, and political ethics in particular.[30]

Needless to say, each of the civilisational currents and cultural formations has its own unique features, but such differences need not be inimical to normative discourse either within or between the major civilisational traditions. All of the world's major religious and ethical traditions (e.g. Hinduism, Buddhism, Christianity, Judaism, Islam, Confucianism and secular humanism) have in any case experienced over

---

[29] Chandra Muzaffar, "From Human Rights to Human Dignity," in *Debating Human Rights: Critical Essays on the United States and Asia*, ed. Peter Van Ness (London: Routledge, 1999), pp. 25–31.

[30] Friedman, Edward, "Asia as a Fount of Universal Human Rights," in Peter Van Ness (ed), 32–55.

time a multiplicity of influences, both indigenous an external. In many societies they have furiously interacted with each other and have in the process contributed to the slow but steady transformation of norms and expectations. The emerging inter-civilisational dialogue may benefit as much from difference as from commonality.

The contribution, then, of civilisational dialogue to the contemporary crisis must by definition be multi-faceted. Six dimensions merit special attention.

Dialogue can provide a richer and more varied conception of political community and humane governance by establishing a closer connection between human rights and the range of human needs, not least those of the disadvantaged (hence the emphasis on social and economic justice).

It can offer a more holistic understanding of the human condition by establishing a closer connection between rights and responsibilities and between the individual and the community.

It can help to situate human rights within a larger social context so that their application is not confined to individuals as disaggregated atoms but as members of larger collectivities, and of the international community as a whole. Hence the emphasis on the rights of peoples—not only the right to self-determination but the right to a healthy environment, the right to peace, the right to food security, the right to share in the common heritage of humanity.

The fourth dimensions flows from the preceding three but has an importance of its own. Dialogue cannot be based on domination or notions of superiority. We in the West cannot approach the task of dialogue with the presumption that the West enjoys a monopoly on the definition of human needs and good governance. The Western liberal model and the particular view of progress on which it rests cannot apply universally across time and space. Human rights and governance standards may be universal in scope at any one time, but how these standards are defined and applied is likely to change over time.

In dialogue the emphasis must be on respectful communication and interaction. The development of a world society must proceed by way of negotiation and involve all of the parties concerned.

In many ways our challenge is to practise a dialogue that appreciates and celebrates the diversity of our civilisational inheritance. Indeed, one of the valuable spin-offs of such a dialogue is that it forces the participants to hold their respective traditions up to critical examination, to rediscover the fundamental ethical impulse which sustains that tradition and to consider ways of adapting it to the new circumstances of our epoch. Civilisational dialogue works best when it fosters a profound soul-searching within as much as between civilisations.

To put it simply, inter-religious and intercultural dialogue can help articulate a new internationalism that goes beyond mere economic or technological interdependence, and subjects economic and political orthodoxy to ethical scrutiny.

CIVILISATIONAL DIALOGUE: ITS CONTEMPORARY FUNCTION AND SIGNIFICANCE

But how are we to approach the dialogue of civilisations? How are we to apply dialogical principles in the present geopolitical and geocultural context? Here, it may be helpful to draw attention to two influential voices which have in different but converging ways helped to place the dialogue of civilisations on the intellectual and political map. They have much to tell us about the way forward.

The first is Mohammad Khatami, the fifth president of the Islamic Republic of Iran, a religious scholar steeped in the study of philosophy.

For Khatami, dialogue is the common search for truth. Dialogue cannot therefore obscure or evade the differences that separate its participants, which is why for him the act is one in which listening is at least as important as speaking. Dialogue is the encounter across cultural, religious, philosophical, ethical, civilisational boundaries, in which each participant listens to the other, becomes open, even vulnerable to the other. In this sense, dialogue engages the participant in a journey of self discovery:

> It is only through immersion in another existential dimension that we could attain mediated and acquired knowledge of ourselves in addition to the immediate and direct knowledge of ourselves that we commonly possess. Through seeing others we attain a hitherto impossible knowledge of ourselves. Dialogue among cultures and civilisations rests upon rational and ethically normative commitment of parties to the dialogue. [...] [It] is a bi-lateral or even multi-lateral process in which the end result is not manifest from the beginning.[31]

What, then, are dialogue's normative foundations? The recurring themes in Khatami's numerous speeches on the subject suggest the following key elements: a) the dignity of human being—made possible only through will to empathy and compassion—as the measure of world order; b) the refusal of politics without morality; c) the notion that ideas and values, embedded

---

[31] Seyyed Mohammad Khatami, address at the Dialogue Among Civilizations Conference at the United Nations, September 5, 2000.
http://www.un.int/iran/dialogue/2000/articles/1.html

in cultures and civilisations, are an important determinant of political behaviour; d) the sense that intellectuals, poets, artists, scientists, and mystics, precisely because they have the capacity and authority to articulate the large questions of human existence, have a unique role in civilisation dialogue. Many questions remain unanswered: Who participates in this dialogue? What are the modalities of dialogue? What is to be the role of states and governments in the dialogical process?

There is nevertheless one idea, central to Khatami's conception of dialogue, which merits attention. In his celebrated 1999 speech at the University of Florence, he offered the following juxtaposition of East and West:

> Orient, which even in an etymological sense signifies the process of imparting direction and order to things, can beckon Europe and America to equilibrium, serenity and reflection in the context of an historical dialogue [...]. If deeply understood in their Eastern connotations, equilibrium and serenity lie beyond both the Dionysian and Apollonian extremes of western culture. The age of reason is an Apollonian age while romanticism is the opposite pull on the swing of the same pendulum.[32]

Khatami's exposition takes us back to the question of what is to be the discursive framework that guides the post-Cold War era. For Khatami dialogue among civilisations is designed specifically to address the fault line that separates Orient and Occident, a fault line that has a long history, of which the present difficulties between Islam and the West are but the most recent, perhaps geopolitically most troublesome manifestation.

Another influential voice that merits attention is that of Tu Weiming, perhaps the foremost neo-Confucian thinker of our time. Born in February 1940 in Kunming, China, he grew up and was educated in Taiwan and is now Professor of Chinese History and Philosophy and of Confucian Studies at Harvard University.[33]

---

[32] Seyyed Mohammad Khatami, speech at the European University Institute, Florence, March 10, 1999.
http://www.dialoguecentre.org/PDF/Florence%20Speech.pdf
[33] Tu Weiming (ed), *Confucian Traditions in East Asian Modernity: Exploring Moral Education and Economic Culture in Japan and the Four Mini-Dragons* (Harvard University Press, 1996); *Confucian Thought: Selfhood as Creative Transformation* (Albany, NY, State University of New York Press, 1985); Confucianism in a Historical Perspective (Singapore: Institute of East Asian Philosophies, 1989); *The Way, Learning and Politics in Classical Confucian Humanism* (Singapore: Institute of East Asian Philosophies, 1985).

A recurring theme of Tu Weiming's intellectual contribution is the modern transformation of Confucian humanism.[34] Confucian values, he argues, remain highly relevant to modernity and are evident in contemporary social practices, at least as principles of societal organisation. These include: a) the role of the state in the management of the market; b) social civility as the key to civilised mode of conduct (law is useful but not enough); c) the family as the foundation stone of social civility; d) civil society as the indispensable nexus between family and state; e) education as the key to civil society; f) self-cultivation understood as both goal and process.

Confucian societies retain many of these values even as they embrace the fierce competitiveness of the West. The reason is not hard to fathom: modernisation and modernity are shaped by cultural forms rooted in tradition:

Traditions in Modernity are not merely historical sedimentation passively deposited in modern consciousness. Nor are they simply inhibiting features to be undermined by the unilinear trajectory of development—on the contrary they are both constraining and enabling forces capable of shaping the particular contour of modernity in any given society.[35] For Tu Weiming, these traditions constitute the critical elements of sustainable dialogue.

What can Confucianism bring to such a dialogue? Here is where Tu Weiming is at his most illuminating. He draws attention to what he calls the "ecological turn" of neo-Confucian thought, and in particular to the contribution of three modern Confucian thinkers. Qian Mu (1895–1990), Tang Junyi (1909–1978) and Feng Youlan (1895–1990) based in Hong Kong, Taiwan, and China respectively. In their critique of the enlightenment and the discourse of modernity, they take us, he contends, beyond aggressive anthropocentrism and instrumental rationality, and pave the way for an inclusive cosmological and humanist vision that transcends the either/or mode of thinking in favour of a non-dualistic understanding of the continuity of heaven, earth and humanity.

The theme is a highly instructive one, for it offers another path to East-West dialogue. Placed in this context, it is not hard to see why Tu Weiming sees the long-term stability of the Sino-American relationship as likely to depend on China widening the frame of reference offered by its own

---

[34] W. Theodore de Bary, "Neo-Confucianism and Human Rights," in *Human Rights in the World's Religions*, ed. Leroy S. Rouner (Notre Dame: University of Notre Dame, 1988), pp. 183–98.

[35] Tu Weiming, Lecture delivered Colorado College, February 5, 1999. http://www.coloradocollege.edu/academics/anniversary/participants/Tu.htm

civilisation. For its part, the United States, which has hitherto functioned principally as a teaching civilisation, may have to acquire more of the qualities of a learning culture. Put simply, Tu Weiming suggests that we may be entering a "second axial period" in which all the major religious and ethical traditions that arose during the "first axial period" are undergoing their own distinctive transformations in response to the multiple challenges of modernity. It is possible that such reassessment will make possible, through a process of mutual learning, an "anthropocosmic" worldview where the human is embedded in the cosmic order. This period of transition is the "dialogical moment," the beginning of a new history that is simultaneously global and plural. Such a moment, Tu Weiming tells us, can flourish when "the politics of domination is being replaced by the politics of communication, networking, negotiation, interaction, interfacing and collaboration."[36]

Despite the vastly different cultural and ideological backgrounds from which they spring, influential voices have emerged calling for a distinctive approach to world order, sharply at variance with western triumphalism or imperial discourse. This approach lends itself to the following propositions:

- Dialogue, that is encounter with the other, is the path to self-discovery and is therefore a profoundly transformative process;
- Dialogue can proceed only with the renewal of tradition against the backdrop of modernity;
- The dialogue of civilisations proposes first and foremost the dialogical encounter between East and West;
- Such an encounter will involve a new synthesis constituted of both differences and commonalities;
- The dialogue of civilisations offers a particularly promising cultural underpinning for a new conception of global citizenship and governance;
- The encounter of civilisational insights should inform and even guide the political processes of states, but also the international rule of law and the constantly expanding network of regional and global institutions.

---

[36] Tu Weiming, presentation to the seminar organised by the Danish Foreign Ministry, Copenhagen, June 2001. Proceedings edited by Jacques Baudot, *Building A World Community: Globalisation and the Common Good* (Copenhagen : Royal Danish Ministry of Foreign Affairs in association with University of Washington Press, Seattle, 2001).

One other observation is highly relevant. Dialogue is no simple or easy remedy for the world's current ills. If the philosophy and method of dialogue are to be applied to the theory and practice of citizenship and the wider normative framework governing state conduct, this will inevitably involve a good deal of pain. For citizens and the various communities to which they belong (as well as states themselves) must come to terms with the difficult task of reconciliation. Many communities have suffered from past violence, some continue to suffer today. Yet, we also know that many of these same communities have been the perpetrators of violence. Reconciliation will require citizens and authorities of different communities to share their stories, to listen to one another's experience of pain, to confess past wrongs, to acknowledge collective responsibility for righting the wrongs of the past. Civilisational dialogue can become a force for healing to the extent that it nurtures a radical ethic in the evolving organisation of human affairs. The strong have to cultivate the virtue of humility

In this unfolding transitional moment, the initiative is likely to lie as much with civil society as with the state—though there is a great deal that states can and must do. If we as members of civil society (locally, nationally, and transnationally), are to address the immense challenges of the next several decades, we will need to participate in a dialogue of global proportions—global not simply in geographic terms, but global in the sense that it cultivates a "global spirituality." This will be a dialogue tailored to a new conception of citizenship that puts an entirely different complexion on unity and difference, and allows them to coexist, illuminate, and reinforce each other.

The obstacles to such a project are obvious and daunting. Yet the opportunities for moving forward may be greater than is often assumed. We are in fact witnessing the emergence of a new kind of universalism and the slow, at times erratic, but unmistakable diffusion of power. Despite periodic setbacks, we are seeing the increasing universality of the UN system, as measured not only or even primarily by the number of member states, but by the increasing participation of a wide range of non-state actors, the widening scope of consultation, and the UN's steadily expanding agenda and forms and techniques of involvement. Increasingly, the world's global and regional institutions are in practice, if not in theory, rethinking the centrality of the principle of sovereignty. Mirroring and reinforcing that tendency is the embryonic development of a global civil society, which is giving rise to new processes of global communication and co-operation

A new universalism, nurtured by the dialogue of civilisations, may also facilitate the growth of a multipolar system if the United States is joined by Western Europe, Russia, China, Japan, India and possibly an Islamic coalition in defining the priorities of the international agenda. A dialogical universalism, attuned to the cultural, religious, and philosophical plurality of the world, may be better able to handle the North-South divide, whether on issues of trade, debt, or environment. It may in time give rise to a global reform coalition that includes a number of states and their agencies, international organisations, knowledge communities, and the rapidly expanding groups, movements, and networks that comprise civil society. Participants in the dialogue of civilisations must stand ready to reimagine the future and so transform the present.

GLOBAL MULTICULTURALISM
VERSUS THE "WAR OF CULTURES"

Ada Aharoni

How beautiful upon the mountains are the feet of the messenger
of good tidings that announces peace!
The Bible, Isaiah 52

He who walks with peace–walk with him.
The Koran, Sura 48

INTRODUCTION

In our world today, the conflict of cultures has become one of the most
prominent risk factors for the sustainability and future development of
human civilization. Following the terrorist attack on the World Trade
Center in New York (September 11, 2001), it became obvious that the
opening of the third millennium has ushered a dangerous and unprecedented
"war of cultures." This new global development (which includes the trend
of suicide bombings) cannot be overcome by guns and bombs, but rather by
a vehicle of culture itself, by an openness, understanding and respect of the
values, beliefs, and norms of "the other," or in other words, by the
promotion of "Multiculturalism." The fear that the opponent, or "enemy,"
disdains one's culture and religion and is anxious to eliminate it is one of
the profound causes of the clash of cultures which has led to the present
dangerous "War of Cultures."

The "Webster New World Dictionary" describes "Culture" as: "The
development, improvement and refinement of the mind, emotions, interests,
manners, tastes, as well as: the arts, ideas, customs, and skills of a given
people in a given period." The Oxford English Dictionary adds to this
definition, that culture is "The intellectual side of civilization." Hence,
"Multiculturalism" is all the above, when applied to many various cultures.

In the era of globalization, there is a new wave of global culture
spreading all over the world, parallel to the spreading of a global economy,
international relations, markets, information, and technology. However, it is
unfortunate that the emerging global culture instead of promoting a culture
of peace, harmony, and positive ethical values, is often influenced by the
predominance of the presentation of violence, crime, and homicide films
daily shown on global television, and other electronic media.

Multiculturalism and harmonious intercultural communication can
effectively overcome the social culture of violence and war by promoting

the awareness of the oneness of humankind, as well as the promotion of the consciousness of common positive ethical values shared by different cultures. Multiculturalism can also promote a new positive identity of the "global citizen" in addition to the various ethnic identities of specific groups and nations. Instead of being in opposition to each other, the new global identity and the national identity can nourish and strengthen each other. Together, they can create a dynamic and symbiotic enrichment of the individual, of societies, and of nations, at various significant levels.

It is therefore crucially important in our present global configuration, to build an effective multicultural system and network, at the regional and global levels, that would encompass: all levels of society, the media, and education. The main goals of such a system would be to develop through interconnected international institutions, an innovative and revolutionary peace culture, and to spread its various aspects and values to the wide masses around the world.

To accomplish this important gigantic task, the following measures are recommended:

1. Institutions and governments should invest in developing a harmonious multicultural system and network that would help people and nations to understand and respect each other. Such an endeavor would reduce the misunderstanding and fear of "the other," as well as the possibility of violent conflicts, and save in the cost of armaments and defense. The developing and spreading of a multicultural peace system and network could indeed be the best investment for defense. As in "preventive medicine," the promotion of a harmonious multicultural social system can be considered as the "prevention of Wars of Culture." An influential multicultural Global TV for Peace Network could change dangerous influences and trends caused by ignorance, fear, mistrust, and hatred of "the other" that leads to conflicts and wars into attitudes of understanding, trust, and respect for that previously unknown and threatening "other."

2. Governments of all states should consider establishing Ministries of "Multicultural Peace" with appropriate budgets that can accomplish the great task of changing the trends in various national cultures from bigotry, violence, and terror, to multicultural openness toward other cultures and other religions, and to the promotion of an intercultural communication based on harmony and peace. Literature and the arts in the pursuit of peace, collected from various civilizations and cultures, should be researched, translated, and widely used. Multicultural peace education and peace studies at all levels, should be initiated and established, not only for children and young people, but also for leaders, teachers, and parents, as well as the public at large.

3. Finally, wide support for global Peace NGO's should be initiated and established. Non-governmental organizations in the various countries should be intrinsically involved in the creation of the required new multicultural peace system. The NGO's should be largely sponsored, to be able to operate effectively and in a global interconnected fashion. NGO's could help in the collection and diffusion of the various cultural contributions of peace literature, poetry, drama, and the arts, from the best that is available in various cultures and civilizations. This would help to reflect the great majority of the "Voices of the Earth," yearning for a peaceful world without violence, destruction, terror, and war.

THE ROLE OF A PEACE MEDIA: CREATING A NEW PEACE CULTURE

> Ours is a world of nuclear giants and ethical infants! We know more about war than we do about peace. We know more about killing than we do about living […]. It is not the magnitude of the problem that is the great obstacle. It is our colossal indifference to it.
>
> General Omar Bradley[1]

The media and telecommunications should play an important role of interconnection between people and nations, as they are key factors in the process of the globalization of culture and the spread of multiculturalism. Until recently, people in each society mainly read news concerning their own societies, and they chiefly listened and watched to their own local electronic media. The growing global telecommunications networks promote the knowledge, understanding, and interconnection of different societies and they open new realms of other civilizations and cultures. In doing so, the global media can break up stereotypes and bring about the required openness and changes in the consciousness of individuals and in global society. Hence, the modern electronic communications, especially TV networks and global Satellites, can play a key role in the creation and the promotion of the required innovative multicultural peace system.

The electronic media therefore, due to its capacity to ensure fast movement of information and to reach global multitudes simultaneously have a great responsibility in shaping perceptions and opinions of people, and they can fulfil a crucial role in the building of a global village beyond war. The economic globalization that is currently taking place has increased people's consciousness concerning the notion of the oneness of humanity. The electronic media: satellites, television, radio, and the Internet, can have

---

[1] Armistice Day Address, November 11, 1948, in *Collected Writings*, 4 vols (Washington D.C.: [n.p.] 1967–71), Vol. 1.

a meritorious impact in promoting this consciousness. Links in cyberspace between people and institutions, through the use of the Internet, are an added dimension for the formation of multicultural partnerships and they can render possible a wide expansion of varied inter-cultural influences.

Furthermore, a balanced, responsible and conscientious media can greatly help in the process of healing our planet of its violent characteristics such as terror and wars, which are infesting many parts of the world, where violence is often erroneously equated with strength. The media should be brought to regard "Peace News" as "newsworthy," and a balance should be achieved between the reporting of "good and hopeful news" and the sensational reporting of violence and crime. The disproportional amount of homicidal and crime news inflates the negative aspects of society and is a deformation of reality and normality. Hence, it is crucial to quickly create and develop an ethical multicultural peace media and network to counteract destructive influences and trends and to build global peace. The "Peace Radio," linked to the UN University based in Porto Rico, is an example of the suggested multicultural peace media system.

Governments, decision makers, and people responsible for the media and telecommunications, should strive to reform them in such a way that they can become reliable vehicles for the promotion and diffusion of multicultural peace. In addition, the leaders and people in each country, who usually have an impact on popular consciousness concerning issues of war and peace, such as: journalists, culture researchers, TV and films directors, as well as dramatists and writers—should be personally involved and motivated to contribute the best of their talents toward the creation, development and promotion of the global multicultural peace system.

The media should give a priority to "peace news," and cover the aspects of society and culture that are positive and constructive. They should also widely present and positively expose writers, poets, playwrights and artists who are consciously contributing to the creation of the new "global peace system."

Thus, telecommunications and the media are indeed key figures for the creation of the innovative multicultural peace system that would promote global advancement of humankind. They could also contribute in a major way, toward the individual's global identification and the notion of the unity of humankind, while keeping one's own culture, traditions, and intrinsic cultural diversity.

THE GLOBAL TV BY SATELLITE FOR PEACE CULTURE: A MULTICULTURAL MODEL

It is not too late for the world to be what it might have been.

While most television networks are chiefly framed from the point of view and perspectives of the sensational and what is violent in our world, the "The Global TV by Satellite Network for Peace Culture"—the GSPC, will be directed and framed by peace culture researchers, and it will have an agenda set by peace writers and media. Most citizens of the world share universal values: love of the family and love of life, as well as the basic values of caring and sharing. These are the basic values and ethics that will govern the frame of reference and perspectives for choosing the issues for the agenda and the programs of the GSPC. They will all be relevant to the sustenance and flourishing of humankind and to the building of a world beyond war, terror, violence, and famine.

The IFLAC "Global Television Network by Satellite for Peace Culture," will be an independent, not-for-profit project. It is initiated by IFLAC PAVE PEACE: The International Forum for the Literature and Culture of Peace: www.iflac.com, www.iflac.com/ada

It will function in collaboration with major networks and institutions, and it will receive counsel from an International Advisory Board comprised of the Directors and of IFLAC in various countries. These leaders are outstanding individuals from the academic peace research sector, literary, social, and philanthropic segments of society.

Major television networks and government agencies devote considerable resources to the covering of conflict, violence and war, and there are almost no peace programs on television, or programs for the promotion of peace culture. Hence, there is a great need for a systematic plan of action in all-global networks to provide meaningful and resourceful guidance on the subject of the humane values of peace and multiculturalism. The programs should be involving, exciting, of a high professional quality and suitable for all sectors of society, including for leaders, teachers, parents, and students. They should make use of the voices and qualities of peace researchers, writers and intellectuals, as well as authentic voices of peace loving citizens, representing the great majority of global citizens that yearn and clamor for peace.

Generations repeat the mistakes of former generations, and mainly conflicts, violence, wars, and the recent disastrous phenomenon of suicide bombings—become preferred priority news and permanent facets of societies. The GSPC will be a model for the coverage of peace news and for the promotion of the notion that peace culture news is "newsworthy."

Major Television Networks not only choose to cover mostly disastrous news, but furthermore, they constantly air violent homicide and murder films that have a negative and destructive influence on society. The predominant coverage of mostly violent and destructive events in the global media and the airing of violent and unethical films will have to change.

The GSPC network will instead, aim at airing hopeful, positive, and exciting programs and films about how people and leaders tackle their problems, avoid violence, and solve conflicts. It will function as "preventive medicine" against the possibility of rampant violence, terror, and wars. Toward this aim, the GSPC will develop and implement programs of peace news, peace films, literature and poetry, as well as multicultural and inter-generation dialogues and exciting personal peace stories from all around the globe. The network agenda will also develop and air alternative educational peace programs for all ages and promote multicultural leadership models. These various peace programs and films will be available in all parts of the world through powerful global Satellites and they will serve all segments of global society. The GSPC Programs will also be made available on the Internet and a vast network of Internet Clubs will be built in third world countries, with access to all its various resources and programs.

Through these in-depth, systematic and sustained programs of the GSPC, leaders, as well as all citizens of our global village, will be able to absorb peace values, skills and ideas, and to dedicate their talents and energies toward the building of a world beyond war and violence. Leaders, men, women and youth, will be equipped with the necessary ethical values, insights and skills to overcome the occurrence of conflicts, and to prevent their descent into violence and war.

The peace loving people of the world, who comprise the great majority of the citizens of the global village, will be inter-linked by the GSPC programs on the Internet, and it would strengthen them in their endeavor to create a better world beyond war. Through various informative links, and exciting video programs, people will be able to express their hopes, dreams, and shared concerns. The GSPC will also initiate, create, and support peace inter-communications and peace programs and actions by institutions, governments, corporations, and Non Governmental organizations that will enable humankind to live together in a balanced, harmonious, and peaceful world.

It would be a valuable and important step if this prestigious Conference in Istanbul, on "Globalization for the Common Good," would recommend the foundation of the "Global TV by Satellite for Peace Culture" (GSPC), to the Turkish government and that it would indeed implement it. Turkey is the ideal place for the establishment of such a major global project as it is a natural cultural bridge between East and West.

The GSPC could start from some weekly hours, and gradually work up to twenty four hours a day, broadcasting at the beginning from Istanbul, Haifa, and Ramallah, in English, Turkish, Hebrew and Arabic, and it can gradually add other major languages, so as to make it a real multicultural Global Television for Peace Culture. When more support becomes available, by the UN and other major Institutions, it is hoped that in time, the GSPC will become fully multicultural and be globally available through a powerful global satellite.

GSPC TRANSFORMATION OF VIOLENCE TO MULTICULTURAL PEACE

The same stream of life that runs through my veins day and night runs through the world.

Rabindranath Tagore[2]

The GSPC will attempt to transform the world from a violent planet into a peaceful one, and to make it a better, more harmonious, and safer place for all through the global spreading of a Multicultural Peace agenda. The highly professional coverage will be humane and democratic and it will promote the basic notion that all individuals are part of one humanity and they should be dedicated and faithful to it. To preserve the planet in these dangerous nuclear-bomb-times, leaders and citizens will have to radically change their thinking concerning the waging of wars. One of the major challenges of the GSPC programs will be to guide leaders and citizens as well as youth to become peacemakers and to devote their talents, capacities, and energies towards the creation of a global civilization of well-being and harmony.

As the GSPC will be multicultural, it will have to initiate the translation of works by major global writers, philosophers, and poets that promote multiculturalism and peace culture. It will cover and air illuminating interviews of multicultural peace writers, poets, and artists, from all over the globe and make their works and peace messages accessible to the whole world.

The GSPC will also include a "Peace Culture University of the Air," that will develop a systematic and sustained program of study on the theory, principles, and practice of multiculturalism and the culture of peace. Among various other subjects, it will provide the study of the lives, thoughts, and examples of great peace leaders, such as Mahatma Gandhi, Luther King, Anwar Sadat, and Yitzhak Rabin, and the various remarkable and

---

[2] Rabindranath Tagore, "Stream of Life," in *Gitanjali: Song Offerings* (London: MacMillan, 1913).

outstanding women peace leaders and thinkers, throughout history, such as Queen Hatshapshut of ancient Egypt, Florence Nightingale, Sister Theresa, and Sister Thea. Thea Woolf was the Head Nurse of the Jewish Hospital in Alexandria, who saved Jews from the Nazi Holocaust, with the aid of Moslem Egyptian officials, as related in *Not In Vain: An Extraordinary Life*.

The principles and theories of these various Peace Leaders will be integrated into the agenda of the "GSPC University of the Air." Its curriculum will include various subjects, such as: Sociology, Literature, Interrelated-Religions, History, Psychology, Science, Media and Communications, Women Studies, and Art—all from the point of view of Peace Studies. It will also establish interrelated programs of intensive "Regional Culture for Peace" units, which will objectively examine in depth specific conflicts, such as the long and acute Israeli-Palestinian conflict, and offer ways to resolve them. For example, at this juncture, if it were to comment on this, it would probable state that the best way to solve the Palestinian-Israeli conflict is the "Two States" solution proposed by the European Community, the Quartet, and the Arab League Initiative. Former Member of the Knesset, Prof. Naomi Chazan, recently commented on that: "It would be a genuine investment in Palestinian-Israeli peace negotiations on permanent status issues, to conduct the talks within the framework of the Arab League Initiative. Such a commitment—with all it entails in terms of energy and resources—is the only way to correct the frightening illusion that war and peace can go together." (*Jerusalem Post*, May 18, 2007).

The GSPC will moreover establish "Global Peace Culture" programs that will attempt to develop a global identity and consciousness of the individual as well as of ethnic groups and nations, stressing their responsibility to the whole of humankind and to the planet. These programs will particularly cover those regions where the ravages of war, terrorism, and racial prejudice, such as in the Middle East, have created conditions of misery, fear and insecurity, and they will research ways to solve the crises and conflicts.

The programs for children will include the IFLAC PEACE TRAIN Project, which will run in several countries, where children will exchange peace greetings drawn on wagons of trains, with children across conflicted borders, as for instance, Israeli and Palestinian children, and Turkish and Greek children. Beautiful and humanistic films for children, both modern ones, and old ones, such as for example, those of Shirley Temple and Margaret O'Brien, will be aired, in which children will be able to identify with positive, live, and lovable heroic models.

The GSPC will condemn the global social and electronic media culture of violence as the worst enemy of humankind and it will strive to powerfully change the belligerent violent lens to a peace culture one. The GSPC will be a reaction to the disastrous violent mess on the planet earth: it will help to clean the mess and install sanity, beauty, and joy throughout the global village. In doing so, it will use various modes and structures. This will include humor and comedy, together with some other effective vehicles and tools. Humor will be one of the ways to strip the glorification of violence, murder, and homicide, and to ridicule and condemn their association with the sensational and with sexism. The GSPC will pulse with reason and hope, and with the vast celebration of peaceful and caring womanhood and manhood, working together for the creation of a better world.

For those who doubt that the GSPC can be effectively created and have a major revolutionary impact on the world, let us consider for example, the Al-Jazeera Television. A few years ago it was difficult to imagine that a small new Arabic channel would lead the news agenda, stir the world and throw serious challenges to media monopoly. Today, Al-Jazeera, a Qatar-based independent television channel, stimulates and creates controversies in and out of the Arab world, as well as in Europe and America.

This year Al-Jazeera has established programs in English that provide English speakers in the United States, Europe, and elsewhere, with their particular version of reporting. Its inflammatory and sometimes biased programs often project one-sided views about the Middle East, the world's most turbulent region. In spite of this lack of professional objectivity and one-sidedness, Al-Jazeera has become a powerful reality, and no major international TV station can afford to ignore it. The CNN, ABC, NBC, Fox, BBC, German ZDF, and NHK of Japan, have signed agreements with Al-Jazeera and they co-operate with it. Although Al-Jazeera was known to the western world only in 2001, from the very beginning of its establishment in 1996, it became a center of attention and a powerful global influence.

The "Global TV by Satellite for Peace Culture," will air a quite different tune—its reporting will concentrate on an objective and serious analysis of present predicaments and conflicts, with the intent to solve them with equity and to promote peace among nations. It will forcefully counteract biased, fanatical, and violence-oriented reporting in the global media, and it will widely air objective Global News including Peace News, as well as Regional News. It will also deeply analyze and project global and regional political perspectives, together with the systematic delineation on a daily basis of the global and national peace culture progress, in an honest and objective way, and with a high standard of professionalism. This will give hope to the masses of citizens who yearn for peace, especially in conflicted and war-torn regions of the Global Village.

PEACE CULTURE LEADERSHIP

> If ever the world sees a time when women shall come together purely and simply for the benefit of mankind, it will be a power such as the world has never known.
>
> Matthew Arnold[3]

In the above illuminating quotation, the British poet, Mathew Arnold, wisely writes about the latent possible peace power of women. Indeed, if women—who are more than half the population of the world and the best allies for peace—unite and succeed to attain equal leadership status with the men, it would be a tremendous step toward the creation of a world beyond war and terror. Therefore, women should be trained on an equal basis with the men, to be able to acquire the knowledge and skills for successful peace-centered leadership. "The Peace Culture Leadership Program" will be one of the intensive training programs on the GSPC agenda, aimed at equipping men and women with a strong background of peace values, peace culture, knowledge, and skills. It will prepare prospective Peace Leaders for positions in all segments of society: government, civic, religious institutions, business, NGOs, professional institutions, and in work places. The peace culture leadership program will focus on developing the capacity of women and men leaders so that they will be empowered to create suitable strategies for a wide implementation of the culture of peace in their respective communities, governments, institutions, and organizations. In particular, the program will:

- Equip participants with the principles of the equality of women and men;
- Provide the conceptual understanding of an enlightened and progressive peace-based leadership, formulated according to the principle of unity in diversity;
- Provide a strong basis of the ethics and practice of democracy, characterized by inter-ethnic harmony and cooperation, as well as a deep respect for the human rights of all citizens.

Methods of conflict resolution will be taught and applied. Participants will be trained to acquire the skills for diffusing the Peace Culture Program

---

[3] Cited in Steven M, Gelber and Martin L. Cook, *Saving the Earth: The History of a Middle-Class Millenarian Movement* (Berkeley: University of California Press, 1990), p. 166.

ideals into the public consciousness, including religious and educational institutions, municipalities and governments all around the world.

FUNDING

> In the fullness of time, war will come to an end, not for moral reasons—but because of its absurdity
>
> Evelyn Hardy

Funding for such a colossal and urgent project such as the GSPC will be solicited from Governments, as well as the UN, UNESCO, the WORLD BANK, and major institutions, including national and private corporations, foundations, and individuals. The creation of the GSPC is crucial to the whole of humanity and to the whole global village. It will function as "Preventive Medicine" to overcome conflicts and avoid wars, terror, and violence, and it will support the global development of a culture of peace, instead of the prevalent culture of violence and militarism.

A frequently asked question by peace-loving individuals is, "How can I help?" There are many ways in which people can help to promote the foundation and the firm establishment and development of the "GSPC: The Global TV by Satellite for Peace Culture":

- Individuals can help by writing to their Senators and Congress representatives in their Governments, as well as to the UN, UNESCO, and the WORLD BANK, about the urgent need to create the IFLAC GSPN, and ask them for their sponsorship, financial help, and participation.
- Participants can send the GSPC Project to additional various local and global institutions that share the commitment to global peace and to the building of a world beyond war, and ask for their support and help.
- Individuals and corporations can help by making donations toward the establishment of the GSPC and encouraging friends and associates to do the same.
- People, who are versed in the Technology of Television and Satellites, can be solicited to offer their voluntary services in all aspects of setting up the "Global Television Network by Satellite for Peace Culture."
- Fund Raisers, Public Relations persons and Secretaries, can offer their services for coordinating communications and activities in the various countries and sectors they belong to.

- The organization of fund-raising dinners and events for the launching of the GSPC, in major cities all over the world, requires good, creative, and skilful administrators. At such fund-raising events, Peace Culture Researchers will be glad to address such themes as how the GSPC can create "A Healing Among Nations and Promote Global Understanding," toward the creation of a better world beyond war. In addition, writers, actors, and poets would be glad to present artistic "Peace Presentations, Poetry, and Music."

MULTICULTURAL PEACE LITERATURE AND ART

He playfully showed
With a smile and a wink,
and a Teddy Bear hug –
It could be the beginning
Of a honey-laden decade
In a brave new world –

By wisely trading
Guns
    For Teddy Bears"

Ada Aharoni[4]

Culture and literature are an important part of our lives, we absorb them daily as we do our daily bread, and they constitute the building blocks of our identities and personalities. However, we do not give their contents and impact enough attention. The major components of literature—novels, fiction, poetry, and drama—are often made into films and television programs, and as various studies have shown, fiction, drama and stories can often influence more than facts.

Both classical and modern peace creations, collected from multicultural resources around the world, should be used as models for building the harmonious peaceful culture needed to repair the world from the violent phase it is going through. Outgoing multicultural major works of peace literature and art should influence and characterize the dawn of the third millennium.

There should be a thorough examination of what has already been achieved in national cultures that can help the building of a multicultural climate of peace. Despite the fact that our global village has been affected

---

[4] Ada A. Aharoni, "Teddy Bears for Guns," in *Not in Your War Anymore* (1997). http://tx.technion.ac.il/~ada/peace-p.html#notwar

by major destructive cultural upheavals caused by conflicts, wars, and differences in development and standards of living, peace culture traditions and literary heritage exist in all civilizations. They have been developed at different periods of history, and in different region, and they should now be collected and used for the reinforcement of the common cultural ties of humankind and the new global citizen consciousness. Those collected peace works can constitute important stepping-stones toward the required innovative multicultural peace developments.

The manifold benefits of a multicultural literature in the pursuit of peace should be made available to the wide public all over our global village. Various valuable classical literary peace sources that have stood the test of time, such as Rabindranath Tagore's philosophical poems, Wilfred Owen's peace poetry, Jubran Khalil Jubran's *The Prophet*, and Leo Tolstoy's *War and Peace*, Hafez and Omar Khayam's beautiful poetry, and many other valuable creative works, should be presented widely to audiences around the world, through satellite television programs and radio. They should also be utilized in education programs at all levels and in cultural entertainment as well. Peace culture research studies of world literature could highlight new angles of peace themes in great classical drama, as for instance, the condemnation of violence and war in the works of Shakespeare, as can be seen in his tragedies, *Romeo and Juliet, Hamlet*, and *Othello*.

Multicultural peace literature should also be intensively researched in contemporary culture and literature, and new peace books should be explored and utilized, such as the historical novel, *From the Nile to the Jordan*, which shows multiculturalism in Egypt, and the biography of the peace heroine Thea Wolf, *Not in Vain: An Extraordinary Life*, as well as Prof. M. Fawzi Daif's book on *The Significance of Peace in the Poetry of Ada Aharoni*, and the book for children, *Peace Flower*.[5] The first three books describe the cooperation of Jews and Egyptians in Egypt, before 1948, and they should be made widely known, as they give hope for possible cooperation and reconciliation in the present between Israelis and Arab/Palestinians.

We find words and descriptions of peace in all cultures and in all religions. For instance, in the Holy Bible we find, "How beautiful upon the mountains are the feet of the messenger of good tidings that announces peace!" (Isaiah 52), and in the Koran: "He who walks with peace—walk with him!" (Sura 48). And in our own times, the late Pope John Paul II

---

[5] Ada Aharoni, *From the Nile to the Jordan* (Haifa: Lachman, 2001); *Peace Flower: A Space Adventure* (Haifa: Lachman, 1994); *Not in Vain: An Extraordinary Life* (San carlos: Ladybug, 1997); Mohammed Fawzi Daif, *The Significance of Peace in the Poetry of Ada Aharoni* (Cairo: Nile Publications, [n.d.]).

admonished, "War is a defeat for humanity. Only in peace and through peace can respect for human dignity and its inalienable rights be guaranteed."[6]

Governments, relevant institutions, NGO's, and the wider public, should be made aware of the power of multicultural literature in the pursuit of peace, to render the world a safer place to live in, and to enrich the intellectual and ethical standard of living. This view of a constructive, ethical, and harmonious peace culture does not imply an escapist or unrealistic attitude. The concrete problems in conflicts, such as land, water, work opportunities, and education possibilities of nations should be thoroughly investigated and solutions that are acceptable by both sides of the conflict should be provided. These materialistic and concrete grievances should not only be addressed socially and politically, but also aided and exposed through the projection of effective cultural programs on television, as well as in films, literature, and drama.

The multicultural works of peace literature and art could promote powerful components of CBM's: "Confidence Building Measures," among people and nations, including the values of appreciation and respect for the culture, religions, and art of "the other."

In a conflict situation, there are several benefits to be reaped from the development of a multicultural and intercultural peace system. These can be grouped in three major stages: before, during, and after, the occurrence of a conflict or a war:

a) *Before* a tense situation, multiculturalism based on openness and peace values, can function as a preventive remedy. Coming into contact with the culture of "the other" and listening to his side of the "story" or the conflict, an acceptable agreement by both sides becomes easier and he ceases to be a threat, for, as the popular saying has it, "An enemy is someone whose story we have not listened to."

b) *During* the conflict: An open, pluralistic culture, based on values of understanding, respect, tolerance and moderation, can help in arriving at a solution, even during the conflict or war. When conditions for a settlement may have developed, attainment of peace can be delayed by the mistrust created by the conflict situation. The building of bridges of understanding of the "other's" view, and

---

[6] Pope John Paul II, "Message for the World Day of Peace," January 1, 2000. http://www.vatican.va/holy_father/john_paul_ii/messages/peace/documents/hf_jp-ii_mes_08121999_xxxiii-world-day-for-peace_en.html

respect for the other's culture, religion, and identity, can greatly help to overcome the mistrust and hatred.

c) *After* the conflict or war is over, the multicultural peace system can also help in building renewed trust between people and nations. During a war not only buildings are destroyed, but also the image of the enemy, who is usually portrayed as a "demon," by each of the sides. Deep residues of fear, hatred, and mistrust linger in the hearts of former opponents. These sentiments cannot be overcome only by the signing of a peace treaty by leaders, but require also a thorough re-construction of a positive image of each other by the people themselves by acquiring knowledge, understanding, and respect for each other's identity, ethnicity, culture, and religion.

Literature, poetry and the arts, are suitable vehicles for this required "reconstruction," of each other's image, as they have the ability to reach the deeply emotional layers of mistrust and hatred built over the years in the hearts of enemies, and they have the power to dissipate them. It is also necessary to know and respect the core identity of the previous "enemy," consisting mainly of: cultural heritage, values, ethics, history, and religious beliefs, to be able to reach a full reconciliation.

INTERACTIVE PEACE MUSEUMS

> Dear Descartes, not only
> "I think therefore I am,"
> But mostly
> "I create therefore I am."
> Ada Aharoni[7]

Another possible innovative aspect of the building of a new multicultural system, which municipalities and governments should consider, is the founding of "Interactive Peace Museums." This development has recently been established in various countries to help propagate multiculturalism and the peace cultural and historical heritage of nations, and to make it accessible to the whole of humankind. Peace museums have been founded in various countries, including Japan, England, Samarkand and other countries. Japan, which has suffered so much from the atomic bomb during World War Two, is a leading figure in this new trend, and it has already founded more than eighty peace museums. These museums demonstrate the

---

[7] Ada Aharoni, "Dear Descartes."
http://www.authorsden.com/visit/viewpoetry.asp?AuthorID=27219&id=134122

great yearning of the Japanese people for a global multicultural peace system, after having suffered the atrocities of the atomic bombs on Hiroshima and Nagasaki. The Peace Museum in Kyoto has a whole floor dedicated to the condemnation of the Jewish Holocaust by the Nazis, which is one of the examples of the openness to the cultural history of other nations.

Creative, interactive and Multicultural peace museums represent a new conception of what a museum should be. They are "alive" and full of vital activity and multicultural programs for all ages and are becoming increasingly popular. School children and students regularly visit them, and use their peace materials for their works and research on multicultural peace. In addition, public lectures, exhibitions of arts, peace literature and poetry, and peace concerts for all ages, are organized and presented to the wide public.

Ideally, multicultural peace museums should become a "must" in every major city and town in our global village. A well-financed governmental and municipal budget, as well as the UN, UNESCO, and the World Bank, should sponsor the building of peace museums in every city and major town of our global village.

CONCLUSION

I am the enemy you killed my friend.
                              Wilfred Owen[8]

In view of the fact that the conflict of cultures and religions has become one of the most prominent risk factors for the sustainability and future development of human civilization, ways to curb it and to replace it with an ethical and peaceful multicultural system and network are suggested. The new regional and global multicultural system would include ethical and peace values from various cultures, and it would be based on the best of peace heritage, cultures and literature from various civilizations and nations around the globe. It would be spread and promoted by telecommunications and the media in general, as well as by the IFLAC GSPC project consisting of a powerful Global Television Network by Satellite for the spreading of the Culture of Peace and to counteract the global terror and violence and the "War of Cultures."

The establishment of the IFLAC GSPC can also help to impart to humanity a new multicultural identity, in addition to national and ethnic

---

[8] Wilfred Owen "Strange Meeting," in *The Collected Poems of Wilfred Owen*, ed. C. Day Lewis (London: Chatto and Windus 1963), p. 35.

cultures and identities, and it can guide humankind in making the world more secure. The development of a multicultural peace satellite over conflicted areas would spread the best of what is available in neighbouring cultures, religions, and civilizations, and it would help to promote intercultural bridges of understanding and respect, and to promote a world beyond violence, terror, and war. It would, furthermore, abate the fear and mistrust of the "other," and create bridges of understanding between people and nations, especially in conflicted areas such as the Middle East.

The foundation of a powerful global multicultural Peace System and Network should be pursued by human society on a large scale, comparable to the efforts for creating a global economy, or for obtaining petroleum, and with as much perseverance and tenacity. This colossal task should be considered one of the major goals of humankind near the end of the first decade of our third millennium. The endeavor would gain momentum by involving all governments and major institutions—the UN, UNESCO, and the World Bank, as well as the private financial sectors. These would gain in investing in such a venture, as they would be protecting themselves in the best and most profound manner from possible future violence and terror as witnessed on September 11.

The GSPC will powerfully weave the global voices and strengths of peace-yearning people, who indeed comprise the great majority of the citizens of the world. With commitment, determination, and vision, it is indeed possible to create and promote a resourceful, effective, and influential Multicultural Global Peace Television Network that will curb and dispel the present dangerous "War of Cultures." Turkey is certainly the ideal place for creating the Global TV by Satellite for Peace Culture (GSPC), as it is a natural multicultural bridge between East and West.

IN VAIN: VIOLENCE IN GOD'S NAME

Jim Kenney

KEY ANALYSES OF RELIGION AND VIOLENCE

Violence, terror, and war defaced the twentieth century. Their awful discoloration of our era was heightened by the exacerbating role of religious (and ethnic) identity. The conjuring of evil in our time has all too often been intensified by the admixture of "good." That frames the questions at issue. What are the sources of violence, terror, and war? How does "good" intensify "evil"? Finally, when and how did religion become the most terrifying face of our age? When, in the modern period, did violence and religion become intertwined in the minds of so many thoughtful people?

And how, in the enlightened twentieth century was God's name taken so often and so destructively in vain? Of course the concepts of religion and violence have hardly been estranged in human history. But by the early twentieth century, the hope (at least in religious circles) was that religion would at last become a steadily flowing wellspring of peace and justice.

It wasn't to be. Try this question in your group, your family, congregation, circle of friends, or workplace: "What are the principal sources of violence in today's world?" I'll wager that "religion" places number 2 or 3 in the tally. What would Jesus say? Or Moses, Muhammad, or Buddha? Well, of course, they knew the power of religion to unite and to bring harmony; but just as surely they knew religion's potential to divide. And each must have understood (as so many scriptures attest) the power of religion to conjure up violence.

Perhaps a better question would be, "What would Gandhi or King say?" Mohandas Gandhi, Martin Luther King—or many of the tens of thousands of peace and justice workers giving their all and often their lives in the struggle—would attest to the power of religion to unite and to uplift. They would also testify to the power of pseudo-religion to incite, to inflame, and to enrage. Ultimately, a religious group, cult, or community can indeed become evil.

When that happens, says Charles Kimball in *When Religion Becomes Evil*, the group begins to exhibit characteristic manifestations, "five warning signs":

1. Absolute truth claims made with rigidity and certainty;
2. Blind obedience to charismatic leaders;

3. Pursuing an ideal time ("groups that are certain when God's future should happen—or is going to happen");
4. The end justifies any means;
5. Holy war.

I'd add another to his list:

6. Anti-intellectual and anti-scientific pronouncements.

Kimball, an expert on religion and Middle East policy, stakes out the cultic center of reference. The "truths" of the group attract followers, searchers desperate for solid "meaning claims." The hunger for easily digestible truth, fed by cultic certainties, drives the modern religious far right. He notes, however, that just as the source of religious violence is to be found in the several traditions he explores, the antidote is to be found in religion as well. Kimball's concluding chapter introduces the concept of the spiritual compass, with God or the transcendent as "true North" and faith, hope, and love as the other cardinal points.[1]

Jessica Stern spent many precarious months with terrorists of several groups (Jewish, Christian, and Muslim) in researching her book, *Terror in the Name of God*. Her extraordinary analysis distills from those encounters five grievances that drive religious terrorism, while offering a socio-cultural frame for Kimball's warning signs. Each grievance is examined in a chapter that focuses on a particular religious Jewish, Christian, or Muslim group engaged in acts of terror. The grievances are as follows:

- Alienation: the feeling that one (or one's community) is cut off from the larger social order by changing cultural values, injustice, declining morals, etc. (e.g., Christian anti-abortion movements);
- Humiliation: real and perceived personal and national humiliation of one people at the hands of another leads to desperation and uncontrollable rage (e.g., Hamas and the Muslim suicide bombers in Israel/Palestine);
- Demographics: dramatic population shifts (often government mandated) that upset regional religious, tribal, cultural balances (e.g., Christian-Muslim violence in Indonesia);
- History: the understanding and/or manipulation of ancient history as a powerful weapon in extremists' hands, including their

---

[1] See Charles Kimball, *When Religion Becomes Evil: Five Warning Signs* (New York: Harper Collins, 2003).

efforts to expand national boundaries and to seek redemption (e.g., Jewish extremists like the Temple Mount Faithful);
* Territory: long-standing political disputes over territory as raisons d'être for holy war (e.g., Muslim-Hindu violence in Kashmir).

Stern's timely perspective on the psychological dimensions of militant religion provides the foundation for the book's second half, an examination of the structures of terrorist organizations. Finally, Stern examines the particular vulnerability of Islamic states to terrorism, emphasizing rampant globalization, American support for Israel, the deepening of poverty, and the turbulence of the movement toward popular democracy.

She concludes with a thought-provoking but unfortunately brief set of recommendations for the architects of modern western policy. The central question posed by this section is "How can we address the crisis of religious violence without exacerbating hatred of the West?"[2]

In *Violence in God's Name*, Oliver McTernan offers a different perspective on the issues addressed by Kimball and Stern.[3] A former Jesuit priest, broadcaster, and peace activist, he challenges two tendencies that weaken modern journalistic and scholarly analyses. The first is to deny the role of religion in terrorist violence, emphasizing instead factors such as perceived economic and social injustice, struggles over land, political power, etc. The second tendency exaggerates the role of religion, ignoring other contributing factors and cultural dynamics. He argues that "Religion does matter and [...] needs to be seen as an actor in its own right," but adds that "The preciseness of role that religion plays will vary from conflict to conflict." (p. 44)

McTernan's chapter on "Religon and the Legitimization of Violence" is particularly powerful, demonstrating that "without exception" each of the world's great faith communities—when faced with a significant threat to its existence or with a dramatic opening to expansion—has sanctioned the use of violence in its own interest.

> In each faith tradition one can find sufficient ambiguity in its founding texts and stories to justify killing for the glory of God. Each tradition has also its heroes who saw themselves as acting on divine authority as they plotted the destruction of those whom they perceived to be enemies of God. Today's

---

[2] See Jessica Stern, *Terror in the Name of God: Why Religious Militants Kill* (New York: HarperCollins, 2003).
[3] Oliver McTernan, *Violence in God's Name: The Role of Religion in an Age of Conflict* (New York: Orbis, 2003).

religious extremists can find their rationale for inflicting terror in the name of their God in the ambivalence towards violence that is found in each faith tradition. (p. 76)

The book's closing passages may, however, be the most evocative of all. He quotes the Hindu sage, Swami Vivekenanda at the 1893 World's Parliament of Religions.

The Christian is not to become a Hindu or a Buddhist nor a Hindu or a Buddhist to become a Christian. But each must assimilate the spirit of the others and yet preserve its own individuality and grow according to its own law of growth. (p. 164)

IDENTITY, RELIGION, AND VIOLENCE

In our own age, many find the world-shrinking forces of globalization unbearably threatening to personal, family, religious, cultural, or national identity. In his remarkable book, *In the Name of Identity: Violence and the Need to Belong*, Amin Maalouf offers a simple and moving reflection:

To tell the truth, if we assert our differences so fiercely, it is precisely because we are less and less different from one another. (p. 103)

He focuses on the tendency of the identity-challenged to *re-identify* themselves over and against other groups. Maalouf recognizes the critical role of self-acceptance in interaction with the *other*, recognizing the dangerous temptation to define oneself in terms of the perceived vices of the other—rather than in terms of one's own virtues or aspirations. Thus, we encounter the familiar formula, "Thank God I'm not […] (a Serb, a Croat, a Jew, a Muslim, white, Christian, black, a woman […] the other)."

The remedy is to be sought in the conscious effort to nurture cultural diversity. (This, of course, is one of the essential themes of Globalization for the Common Good.) One of Maalouf's most powerful insights comes near the end of his book, as he reflects:

I do not deny that my recommendations for preserving cultural diversity call for a certain amount of effort. But if we were to let ourselves off this task and just let things take their course; if the world civilization taking shape before our eyes were to go on seeming essentially American, Anglophone or even occidental; then I think everybody would lose by it. The United States, because they would alienate a large part of the rest of the world, which already chafes at the present imbalance of power; the members of non-Western cultures, because they would gradually lose all that makes up their raison d'être and find themselves in a rebellion doomed to failure; and, perhaps above all, Europe, which would lose on both counts [...]. (p. 142)

In each of the analyses I have sketched (Kimball, Stern, McTernan, and Maalouf) identity and identity crisis loom as central themes. The person or community caught in the throes of identity crisis is extremely vulnerable to manipulation by religious demagoguery and—often less obviously—by unscrupulous groups and individuals whose wealth and/or power have been challenged. Often, the forces of globalization not only shape the patterns of identity crisis but also generate the very significant threats to wealth and power. Ironically, these dynamics can combine in the "perfect storm" of religious violence.

Religion has power to unite and to uplift. Just as surely, however, what Quranic scholar Dr Irfan Ahmad Khan has termed "pseudo-religion" has the power to incite, to inflame, and to enrage. (See his paper, "The World is in Danger" in this collection.)

We can trace the incendiary cycle of religion, identity, and violence as follows. Cultural absolutism arises from ignorance of the other. It is often manifest in the charismatic leaders, absolute truth claims, and blind obedience that Kimball identifies as key symptoms of a religious community's turn toward evil. By its very nature, absolutism generates religious and cultural exclusivism. In a globalizing world, however, the ignorance of "the other" that absolutism requires is increasingly difficult to maintain. Inevitably, the encounter with the other becomes more intense. Each of Stern's key grievances is rooted in a failed encounter with some other. And each is fed by cultural confusion, identity crisis, and the growing tendency to define oneself (to carve out a new identity) *over and against that other*. Pseudo-religion unfailingly abandons the core teachings of whatever community it infects.

Once a distorted religious understanding becomes an individual's or a community's ground of identity, manipulation by the forces of threatened wealth and power is a likely next step. At this point, the process surges into the deadliest stage of the process, the sacralization of violence. Almost inevitably, it culminates in the seemingly perpetual exchange of atrocities and the regeneration of the entire cycle.

The key to ending the nightmare lies in understanding, slowing, and eventually halting the movement from absolutism to identity crisis to demagoguery to the crisis stage of religious violence. In this connection, the significance of the global interreligious movement and of a more nuanced understanding of globalization can hardly be overstated.

276

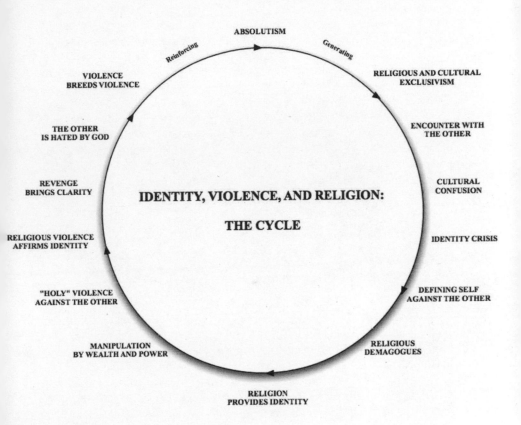

ABSOLUTISM

Reinforcing

Generating

VIOLENCE
BREEDS VIOLENCE

RELIGIOUS AND CULTURAL
EXCLUSIVISM

THE OTHER
IS HATED BY GOD

ENCOUNTER WITH
THE OTHER

REVENGE
BRINGS CLARITY

CULTURAL
CONFUSION

IDENTITY, VIOLENCE, AND RELIGION:

THE CYCLE

RELIGIOUS VIOLENCE
AFFIRMS IDENTITY

IDENTITY CRISIS

"HOLY" VIOLENCE
AGAINST THE OTHER

DEFINING SELF
AGAINST THE OTHER

MANIPULATION
BY WEALTH AND POWER

RELIGIOUS
DEMAGOGUES

RELIGION
PROVIDES IDENTITY

GLOBALIZATION, CULTURAL EVOLUTION, AND EDDIES OF RESISTANCE

At the 2006 *Conference on Globalization for the Common Good*, held in Honolulu, Hawaii, I argued that globalization can be viewed from at least two contrasting perspectives. As a "top-down" phenomenon, it is often marked by the locally destructive global interpenetration of markets, by a disconcerting cultural homogenization with a distinctive western and American flavor, and by a corresponding perceived threat to social, political, economic, cultural, and religious identity in many regions of the world. Top-down globalization—as is evident in the astonishing range and complexity of current worldwide tensions—lends credibility to the otherwise questionable notion of an impending "clash of civilizations." On

277

the other hand, considerable evidence suggests a countervailing phenomenon that we can call "globalization from the bottom up." It is manifest in an *emerging global consensus* of values with respect to peace, social and economic justice, gender equity, human rights, and ecological sustainability—a consensus that is observable among activists to be sure, but increasingly evident in significant segments of the larger world population.

In a time of major evolutionary culture change, as newer, more constructive values emerge, prevailing patterns are challenged and disrupted. In the process, a disturbance can be created in the life experience of individuals or groups. If the perturbation is severe enough—if a sufficient number of persons or groups are affected or if significant concentrations of power are challenged—a major counterflow can form; an eddy. When the rhythm of a smoothly flowing stream is disturbed, eddies can form, usually as temporary whirlpools, roiling the water in their immediate vicinity but not significantly affecting the prevailing flow.

The analogy is apt. A reaction like fundamentalism, for example, may create enormous (and dangerous) turbulence in a changing world; it is extremely unlikely, however, to reverse a powerful evolutionary flow. It is also extremely important to note that those who create and inhabit such patterns of resistance may often claim to be faithfully representing older traditions. In actuality, however, eddies usually involve extreme distortions of those older values. Religious exclusivism is a familiar (and essentially benign) feature of the modern culture complex. Extreme religious fundamentalism is decidedly not: it is instead a twentieth-century reaction against early manifestations of the newer value wave. By the same token, patriarchy was, in its time, a relatively benign force; intensified intimate and societal violence against women is in large part a reaction against new wave gender-equity. Many of the most critical problems of our age need to be understood not as aspects of declining older values and certainly not as features of the newer value complex, but as phenomena of the our evolutionary moment, dangerous but temporary counterflows that can slow but not stem the new tide.

There are at least three categories of eddy, rooted in three very different aspects of human experience and behavior: *culture, identity,* and *power.* When any or all are threatened, dangerous and destructive patterns of counterflow or backwash can form. Each category is listed here with a few examples of its characteristic expressions.

Cultural Confusion	Identity Crisis	Threats to Power
Incivility	Identity Extremism	Corruption
Relativism	Fundamentalism	Unilateralism, Imperialism
Apathy, Anomie, Amorality	Religious Violence, Terrorism	Tyranny

Eddies of the first category ("Cultural Confusion") are patterns of resistance to changing life conditions and altered behavioral expectations. The decline of the older ways challenges or undermines a whole range of social/cultural patterns, etiquettes, and standards. The affected individual or group simply abandons all attempts to "go along" and wanders (in apathy, anomie, and/or amorality) through an unchartable new world.

The second category ("Identity Crisis") includes eddies of the most visible type: those born from individual or group identity crisis. When a long-ascendant complex of values and behaviors is suddenly challenged or even destroyed (as has happened in recent years in many troubled parts of the world), identity crisis is inevitable. Here again we encounter a dangerous but all too common response: defining oneself over against the members of some other group: "I am opposed to all that Americans (or Jews, or Serbs, or Muslims, or blacks, or women, or environmentalists) stand for." Identity crisis is the essential disturbance that gives rise to some of the most destructive eddies, including ethnic cleansing, fundamentalist intolerance, and most forms of religious violence.

The third category ("Threats to Power") includes the most powerful systemic eddies, born of disturbances in what might be termed the "power-grid" of the older order. Political and corporate corruption, new patterns of regional and global imperialism, and a new breed of twenty-first-century tyrannies and "illiberal democracies" are among the most characteristic of the eddies of resistance to cultural evolution. More disturbing still is the growing evidence that identity-challenged religious communities and their demagogues are frequently manipulated by powerful interests groups determined to secure their own dominant positions. It's a bitter irony that the blunt instrument of religious violence may often be wielded by those who have no real interest in or commitment to the spiritual.

CONCLUSION

Though modern thinkers debate the merits of religion, it has been the principal wellspring of meaning and source of identity for most of humankind throughout prehistory and history. There can be no doubt, however, that religion as a cultural expression in the early twenty-first century is severely damaged. Among the worst of the eddies of our time are the rise of fundamentalism in every major tradition, the role of religion in destructive identity politics, and the awful modern rebirth of violence in the name of religion.

Religion, though, assumes a key role in the current cultural evolutionary dynamic. Those who suggest that humanity would be better off if religion were somehow erased from the historical record and absent from the present drastically underestimate the contributions that the world's religions have made to culture and its evolution. Naysayers often point to religion in the early twenty-first century as a clear source of evidence for devolution, rather than cultural advance. Yeasayers, on the other hand, tend to see genuine epochal movement in religious and spiritual circles worldwide and to argue that real cultural advance is underway.

Theologian Ewert Cousins and many others insist that ours is a "New Axial Period" that "will shape the horizon of consciousness for future centuries."[4] It is shaping and being shaped by the transition from *exclusivism* (complete denial of the truth of the other), toward *inclusivism* (acknowledgement of the possibility that the other's truth may be an acceptable variant of one's own, defining truth), toward *pluralism* (openness to the likelihood that religious truth may be found in many cultures and traditions).

Here I draw on my own experience over the last twenty years in the emerging field of interreligious engagement. This global effort encourages the world's many religious and spiritual communities to come together in encounter, dialogue, and constructive common action. I contend that a significant number of these communities are in fact increasingly engaged with the great issues of the age:

- non-violence and the building of cultures of peace;
- the nurturing of economic and social justice and human rights;
- honoring and preserving the Earth and all her life systems.

This engagement represents what one of the deepest reserves of hope in a troubled time.

---

[4] Ewert Cousins, "Christ of the 21st Century," *Monastic Interreligious Dialogue Bulletin*, 64 (May 2000).
benedictsdharma.com/a.php?id=302

THREE FAITHS FORUM:
A PATH TO PEACE BUILDING

Sidney L Shipton

Firstly let me thank you for inviting me once again to take part in an important conference on Globalisation for the Common Good. I had the privilege of participating in the first conference in Oxford and the second conference in St Petersburg and regretfully was not able to be with you again until now.

I am not an academic but a lawyer by profession and as Co-ordinator of the Three Faiths Forum (Muslim-Christian-Jewish trialogue) I am pleased to have the opportunity of discussing a non-violent path to conflict resolution and peace building.

Today, more than ever and in spite of the great strides that have been made in science and technology and in achievements in so many fields of endeavour we live in a violent age, an age of violence growing year by year in intensity.

It may well be that the age of world wars is over. No great power it seems wishes to use such fearful weapons of war that have been developed in recent years since the first atomic bomb was dropped in Hiroshima which, let it be said, brought the second world war to an end but at a terrible cost.

Today we find what I would call mini-wars taking place world wide where the weapons used are misguided individuals who become suicide bombers believing they are giving their lives for a cause and that they will end up in heavenly paradise as the consequence of their naïve actions. Terrorists (I decline to call those who kill civilians, young and old, indiscriminately, freedom fighters) wage such wars which are in effect often civil wars and this is the order of the day.

The civilised world still hesitates to rid the world of terrorists and insurgencies grow—so what is the answer? What is the non-violent path to be?

To me from a practical point of view there are five major ways of tackling terrorism and these in fact precede defence and security considerations.

First, it is essential to cut off at source the fuelling of terrorists by preventing them from receiving the necessary funding and financial support in many cases from countries in the area or on the borders since no terrorist organisation can exist without funds fuelling their activities.

Secondly it is essential to cut off the supply of explosives, munitions, weapons, uniforms, bomb-making equipment and all the trappings of a secret army.

Thirdly it follows that it is essential to eradicate these countries and people who train and teach would-be terrorists often in terrorist training camps set up in other countries.

These ways of tackling terrorism are self evident and obvious, but I make no apology for mentioning them.

Action should and must be taken by international bodies such as the United Nations, NATO, and the European Union against countries who feed and fuel terrorism. They must be ostracised and become the pariahs of the world. Sanctions must be effective and forthright.

However the fourth and fifth ways of tackling terrorism are the non-violent paths we must take to resolve conflict (usually in the nature of civil war) to lead to peace.

Fourthly, from a long term point of view it is necessary in many cases to provide work and job opportunities in deprived areas. The seeds of dissension find fertile soil in the unemployed, giving the backroom organisers of terrorism the opportunity to turn them into terrorist and suicide bombers.

Fifthly, and this is the way forward I wish to concentrate on, it is necessary, indeed essential, to promote dialogue or as the late Sir Winston Churchill, Prime Minister of Great Britain, put it, it is better to have Jaw Jaw than War War.

Dialogue and the educational processes which go with them are the paths that lead to conflict resolution and peace building nationally and internationally.

Regretfully the media and press do not usually publicise the "moderate." Religious texts regretfully are open to different interpretations, for example, the wonders of paradise instilled into suicide bombers are really fragments of imagination. (It was the late Sheikh Dr M.A. Zaki Badawi KBE, Co-founder of the Three Faiths Forum and my mentor for some ten years in the principles and practices of Islam, who told me categorically that a Muslim committing suicide is committing a sin and is not a martyr).

With the above in mind, and understanding, particularly in the UK, that it was necessary to assist the growing Muslim community in integrating and fighting Islamophobia, the Three Faiths Forum came into existence. My work in the Forum, I feel, may be used as an example and model in our discussions at this conference.

The Three Faiths forum was founded by Sir Sigmund Sternberg, Rev. Dr Marcus Braybrooke, and the late Sheikh Dr M.A. Zaki Badawi. I became the Co-ordinator and this year we are celebrating ten years of activities endeavouring to bring Muslims, Christians, and Jews (the three Abrahamic monotheistic faiths) together by dialogue in a spirit of mutual respect and understanding. Regretfully there is still a long way to go. Although we work at different levels including the leadership level through our Advisory Board which acts as a think tank and sounding board for our ideas and projects, the major thrust of our work is at grass roots level. Let it be made quite clear that Muslims, Christians, and Jews are not monolithic faiths. There are different types of Muslims, different types of Jews, and different types of Christians. Our Advisory Board endeavours to be comprehensive and representative but I cannot say with hand on heart this it represents 100% of all of the three Abrahamic faiths.

We set up Medical and Lawyers groups and we form local and regional groups particularly which are of major importance. In addition, as of last year having received a grant from the Home Office, we are now working in schools, colleges, and universities. Also we endeavour to work jointly with active Muslim groups such as City Circle (young professionals and business people) and Muslims in Dialogue, The Ismaili Centre, and many other Muslim organisations which because they have a positive approach do not make the headlines.

Let me elaborate on how we try to achieve our objectives as a long term non-violent response to overcome the domestic threat and lead to peacebuilding. I have already referred to our Advisory Board but probably the real work is done within smaller groups. Our Medical group works on the basis of Chatham House rules. A paper is prepared on a particular subject alternatively by a Muslim, Christian, or Jew and is then discussed. Through the subjects of genetic engineering, abortion, mental health, etc., those present find much upon which they can agree and probably more on which they can agree than they thought before coming to such a discussion. Similarly, as far as the Lawyers group is concerned (which has been recognised by the Law Society) we have discussed subjects such as the blasphemy laws. All these discussions are open ended but the real purpose of the meetings, dare I say it, is to get Muslims, Christians, and Jews talking to each other and getting to know each other.

Our Three Faiths Forum local groups, once they have been set up, work on their own initiative and as long as they bring together their members in a spirit of understanding we leave the subject matter to them. Some do what I call a "religious pub crawl" which means usually that on a Sunday, the groups visit a local Church, then a local Mosque, and then a local Synagogue, and in each place they learn a little of what occurs on Friday, Saturday, or Sunday (that is to say the appropriate Sabbath of each of the three faiths). Here let me say that as a matter of principle all our meetings take place not in a fixed venue but alternate between a Mosque, a Church,

283

and a Synagogue and this includes our local and our specialist groups as well as our Advisory Board.

Our work with schools and colleges in addition is based on the Tools 4 Trialogue, that is to say discussing texts and looking for similarities and differences.

Our work does not end there as we carry out joint activities with whoever wants to work with us. Let me give you some recent examples; The Three Faiths Forum held a joint seminar with the Institute of Education and Muslims, Christians and, Jews discussed faith schools and whether they were good or bad.

A three day consultation was held on the subjects of Christian, Muslim, and Jewish music. This took place in St Georges House, Windsor Castle under the auspices of the Institute of Ismaili Studies, the Festival of Muslim Culture, the Jewish Music Institute, and the Three Faiths Forum. The highlight of the conference was a unique concert in the chapel where for the first time a Jewish Choir and a Muslim Music group performed as well as the Christian Chapel Choir itself.

Recently the Three Faiths Forum held itd Fourth Annual meeting with all the ambassadors and heads of mission in London called together on our behalf by Sir Anthony Figgis (HM Marshal of the Diplomatic Corps) where, in addition to speakers from the World Economic Forum and the Foreign and Commonwealth Office, presentations on the work of the Three Faiths Forum are given to the participants (which incidentally has led to interfaith contacts in Bulgaria and Romania and indeed the setting up of a Forum Abraamico in Lisbon last year).

From what I have said I hope it is quite clear that we believe the long term non-violent path to conflict resolutions and peacebuilding is to get people to know each other and to understand each other and to respect each other and particularly to realise that the stereotypes that exist (particularly when you have never met a Muslim or indeed a Christian or a Jew) are generalisations which do not relate to the majority of Muslims, Christians, and Jews.

Let me conclude with a short experience I had once on holiday with my wife some time ago. We met a young couple of people and got to know them and towards the end of the holiday when I was alone with my new friend he said to me, "Sidney when did you convert to Judaism?" It surprised me at first and then I realised that he lived in a rural environment in the UK and he had never met or befriended a Jew before. Because I spoke reasonable unaccented English I did not fit his stereotype of what a Jew should look like. (Perhaps like someone with a beard and an accent like in *Fiddler on the Roof*?) The story has a happy ending: I am the godfather of his son Thomas (the couple got married on the Island of St Thomas; my wife and I were on a cruise) and he is now at Oxford University.

The Three Faiths Forum is playing a significant role not only in the UK but also internationally as an affiliate of the Abrahamic Forum of the International Council of Christians and Jews and through its contacts with the Ambassadors and Heads of Mission based in London where, as I have said, we meet every year. The Foreign and Commonwealth office send delegations to us to listen to presentations similar to this one and interfaith conferences have taken place in several countries as a result of the above. Indeed as I have already said we have a Forum Abraamico in Lisbon, Portugal and groups being formed in Bulgaria and Romania. I hope what I have said will provide some food for thought at this important Sixth Annual Conference in the City of Istanbul.

SECURITY AND PEACE: SOCIO-POLITICAL, ECONOMIC, AND CULTURAL PERSPECTIVES

THE ARROW THAT PIERCED DUALITY: FROM DUALISM TO HOLISM—CULTIVATING A CULTURE OF PEACE IN THE "FIRST WORLD"

Mayumi Futamura

Since wars begin in the minds of men, it is in the minds of men that the defenses of peace must be constructed (UNESCO 1945).

When thinking about peacebuilding, people generally focus on the "Third World" or conflict areas that are marred with violence, human rights abuses, and poverty. Not many people think about building peace in the "First World." But peacebuilding in the "First World" is necessary because the root causes of violence/war/conflicts in the "Third World" often originate in the "First World," and people living in the "First World" actually face their own unique suffering: things are not as peaceful as they may seem.

The "First World" is an economically developed and industrialized "modern world." The current mode of modernity is synonymous with economic development. As such, it manifests in materialistic advancement and discourages the contemplative side of life. As a result, people in the "First World" suffer from spiritual deprivation. While a degree of peace has been achieved materialistically, in order to build a holistic state of peace we must address this spiritual deprivation.

In this paper I will examine the conditions of the "modern" world and argue that building peace within it means transcending dualism. Dualism, in contrast to holism, is a system of two opposing views. It is the dominant doctrine that permeates social discourse and shapes our frame of reference.[1] Dualistic polarities attempt to describe and contain social reality in artificial ways.[2] The dualistic perspective inevitably creates division, hierarchy, and discrimination. Hence, transcending dualism is a step towards creating peace. But how can we transcend dualism?

To answer the question, I will explore the holistic wisdom and insights that Buddhist literature offers. Buddhism is a "dynamical system of interpretation" that can help us transcend ideology and hierarchical structures (Del Collins, p. 265). Buddhism is a philosophy and practice that reminds us of the interconnectedness of the world. The philosophy of

---

[1] Marla Del Collins, "Transcending Dualistic Thinking in Conflict Resolution," *Negotiation Journal*, 21:2 (April 2005), 263–80 (p. 264).
[2] John Paul Lederach. *The Moral Imagination: The Art and Soul of Building Peace* (New York: Oxford University Press, 2005), p. 35.

Buddhism assists us to enter into a different, holistic paradigm. The core principles of peace, or a culture of peace, can be found in Buddhism.

First, I will begin by discussing how, although the barren branches of violence reach around the globe in all directions, the causes of war and violence in the "Third World" are firmly rooted within the "First World."

WHY PEACEBUILDING IN THE "FIRST WORLD"?

I will never forget the day when the United States began the "Shock and Awe" bombing of Baghdad. The anger and dread and tremendous sense of violation I felt that day are still vivid in my heart. According to the authors of *Shock and Awe: Rapid Dominance*, the aim of "Shock and Awe" bombing of Baghdad was to impose the "non-nuclear equivalent of the impact that the atomic weapons dropped on Hiroshima and Nagasaki had on the Japanese."[3] The bombing directly targeted the civilian infrastructure necessary for the survival of the Iraqi civilian population. Shopping malls and markets and many other civilian infrastructures were bombed and destroyed. It was an act of terrorism committed by the world's most powerful state.

The invasion resulted in prolonged internal conflicts. A study in *The Lancet*, one of the two major medical journals in the U.K., reports that an estimated 655,000 Iraqi people died as a result of the US-led invasion.[4] The civil wars, or new type of wars that the world is witnessing, contain a "myriad of transnational connections."[5] The new wars in the "Third World" are not "symptomatic of local failures in governance."[6]

The connections are not limited to war, but violence and human rights abuses in the "Third World" also have a direct relationship to the "First World." Kevin Bales, sociologist and author of *Disposable People*, writes

---

[3] Harlan Ullman and James P. Wade. *Shock and Awe: Achieving Rapid Dominance* (Washington: National Defense University Press, 1996), http://www.globalsecurity.org/military/library/report/1996/shock-n-awe_index.html
[4] Gilbert Burnham, Riyadh Lafta, Shannon Doocy and Les Roberts, "Mortality after the 2003 Invasion of Iraq: A Cross-Sectional Cluster Sample Survey," *The Lancet*, October 11, 2006. http://www.thelancet.com/webfiles/images/journals/lancet/s0140673606694919.pdf
[5] Mary Kaldor, *New and Old Wars: Organized Violence in a Global Era* (Cambridge: Polity, 2001), pp. 7–9.
[6] Oliver Ramsbotham, Tom Woodhouse and Hugh Miall (eds), *Contemporary Conflict Resolution: The Prevention, Management and Transformation of Deadly Conflicts*, 2nd edn (Cambridge: Polity, 2005), p. 90.

that modern slavery grows and thrives best in extreme poverty"[7] and the lives of slaves directly and indirectly touch our lives in today's globalized economy. Bales write:

> Shoes you wear, carpet you stand on, sugar pot in your kitchen and toys in the hands of your children may be made by slaves in Pakistan or India or Caribbean. Slaves touch your life indirectly as well. Slaves made the charcoal that tempered the steel that made the springs in your car. Slaves grew the rice that fed the woman who wove the cloth you've put up as curtains. Your investment portfolio and your mutual fund pension own stock in companies using slave labor in the developing world. Slaves keep your costs low and returns on your investments high (p. 4).

By simply looking for the best deal, we may be choosing goods that are made by slaves; we may all be participating in the ultimate violation of human rights without even noticing.

The impact of slave-made goods reverberates through the world economy in ways even harder to escape. Workers making computer parts or televisions in India can be paid low wages in part because food produced by slave labor is so cheap. This lowers the cost of the goods they make and leads to closure of factories unable to compete with their prices in North America and Europe. Slave labor anywhere threatens real jobs everywhere (Bales, p. 24):

> The new slavery is an international economic activity; slavery is committed by states and transnational corporations (TNCs) as well. In Burma, for example, the dictatorship enslaved its citizens to carry out a project— building a natural gas pipeline—in partnership with the US oil company Unocal, the French oil company Total, and the Thai company PTT Exploration and Production. (Ibid., p. 8)

There are about 27 million slaves throughout the world (Bales, p. 8). The total annual profit generated by these 27 million slaves is estimated at around $13.6 billion, of which $10.5 billion is generated by 200,000 women and children enslaved in the sex trade (ibid., p. 23). Businessmen from the "First World," especially Japanese men, are notoriously sighted "buying" girls at brothels in Asian countries.

The "First World" financial institutions are involved in the perpetuation of poverty and the "astonishing prevalence of slums."[8] In *Planet of Slums*,

---

[7] Kevin Bales, *Disposable People: New Slavery in the Global Economy* (Berkley and London: University of California Press, 2004), p. 31.
[8] Mike Davis, *Planet of Slums* (London and New York: Verso, 2006), p. 20.

Mike Davis writes that it is the policies of agricultural deregulation and financial discipline enforced by the IMF and World Bank that "generate an exodus of surplus rural labor to urban slums" (ibid., p. 15). The "landmark" UN report, *The Challenge of Slums*, which provides a "comprehensive balance sheet of the damage done by 30 years of structural adjustment, debt and privatization," was completely ignored by policy makers and development agencies, except by the Pentagon, which looked at the report with great interest as it regards slums as labyrinths where future battles take place.[9] It is estimated that more than one billion slum dwellers "squat in squalor, surrounded by pollution, excrement and decay" (Davis *Planet*, pp. 19–37); and the number is increasing. In the next year or two, the "urban population of the earth will outnumber the rural"; furthermore, all future world population growth, which is "expected to peak at about 10 billion in 2050," will concentrate in cities, of which 95 per cent will converge in the urban areas of developing countries (ibid., pp. 1–2). Residents of slums constitute 78.2 per cent of urbanites in the least-developed countries, or a third of the global urban population (ibid, p. 23).

Many NGOs and development agencies go to the "Third World" to "help" undertake important work. However, how can we hope to stop violence and build peace in far away places without first addressing the root causes of the conflict originating in the "First World"? Without first building peace within, might we not end up disturbing the area that we hope to help?

Tetsu Nakamura, a medical doctor and executive director of Peshawar-kai Medical Services, who has served in Pakistan and Afghanistan since 1984, writes that the presence of the Western development agencies seems to corrupt the invaluable treasure of heart that Afghan people used to have. He writes: "Peshawar used to be serene and quiet, but now it's filled with cars and emissions. Many local staff at regional clinics and the office in Jalalabad left us in pursuit of higher wages. I can see people's heart and focus changing. There is now this overt mammonism, which used to be a characteristic of people with higher education, or intellects in big cities. In Kabul, the pursuit of enjoyment and decadence is becoming the major social energy."[10] He also observes that young men coming from Japan to help seem to be more depressed and unhappy than children in Afghanistan who

---

[9] Davis, Mike. "The Rising Tide of Urban Poverty," *Socialist Worker*. May 12, 2006. http://www.socialistworker.org/2006-1/588/588_06_MikeDavis.shtml

[10] Tetsu Nakamura, "Overall Review of the Year 2003," *Peshawar-kai Newsletter* 80, July 7, 2004. http://www1a.biglobe.ne.jp/peshawar/eg/e_2003gaikyo.html

live in an uncertain and dangerous environment.[11] Why is it the case? I will now look at the conditions of the "modern world."

THE CONDITIONS OF THE "FIRST WORLD"

The "First World" is a "modernized" and "developed" world where the complex web of communication networks, capitalist economies, and consumerism are facts of life. Modern life is "characterized by uncertainty, rapidity of change and kaleidoscopic juxtapositions of objects, people and events"; modern minds are "forged in the context of instability of a cataclysmic kind."[12] The current mode of modernity is synonymous with economic development. As such, it manifests in materialistic advancement and discourages the contemplative side of life.

In an article, titled "Tourists and Vagabonds," Zygmunt Bauman, Emeritus Professor of Sociology at the Universities of Leeds and Warsaw, vividly describes the ultimate reality of the "modern" world. He sees that the world is "sedimented on the two poles, at the top and at the bottom of the emergent hierarchy of mobility."[13]

At the higher end of the two poles are the "inhabitants of the First World," or the "tourists." At the lower end are the "inhabitants of the second world," or the "vagabonds" who endure a kind of deprivation "made yet more painful by the obtrusive media display of the space conquest and of the 'virtual accessibility' of distances that stay stubbornly unreachable in non-virtual reality" (p. 88). While the tourists "live in time," traveling every distance instantaneously, the vagabonds are confined in space. All that the vagabonds have is the "burden of abundant, redundant, and useless time," which they have nothing to fill (ibid.). The tourists are the "cosmopolitan, extraterritorial world of global businessmen, global culture managers or global academics" (p. 89). They travel "at will," get much fun from their travel in first class or using private aircraft, and are "cajoled or bribed to travel and welcomed with smiles and open arms when they do" (ibid.). State borders do not exist for them. On the contrary, the walls of immigration controls are still the reality for the vagabonds. They travel "surreptitiously, often illegally, sometimes paying more for the crowded steerage of a

---

[11] Tetsu Nakamura, "ZETSUBOU TO KIBOU NO Afghan FUKKOU" ("Hope and Despair in the Reconstruction of Afghanistan"), *Peshawar-kai Newsletter* 83. (April 1, 2005). http://www1a.biglobe.ne.jp/peshawar/kaiho/83nakamura.html

[12] Stephen Frosh, *Identity Crisis: Modernity, Psychoanalysis and the Self* (New York: Routledge, 1991), p. 7.

[13] Zygmunt Bauman, *Globalization: The Human Consequences* (Oxford: Polity, 1998), pp. 87–88.

stinking unseaworthy boat than others pay for business-class gilded luxuries—and are frowned upon, and if unlucky, arrested and promptly deported, when they arrive" (ibid.).

The tourists stay or move as they wish while the vagabonds move because they have no other choice. The vagabonds are involuntary tourists who are "refused the right to turn into tourists" (Bauman, p. 93). The tourists and the vagabonds are the same in a sense because they are both consumers and thus "sensation-seekers and collectors of experiences," "attracted or repelled" by the same external stimuli (p. 94). However, because of this similarity, the vagabond is "the alter ego of the tourist," as well as the "tourists' nightmare" (p. 94). The vagabonds remind the tourists of the possibility of becoming vagabonds.

While Bauman's polarized depiction of tourists and vagabonds provides a useful lens to view "modernity," one can sense an extremely desolate state of mind at work in his argument. Trapped in dichotomy, Bauman colorfully exhibits the characteristics of dualistic thinking, with added disdain.

The observations Bauman makes are accurate. Rich people like Donald Trump are adored, as evident in the popular TV show, *The Apprentice*. And more than that, rich people do enjoy luxuries that are pleasant and can result in happy, if not joyful, experiences. However, Bauman's characterization of the vagabond as the alter ego of the tourist exposes his shallow appreciation for the value of a given individual life. The vagabond is just one of many identities of the privileged tourist (or the global academic). Furthermore, the tourist's alter ego being his nightmare illustrates his own fearful state. This is the ultimate sign of spiritual deprivation. He is scared of himself. The author's notion of consuming reality or external stimuli is the definitive sign of a disconnection with reality.

But Buaman's condition is not unique. Modernity provides very few spaces for self-reflection. Consequently, there is a drastic imbalance between the degree of technological development and spiritual development. We have cars, but we do not know how to share the roads. The conditions of modernity deter people from a contemplative life and make people forget about cultivating the treasures of the heart—the internal wealth that resides in the heart and mind. The greatest challenge for people in the "First World" is to cultivate the treasures of the heart, not external wealth.

Evidence of disconnection from fellow human beings and spiritual impoverishment is found through looking at one dimension of the state terrorism committed against the people of Iraq. It was terrorism supported by "free people" who live in a "civilized" "modern" society, in a "liberal democracy," who are reasonably rich and powerful.

Within a second after the bombing of Baghdad began, Americans, or whoever had access to the Internet and could write English, started writing comments on the web as the world witnessed it on the TV screen. There was a complete lack of imagination about the reality of Iraqi people on the ground. It was surreal. It was simply inhumane. It was the moment the most despicable act of violence became "'entertainment."

One thread with the first message, "Shock and Awe Begins," was posted on 21/3/2003 9:19:31 AM PST and is followed by the following comments:

> First confirmed explosions reported! Lets hope this is the real thing and not just another teaser! (9:20:17 AM PST)
>
> I heard it called "Operation Exemplary Destruction". Cool... (9:20:33 AM PST)
>
> GOOD!!! About time for the beginning of the end starts. Go Get 'em guys!!!!! (9:22:00 AM PST)
>
> Maybe it'll be a late nominee for the Academy Awards. (9:20:48 AM PST)
>
> Watching! God protect our troops and our Allies! Let this be over asap! My daughter just joined the Army today! (9:22:55 AM PST)
>
> What a beautiful site and wonderful noise! (9:23:31 AM PST)
>
> I don't care what time it is in Baghdad....the real time is high noon for Iraq. (9:23:32 AM PST)
>
> Not too much in sky over Baghdad. So if this is S&A, it's a lot tamer than we thought it would be. (9:24:03 AM PST)
>
> MSNBC states Pentagon notified press that it has indeed begun. (9:24:27 AM PST)
>
> Bake 'em an' shake 'em! (9:24:38 AM PST)
>
> Message to Iraq: SURRENDER NOW. (9:24:56 AM PST)
>
> My tax dollars at work. Finally, an urban renewal program I can agree with. (9:25:29 AM PST)
>
> (Robinson-DeFehr Consulting, LLC, 2003)

One must wonder how on earth these people can be so callous, utterly ignorant, and aggressive. These people, though they were using pseudonyms, are real. By the end of the day, 850 messages were posted under this single thread alone. Who knows how many people watched the "event" real-time on the TV screen and cheered on that day. The fact is that many ordinary citizens in the "First World" participated in the act of terrorism, committed by a state.

We can clearly see that there is more to the picture than meets the eye when looking at seemingly "peaceful" societies. What, then, needs to be done? How can the peacebuilding community address the spiritual deprivation in the "First World"?

The answer can be found through seeding new ideas into Western thought. This is because when the discussion regarding history, culture, and modernity takes place within the confines of the Western vocabulary, not surprisingly the result is a deterministic narrative of the world and man's place in it. For example, the mind/body split of Cartesian dualism approaches the issue of spirituality in a dramatically different way from the holistic Buddhist view based on the interconnectedness of life. Dualism is a system of two opposing views. It is the dominant doctrine that permeates social discourse and shapes our frame of reference (Del Collins, p. 264). Confronting and challenging the basic tenets of Western thinking in a supportive and non-critical way can lead to a richer understanding of the present.

FROM DUALISM TO HOLISM

The spiritual depravation in the "First World" can be addressed by a shift of paradigm—from dualism to holism. Dualism is a defining characteristic of social discourse around the world. Dualism is "intricately woven into long-held views of reality"; it "permeates all forms of social discourse" and thus it shapes the dominant frame of reference (Del Collins, p. 264). Abstract dichotomies, such as materialism or idealism, capitalism or communism, democrat or republican, are examples of this frame of reference.

Dualism is a component of modernity and has a long history (ibid., p. 265). *Classics of Western Thought: The Modern World* showcases the foundation of dualism in today's world. Rene Descartes believed that "mind and matter are essentially different substances subject to different laws."[14] Aristotle was one of the first philosophers to "codify and record dualistic thinking to be absorbed and repeated by posterity as a universal truth, the natural order of things" (Del Collins, p. 266). The "astonishing achievement" of modern Western civilization can be attributed to its characteristics of "placing greater emphasis upon direct observation of natural phenomena and on novel ways of thinking about facts." (Knoebel, p. 1) In other words, modern Western civilization is build upon dualistic thinking.

As a doctrine, dualism can encourage conflict; it is a "system where there are only two points of view" (Del Collins, pp. 263–64):

> Arguably, hierarchical social structuring arose from dualistic thinking because such dichotomies lend themselves to a socially constructed moral overlay, and dualism not only divides everything into opposites but judges them as either inferior or superior. [...] There is little or no room for

---

[14] Edgar E. Knoebel (ed.), *Classics of Western Thought: The Modern World*, 4th edn (Toronto: Nelson Thomson Learning, 1992), p. 20.

divergence, and this imagined dichotomy creates divisiveness (Del Collins, p. 267).

Dualism, in contrast to holism, "limits options to one of two choices" as it does not recognizes the third choice; it establishes a hierarchy; it sets up "moral dichotomies"; it "encourages discrimination" (Del Collins, p. 271). The either/or thinking of dualism "fails to recognize that reality consists of intermediate degrees, flexible borders, and ever-changing vistas" (p. 264). It is a "fight against ambiguity," or a "battle of semantic precision against ambivalence" (p. 266). These features of dualism stand in direct opposition to the features of a culture of peace—flexibility, cooperation, pluralism, and inclusiveness.

Peacebuilding, then, can be seen as assisting the human mind to transcend dualism. Marla Del Collins, Assistant Professor of Communication Studies at Long Island University, suggests that, in order to transcend dualism, we need "complex dynamical systems of interpretation originating from a broad range of disciplines," such as chaos theory, quantum mechanics, and Buddhism (pp. 264–65). Dynamical systems of interpretation can (1) offer multiple perspectives, (2) encourage "cooperative and interconnecting models of multidisciplinary inquiry," and (3) create an "atmosphere of flexibility, reminding us that reality is in a constant state of flux" towards pluralism, thus helping us to transcend ideology (p. 265).

As suggested earlier, confronting and challenging the basic tenets of Western dualistic thinking in a supportive and non-critical way can lead to a richer understanding of the present. Hence, I will now explore what it means to build peace in the "First World" by searching for insights in Buddhism. Specifically, I will look at some of the world's oldest literature that describes the peaceful outcomes Buddha assisted in manifesting and the wisdom behind Buddha's words and deeds.[15] These accounts will highlight the elements of a culture of peace found in the stories. Buddhist scriptures can be seen as classic literature of peacebuilding that have survived for thousands of years. They were written by the scholars of their time and contain profound wisdom and hints on how we can resolve the root cause of conflicts and build healthy relationships and communities.

---

[15]In addition to the original translations by the Pali Text Society, I consulted other available texts in Japanese and English.

BUDDHISM AND THE CULTURE OF PEACE

Gotama Siddhartha, or Buddha, assisted in transforming disputes and conflicts, including a dispute between two villages over water rights.[16] He assisted in transforming people in deep trouble, including a serial killer who had terrorized communities.[17] He even helped to avert a war from happening.[18]

This essay looks at one of the stories in *Majjhima Nikaya*, the 152 conversations, or *suttas*. It is about how Buddha transformed the life of a serial killer who was terrorizing communities (Verse 86, p. 710). *Majjhima Nikaya* is regarded by the Theravada school of Buddhism as the "definitive recension of the Buddha-word" and is generally considered the most reliable source for the original teachings of Buddha. It contains the "richest variety of contextual settings" and is "replete with drama and narrative."[19]

In King Pasenadi's territory, there was a brutal serial killer who showed no mercy to living beings and terrorized communities. He was called Angulimala because he wore a necklace (*mala*) made of fingers (*anguli*) cut out of his victims.

One day, upon hearing about Angulimala, Gotama went along the road to where Angulimala was staying. People tried to stop Buddha but he would not stop. Angulimala saw Buddha coming alone and thought: "Isn't it amazing! Isn't it astounding! Groups of ten, twenty, thirty, and forty men have come along this road, but I killed them all. Now this contemplative comes alone, without a companion. Why don't I kill him?"

So Angulimala, taking up his sword and shield, approached Gotama. He tried to approach him from one side and then the other. He ran this way and that. However, no matter how he tried, Angulimala could not catch up with Buddha. Buddha would always remain at the same distance. If Angulimala took ten paces forward, then Buddha would take ten paces back. When Angulimala took five paces to one side, then Buddha would take five paces to the other.

---

[16] *Sutta Nipata (The Group of Discourses)*, 2nd edn, trans, K.R. Norman (Oxford: Pali Text Society, 2001), IV, 15.

[17] *Majjhima Nikaya (The Middle Length Discourses of the Buddha: A New Translation of the Majjhima Nikaya)*, trans. Bhikkhu Nanamoli, ed. Bhikkhu Bodhi (Boston, Mass.: Wisdom Publications, 1995), verse 86.

[18] *Maha-parinibbana Sutta (Last Days of the Buddha)*, trans. Sr. Vajira and Francis Story (Kandy: Buddhist Publication Society, 1998), Vol. 16, 5.6.

[19] Bhikkhu Bodhi, 'Preface', in *Majjhima Nikaya*, pp. 13, 20.

Aghast, Angulimala called out to Buddha to stop moving. Then Buddha said to him, "I have remained in the same position. You, Angulimala, cease to move."

Angulimala was baffled because it was Buddha who was moving around swiftly. He could not help but ask: "Why do you say that? You are the one who is moving. Why am I the one who must stop?" Buddha replied to him:

"Angulimala, I have stopped forever,
I abstain from violence towards living beings;
But you have no restraint towards things that live:
That is why I have stopped and you have not." (*Majjhima Nikaya 86*, p. 711).

The Buddha's words hit Angulimala like thunder. He threw aside his weapons, knelt down, and asked Buddha if he could be one of his disciples. Buddha replied, "My dear disciple, would you please come here." Buddha used the word *ehi*, the highest honorific term, to a man who killed hundreds of people and terrorized surrounding communities.[20] The scripture explains that Angulimala took a vow to follow the Buddha's path worthy of this "highest respect" conferred onto him.

When Buddha decided to seek out Angulimala there was a chance that Buddha could have been killed. Buddha was dead serious about speaking to the killer's frozen heart. That seriousness, which came from Buddha's profound compassion, startled and revolutionized Angulimala. It was his authentic and creative attempt to engage with the killer, made possible by his intuition and his willingness to risk his life that made the transformation possible.

Buddha's words transformed Angulimala because he touched Angulimala's heart. Buddha's action was based on the genuine trust and respect for humanity, which is backed up by the empirical understanding that he attained through his contemplative practice. Buddha knew that, no matter how vicious and brutal and insane a person may appear to be, deep in the life of the person there must remain the ability to feel and think rationally and thus there must be a way to build a connection with Angulimala. That is what he sought within Angulimala when he engaged him.

Later, Angulimala is quoted in another scripture as saying, "Where once I stayed here and there with a shuddering mind, in the wilderness, under a tree, in mountains, in caves, now, with ease I lie down; with ease I live my

---

[20] Masaya Tomooka, *Buddha WA AYUMU, Buddha WA KATARU (Buddha walks, Buddha talks)* (Tokyo: Daisanbunmei-sha, 2001), p. 30.

life. What a great blessing Buddha my mentor has given me!"[21] This confession reveals that, although Angulimala was terrorizing the society, he was being terrorized and tormented by his own fear. Buddha was adamant about going to see Angulimala not only to solve the cause of terrorism in the communities but also because he could see the state of suffering Angulimala was in. Buddha's intuitive and authentic action resonates with John Paul Lederach's words: the mystery of peace is located in the nature and quality of relationships developed with those most feared (Lederach, p. 63). Unraveling that mystery is open to us when we free ourselves of the dualistic logic and attachment to self.

Therigatha, a compilation of the "earliest evidence of women's experience in any of the world's religious traditions,"[22] contains a story of a grieving mother whose baby boy had just died (*Therigatha*, Verse 11, p.88). Her name was Kisa-gotami. Having lost her son, she was overcome by deep grief and started to act insanely. She took the dead corpse, carried him on her back and wandered around the community, asking people for medicine. Due to her actions, the community began to despise her. Somehow Kisa-gotami managed to see Buddha and asked him, "Please give me medicine for my boy!" Having listened to her cry, Buddha assured her he would make the medicine. However, he needed one particular ingredient. Buddha told Kisa-gotami, "Go to the city, find a household that has never before seen death, and take some mustard seeds from them."

Delighted, she hurried to the city and started looking for such a household. At one house after another, she asked, "If this house has never before seen any death, give me some mustard seeds. Buddha has told me to obtain some in order to make medicine for my son." Of course she could not find such a household, but while going around, her madness left her. By going from door to door, she realized that death comes to everyone and that her grief was not unique.

Within the world of interconnectedness, everything exists in relation to everything. People live in relationships and create meaning through social interaction and, as such, people need each other to heal. Kisa-gotami needed to talk, be heard, and have her experience validated. What healed her heart was the interaction she had with people. When people see someone in the midst of trouble or despair, they generally pity, despise, or distance themselves from that person in some way. Kisa-gotami was alone. The task

---

[21] *Theragatha (The Elders' verses)*, trans. K.R. Norman (Oxford: Pali Text Society, 1995), verses 866–91.

[22] Steven Collins, "Introduction" to *Poems of early Buddhist Nuns (Therigatha)*, trans. C.A.F. Rhys Davids and K. R. Norman (Oxford: Pali Text Society, 1989), p. vii.

Buddha provided Kisa-gotami assisted her in getting rid of the partition between herself and the society. People used to look at her with contempt, but now they looked at her as one of them because, having had a chance to engage with her, they were able to understand her. Buddha intuitively knew that "genuine constructive change requires engagement of other" (Lederach, p. 49).

There is one more remarkable aspect in this story. When Kisa-gotami went back to Buddha, he asked if she had obtained the mustard seeds. When she told him that matter was over, Buddha said that her words restored him (Tomooka, p. 60). Here, we see his profound compassion and the extraordinary ability to empathize with others. Buddha was literally grieving as much as Kisa-gotami. From the moment he heard her cry, his heart was torn apart. And that ability to empathize enabled him to engage with Kisa-gotami in authentic way, listen to her cry, and understand what was really going on.

We can identify some fundamental principles of a culture of peace from these stories of Buddha:

(1) A culture of peace affirms life. It recognizes the humanity of others regardless of the situation. It innately comprehends the sanctity of all living beings. It translates doubt into a belief that the creative act and response are permanently within reach (Lederach, p. 38).

(2) A culture of peace comprehends and accepts the complex web of human relationships. It recognizes that the "quality of our life is dependent on the quality of life of others" (Lederach, p. 35). It intuitively recognizes the value of one single individual. Within the world of interconnectedness, everyone matters.

(3) A culture of peace means resilience. And resilience of mind is what enables us to remain hopeful, "suspend judgment in favor of exploring presented contradiction," and maintain healthy curiosity. Curiosity is an ingredient that enables us to respect complexity and refuse to "fall into the forced containers of dualism" (Lederach, p. 36).

(4) A culture of peace means profound compassion. It cannot remain indifferent when someone is suffering.

These principles reverberate with the four essential disciplines that make peacebuilding possible—the recognition of relational mutuality, paradoxical curiosity, creativity, and the willingness to take a risk—indicated by Lederach (pp. 34–39). They also echo the six principles of the culture of peace defined by UNESCO—respect all life, reject violence, listen to

299

understand, share with others, rediscover solidarity, and preserve the planet.[23] We can make these principles of the culture of peace a guide for our journey to build peace in our society.

THE INVISIBLE ARROW AND ROOTS OF PEACE

> Reach out to those you fear.
> Touch the heart of complexity.
> Imagine beyond what is seen.
> Risk vulnerability one step at a time
> (Lederach, p. 177)

In *The Moral Imagination*, Lederach writes that people who have worked professionally in "settings of violent conflict" struggle with the deeper questions posed by the setting itself: "Who are we? What are we doing? Where are we going? What is our purpose?" (p. 176)

These questions are exactly what Buddha asked and contemplated. Why do people fight? Why can't people help discriminating between "us" and "them"? After a long deliberation and various attempts to understand, he became enlightened, or in other words, he realized the cause of human suffering. It was more accurately described as awakening (to the reality) rather than a realization (Tomooka, p. 127). What he attained was not mystical but rather it was a principle of attaining peace within.

Buddha described the cause of suffering, or conflict, as an arrow piercing people's hearts. (*Sutta Nipata*, iv) Thus, assisting people to recognize the arrow was his main focus in teaching. The root cause of conflict is the invisible arrow; the arrow signifies the deep desire for self-preservation. Deep inside, people intuitively know that things constantly change and their current selves also change and disappear (Tomooka, pp. 126–131). That is why people discriminate against the old, ill, poor, and death.

I will conclude the paper by recounting one more story that reveals the level of inner peace Buddha possessed and how one person who has attained inner peace can create peace outside.

One day, an angry man named Akkosaka stormed into the monastery where Buddha was resting and started yelling, swearing, and cursing at Buddha (*Samyutta Nikaya*, Ch.7, 1.2). Akkosaka was fuming because young men from his clan abandoned his village to become Buddha's disciple.

---

[23] UNESCO, "The Six Key Points of the Manifesto 2000" (2000).
http://www3.unesco.org/manifesto2000/uk/uk_6points.htm

Buddha remained silent and listened to Akkosaka, until Akkosaka was finished yelling.

When Akkosaka finally stopped, Buddha abruptly but calmly asked him, "Do guests, friends, and relatives sometimes visit you?" Taken aback by the calmness of Buddha, Akkosaka replied, "Yes."

Buddha: "Would you then serve tasty food, treats, and drinks for your guests?"

Akkosaka: "Yes."

Buddha: "But if the guests declined to accept it, who would get the food, treats, and drinks?"

Akkosaka: "Well, if they would not accept, I have no choice but I have to have them back."

Buddha: "That's right. Now I decline to accept the treats you just served me. Therefore, you must have them back."

Akkosaka was said to have become Buddha's disciple on the spot. This story illustrates how the ability to maintain one's inner peace is so incredibly powerful. Inner peace and mindfulness are crucial not only to deal with a stressful environment but also to assist other people in trouble.

Perhaps the strongest argument about how we can build peace in "seemingly peaceful societies" can be missed because it is very subtle. Buddha himself said very little, if anything at all, about the techniques or methodologies on how to build peace. Instead, he taught how to cultivate one's own life state, presumably because he believed this to be the most fundamental issue. In addition to what has been outlined in the paper, this fact alone should be reason enough for us to strive to build inner peace within.

Peacebuilding in the "First World" is about people trying to transcend dualism in their everyday life. Cultivating peace is developing one's being to "create a life worth living."[24] We can transcend dualism by consciously watching our own mind and thought—in other words, becoming mindful. It is a daily effort to have a self-reflective moment to keep reminding ourselves of and reconfirming the principles of a culture of peace. To build peace we must keep aligning ourselves with these principles. In this sense, literally, all aspects of our ordinary daily life can be peacebuilding; working, eating, creating, reading, watching, talking, playing, studying, and thinking. One can start right in his or her living room.

---

[24] Daniel Bowling, "Mindfulness Meditation and Mediation: Where the Transcendent Meets the Familiar," in *Bringing Peace into the Room: How the Personal Qualities of the Mediator Impact the Process of Conflict Resolution*, ed. Daniel Bowling and David Hoffman (San Francisco: Jossey-Bass, 2003).

But culture is not static. A culture of peace needs constant and strenuous input and maintenance. It has no absolute form or shape. The principles remain the same, but how it is expressed or manifests will change over time and space. A culture of peace means keeping balanced, or staying on the middle way. If things lean toward one direction too much, then the equilibrium is lost. A culture of peace would need some sort of mechanism to shift itself toward the other direction.

If many of us start living life with the conscious intention of being mindful in the spaces where we exist and having dialogue about the values of a culture of peace, then peace will manifest right here where we live. Moreover, as the roots in the "First World" are nurtured by the culture of peace, they will inevitably transform the barren branches of violence into a blossoming of peace in the "Third World." The culture of peace follows the person who possesses it wherever he or she goes.

THE UNITED NATIONS PEACE FORCE IN CYPRUS AS THE PSYCHIATRIST OF GLOBAL GOVERNMENTALITY ON THE "DANGEROUS" CYPRIOT POPULATION

Nejdan Yildiz

INTRODUCTION

The United Nations Peacekeeping Force in Cyprus (UNFICYP) was deployed to the island on March 1964 on the basis of United Nations Security Council (UNSC) Resolution 186. The mandate has three major goals which are preventing a recurrence of fighting, contributing to the maintenance and restoration of law and order, and contributing to a return to normal conditions (United Nations Security Council [UNSC], 1964). Since the peacekeeping force is still positioned on Cyprus after more than forty years, it seems that these goals must not have been achieved. But it is difficult to evaluate, since neither normal conditions nor order were defined in the UNSC Resolution 186. Furthermore it is not clear whose interests the peacekeeping force serves. Moreover, the immense international efforts put into the resolution of the Cypriot conflict, the accumulating military and civilian aspects of peacebuilding, reflect that this small flashpoint contains greater significance for the international community than it seems. That is why my research focuses on the functions of UNFICYP. The objective of this research paper is to expose how the governance of the Cypriot population via the United Nations is directly linked to governance on a global scale, in other words to the global government of liberal peace. In order to attain this objective, as Foucault argues in defining how to practise criticism, conflicts must be made more visible, not for their own sake, but to show that they are essential and more than mere happenstance confrontations.[1] By doing this, unchallenged assumptions, uncontested modes of thought, or basically the truth which justifies certain practices can be problematized. The legitimizing discourse of UNFICYP activities is the discourse of UN peace operations which has a modern character due to its

---

[1] Michel Foucault, "Practicing Criticism," in Michel Foucault, *Politics, Philosophy, Culture: Interviews and Other Writings, 1977-1984*, ed. L. D. Kritzman (New York: Routledge, 1988), pp. 152–158 (pp. 153–57).

representation of a problem-solving attitude and expert institutions.[2] That character leads UNFICYP to respond to the Cyprus conflict by looking for an appropriate policy to enhance the geo-strategic interests of global powers: in other words, UNFICYP attempts to de-escalate violence in the short-term rather than to comprehend the deep, historical causes of the conflict. Hence, this modern attitude shall be problematized in a global, political context. However, this task should not be interpreted as replacing one regime of truth with another. As Paris suggested, studying peace operations should focus on investigating fundamental presumptions of peacebuilding rather than providing practical policy-options aimed at enhancing the ability of peace-builders to control the local conflict.[3] Therefore, in Pugh's terms, "deconstructing the simulacra of peacekeeping offers no alternative teleology of progress and no prescription for change other than continual creative opposition to hegemonies of all kinds."[4] In short, the methodology of this research paper is to pose problems rather than proposing new policies which are doomed to create unintended problems. By making the confrontation between UN activities and the Cypriot population visible, it will be possible to expose the relationship between the discourse of UN peace operations and the power exercised by UN activities upon Cypriots, constituting a critique aimed at, in Foucault's terms in "Practising Criticism," "the de-subjugation of the subject" (pp. 152–58).

This research consists of two parts. In the first part, the activities of UNFICYP are evaluated in a wider, political context. Those functions include not only peacekeeping, but also humanitarian and policing works, UN mediation, shuttle diplomacy, UN Secretary General good offices, and negotiation. Exhibition of conflicts will be achieved in that part through three analyses: of the objectification of Cyprus conflict, of the power relations subjugating the Cypriot population, and of Cypriot resistance as an anti-authority struggle. Exposing the power exercised through the UN peacebuilding activities in Cyprus enables us to problematize its underlying, unchallenged, and taken for granted assumptions and modes of thought. In the second part, how the conduct of world populations, or in other words their government, is made possible through the control of discourses is articulated. Discourses that legitimize UN peacebuilding

---

[2] Tarja Vayrynen, "Gender and UN peace Operations: The Confines of Modernity," *International Peacekeeping*, 11:1 (2004), 125–42 (p. 129).

[3] Roland Paris, "International Peacebuilding and the 'Mission Civilisatrice,'" *Review of International Studies*, 28:4 (2002), 637–656 (pp. 655–56).

[4] Michael Pugh, "Peacekeeping and IR Theory: Phantom of the Opera?" *International Peacekeeping,* 10:4 (2003), 104–112 (p. 111).

activities in Cyprus restructure other possible actions both in Cyprus and in other parts of the globe. Those discourses, while constraining several possible actions by making them difficult to be exercised, induce other actions by making them imperative. In the light of the arguments made in this paper, the author finally suggests that UNFICYP plays the role of a psychiatrist who has the task of curing the disease posed by a dangerous individual against the social body. The prescription is the transformation of the dangerous subject and continuous surveillance of it.

Part One

A power relationship has two inherent elements: first is the existence of "the other" on which the power is continuously exercised. "The other" is forced to give consent to the power exercised upon it. This consent is acquired by objectivizing "the other" which transforms it into a subject. On the other hand, once faced with a relationship of power, the subject reacts, responses, and rebels, which constitutes the second element of a power relationship (Foucault, "Subject and Power," p. 220).[5] This part of the research will explore the power relationship between the Cypriot population and UNFICYP via three analyses. First, the process of subjectivizing the Cypriot population through internationalization, in other words objectification, of the inter-communal conflict in Cyprus will be analyzed. Then, by using analytical tools provided by Foucault ("Subject and Power," p. 223), power relations targeting Cypriots will be elaborated. Thirdly, Cypriot resistance will be examined to determine whether it is an anti-authority struggle or not.

ANALYSIS OF THE SUBJECTIVIZATION OF THE CYPRIOT CONFLICT

Internationalization of the Cyprus problem in 1963 opened up all the possibilities of intervention whether military, political, or social. Through the discourse of peacebuilding and conflict resolution, the involvement of a variety of foreign actors ranging from guarantor states and regional powers to international peace operators was legitimized. The Cyprus conflict was first transmitted to an international field by the United Kingdom's initiative of staging an international conference in London in January 1964 immediately after the local upheavals of December 1963. Fearing the complete breakdown of the Cyprus Republic and escalation of a local

---

[5] Michel Foucault, "The Subject and Power," in *Michel Foucault: Beyond Sstructuralism and Hermeneutics*, ed. H. L. Dreyfus and P. Rabinow (Chicago: The University of Chicago Press: 1983), pp. 208–226 (p. 223).

conflict into a regional one between Greece and Turkey, the UK and USA came up with the idea of NATO peacekeeping.[6] However, after negative responses by the USSR and Makarios to that idea, UN peacekeeping was introduced as an alternative. Makarios, the Greek-Cypriot leader and recognized president of Cyprus, believing in the principles of the UN Charter, and relying upon its framework, preferred a UN force to NATO which he believed could have increased Anglo-American influence on Cyprus.[7] Assuaged by the discourse of the United Nations, Makarios gave his consent to the deployment of an international force on Cyprus.

Internationalization of the Cyprus conflict was not determined by the eruption of violence on the island. During the 1950s, a substantive amount of terrorist acts had been executed. However, at that time, the USA and UK had tried to prevent the internationalization of the problem, which was contrary to their behavior in 1960s. Several attempts by Greece to bring the issue to the UN General Assembly were defeated by NATO members in the assembly.[8]

Internationalization of the conflict increased direct interference by Turkey and Greece in Cyprus. Totalization and individualization of Cypriot identities have been perceived as normal and legitimate. Whereas the Turkish authorities via the Turkish Defense Organization (TMT) crushed dissident voices among Turkish-Cypriots and created a homogenous, total Turkish-Cypriot identity, they also individualized Turkish-Cypriots and forced them back onto themselves by isolating them from Greek-Cypriots. The same process was experienced in the Greek side through EOKA-B, although it was slower due to Greek-Cypriot resistance to that process.[9] Government of individualization was not only exercised by local authorities but also by UNFICYP. Penetration of UN activities into the everyday lives of Cypriots through patrolling of streets and countryside and guarding Nicosia's stores and hotels imposed a sense of law and order on

[6] Van Coufoudakis, "United Nations Peacekeeping and Peacemaking and the Cyprus Question," *Western Political Quarterly*, 29:3 (1976), 457–473 (pp. 462–63).

[7] Oliver P. Richmond, *Mediating in Cyprus: The Cypriot communities and the United Nations* (London: Frank Cass, 1998), p. 93.

[8] Suha Bolukbasi, "Boutros Ghali's Cyprus Initiative in 1992: Why Did it Fail?" *Middle Eastern Studies*, 3:1, 460–482 (p. 413).

[9] Adamantia Pollis, "Colonialism and Neo-Colonialism: Determinants of Ethnic Conflict in Cyprus," in *Small States in the Modern World: The Conditions of Survival*, ed. P. Worseley amd P. Kitromilides (Nicosia: Cyprus, 1978), pp. 45–79 (pp. 62–69).

Cypriots in a lawless and disorderly state.[10] Apart from those activities, UNFICYP undertook the role of a link between two hostile communities. Several projects aimed at encouraging Greek-Cypriots and Turkish-Cypriots to face each other in public life were carried out (Stegenga, p. 8). However, those projects, presuming the bi-communality of two primordially distinct ethnicities, included the excluded as excluded in the lives of each community. In other words, in the process of coming together, for both of the communities, the differentiation of inside/outside is instituted. As Agamben suggests in *Homo Sacer*, the distinction between "us" and "other" was secured by including the excluded as "the other."[11] Therefore, after a period of mutual killings and in an environment of distrust, when those two ethnicities face each other, they attach themselves to their communities for the sake of security.

The de-facto transformation of the functions of UN peacekeeping after the 1974 Turkish occupation of the island caused irrevocable segregation of the two communities. UNFICYP, by 1974, turned from a force spread throughout the island into one that protects the demarcation line cutting the whole island into two pieces.[12] In order to stop violence and to prevent recurrences of fighting, UN peacekeepers were interposed between two antagonistic communities as a part of "de-confrontation" process (Stegenga, p. 9).

Therefore, this kind of foreign intervention furthered the bi-communality on Cyprus which was already institutionalized by the 1960 Constitution. The new phase of involvement that had begun in 1963 consolidated it by defining the conflict as inter-communal between two primordially distinct ethnicities. Hence, there is a reciprocal relationship between the objectification of the Cypriot population via the internationalization of the Cyprus conflict and the government of Cypriot identities.

---

[10] James A. Stegenga, "UN Peacekeeping: The Cyprus Venture," *Journal of Peace Research*, 7:1 (1970), 1–16.

[11] Giorgio Agamben, *Homo Sacer: Sovereign Power and Bare Life* (Stanford: Stanford University Press, 1998), cited in Michael Dillon, and Julian, "Global governance, Liberal Peace, and Complex Emergency," *Alternatives: Social Transformation and Humane Governance*, 25:1 (2000), 117–145 (Section 1, para. 8).

[12] Alan James, "The UN Force in Cyprus," *International Affairs*, 65:3 (1989), 481–500 (p. 484).

Analysis of the Power Relations Directed upon Cypriots:

Power relations can only be analyzed by exposing the exercise of power. In order to do so, one needs not to look for the source of power, but to investigate by what means the power is exercised (Foucault, "Subject and Power," p. 217). Foucault further pointed out some tools to analyze power relations which are the degrees of rationalization, the system of differentiations, the types of objectives, the forms of institutionalization, and the means of bringing power relations into being (ibid., p. 223).

I

Bauman argues that since our response to death remains traumatic due to our inability to comprehend it, dichotomizing pairs are a means to overcome that ambivalence (cited in Vayrynen, p. 128). Binary oppositions, by fixing the limits of interpretation, conceal the ambiguities of any given dichotomy. Those pairs, boundaries, distinctions, inside-outside explanations provide us with the necessary interpretation to rationalize the ambiguities and contradictions of the modern world (ibid., p. 129). The conflict and peace dichotomy is the binary pair that lets us overcome the discontinuities in the field of peacebuilding. In any given society, if conflict erupts, the international community deems it necessary to intervene and transform that society. However, even if peace is attained, intervention is not terminated because of the possibility of relapsing back into the conflict. Thus, continuous surveillance is rationalized.

Since 1964, many times, the changing dynamics of the Cyprus conflict led UN peacekeeping to alter its functions. However, its mandates have never been re-defined by the UN Security Council (James, p. 485). This pragmatic and illegal nature of UNFICYP could not have been legitimized without the discourse of peace/conflict. Another discontinuity was embedded in the UN mediation of the Cyprus conflict. In June 1992, during the proximity talks held in New York City, UN Secretary General Boutros Ghali, by departing from traditional low-profile UN mediation, strongly asserted that the status-quo in the island cannot be maintained (Bolukbasi, p. 460). The pressure put on both community leaders reflected the UN's departure from its traditional impartial policy which had been prevalent for three decades. Discontinuity between Cold War and post-Cold War peacebuilding was not problematized, and norms and principles of peacebuilding were modified rapidly.

II

The system of differentiations is composed of constructed binary oppositions which rationalize several hegemonic undertakings. Those differentiations are both reasons for and results of power relations. They "permit one to act upon the actions of others" (Foucault, "Subject and Power," p. 223). In the case of the global governmentality of Cyprus, they take the form of binary oppositions between the intervened—Cypriots— and the interveners who are the economically developed states and societies based on the neo-liberal norms of Western periphery. That dichotomy constructs the differentiation of enlightened, safe areas of the globe vs. dark regions lapsed into violent conflicts. On the one hand, market democracies are portrayed as models of welfare and security; on the other hand, regions imbued with conflict are ghettoized.[13] Another key differentiation is the inside/outside dichotomy. It is perceived that the causes of problems in excluded regions stem from their own culture or political system. Thus, superior market democracies need not feel any guilt over those conflicts, assuming that there is no causal link between "our" actions and "their" wars.[14] Furthermore, perception of zones of conflicts as "excluded" preserves consolidates the powers of Western nation-states in global governance (Dillon and Reid, Section I, para. 13).

III

Those who act upon the actions of others have several types of objectives. In the case of Cyprus, there are three types of objectives that are pursued by the hegemon: riot control, consolidation of the Westphalian international system, and enhancement of geo-strategic interests.

UN peacebuilding during the Cold War took the form of riot control targeted on unruly states which threatened the existing order. Thus, peacekeepers aimed to preserve order by keeping tensions minimal during which problem-solving adjustments can occur (Pugh, "Peacekeeping and Critical Theory," p. 40). Those problem-solving tactics were usually composed of preventing open-violence, monitoring cease-fires and status-quos which were complemented by low-profile mediation and negotiation

---

[13] Michael Pugh, "Peacekeeping and Critical Theory," *International Peacekeeping*, 11(1) (2004), 39–58 (p. 47).
[14] Alex J. Bellamy, "The 'Next Stage' Stage in Peace Operations Theory?" *International Peacekeeping*, 11:1 (2004), 17–38 (p. 28).

activities whose success depended upon independent external variables.[15] Hence, conflict resolution during the Cold War could be defined as the transformation of conflict into a peaceful, non-violent process of social and political change (ibid., pp. 326–27). That definition was confirmed by UN peacekeeping activities in Cyprus. In cases of conflict, UN troops only attempted to halt the violence by situating themselves between the sides. They also aimed to deter violence by continuous patrolling and reporting of incidents to headquarters.[16] Thus, UNFICYP served to preserve order rather than to make peace. Even after 1974, peacekeeping activities were limited to preventing armed build-ups in and along the buffer zone, hindering provocations across the zone, and precluding unauthorized civilians from entering the zone (Lindley, p. 85). This clearly shows that UNFICYP aimed at defusing the crisis, thus, being "a barrier against an unwanted war" (James, p. 500).

During the 1960s, Cypriot diplomats sought a UN resolution which would refer to the independence, sovereignty, and territorial integrity of the Cyprus Republic without the threat of foreign intervention (Coufoudakis, p. 465). As Cyprus had been a UN member since its independence in 1960 and the UN Charter responded to all concerns of Cypriot diplomats, what was the motive behind their undertakings at the UN General Assembly? Those diplomatic attempts exposed the discontinuities or gray areas of the international system. As Richmond argues, peacekeeping intends to protect the Westphalian international system by concealing the problems that occur in the grey areas of the system, such as the discrepancy between popular and legal definitions of self-determination and national minorities ("UN Peace Operations," pp. 86–87). Another means to protect the system is replication of it. Peace-builders promote an internationally sanctioned model of legitimate domestic governance, based on state-centrism and neo-liberal values, in the war-shattered states in which they are deployed (Paris, p. 650). Thus, a particular type of governance is globalized. This reproduction of particularity serves the interests of dominant powers. Peacebuilding "reproduce[s] the frameworks that underpin the socio-political and international system that its proponents are constituting and are constituted by" (Richmond, "A Genealogy,"). This kind of reproduction

---

[15] Oliver P. Richmond, "A Genealogy of Peacemaking: The Creation and Re-Creation of Order," *Alternatives: Global, Local, Political*, 26:3 (2001), 317–43 (p. 320).

[16] Daniel A. Lindley, "Assessing the Role of the UN Peacekeeping Force in Cyprus," in *The Work of the UN in Cyprus: Promoting Peace and Development*, ed. O. P. Richmond and J. Ker-Lindsay (New York: Palgrave, 2001), pp. 77–100 (p. 78).

was obvious in the UN mediation efforts in the Cyprus conflict. The normative standard in mediation process was the infallibility of the Cyprus state (Richmond, *Mediating in Cyprus*, p. 133). If Cyprus was partitioned legally into two, the Westphalian system would be jeopardized and destabilized. Therefore, all points of departure during mediations from 1964 to the present were about degrees of federalism within the unitary Cyprus state, which was within the limits of Westphalian principles.[17] The latest outcome of those efforts was the Annan Plan which was formulated on the basis of a consociational power-sharing model in one state. The plan envisages autonomy and confederal arrangements for both communities, together with a highly proportional electoral system.[18]

During the Turkish occupation of Cyprus in 1974, UNFICYP declared Nicosia Airport a UN Protected Area in order to forestall Turkish capture of the airport (James, p. 492). UN troops, who remained inactive during the Turkish military occupation of northern countryside of Cyprus, responded and fought back for the strategically crucial Nicosia airport. That incident reflects that UNFICYP were deployed on the island to serve Western geo-strategic interests rather than Cypriot ones. In other words, the formation of international organizations to deal with security threats posed by states in conflict, and their interventions in those unruly geographies, are motivated by the perceived geo-strategic and economic interests of the hegemon (Dillon and Reid, Section 1, para. 13). Moreover, when the violence erupted in Cyprus on December 1963, the dominant powers rapidly sought to protect their geo-strategic concerns against the perceived threats posed by the failed Cyprus Republic. The UK and USA introduced the idea of peacekeeping through which the escalation of conflict would be precluded, the south-eastern flank of NATO would be preserved, and Soviet involvement in the Mediterranean would be negated (Richmond, *Mediating in Cyprus*, p. 92).

IV

Institutionalized apparatuses are integral part of power relations. In the case of the global government of the Cypriot population, there are two forms of institutions with their own regulations and structures that can be

---

[17] Ronald J. Fisher, "Cyprus: The Failure of Mediation and the Escalation of an Identity-Based Conflict to an Adversarial Impasse," *Journal of Peace Research*, 38:3 (2001), 307–326 (p. 312).

[18] Ahmet Sozen, "A Model of Power-Sharing in Cyprus: From the 1959 Zurich Agreements to the Annan Plan," in *Greek-Turkish Relations in an Era of Détente* ed. A. Carkoglu and B. Rubin (New York: Routledge, 2005), pp. 61–77 (p. 72).

categorized as an "elite-led Cold War" on Cyprus, and "emerging strategic complexes."

The term "elite-led Cold War" on Cyprus was coined by Richmond ("UN Peace Operations," p. 86) to define big power agreements to prevent regional escalation of conflict.[19] Since the establishment of UNFICYP, there has been a flexible cooperation between two rival powers. The USSR joined Western powers in extending the mandate of the UN force in Cyprus every three months. Moreover, the USSR gave its consent to the de-facto alteration of UN peacekeeping functions on Cyprus after 1974 (James, p. 485). More crucially, at the dawn of the Turkish invasion of Cyprus in 1974, the USSR, which had the image of being a staunch supporter of Cypriot sovereignty, refrained from defending it (Coufoudakis, p. 471). Despite its loose structure and being dependent on the flexible tacit approval of one side, "elite-led Cold War" nurtured the global government of the Cypriot population.

"Emerging strategic complexes" as a response to perceived threats emanating from political emergencies are formed by a strange alliance of nation-states, international organizations, international non-governmental organizations, and local civil society. Increasingly overlapped discourses of security and development rationalized their intervention in turbulent societies (Dillon and Reid, Section 1, paras 7–12). Despite its hierarchical regulations and sophisticated structure, this division of labor accelerated and strengthened the surveillance of the Cypriot population. It is this kind of complex that brings an "unusual blend of soldiers, diplomats, policemen, and civilian staffers and technicians" under the roof of UNFICYP (Stegenga, p. 6). It makes possible the involvement in the mediation process of a variety of third parties, ranging from representatives of the United Nations and European Union and UN Secretary-Generals, to foreign ministers of the USA and UK, as was also observed by Fisher (p. 312). There is such a complementary relationship among the bodies of the complex, that UN peacekeeping and UN mediation can rationalize each other's functions.[20] This "Emerging strategic complex" even has its own logic of authority. Although UNFICYP is technically responsible to the UN Security Council, in fact the UN Secretary-General decides on substantive issues (Stegenga, p. 6).

---

[19] Oliver P. Richmond, "UN Peace Operations and the Dilemmas of the Peacebuilding Consensus, *International Peacekeeping*," 11:1 (2004), 83–101 (pp. 86–87).

[20] Oliver P. Richmond, "UN Mediation in Cyprus, 1964-65: Setting a Precedent for Peacemaking?" in Richmond and Ker-Lindsay (eds), pp. 101–26 (p. 102).

V

The instrument for bringing power relations into being is "strategic conflict management": a never-ending task of peacebuilding. Cypriots are forced to participate in conflict resolution activities by the effects of UN discourse. Those activities consist of third party mediation and negotiation, inter-communal talks under the auspices of the UN, shuttle diplomacy, UN Secretary-General good offices, UN humanitarian works, and so on. Once Cypriots become subject to those activities, the means of bringing power relations on Cypriots into being becomes possible. UNSC Resolution 186 was decisive in creating such a comprehensive conflict settlement structure. Peacekeeping, peacemaking, and peacebuilding activities are executed simultaneously on Cyprus (Richmond, "UN Mediation," p. 102).

The most powerful discourse that entrapped Cypriots in conflict resolution activities is that of international recognition and legitimacy. Since the Turkish-Cypriot leaders considered themselves lacking only recognition and equality, which can only be supplied by the United Nations, they could not risk being isolated from the UN framework. On the other hand, Greek-Cypriot leadership had to be on good terms with the UN to prevent Turks from getting what they want (Richmond, *mediating in Cyprus*, p. 154). Moreover, the ability of Greek-Cypriot politicians to exercise power on the Turkish-Cypriot leadership stems from the fact that they were recognized by the UN as the legitimate government of Cyprus (Richmond, ibid., pp. 181–82).

ANALYSIS OF CYPRIOT RESISTANCE

Since forms of resistance are forged against power relations, they can be used as a catalyst in order to bring power relations to light, locate their positions, and discover their application and methods used (Foucault, "Subject and Power," p. 211). These oppositions or anti-authority struggles have a number of features. First of all, their aim is not to attack particular groups, institutions, or classes, but power effects: in other words specific form of power. These struggles are anarchistic in nature. Because they cannot find "the chief enemy" due to its complexity, they criticize and attack "the immediate enemy." In addition, those oppositions do not expect to find a solution to their problems, but to demonstrate their discomfort with the present situation. Their most crucial characteristic is the struggle against "the government of individualization," against the control and transformation of their identity. They also reject the imposition of certain forms of knowledge. The truth, through which power circulates, is questioned. In short, anti-authority struggles are spontaneously formed against being subjectivized (ibid, pp. 211–12).

On the level of the Cypriot leadership, the most obvious resistance was performed by Cypriot diplomats. Especially after 1963 when Turkish-Cypriots were forced to withdraw from governmental offices, diplomats had tried to annul the Treaties of Guarantee and Alliance within the framework of UN in order to secure independence and sovereignty for Cyprus (Bolukbasi, p. 412). Those treaties are a means to intervene in domestic affairs of Cyprus. Power relations are engaged through the legitimacy created by those treaties. Thus, attempts by diplomats were struggles against a technique of power rather than its source. Furthermore, efforts to abrogate those agreements demonstrate Cypriot struggle against subjectivization, since those treaties treated the Cypriot population as a mere object to be acted upon.

One should not perceive the Greek-Cypriot attacks on Turkish-Cypriots as mere hatred towards another ethnicity. Those acts could also be interpreted as revolts against the government of individualization. The more the UN imposed the negative peace and the more the international community ordered Cypriots how to behave, the more their antagonism increased. For example, when the National Guard launched an attack on Turkish-Cypriots in August 1964 which the Turkish air-force retaliated against, the UN Security Council immediately appealed for a cease-fire and enforced it. However, after a short period of calm, the National Guard initiated another violent attack in November 1967 (Lindley, pp. 80–81). Leaving the indefensible acts of these paramilitary groups aside, it is a fact that they were subject to a form of power. As those groups wanted to break the state of negative peace and status-quo, it is further imposed on them. As a result, they fought back as much as possible and as long as they found means to escape from the global governmentality.

A thousand incidents in the buffer zone that occur every year further reflects the Cypriot protest of imposed bi-communal order. Those incidents usually include stone-throwing to the other side, verbal harassment and insults between the two sides, illegal encroachments into the buffer zone, and non-lethal gun shootings (Lindley, pp. 85–87). Responses by UNFICYP, which are composed of attempts to calm the tensions and ordering both sides to back down, further constrain the Cypriot's conduct by telling him/her how to behave. Therefore, Cypriot demonstrations of discomfort turn out to be unpredictable and ungovernable. Demonstrations beginning with display of lack of discipline can end up in gunfights as happened in April 1993 (Lindley, p. 88). Furthermore, a major motorcyclist demonstration of August 1996, which was another display of utmost discomfort with present situation, led to two deaths and many injuries

(Lindley, p. 90). It is obvious that those anarchistic demonstrations aimed to destabilize the imposed order on Cyprus, protesting the enforced segregation of communities, and they did not seek to solve the problem, but only to express it.

Shootings and stone-throwing between the sides means more than an inter-ethnic antagonism. Each side perceives the other as responsible for the current negative peace. Because the sophisticated structure of global governmentality obscures actual culprits, enemies behind the border become an easy target. Furthermore, UN peacekeepers also become subject to those attacks and harassments. The demonstrators may throw rocks, bottles, and even Molotov cocktails at UNFICYP personnel if given the opportunity (Lindley, p. 89).

Part Two

As Foucault (cited in Dreyfus and Rabinow, pp. 202–4) argued, because power cannot be held and maintained at a centre or in particular institutions, it becomes effective only as long as being exercised. The execution of power relations becomes possible through several discourses. Those discourses legitimize certain actions while de-legitimizing others. As the regime of truth produced by subjectivizing discourses is taken for granted by Cypriots, they open the way for a variety of possible actions to be acted upon themselves.

Zones of indistinction like "the excluded," which are separated from "the exceptional self," are crucial in constructing the inside/outside dichotomy which serves to consolidate and maintain sovereign power. The construction of the prevailing state of anarchy as somewhere "outside" but close enough to affect the "inside" deems necessary the strategic formation of a state of emergency on the "inside." The distinction of chaos and normal conditions specifies the domains of anarchy, lawlessness, dislocation as opposed to the domains of peace, justice, and belongingness. In the case of global governmentality, that system of differentiations is produced between political systems, cultures, and populations rather than nations and states (Dillon and Reid, "Sovereign Power and Bare Life," para. 5).

The dichotomy of zomes of peace/conflict is the fundamental discourse that lets other regimes of truth be built in order to make global governmentality possible. It is the presentation of Cyprus as plunged into an inter-communal ethnic conflict that requires "intervention from" and "surveillance of" the regimes of peace and stability.

The peace operation is required to be successful fulfilling its mandates in order to justify future operations. Thus, the longer the operation takes, the less successful it might be. Consequently, the deployment of UNFICYP over forty years should represent a failure. However, Debrix has argued that its representation is not significant for its assessment.[21] If peacekeeping is evaluated from the perspective of simulation rather than its referentiality, peace operations turn out to be great achievements for global security. This is achieved by promoting images of virtual peace. Concealing the real effects of peace operations and believing in ideological configurations of keeping, building, and enforcing peace simulates peacekeeping as an eminent and essential operation. Therefore, the continuous surveillance of the Cypriot population via UNFICYP is perceived as a precondition for peace and prevention of relapsing back into conflict.

Another effect of virtual peace is hiding the structural causes of conflicts. "The discourses [...] neglect the political understanding of violence and its sources, and reduce political violence into technical problems to be solved by outside expertise" (Vayrynen, p. 130). Since the representation of peacebuilding does not matter due to its virtual realization, then why should peacekeepers invest time and energy in understanding the real causes of inter-ethnic violence when they are able to seem to be solving the problems? That is what happened in Cyprus. The structural causes of inter-communal violence in Cyprus go back to the British colonial policies and were further augmented by direct foreign intervention (Pollis, p. 74). However, these causes were neglected and what has been prescribed for Cyprus is a highly federative, consociational state and a bi-communal, segregated society, despite the fact that the conflicts had not arisen out of the absence of such a federative state system in Cyprus.[22]

Dividing the globe into zones of affluence and of anarchy depict particular cultures as superior to the rest. Thus, peacebuilding might be interpreted as the white man's burden–an updated version of the *mission civilisatrice* which assumes that the developed market democracies of the West have a moral responsibility to "civilize" backward people, and to enlighten the dark regions of the globe. Despite the fact that the current practice of peacebuilding is pristine from the brutal acts of colonial times, assistance that is provided by peace operations comes with an ideological

---

[21] Francois Debrix, *Re-Envisioning Peacekeeping: The United Nations and the Mobilization of Ideology* (Minneapolis: University of Minnesota Press, 1999), pp. 216–18.

[22] United Nations, *The Comprehensive Settlement of the Cyprus Problem* (2004). http://www.un.org/Depts/dpa/annanplan/annanplan.pdf

attachment that restructures the political systems and cultures of subjectivized populations (Paris, pp. 651–53).

Assistance to war-shattered societies also promotes what Lacy called the "sentimental moral equilibrium" of the West.[23] Acting as the sole power in trying to solve global problems, the moral security of the West is enhanced because it becomes "the responsible" global authority. Therefore, the sense of Western superiority embedded in global governmentality is furthered again by global governance.

Global governmentality cannot function without the discourses of "ideal" norms and governance. Subjectivized populations have to perceive particular norms and form of governance as universally good in order to give consent to the imposition of those norms and form of governance on themselves. Promoting that perception is achieved through the globalization of those norms and that model of governance. And, in the globalization of particularity, UN activities have a crucial role. As Paris pointed out, what is happening through UN peacebuilding is the globalization of the concept of ideal state formation and functioning. UN peacebuilding presents the liberal market democracy as "an internationally-sanctioned model of legitimate domestic governance" (p. 639). Thus, UN peacebuilding is more than a tool of conflict management: it is "a transmission belt" conveying the standards of the core to the periphery (Paris, pp. 650–53). In other words, UN peacebuilding defines and sets the standards of "normal behavior," disciplining the defective which is the task of a psychiatrist in modern societies according to Foucault.[24]

The examples above are disciplinary agents and discourses of panoptic governance. Power is exercised through them without centralized power structures. That is why disciplinary power cannot be recognized by the disciplined subject. It is embedded in sophisticated networks, and obscured by regimes of truth.[25] What Dillon and Reid called "emerging strategic complexes" is an example of those systems functioning with the legitimacy provided by several discourses such as the peace/conflict dichotomy and through disciplinary agents such as UN peacebuilding. Furthermore, evaluating international affairs in the contexts of disciplinarity, governmentality, and panopticism leads us to interpret the continuous

---

[23] Mark J. Lacy, "War, Cinema, and Moral Anxiety," *Alternatives: Global, Local, Political*, 28 (2003), 611–636 (p. 634).

[24] Michel Foucault, "Confinement, Psychiatry, Prison," in *Politics, Philosophy, Culture*, pp. 178–210.

[25] Francois Debrix, "Space Quest: Surveillance, Governance, and the Panoptic Eye of the United Nations," *Alternatives: Social Transformation and Humane Governance*, 24:3 (1999), 269–295 (pp. 290–91).

surveillance of societies in conflict by UN agencies, in other words global governmentality, as an attempt to normalize international political behavior (ibid., p. 291). However, that surveillance is applied not only to states, but also to populations and individuals. That is why UNFICYP precipitates responses not only from community leaders, but also from ordinary Cypriots whose life is subject to discipline. Hence, UNFICYP is a mechanism to insert and establish a form of administration and continuous regulation of everyday life. Therefore, UN peacebuilding as a disciplinary agent of the global governmentality is a panoptic technology which, in Foucault's terms has the ability "to make the spread of power efficient; to make possible the exercise of power with limited manpower at the least cost; to discipline individuals with the least exertion of overt force by operating on their souls; to increase to a maximum the visibility of those subjected; to involve in its functioning all those who come in contact with the apparatus" (cited in Dreyfus and Rabinow, p. 192).

Conclusion

In order to comprehend the functions of UNFICYP as those of a psychiatrist, the latter's functions have to be examined. Foucault's work on the genealogy of expert psychiatric opinion in penal cases is extremely helpful in discovering the role of psychiatrist in modern societies.[26]

Expert psychiatric opinion is highly effective in legitimizing the transformation and normalization of individuals. It does so first by, as Foucault argues, "transferring the application of punishment from the offense defined by law to criminality evaluated from a psychologico-moral point of view" (p. 18). This is achieved through two processes. First, the offense is mentioned redundantly in order to constitute it as an individual trait rather than as something acted. Second, standards such as an optimum level of development (psychological immaturity, profound imbalance), moral qualities, and ethical rules are created in order to evaluate the forms of conduct (p. 16). The transformation of the individual is legitimized, secondly, by turning the author of the crime from a legal subject to "an object of a technology and knowledge of rectification, readaptation, reinsertion, and correction." Expert psychiatric opinion attains this by blurring the status of the legal subject, in other words by establishing juridical indiscernibility around the responsibility of the author of the crime (pp. 20–21). The third function of expert psychiatric opinion is the

---

[26] Michel Foucault, *Abnormal: Lectures at the College de France 1974-1975* (New York: Picador, 2003).

constitution of a doctor-judge. Psychiatric expertise transforms the accused into the convicted by demonstrating the potential criminality embedded in his character. Furthermore, those measures constitute a homogenous social response justifying continuous protection of the social body by means ranging from medical treatment to penal institutions. However, that response is neither aimed at an illness nor at a crime. It is aimed at the dangerous individual who is not completely ill or criminal. Thus, it is that a combination of perversion and danger legitimizes the continuous intervention by medico-judicial institutions on individuals (pp. 33–34). The merging of the medical and the judicial is made possible by the discourse of fear whose objective is to detect and counter social danger (p. 35). Social danger stems from a partly ill, partly criminal individual who is exactly "abnormal." Defining the abnormal paves the way for activities to normalize that abnormal individual (pp. 41–42). Normalization, however, should not be perceived as something negative whose primary objective is to preserve and repress. On the contrary, it is a positive technique of intervention and transformation, a discipline of normalization (pp. 49–50).

Psychiatry as a medical discipline has been endowed with particular mechanisms of power such as the compulsory hospitalization order. Confinement of the insane and continuous surveillance of them in a psychiatric institution requires three conditions. Firstly, the medical institution must be established with the objective of accepting and then curing the ill. Secondly, hospitalization must be legitimized by particular forms of public administration accompanied by medical reports. Thirdly, hospitalization must be motivated by the mentally ill condition of an individual which threatens public order and social security. These developments give psychiatry the authority to determine if the individual is capable of creating social disorder or danger, unlike the previous authority to decide whether he is responsible for his actions or not (pp. 140–41).

The generalization of psychiatry needs a justification and a rationalization to intervene on abnormal individuals without being required to explain the pathological processes of that abnormality. Once that becomes possible, psychiatrists are able to implement techniques of normalization on all abnormal individuals without demonstrating the actual, but only potential, symptoms of illness or madness (p. 307).

To sum up, psychiatry claims a role of social defense by becoming the scientific discipline for social protection. It attempts social interventions and controls in the name of justice and management of abnormalities. It lays claim to be "the general body for the defense of society against the dangers that undermine it from within" (p. 316).

In the case of the global governmentality of the Cypriot population, the legitimization of disciplinary interventions is accomplished in a same way that expert psychiatric opinion has done for the management of abnormalities. The activities of UNFICYP resemble the punishment of Cypriots not because of an offense they exercised, but because of their condition. Cyprus had not violated any principle in the UN Charter. It did not violate the rights of another sovereign nation-state, nor did it threaten the use of force against the political independence or territorial integrity of another state. The only felony of Cyprus was to be entrapped in an intra-state conflict and facing being a failed state. Inter-communal conflicts, civil wars, and failed states are stigmatized concepts in the field of international relations. Despite the fact that those conditions are not breaches of international law, they constitute a condition of being politically under-developed compared to other established nation-states. Thus, in order to justify transformative intervention, states like Cyprus are evaluated on the basis of moral and ethical standards. For example, a failed state is perceived as unable to provide universally required services and rights to its citizens. Those moral qualities distract attention from the acts of Cyprus, and focus on the nature of its being, its qualities. By doing so, a shift from "the punishment based on an offense defined by law" to "the criminality evaluated from a psychologico-moral point of view" is successfully achieved.

Moreover, the international community does not try to discover the responsible of Cyprus' state of being. By overlooking the pathological processes behind the "dangerous" characteristics of the Cypriot state and society, Cyprus as a whole was turned into a state which is subject to the corrections and reinstitutions of UNFICYP. A lack of need to demonstrate the causes of problems brings a lack of need to provide evidence for actual adverse effects of those problems. For example, if one believes in the supremacy of a nation-state based on liberal normative value systems, one will conceive of the collapse of such a state as something dangerous and undesired. Thus, one does not need to see the occurrence of an offense as long as one sees a way of being which is stigmatized. It does not matter how the Cypriot state failed, how Cypriot society fell into a civil war, or how those developments affected the international order, but how they might affect it in the future. Therefore, the normalization of the dangerous Cypriot population is rationalized without the need to demonstrate the dangers that are posed by them. It is potential outcomes, which can be pre-emptively responded to, rather than actual ones, that matter. Hence, the Cypriot population is turned into a "dangerous individual." Fear of intra-state conflict de-stabilizing the Westphalian international order is the main discourse behind the perception of a "dangerous population." The international community is afraid of Cypriots who problematize the normative value systems of liberal market democracies by terminating the imposed peace and destroying a state created on the basis of liberal presumptions. If a collapsed Cyprus state, which used to be structured on the basis of a federative and consociational model, and a society which failed to unite in diversity, are perceived as threats to the universal legitimacy of state-centrist liberal norms and values, then it becomes legitimate to define the Cypriot population as dangerous and to normalize the abnormal Cypriots. Likewise, once it is claimed that Cyprus in conflict carries the danger of escalation to regional conflict that might destabilize the global order, then it becomes imperative to intervene in Cyprus in the name of protecting the international society of nation-states from disorder.

When the potential global implications of inter-communal conflict in a failed Cyprus are analyzed, instrumental rationality requires suggesting policies and means to alter prevalent conditions, a task being undertaken by peace studies. What is extremely crucial in those analyzes is the unpredictability of how and when the nature of Cypriot state and society will pose an actual problem. Hence, pre-emptive response becomes imperative. Therefore, a huge field of possible interventions by strange alliances of institutions such as "emerging strategic complexes" is opened. The abnormal Cypriot state shall be normalized. However, the process of normalization will not be a negative one. It will be an application of positive power by re-promoting peace in Cyprus and re-establishing a state which will be a replication of the Western model.

There are several preconditions of the normalization process, of "promoting peace" in Cyprus. First of all, there should be institutions which have the legitimate task of transformation and surveillance. UNFICYP operating under the authority of the United Nations is a perfect candidate for such a job. Apart from this, those activities are required to be legitimized by a group of expertise. Academic works and reports by inter-governmental institutions and peacekeeping personnel fulfil that necessity. Finally, transformation and surveillance activities are motivated by the threat posed by Cyprus. It is the conditions of Cypriots that precipitate the intervention.

In conclusion, similarities between the functions of UNFICYP and the psychiatrist suggests that UNFICYP has the role of protecting the social body, which is the international system based on Westphalian principles, against the threats posed from within which are the collapse of regional balances of power and de-legitimization of universally accepted norms. Thus, the dangerous individual in this case is the Cypriot population. Finally, the technique that is exercised by UNFICYP in the government of the dangerous Cypriot population is panoptic and disciplinary in its nature.

EDUCATION FOR SECURITY IN ROMANIA: A SURVEY OF YOUNG PEOPLE

Ella Magdalena Ciuperca

INTRODUCTION

The events of September 2001 brought terrorism onto the list of fundamental problems of the present-day world. Numerous approaches in sociology, psychology, political and security studies demonstrate interest in the causes, motivations, or explanations for such an unpredictable phenomenon. This is necessary in order to understand how conflicts such as those between Israel and Palestine, the wars in Afghanistan and Iraq, or the devastating terrorist attacks in the USA, Russia, Turkey, Spain, and Great Britain were possible.

Research literature on terrorism has expanded dramatically since the 1970s, and especially since September 11, 2001. In psychology, for example, a search of the PsycINFO database (the largest psychology database in the world, with entries dating back to the 1880s) reveals that more research on terrorism has been published since 2001 than in all previous years combined.[1]

However, the number of studies based on systematic empirical analysis is surprisingly limited—one of the main reasons for this being the low quality of available statistical data. Nevertheless, social scientists have succeeded sometimes in understanding and predicting terrorism even long before the events of September 11. For example, Hudson underlined, in his report on "The Sociology and Psychology of Terrorism," the possibility that a terrorist attack might occur in the United States. He was even more specific because, among some other suggested scenarios, there was one about suicide bombers of Al-Qaida who might crash an aircraft into the Pentagon or other buildings.[2]

This represents only one argument in favour of a more active involvement of social scientists in the prevention and annihilation of terrorism. In trying to accomplish such a desirable objective, Romanian researchers could notice that terrorism is a theoretical field which has not

---

[1] Scott Plous, and Phil G. Zimbardo, "How Social Sscience can Reduce Terrorism," *Chronicle of Higher Education*, 51:3, September 10, 2004, pp. B9–B10. www.socialpsychology.org

[2] Rex A. Hudson, *The Sociology and Psychology of Terrorism* (Washington D.C.: Federal Research Division of the Library of Congress, 1999). http://www.loc.gov

been sufficiently well investigated in their own country also. In fact, after consulting the existing specialised literature from Romania, one can see that the great majority of studies related to the terrorist phenomenon have a generalist, historical, and descriptive character, without using any of the specific techniques of scientific research. The real identification of the manner in which the civil population perceives the activities of terrorist groups has never been studied.

So, because of the insufficiency of the institutional and sociological approach to the terrorist phenomenon in the specialised literature, I consider that the originality of this study consists in exploring the epistemological discrepancy between the historical and descriptive approaches to the terrorist phenomenon and the way people perceive those items which aim to identify the level of knowledge and understanding of the terrorist phenomenon by the Romanian population.

RESULTS AND DISCUSSION

The goal of this survey was to identify the information level of the population regarding the terrorist phenomenon and its understanding, bearing in mind that a good knowledge of the processes involved is of great importance for the appropriate handling of such a danger.

I have chosen to use in this research only young, educated people, students, or graduates in different fields. I chose them as I considered they were the most amenable to education and more interested in civic issues. So the sample comprised 332 subjects distributed as follows: 184 women and 147 men, 28 from rural areas, with ages ranging from 18 to 35 years— although most of them, 140, were aged between 21 and 30 years old). As a rule, their occupational, residency, and gender characteristics follow those of the general population of Romanian young people.

They answered a self-administered questionnaire during the period October 2006–January 2007. The collected data were interpreted using Windows Statistical Package for the Social Sciences, in order to confirm or refute the following general hypotheses of this research:

1. Regarding the terrorist phenomenon Romanian young people have a coherent pattern of knowledge connecting its causes, financing sources, actions, and prevention methods.
2. Age has a significant influence on the perception of the terrorist phenomenon by Romanian young people.
3. Gender has a significant influence on perceptions concerning the terrorist phenomenon within the population of young people in Romania.

Contrary to my expectations, young people in Romania have well-defined opinions about terrorism. So that, 52.7% of the respondents consider that terrorists have a good education, 60.2% believe that they are mostly young people, and 41.6% of the respondents understand the fact that the communities to which they belong do not reject terrorists. That means that the members of their belonging groups accept their activities, thinking of them as the only way to achieve some, often common, goals.

These findings are consistent with those of the specialist researchers which show that terrorists have, in general, more than average education and that only a very few of them are uneducated or illiterate.[3] To exemplify, Taylor identified the average age of terrorists as about 20 years, although there are many organisations which use persons of about 14-15 years old, especially for dangerous missions. Russell and Miller also assembled demographic data about 350 individuals engaged in terrorist activities in Latin America, Europe, Asia, and the Middle East and found that about two-thirds of terrorist group members had received some form of university training.[4]

My respondents' answers to the item "Terrorists are mostly uneducated persons" correlate (underlined through the Spearman test) with those to "Terrorists are mostly women" ($S=0.229$, $p\leq0.001$) and with those given to "Terrorists are mostly young people" ($S=0.192$, $p\leq0.001$). To explain such perceptions I have to recall that, because of the latest international events, many people make an incorrect assumption, superimposing the image of Islamic terrorism over the multiple types of it. In such conditions, being questioned about terrorism, people activate the stereotype about Islam. So that women, here terrorist women, should be uneducated persons because of the belief that they have fewer chances to gain a high level of education in their communities. In addition, those who answer that terrorists are mostly women believe that media objectively reflect the terrorist phenomenon ($S=0.118$, $p\leq0.044$). Considering the fact that the media have a tendency to present more cases involving women terrorists than men (because of the greater impact of such news) and because people trust the media, they could wrongly perceive that women terrorists are the more numerous in spite of the fact that they are greatly outnumbered by men.

---

[3] Ariel Merari, "Suicide Terrorism in the Context of the Israeli-Palestinian Conflict," in *Assessment, Treatment and Prevention of Suicidal Behaviour*, ed. R.I. Yufit and D. Lester (London: Routledge, 2005); Max Taylor, *The Terrorist* (London: Brassey's, 1988).

[4] Charles A. Russell and Bowman H. Miller, "Profile of a Terrorist," *Terrorism: An International Journal*, 1 (1977), 17–34.

People from the rural areas think that terrorists are persons rejected by their own communities (U=2638.00, $p \leq 0.045$). Such a belief could be the result of the values shared and internalised in rural communities, in harmony with a high sense of moral value and also the power that social control has. Therefore, in their opinion, a person involved in those types of acts has no option but to be ostracised by his/her group.

Analysing the answers regarding the population's perception of the main causes and motivations of people who become terrorists, it is noticeable that many subjects consider religious extremism as an important source of the phenomenon. The discrepancy between these subjects and those reflecting reasons such as territorial problems, political regimes, or nationalism permits us to conclude that the population is not well informed on these issues. Therefore, their social representation of reality is based on only disparate pieces of information without any further, more profound, inquiry into the inner mechanisms of terrorism.

	Very low level	Low level	High level	Very high level	Total
The lack of dialogue and of a reconciliation framework	9.00	33.70	38.30	16.00	98.50 (327)
Religious extremism	0.90	3.30	33.70	60.80	99.70 (331)
Nationalism	2.40	20.50	44.90	30.70	99.40 (330)
Territorial problems	1.80	15.10	47,.00	33.40	98.20 (326)
Need to control resources	6.90	23.20	34.60	29.20	97.90 (325)
Poverty	13.00	35.50	32.80	14.50	97.90 (325)
Totalitarian political regime	18.10	34.30	28.30	12.00	96.40 (320)

It is very interesting that those people who have as their only information sources their family and peers consider that the main causes of terrorism are the lack of proper dialogue and reconciliation conditions and the presence of dictatorial political regimes. Learning about terrorism from familiar sources leads to emphasising the perception of external motivation for individuals who join terrorist networks over internal motivations such as beliefs, patriotism, and so on. It is also possible that those respondents who are well integrated into their social networks understand less about reasons such as revenge and violence.

	Reasons for terrorism are the lack of a proper dialogue and conciliation framework	The reason for terrorism is the existence of a political totalitarian regime
Your main source of information on terrorism is your family	.116 .040 317	.214 .000 313
Your main sources of information on terrorism are your peer groups	.115 .041 317	.158 .007 312

In addition, the subjects' answers to the item "The reason for terrorism is the existence of a political dictatorial regime" correlate with those referring to the cause of terrorism as the poverty of a population (Rp=0.360, $p\leq0.001$). In this matter, researchers have not identified a general pattern to use in an endeavour to understand people who join terrorist organisations. But Russell and Miller found that more than two thirds of the terrorists surveyed came from middle-class or even upper-class backgrounds. Nevertheless, terrorists in much of the developing world tend to be drawn from the lower sections of society. Also, according to Hudson, the rank and file members of Arab terrorist organisations include substantial numbers of poor people. So in this particular matter, these people have appropriate perceptions of the terrorist phenomenon.

If people consider religious extremism and nationalism as the causes of terrorism, they believe that terrorist networks intend to attack public places with bombs and to take hostages. It is possible for people to make such correlations having in mind that because of their profound beliefs terrorists would engage themselves in actions characterised by a great amount of visibility.

	The reason for terrorism is religious extremism.	The reason for terrorism is nationalism.
Terrorist networks intend to attack public places using bombs.	.201 .000 327	.135 .015 326
Terrorist networks intend to take hostages.	.191 .001 323	.109 .050 322

One dimension of a mental model of terrorism is reflected in the correlation between the answers to the question whether the lack of dialogue and of a reconciliation framework could be a cause of terrorism and the idea that terrorist networks have as an objective gaining support from the world population (Rp=0.135, $p\leq0.015$). So it seems to be easier for everybody to accept terrorist actions because of this rationalisation. This way, their violence and irrationality could be considered as a result of despair, a way to express themselves and to make everybody know and understand theirs grievances. So people tend to believe in a logical development of terrorist actions.

An interesting negative correlation appears between the items "The reason for terrorism is the lack of dialogue and a reconciliation framework" and "When do you think that Romania could become a target for a terrorist network?" (Rp=-0.172, $p \leq 0.003$). So the respondents who believe in those as causes of terrorism outnumber those who believe that within a short time period Romania could became a terrorist target. This finding signifies that in their inner conscience the respondents believe that Romania is not a country with a proper interinstitutional dialogue, but instead is characterised by the lack of an efficient framework for reconciliation—all of this in spite of its democratic regime. Thus, it is important to understand when constructing a future educational model that young Romanian people tend to have little trust in their country's institutions.

An additional argument is that people who think that political dictatorial regimes and the gaining of resources are the most important determinants of terrorism also think that terrorists aim to destroy strategic institutions and to put the lives of the general public in danger. Therefore, in the opinion of our respondents, those who hate the political regime do not attack innocent people as a form of revenge, focusing their attention on public issues. Although this is not true, as so many terrorist acts have proved, people persist in trying to attach rational explanations to the irrationality of terrorists' behaviour.

Perceptions of the causes of terrorism are influenced by the sources of information used by the perceivers. Those who keep themselves informed through radio tend to consider nationalism (Rp= 0.124, $p \leq 0.026$), dictatorial regimes (Rp=0.119, $p \leq 0.035$), and territorial problems (Rp=0.131, $p \leq 0.019$) to be the main reasons for terrorism, while those who are kept informed through newspapers consider religious extremism (Rp=0.171, $p \leq 0.002$) and nationalism (Rp=0.119, $p \leq 0.032$) as its sources. The lack of dialogue and of a reconciliation framework (Rp=0.162, $p \leq 0.004$) is considered to be an important cause of terrorism, especially by those who are used to reading scientific studies. Such findings are of a great importance in order to be able to choose proper channels to disseminate widespread information within the framework of an educational model.

Regarding the perception of the methods which terrorists use to finance their networks, it appears that Romanian young people consider that illegal weapons trade (89.7%), money laundering (82.6%), and drug trafficking (69.6%) represent their most important sources of money. Their answers reflect, at the same time a series of correlations as follows: drug dealing and the white slave trade (Rp=0.422, $p \leq 0.001$), drug dealing and money laundering (Rp=0.190, $p \leq 0.001$), drug dealing and the illegal weapons trade (Rp=0.156, $p \leq 0.005$), white slave trade and money laundering (Rp=0.222, $p \leq 0.001$), money laundering and the illegal weapons trade (Rp=0.220, $p \leq 0.001$), and legal commercial operations and money laundering (Rp=0.301, $p \leq 0.001$). So that if a terrorist network is suspected of being involved in one form of organised crime it is also suspected of being implicated in other forms of it. This is explained especially through the social psychological notion of the "halo effect" which refers to a situation where a quality or an action of somebody in one field diffuses into other fields where that person has no competence.[5] On the other hand, in spite of the fact that terrorist organisations use mainly legal commercial exchanges to get money, especially donations, this possibility has the lowest rate of answers.[6]

Most of the subjects who believe that terrorism is financed through organised crime methods also agree with the restraining of certain civil rights. For example, if terrorism is considered to be financed through drugs trade operations, they agree that houses should be searched in an endeavour to prevent this (Rp=0.147, $p \leq 0.022$). Subjects who accept the idea that terrorists intend to detonate bombs in public places consider that physical control of access into public institutions should be a normal procedure (Rp=0.239, $p \leq 0.001$) and also the photo-video surveillance of public places (Rp=0.218, $p \leq 0.001$) or giving information about people who are suspected of engaging in criminal activity (Rp=0.135, $p \leq 0.016$). In addition, those who think that terrorists' aim is to take hostages accept the photo-video surveillance of public places (Rp=0.225, $p \leq 0.001$) and would be happy to take part in some actions organised by legally appointed counterterrorist institutions (Rp=0.139, $p \leq 0.013$). It was noticeable that the perception of every type of terrorists' goal is linked with related civil rights the restriction of which could prevent that phenomenon, showing a strong cause-effect correlation of answers.

Most of the respondents consider that military intervention is useful to fight against terrorism, but in order to carry out such a scenario they consider (79.8%) that a united effort of the entire international community is required. Their belief contradicts existing research which shows that military responses to terrorism tend to be ineffective and, more than that, lead to an increase in acts of terrorism. For example, Enders and Sandler

---

[5] Edward L. Thorndike "A Constant Error in Psychological Ratings," *Journal of Applied Psychology,* 4 (1920), 25–29.
[6] Paul O'Neill, *US-European Union Designation of Terrorist Financiers* (2002). http://www.state.gov/coalition/cr/rm/2002/9999.htm

examined 20 years of terrorist activity and found a significant rise in terrorism following US military reprisals against Libya. [7] Military responses to international terrorism can unwittingly reinforce terrorists' images of their enemies as violent and aggressive, make the recruiting of new members easier and strengthen alliances among terrorist organisations (Plous and Zimbardo).

	Do you agree with military intervention to fight against terrorism?
Chi-Square	200.734
df	3
Asymp. Sig.	.000

A large percentage of the persons included in this study consider that the present alliance system of Romania raises the risk of a terrorist attack against our country. In view of this, it is somewhat surprising that most of the subjects (62%) believe that Romania will not be the target of a terrorist attack in the short term. These contradictory findings could be explained by invoking the social psychological "belief in a just world" which is people's tendency to believe that they live in a world where everybody gets what s/he deserves.[8] So, people do not accept that negative events could happen to them only by pure chance. Also "the optimistic bias of individuals" could be fertile in explaining this apparently unusual answer.[9] According to that response, people tend to present an unrealistic optimism about their future life events, considering that negative events are meant for other people, not for themselves, while happy events will probably happen to them—not to others.

Another amazing finding concerns the opinions of the subjects on the degree that the civil population could prevent terrorism. Although 66.5% of the subjects agree with this idea and answered positively to the question "Do you agree to having some of your civil rights constrained in order to prevent terrorism?," they are still reluctant to accept all the implications of

---

[7] Walter Enders, and Todd Sandler, "The Effectiveness of Anti-Terrorism Policies: A Vector-Autoregression-Intervention Analysis," *American Political Science Review*, 87:4 (1993), 829–844; Andrew Silke, *Terrorists, Victims and Society: Psychological Perspectives on Terrorism and Its Consequences* (London: Wiley, 2003).

[8] Melvin J. Lerner, *The Belief in a Just World: A Fundamental Delusion* (New York: Plenum Press, 1980).

[9] Neil D. Weinstein, "Unrealistic Optimism about Future Life Events," *Journal of Personality and Social Psychology*, 39:5 (1980), 806–820.

this—what they might all mean, such as the surveillance of their private communications, the supplying of information about suspects from their surroundings and about their families or acquaintances, the searching of houses, the arresting of suspects, the censoring of mass media, corporal examination as a precondition of access to public institutions, photo-video surveillance of public places, prohibition against the setting up of certain types of organisations, or—on the positive side—being involved in civil volunteers' teams or other actions organised by law enforcement institutions to combat terrorism.

To prevent terrorism do you agree with ...	...the surveillance of private communications?	... the searching of houses?	...the arresting of suspected people?	...mass-media censoring?	...corporal examination before access to public institutions?
Chi-Square Df Asymp. Sig	58. 837 4 .000	70.929 4 .000	215.411 4 .000	85.915 4 .000	125.004 4 .000

To prevent terrorism do you agree with ...	...photo-video surveillance of public places?	...prohibition against the setting up of certain organisations?	..the provision of information about suspected people?	...the supplying of information about persons who are dear to you ?	... being part of civil volunteers' teams?
Chi-Square Df Asymp. Sig	364.194 4 .000	116.219 4 .000	276.137 4 .000	107.968 4 .000	91.000 4 .000

The subjects' anxiety because of a potential terrorist attack and their need to be safe are reflected in correlations between answers such as those to questions regarding bomb attacks in public places and those regarding the acceptance of corporal examination before being allowed access to public institutions ($Rp=0.239$, $p \leq 0.001$) and photo-video surveillance in public places ($Rp=0.218$, $p \leq 0.001$). People tend to be consistent with their own answers, as illustrated by the fact that those who agree with the interceptions of private communications felt the same regarding the searching of houses ($Rp=0.456$, $p \leq 0.001$), the arresting of suspects ($Rp=0.442$, $p \leq 0.001$), and about media control ($Rp=0,171$, $p \leq 0.009$).

Regarding the main sources of information on terrorism, people who keep themselves informed mostly through television, papers, school, radio and scientific works, consider that they do not find relevant information in their peer groups and family, which is an indicator of the low level of knowledge—or of the lack of interest—about the terrorist phenomenon throughout the general population. .

Information sources about terrorism...	...papers	...radio	...television
Chi- Square	112.626	123.000	292.413
Df	3	4	3
Asymp. Sig	.000	.000	.000

Information sources about terrorism...	...scientific works	...school	...family	...peer groups
Chi- Square	136.492	30.090	314.830	279.421
Df	4	3	4	4
Asymp. Sig	.000	.000	.000	.000

The Mann-Whitney test revealed some significant differences between women and men. Men consider that terrorist networks have lower logistic possibilities when compared with the states against which they fight. This is a correct assumption sustained by the fact that men are usually more interested in the army industry so that they are better informed.

On the other hand, all items that concern the necessity of negotiating with terrorists are better scored by women who have a far more sympathetic and sensitive nature. Some significant differences appear regarding the usefulness of negotiations to gain time in serious cases ($U=11481.00$, $p \leq 0.024$) and to release hostages ($U=11744.00$, $p \leq 0.043$). The less submissive nature of men and their high level of independence are shown in the score they have regarding agreement to having some civil rights restrained ($U=9684.00$, $p \leq 0.001$).

The Mann-Whitney significance test reveals also some expected findings regarding certain meaningful differences between the way people who had chosen to work in areas connected to terrorism (psychology, sociology, history, political studies, military studies) perceive terrorism and the others. The former answered correctly that most of the terrorists are young people ($U=9213.00$, $p \leq 0.001$) and that they are not rejected by their own communities ($U= -8752.00$, $p \leq 0.001$). Their level of knowledge about the phenomenon is reflected also in the answers regarding the underequipping of terrorist networks ($U=8627.00$, $p \leq 0.001$) and the fact that the present alliances system of Romania increases the danger of a terrorist attack ($U=10045.50$, $p \leq 0.001$). All their knowledge supplied them with a higher level of responsibility so that they agree to a larger extent to the restraining of their civil rights in order to prevent terrorist acts.

The answers of the age categories considered in this study were discriminated through a one-way ANOVA test. As a general conclusion, the period from 16 to 25 years is the most efficient for an individual to learn about different issues including terrorism. This is supported by the fact that their answers reflect the lowest level of knowledge about terrorism, a level which is significantly different when compared with that indicated by the other respondents. I am not suggesting that there is a significant difference between generations (as there was no significant event to explain this) and I consider that the fact that they have not yet completed their studies is the cause of such data.

In this vein of thinking, teenagers of 16–20 years consider—to a larger extent than do those aged 26–30—that terrorists are mostly rejected by their own communities ($F(4.294)=3.169$, $p\leq0.014$; $R= -0.371$, $p\leq0. 015$), which reflects a lower degree of knowledge of the phenomenon. The age categories gave also different answers about dictatorial political regimes as a cause of terrorism ($F(4, 315)=5.936$, $p\leq0.001$). Thus people from 16 to 20 years appreciate to a lesser extent than do adults aged 26-30 ($R=0.606$, $p\leq0.002$) and 31-35 ($R=0.829$, $p\leq0. 019$) that terrorism is caused by totalitarian political regimes.

Every age category has a different perception regarding the main goals of terrorists' networks. So that those aged 16–20 consider, to a lesser extent than do those aged 26-30 that terrorists intend to attack well-known people ($F(4, 320)= 3.182$, $p\leq0,014$), but they believe—more than do those in other age categories—that terrorists intend to produce panic inside populations ($F(4, 324)= 8.359$, $p\leq 0.001$) as 21-25 shows ($R= -0,336$, $p\leq0, 011$) or 26-30 shows ($R= - 0.494$, $p\leq0. 001$).

Although the respondents from the age category 16–20 do not agree to having their civil rights restrained ($F(4, 321)=3.333$, $p\leq0.011$), they are more accepting of corporal examination before entering public institutions ($F(4,238)= 4.087$, $p\leq0.003/ R= - 0.519$, $p\leq0.022$) and of prohibition against the establishment of some types of organisation ($F(4, 242)=8.019$, $p\leq0.001$, $R= - 0.871$, $p\leq0.000$, $R= - 0.826$, $p\leq0.017$). The same teenagers would agree to a greater extent to supply information about suspects ($R= - 0.401$, $p\leq0. 016$). They are also prepared to supply information about persons who are dear to them to a greater extent than are people of 26-30 ($F(4,312)=2.767$, $p\leq0.028$, $R= - 0.522$, $p\leq0. 034$). These are surprising data, but we could explain them having as a premise the known fact that teenagers are a particular type of population with certain characteristics. Their need for independence, their willingness to prove their value to others or to save the world causes them to simultaneously reject the possibility of having their rights restricted, while also being willing to do almost everything to combat terrorism.

The subjects from the 16–20 age group consider that school is the least efficient source of information regarding terrorism ($F(4,316)=15.426$, $p≤0.001$) compared to the respondents in the 26-30 age group ($R= 0.980$, $p≤0$. 001) and the 31-35 age group ($R= 0.998$, $p≤0$. 001). The same difference of opinion can be found between the age groups 21–25 and 26–30 ($R= 0.713$, $p≤0.001$) and also between the age groups 21–25 and 31–35 ($R= 0.730$, $p≤0$. 026). The phenomenon of social criptomnezy suggests that after a certain period of time the origin of information is forgotten and people tend to attribute it to other sources.[10] So it could be possible for those subjects aged between 26 and 35 years to consider, some time later, that some of the information they have received over the course of time had been provided by school. But one should not neglect the possibility that they did not receive any information from this source as, during their school years, terrorism was not an important civic issue.

As people usually fear the things they know less about, an educational model regarding a better understanding of the terrorist phenomenon and of the methods to deal with it could be a good solution in preventing such acts. All the findings presented here could constitute the base for such a future approach.

CONCLUSIONS

As we supposed in the first place, there are significant influences of gender and age criteria regarding the perception of different aspects of the terrorist phenomenon.

The results obtained indicate also some significant differences and correlations between the given items that confirmed the general hypotheses of the survey, providing some insights regarding the existence of a particular coherent model in representing the terrorist phenomenon. Hence, the population studied was shown to make multiple connections between the aspects investigated (terrorists' characteristics, causes, financing sources, actions, the importance of Romania on the map of terrorism or the methods to prevent and fight against such a danger), their opinion often reflecting the influence exercised by their information sources.

As a conclusion, it may be said that the civil population should be trained in order to correct their false perceptions and to provide them with

---

[10] Gabriel Mugny and Juan A. Péréz, "L'influence sociale comme processus de changement," *Hermes,* 6 (1989), 227–236.

strategies to face terrorism. Such self-protective measures have the benefits of being not in the least provocative and less costly than a war is.

INTER-FAITH DIALOGUE, INTERNATIONAL MEDIATION AND CONFLICT

A FALSE DAWN?: THE OSLO PEACE ACCORD AS A CASE STUDY OF INTERNATIONAL MEDIATION, CONFLICT MANAGEMENT, AND RELIGIOUS FUNDAMENTALISM

Orna Almog

My research examines the Oslo peace process 1993–2000 and will address three main aspects: international mediation, the role of leadership, and opposition to conflict resolution. This paper will focus predominantly on the mediators' role, in particular the US, and to lesser extent on leadership and religious fundamentalism as obstacles to peace.

The year 1993 brought an historical shift in the bloody history of the Israeli-Palestinian conflict. The accord between Israel and the PLO—the Oslo peace accord—symbolised a new dawn in their relationship.

President Clinton, who presided over this historic moment, assured the two sides the support of the only remaining superpower—the US. American involvement as mediators in Middle East conflicts and especially in the Arab-Israeli dispute has a long history. The US role is crucial and central to any conflict resolution and conflict management in the region. However, the Oslo accord was achieved without US active participation. In fact it was Norwegian officials and Israeli academics that initiated the talks. In spite of the fact that the US took a back seat, its blessing and approval was crucial.

It is important to note that every Israeli-Arab-Palestinian peace process has relied on mediation. As Kenneth Stein and Samuel Lewis argue, since World War II, every US administrator has had to deal with the Arab-Israeli conflict in the Middle East: "the role of a third party is as central to the history of the Arab-Israeli conflict as is the tradition that such a third party has a dual obligation. Both sides have expected and continue to expect a 'mediator umpire' to play an active role in resolving differences."[1]

The role of any mediator is delicate and complicated. In many cases the parties have mixed feelings and they would sometimes welcome an excuse to end the negotiations rather than be forced to make difficult decisions. As Stein and Lewis note, "a mediator must demonstrate a knowledgeable grasp of the history behind the issues. History weighs [...] heavily on Arab and

---

[1] Kenneth W. Stein and Samuel W. Lewis, "Mediation in the Middle East," in *Managing Global Chaos*, ed. Chester Crocker, Fen Hampson and Pamela Aall (Washington, D.C.: United States Institute of Peace Press, 1996), p. 463–473 (p. 452). http://www.ismi.emory.edu/BookChapters/MediationinME.html

Israeli leaders [...]. Memories of past injustices, wars, and betrayals crowd and shape today's decisions. All parties fear being pulled by outside forces into a risky negotiating process whose end could be national disaster."

Stein and Lewis continue, "if Israeli or Arab leaders are to acquire any real confidence in a third party mediator, that person will have to demonstrate real understanding not only of the issues, but also of the historical connections, underlying fears, and basic principles that shape the behaviours of both sides." History, in that sense can be seen as a real obstacle to any Arab-Palestinian negotiation and future agreement. So much so, that part of the success behind the secret channel in Oslo was the fact that both parties agreed not to dwell on the past and to forget about history.[2] This helped to move away from traditional problems of conflict resolution: "Traditionally, the task of conflict resolution has been seen as helping parties who perceive their situation as zero-sum (Self's gain is Other's loss) to recast it as a nonzero-sum conflict (in which both may gain or both may lose), assisting both sides to move towards a positive sum direction."[3] The role of the third party is to assist with this transformation, confronting the top dog if necessary. This means transforming hostile, unbalanced relationships into peaceful and dynamic ones.

As Tanya Glazer, summarising Zartman and Touval, notes, "Parties to a conflict accept mediation when they believe it is in their best interests to do so; that is, when they believe that 'mediation will gain an outcome that is more favourable than the outcome gained by continued conflict." Similarly, parties will accept mediation when rejecting it will result in greater harms. Parties may fear incurring bad relations with the proposed mediating nation or international sanctions if they refuse to negotiate." They add, "In addition, mediation may offer parties a way to negotiate compromises without losing face," thus making sure that terrorism and security threats would be eliminated.[4] These two factors are of immense importance as confidence building measures are integral to any resolution.

---

[2] Jay Rothman, *Resolving Identity-Based Conflict in Nations, Organizations and Communities* (SanFrancisco: Jossey Bass, 1997) ; Nadim N. Rouhana, "The Dynamics of Joint Thinking between Adversaries in International Conflict: Phases of the Continuing Problem-Solving Workshop, *Political Psychology*, 16:2 (1995), 321–45.

[3] Oliver Ramsbotham, Tom Woodhouse and Hugh Miall, *Contemporary Conflict Resolution*, 2nd edn (Cambridge: Polity, 2005), p. 15.

[4] Tanya Glazer, "Article Summary–William Zartman and Saadia Touval, 'International Mediation in the Post-Cold War Era,'" *Conflict Research Consortium*. http://www.colorado.edu/conflict/peace/example/zart5857.htm; William Zartman and Saadia Touval, "International Mediation in the Post-Cold War Era," in *Managing Global Chaos*, ed. Chester Crocker, Fen Hampson and Pamela Aall

Norwegian officials were the first ones to be the facilitators of the process. As a country that is not directly involved in the Arab-Israeli conflict, Norway was able to provide a relatively neutral basis. Yair Hirschfeld, member of the Israeli delegation in Oslo, noted that the Norwegians gave the negotiation a real framework. They mediated also with the Americans and without the Norwegians' skills it would not have worked. They also helped secure financial aid and Terje Larsen, the founder and director of the FAFO, made negotiations easier.[5]

When President Clinton became president, the Cold War was over and optimism and belief in a new era dominated the international era. However, the end of the Cold War heralded new challenges. The dominant focus was on domestic issues. But the president made it clear that he wanted to keep the peace process on track. It is clear that the Clinton administration believed that there was a need for an active US role and that the success of the process depended largely on its role.

Some might argue that given the close relations of the US with Israel it is bound to be biased and cannot fulfil one of the main criteria of the mediator which is to be impartial. However, it is this special relationship that empowers the US to be a mediator. In Israel's view there is no force, regional or international apart from the US that Israel trusts. Although Egypt and Jordan also assisted Israel throughout the process, it is the US that has real influence over Israel's decision makers. Furthermore, many Israeli leaders from the right to the left, from Rabin to Netanyahu look towards the US as Israel's main guarantor. Therefore it is the only party that can exercise pressure on Israel. As Zartman and Touval argue, mediators need not be impartial to be accepted or effective. Instead, they argue, "mediators must be perceived as having an interest in achieving an outcome acceptable to both sides and as being not so partial as to preclude such an achievement."[6]

Furthermore, looking at the history of the conflict it is clear that the Arab leaders themselves considered US involvement and commitment crucial. This was the case after the October 1973 war and the following Camp David agreement of 1979 between Israel and Egypt and between Israel and Jordan in 1995. In this respect, the initial stages of the Oslo accord were unique as they were achieved without US aid, but with its blessing and with the assistance of another third party. Nevertheless, the

---

(Washington, D.C.: United States Institute of Peace Press, 1996), pp. 445–61 (p. 452).

[5] See Uri Savar, *The Process: 1100 Days that changed the Middle East* (New York: Vintage, 1999), Ch.1. http://www.nytimes.com/books/first/s/savir-process.html

[6] Zartman and Touval, p. 452.

importance of the US was quite clear after the DOP was signed and especially after Rabin's assassination in 1995.

But even during Rabin's time in office, even before the official ceremony in the White House in 1993, the US had to put pressure on Rabin and convince him to attend the ceremony. Rabin had his own reservations about shaking Arafat's hand in front of millions of people, thus politically recognising what he perceived to be a terrorist organisation.

During Rabin's premiership the US had an easier task, as Rabin and Peres were fully committed to implementing the agreement. There were however, difficulties in that period as well. But, to a large extent the Oslo spirit, was still alive.

After Rabin's assassination the Clinton administration became much more involved in the process. Both Netanyahu and Barak relied heavily on the US and especially on the President's personal involvement. When Benjamin Netanyahu—Bibi—was elected, the entire process was in danger of collapsing. As head of the right wing Likud party, Netanyahu was staunchly opposed to the agreement. Netanyahu's ideology was very different to those in the Labour party and he believed in the ideology of "Greater Israel." He also disputed the legitimacy of the PLO to represent the Palestinians because it was never elected. Furthermore, the slogan "Land for Peace" which was advocated by many in the Labour party was not accepted by Bibi.

When Madeline Albright became secretary of state she consulted James Baker who suggested using the same methods he employed with the former PM Shamir before the Madrid conference in October 1991. According to this strategy it would be wise to accept both sides' demands, indicating the willingness of the US to take the initiative and be patient. Indeed, her patience was put to the test many times. Albright was quick to learn and realised she had difficult "clients." Arafat and Netanyahu, she wrote, lived about twenty miles and one universe apart.[7]

Clinton, the chief mediator put all his weight and credibility into furthering the negotiation. He laid out a detailed plan for a phased withdrawal from the West Bank and during the Camp David summit in 2000 he promised $8 million from the participants of the economic summit in Okinawa putting the total amount available for refugee rehabilitation and resettlement and compensation around $40 billion.

Both the Israeli and the Palestinian delegates share the feelings that Clinton did his utmost and was very familiar with all the details. According to Mohammed S. Dajani, director and founder of the Institute for American

---

[7] Madeleine Albright, *Madam Secretary: A Memoir* (New York: Miramax, 2003).

Studies at al Quds University and the Jerusalem Studies and Research Institite, Clinton encouraged the Palestinans and the Israelis alike to rise above scepticism and animosity. He called upon both parties to seize the opportunity to establish peace between their peoples.[8]

However, Clinton's frustration was evident, especially towards the end of his presidency. A few days before he left office, he and the Chairman had one of their last conversations. Arafat thanked the President for all his efforts and told him he was a great man. But the President replied by saying, "Mr Chairman I am not a great man, I am a failure and you have made me one."[9]

This study will question the effectiveness and the limitations of mediation in conflict resolution. In addition this research will also address the question of CBMs in a lengthy bloody dispute. The other two main issues this research examines are the roles of leadership and of religious groups as opposition to the peace process.

Historians and political analysts have debated whether great moments, or turning points in history are the result of a special momentum and right timing, or due to great leadership. It is no doubt that both are crucial, however, if the right brave leader is not there to seize the opportunity then no progress or process will take place. It was the 1992 election of the Israeli Labour party led by Yitzhak Rabin that paved the way for the Oslo peace accord. Initially Rabin was apprehensive about the back channel negotiations in Oslo, especially in view of the unsuccessful negotiations in Washington at the time. Rabin's main aim was a peace accord with Syria and the negotiations with the Palestinians were secondary. However, once it was clear that peace with Israel's northern neighbour was not on the cards and that there were real chances of agreement with the Palestinans, Rabin was willing to give it a chance.

For many years, successive Israeli governments built their policies around the collective sense of isolation—as "a people that shall dwell alone." It was common to both labour and Likud governments. It was a genuine feeling but also one that was used to justified certain foreign and defence policies. Rabin recognised it was time to break away from the paralysing sense of isolation and victimhood. "We must overcome the sense of isolation that has held us in its thrall for almost half a century. We must

---

[8] Mohammed S. Dajani, "Pathways out of Violence in the Middle East: Assessing the Strengths and Weaknesses of the Oslo Process," in *Pathways out of Terrorism and Insurgency: The Dynamics of Terrorist Violence and Peace Processes in Divided Societies*, ed. L.S. Germani and D.R. Kaarthikeyan (Slough: New Dawn Press, 2005), pp. 103–115.

[9] Bill Clinton, *My Life (*New York: Knopf, 2004).

join the international movement toward peace, reconciliation, and cooperation that is sweeping the entire globe lest we be the last ones to remain, all alone, in the station."[10]

Rabin's orientation was pro-American. He liked America very much despite the critical attitude of some aspects of American society, and greatly enjoyed his five year stay as the Israeli ambassador to Washington. But more importantly, he believed that only the US was able to offer inducements to the parties involved in the Arab-Israeli conflict and to compensate them for the risks taken.

The Oslo agreement had many opponents on both sides. Palestinian organisations opposed to the agreement launched a chain of attacks inside Israel: a series of car bombs, suicide bombings, and nail bombings struck Israeli centres. On the other hand, the incitement campaign against PM Rabin intensified. Oslo's aggressive opponents were comprised of many of the settlers in the West Bank and some Likud members including Netanyahu, who manipulated the situation to his own political advantage. Their campaign against Rabin went beyond legitimate criticism of a leader and his policies. Some of the settlers and their associates believed that the law of the land is subordinate to the law of the *Torah*: God's instructions are paramount, overruling even the laws of the state. The legal system was worthy as long as it did not clash with their views. It was this belief that served to stimulate discussions of "taking necessary action" against the PM. Looking at some of the settlers' publications one cannot but be horrified to see how far these discussions went.

For those that believed that they were God's messengers, murdering the PM was not out of the question. Many Israelis on the right and especially those belonged to "Gush Emunim" opposed the Oslo agreement because it would lead to Israeli withdrawal from the West Bank and the creation of a Palestinian state, in their view a political mistake and a mortal sin. Still, one can argue that in spite of these difficulties there was positive progress. The "Oslo Spirit," which can be described as the spirit of good will and trust, was kept. But November 4, 1995 brought a shock no one thought was possible: At a peace rally in Tel-Aviv Rabin was assassinated by a right wing Israeli Jew.

A fundamentalist and extreme in his views, Amir was a Zionist religious student, influenced by the some of the Rabbis in the settlements perceiving Rabin's actions as a mortal danger to Israel. Hence, although Amir operated on his own, he was a product of a political stream in Israel that did not

---

[10] Yitzak Rabin, "Speech to Knesset," July 13, 1992.

respect the democratic process and who were convinced they were saving Israel from an apocalyptic future.

One would have hoped that the bullet's assassination would not succeed in bringing the peace process to a halt, but Rabin's death created a hole and wounded the process. We can speculate as to what would have happened if Rabin had not been murdered. Would the "Oslo spirit" have carried on? How would he have reacted to the growing Palestinian attacks? Would he have managed to keep the public on his side? We can only guess, as we shall never know the answers. But what is clear is that no one enjoyed the same credibility as Rabin and no one had the same ability to see it through. The renewed optimism following Barak's election in 1999 was short lived. According to the literature, Barak was willing to compromise more than any other Israeli leader before him, in return for an "end of conflict." But the attempts during the summit in Camp David came to a dead end resulting in new outbreaks of violence.

In conclusion, was the Oslo accord the wrong formula or did the political environment change to such a considerable degree between 1993 and 2000? Were there enough CBMs? And was the agreement used as a "hostage" on both sides?

The Oslo process succeeded in changing the paradigm: it created a new reality and mutual recognition, but did not bring an end to conflict or a reduction of violence. However, history also teaches us that wars cannot last forever. Ddisputes are eventually resolved, hatred overcome, and peace secured. In Rabin's words, "We can continue to kill—and continue to be killed. But [...] we can also give peace a chance" (Speech to the Knesset, October 5, 1995).

HAPPINESS AND THE EYE OF THE BEHOLDER: THE DEEPER IMPLICATIONS OF GNH FOR A MORALLY DISTRACTED WORLD

Ross McDonald

In early 2003 I was invited to take part in a series of meetings in the Himalayan kingdom of Bhutan. The gathering was held to explore the practical operationalisation of the country's development goal, Gross National Happiness or GNH. For approximately 20 years this small and self-sufficient nation has been quietly working on this initiative, one established by the fourth king of Bhutan, His Majesty Jigme Singye Wangchuck in the late 1980s. I was asked to review the current understanding of happiness in the Western scientific literature in order that this could be included in the deliberations on GNH and consider how it might be achieved. This task was not overly problematic given the increasing level of theoretical convergence in happiness research, but when brought into the context of Buddhist culture, it exposed layers of underlying assumptions and fundamental differences in the meaning of happiness between Western material culture and the on-going traditions of Mahayana Buddhism. On returning to New Zealand, I was struck by the enthusiasm that GNH evoked in almost everyone I mentioned it to. This approval generally ignored critical connotations however, and as such the real implications of Bhutan's aspirations tended to missed, and indeed continue to be missed. For the Bhutanese, to seek happiness is to simultaneously seek moral maturity while for the majority in modern society it evokes simpler notions of mere good feeling.

It has been said that the Dalai Lama often begins his speeches with the statement that everybody wants to be happy, and no one wants to be unhappy. As Aristotle also affirmed, happiness is for most, the ultimate goal in life, the one that all other apparent goals come to serve. Riches, fame, beauty—each of these acquires its allure by virtue of its ability to confer happiness. For most cultures and for most of history, being happy has rested upon the foundations of a well-rounded personal development and in this sense has long been seen as the final flowering of a virtuous life.

However, as we shall see, this essential connection between feeling good and being good has not survived the disruptions of modernity and particularly those of consumer culture. We live now in a period where the cultural framework of market society demands that any necessary connection between morality and pleasure be severed. It is a fatal flaw in the structuring of market societies, for in shaking off the shackles of personal restraint, commercial culture induces a narrow individualism that denies the legitimacy of any larger ends. As this attitude has become entrenched, collective values have been realigned and the moral connotations of terms like happiness been slowly but surely excised. This paper is an attempt to chart some of these basic perceptual changes and use them to shed light on the particularly provocative case of Bhutan, a Himalayan country that has rejected GNP as an ultimate social aim. As we shall see, this move opens up valuable space to consider new developmental priorities and in particular offers useful insight into just how far from responsibility our own culture has been allowed to drift under the influence of economic doctrine. Bhutan's search for happiness represents a timely challenge to contemporary economic liberalism, and viewed in light of a litany of unfolding global crises it offers us a practical thematic guide on how we might more wisely secure an advance that is simultaneously happy and responsible.

In the history of Western civilisation, happiness begins conscious life as a fickle state of visitation, one largely driven by the whims of fate. This interpretation of happiness as lying beyond the intentional grasp of humanity is particularly apparent in the great Greek tragedies where the interventions of the gods come as unexpected and often undeserved blessings. It is for this reason that the Greek derivative for happiness "*hap*" literally means luck or good fortune and the Latin equivalent "*felix*" has a similar origin. This opaque understanding slowly evaporated as Europe moved towards the Christian era in which happiness was made attainable through the rigorous cultivation of moral goodness. In Christian doctrine, the highest bliss comes from being in harmony with, and of service to the collective. It comes from learning to minimise personal greed and maximise generosity. Through developing these aptitudes, happiness is secured both in this life and, most importantly, in the next. The spread of this doctrine gained significant impetus following the conversion of the Roman Empire in the fourth century CE and effectively dominated European civilisation until the Enlightenment.

Throughout the Christian Era of Western history, ultimate happiness was promised, and still is to contemporary believers, in Heaven. Here, everlasting fulfillment comes to those, but only to those, who led lives of exemplary virtue. The Bible lays out the origins of humanity, our future fate and the principles of a well-led life. The desirable virtues are codified, as in the Ten Commandments, along with the vices to avoid—most noticeably in the form of the Seven Deadly Sins. Such teachings aim to instill a basic morality of self-control and care for others. For Christians then, the message is clear, if one wishes to find happiness in this life and the next, one must aspire to virtue.

345

In providing structure and direction to the search for happiness, Christianity reflects the patient labours of all the world's great religious traditions. Islam, Buddhism, Hinduism, Confucianism, and a host of indigenous forms provide a similar guiding function for the collective. Each specifies helpful codes of conduct to facilitate self-control and all promise punishment for those who fail to seek their good feelings through morally sound actions. For millennia, religious cultures have sought to pull humanity towards goodness by offering instruction on how to avoid conflict and suffering. Christianity accords with this general pattern, but its influence has declined significantly from the period in which it could authoritatively shape public culture. The shouldering aside of religious constraint and the embracing of a secular reinterpretation of happiness have been phenomena of enormous significance in shaping the modern world. In charting this trend we can begin to appreciate the extent of the gulf that separates Bhutanese aspirations from our own.

At its heart, the history of the secularizing West is the history of a search for moral independence driven by a conviction that individual rationality represents the most powerful force for positive collective change. In large part, the hankering after a greater freedom gained its momentum as a fight against unreasonable religious moralising. And indeed the emergence of a cultural philosophy centring upon the freedoms of man as a consumer and citizen could not have been possible within the doctrines of the traditional church. Within these walls, individual freedom had long been likened to a wolf that the church held firmly by the ears. If individuals were granted excessive moral autonomy it was argued, the wolf of selfishness would savage the public interest and it would be almost impossible to bring to heel again. But through the fatal divisions of the Reformation, this beast did step free—in the form of a new man liberated from "religious superstition" and authorised to deny the gravity of any force aimed at his moral improvement.

In many ways the decline in authority endured by the church was the direct result of its own indiscretions. A flagrantly corrupted papacy, an avaricious network of opportunist bishops in the provinces, its bloody military campaigns—these and other indiscretions undermined its legitimacy and sentenced it to a rapid downfall. But equally, by the beginning of the eighteenth century, a new scientific understanding was demonstrating its utility, and discoveries in astronomy, geography, and geology were eating at the foundations of an overly-rigid institution. With a rising faith in the human potential to forge its own decent advance, secular demands coalesced around the search for philosophical, political and economic liberty. The latter was particularly contentious as the Christian marketplace had long been governed by a straightjacket of conditions ranging from bans on lending capital to legislated prices for goods and

346

wages. As the pressure for economic liberation built up and the discoveries of major trade routes and new resources stimulated local appetites, the push for emancipation became an unstoppable force. Thus, in a short period of decades, Western society moved from being theistically accountable to being largely personally accountable for the moral quality of its actions.

The philosophers and policy makers who cemented this revolution in place firmly believed in the rational potential of the individual and their natural preference for an improving morality. In fact it is fair to say that the whole granting of greater freedom was premised upon this faith. Thus, Thomas Paine believed that citizens would diligently monitor political developments and force progressive political change. Adam Smith and other advocates of the free market genuinely believed that "human heartedness" would prevent markets from spreading suffering and harm. We could build a better world through engineering and commerce. We could achieve better justice through a science of politics and morals. Hence, the liberation of the individual was intended not to promote a hedonistic anarchy, but rather to secure a greater maturity. Unfortunately however, lurking behind the benevolent face of eighteenth-century philosophy, were the less elevated calculations of self-interest in all spheres. These constituencies were, and still are keen to throw their weight behind any grand-sounding theory that offers cover. The release of the ideal rational individual was thus accompanied by the release of a less than ideal shadow, one hampered by the usual tyrannies of moral small mindedness—ignorance, greed, and a wholesale disregard for others.

For such types, the ideal endpoint of post-religious ordering comes when moral restraint is rendered irrelevant to the calculations of self-interest. In contemporary commercialised culture we are moving towards this point as our explanations of moral purpose and meaning have become increasingly obscured——to the point that no construction seems inherently more valuable than any other. In the personal and particularly in the market realm, to restrain or indulge, to support fair trade or unfair trade, to pursue a sustainable or unsustainable lifestyle, these are to a very real degree, moral equivalents in modern culture. The only tangible metric that we share is the degree to which phenomena generate good feeling for the individual. Thus, in current parlance, whatever makes you happy must be good.

This troubling trajectory represents a radical departure from the rational ideal and from patterns observable in most traditional forms of culture. In these, the reverse tends to be held true, that what makes you good must make you happy (in both the causal and imperative sense). This formulation forces a moral engagement as a pre-requisite for fulfillment, while its opposite obliterates its relevance. In non-market cultures a systemic divorce of responsibility from freedom would be viewed as being automatically

347

problematic. And indeed our faith in their separability has not been borne out as we have successively witnessed the spread of a wholesale disregard for the well-being of the collective. A morally narrowed mentality now constitutes the most fundamental hurdle to our achieving the happy goals of a progressive society. But despite this, or indeed because of this, it is being actively cultivated in market culture as it provides the ideal psychological grounding for expanding demands and reaping the unrestrained profits that lie in "satisfying" them. When the universal search for happiness is divorced from morality much individual profit can be gained, but ultimately only at considerable cost to others. This being so, the economy must be restrained by an overarching set of virtues strong enough to actively counter its moral myopia.

In the modern era however, these restrictions have been directly challenged as markets have sought to secure greater freedoms through a radical reinterpretation of the meaning of business in the public mind. Beginning in the eighteenth-century writings of the new economists, the market has been reconfigured to constitute an inherently moral force, one whose mechanisms are capable of transforming the questionable commercial motive of personal gain into a force for inclusive social benefit. As long as competition is encouraged within the marketplace, selfishness can be released in the certainty that any harmful effects will be redirected by a "market mechanism" resulting in a general benefit (primarily in the form of ever-more high quality goods delivered at ever-lower prices). Contrary to traditional Christian wisdom then, the way forward to an inclusive and happy world lies in releasing, rather than containing, self-interested appetites. This on-going ideological push is aimed at loosening social constraints on economy and the long-standing connections between feeling good and doing good.

In assuming that liberation from religious restraint would help us find a more direct route to happiness, the main movers of the Enlightenment believed that the majority would come to exercise considerate choices that would balance personal outcomes with those of others. Thus, accompanying the rapid political and economic freedoms of the new era was a vigorous outpouring of moralizing aimed at ensuring the basic need for civility. However, rather than stemming from a singular source, the debate over where society and its individuals "ought" to head descended rapidly into a virtual Babel of disagreement. For a while though, and at least up until the demise of the Victorian era, familial socialisation continued to be guided by an essentially Christian morality. It was only with the relative decline of this institution that individualism was released in its present full-blown form. Liberated from effective familial socialisation, the aptly named "me generation," in particular, spawned a radical shift in global politics during the 1980s and 90s, one manifested by the rolling back of government regulation and the further release of market forces.

All economies exist within the context of culture and as such, they are shaped and defined by its priorities. But just as culture influences markets, markets can come to profoundly influence their hosts in order to make them more accommodating. That the Enlightenment idealists failed to foresee the impacts of modern marketing is deeply unfortunate as much of their optimism might have been accordingly tempered. Today, legions of the world's best psychologists work with singular intensity to identify and exploit the weakest points in our rational defences against commercial manipulation. New value-shifting techniques are tested on the public every day and in ever more aggressive forms. However, all of these techniques employ one central and constant technique—that of incessantly associating increasing consumption with increasing feelings of happiness. Through targeted psychological marketing, influence is continually applied to expand consumer appetites and then profit from satisfying them. With the central moral restraints of religion and central government significantly weakened, the market has now extended its reach deep into the public mind to shape a consciousness perfectly adapted to its own needs for expansion. The spread of market acceptance into popular culture demands an intensification of greed, ignorance and a lack of concern for others. Accordingly, the popular search for happiness has been redirected towards these immaturities as a function of their supposed utility. At this point we can see once again how far commercial culture has allowed happiness to drift from its moral moorings.

To briefly summarise the above argument, then, it seems that happiness in Western culture has shifted in meaning, from being associated irrevocably with being good, to its contemporary meaning where it implies only feeling good. This shift has been driven in large part by a market ideology notable for its naïve faith in the power of freedom to forge a decent order. Under its influence, insatiable desires have been released in the false belief that pursuing these will lead ultimately to the greatest fulfillment The spread of materialism has only been made possible by the relative demise of restraining culture and its ability to transmit moral attitudes of care and cooperation. Religious authority was shouldered aside long ago, the secular institutions of family authority and hands-on government only more recently. Having legitimised self-absorption, western culture now finds itself seeking to secure happiness through enacting a fateful trio of tendencies, greed, ignorance, and a lack of concern for others. This does not represent a happy development.

Bhutan is a tiny kingdom in the Himalayas, a place as yet largely free from major commercial intrusion but one facing rapid change nonetheless.

If events in the broader region had not reverberated against her borders, it is likely that Bhutan would still be largely removed from the global scene quietly pursuing the conscious isolationism it cultivated for centuries. However, with the Chinese invasion of Tibet in the 1950s, Bhutan's sovereignty was actively threatened and so began a programme of rapid integration into a globalising world. Bhutan joined the world's major international institutions, in large part to enhance its status as an independent nation. But to feel ultimately secure against Chinese expansionism requires aligning oneself with the other regional superpower, India. Thus, in 1961 Bhutan began a slow process of integration with its southern neighbour, including signing agreements to coordinate defence and trade. From this point on Bhutan has been subjected to an inrush of foreign institutions and ideals into a country that had no national currency nor capital until 1961. The Bhutanese now find themselves in the front line of globalisation complete with its distractions and temptations. Being still steeped in an overwhelmingly Buddhist culture, much of the insistence of market temptation induces good humoured rejection to begin with, but it is typically a short step from this to full embrace. For a culture that has long sought to encourage virtues of generosity, compassion, and wisdom, the temptation of a dissolving materialism presents a profound challenge in its celebration of greed, carelessness, and ignorance. These vices are known in Mahayana Buddhism as the Three Root Poisons, as they are viewed as constituting the fundamental source of all destructive and damaging behaviours. They represent a recipe for embedding misery and not happiness.

When modern market culture contacts its indigenous counterparts the philosophical underpinnings of conflicting worldviews are rarely debated with much public intensity. Rather, in most instances, globalising markets effect their de-moralising influence by distracting from existing understandings, not engaging with them. This is most effectively achieved by narrowing concern away from the connected whole towards the disconnected self, away from the public realm towards the private; and away from improving moral reasoning towards intensifying amoral feeling. The deeper debate over whether happiness is morally founded or not is effectively sidelined in the process and deemed irrelevant to the simple business of getting on with feeling good.

As individuals fall into the habit of consuming market-based messages they gradually lose sight of larger visions that extend the gaze beyond the limited arena of personal material gain. In the process, the inspirational heart of any traditional culture tends to lose its traction on an increasingly distracted public. Materialism signals a morally convenient option in which good outcomes can be assumed regardless of the virtue of any individual's actions. It is tempting in that it avoids the unpleasant necessities of learning to limit one's appetites through frustrating them and sharing the things you value rather than commandeering them for yourself. Globalising markets spread a pliable culture in which the ultimate freedom lies in the right to be free from both social and personal moral scrutiny. Globally, feeling good for oneself as opposed to doing good for others has proven to be a remarkably popular choice. But fortunately as yet, it does not represent the universal choice.

Bhutan's response to the challenges of material culture has been unique and of enormous importance in retaining some critical alternative space in the international debate over the national end points of development and how they might be achieved. As economic globalisation spreads its influence to shape accommodating attitudes and institutions, it has largely secured Gross National Product as the sole acceptable measure of any society's progress. To represent Bhutan's intentions in the form of Gross National Happiness is to directly challenge not only an inflated measure but the whole mindset that lies behind its inflation. To guide national policy towards Gross National Happiness is to openly declare the insufficiency of economic expansionism as a sufficient measure for human development. In so-doing, the Bhutanese have struck a deeply intuitive chord, as attractive to the harried modern consumer as it is to the quietist monk. Economics, Bhutan reminds us, is not a goal but a process. It is a means and not an end.

It is a wise perspective to adopt as it is indeed true that when one looks at the empirical relationship between happiness and GNP any straightforward correspondence between the two is difficult to find. Hence, for example we note that the Australian economy has doubled in size since 1980 with no corresponding increase in happiness. The post war period has seen the American economy grow four-fold and the Japanese economy five-fold, but in neither case has skyrocketing consumption increased collective happiness. In fact the best indications are that overall happiness levels are decreasing in the advanced economies largely due to the stresses attendant on a materially competitive lifestyle.

Indeed there is now an extensive academic literature that convincingly demonstrates that financial wealth and material consumption are singularly profitless means to securing happiness. To the extent that market driven societies accept the connection between having more and feeling happier, they undermine any real prospects for fulfillment as these lie not in competitive isolation but in cooperative engagement with others. Current work on the correlates of happiness highlights, marriage, friends, health, optimism, a sense of purpose, and self-acceptance as primary factors promoting happiness. Money has little purchase in most reviews of the literature. There would seem to be mounting empirical support, then, to validate Bhutan's relegation of economic materialism to a strictly secondary status.

There are deeper benefits that also stem from deposing economic growth from its self-proclaimed eminence. Viewed as only a contingently beneficent phenomenon rather than a necessarily beneficent one, market expansion can be gauged by its critical impacts not only on collective happiness but also on other related outcomes of importance—ones like global justice, collective harmony and ecological health. When outcomes in these realms are included, the shaping of consumer culture takes on an ominous hue. Globally the expansion of market culture has led to a distribution of well-being that is enormously polarized, with billions suffering inexcusable privation while millions enjoy unbelievable excess. Looked at in terms of its effects on the global ecosystem, market culture is having disastrous impacts, destroying habitats and species at a truly alarming rate. In the space that a deposed economic hegemony creates, it is possible to view markets as manageable processes capable of producing a variety of results in a variety of spheres. In order to make sense of these impacts and so judge the proper place of economy, an integrative morality must be brought to bear on the problem of development and the proper ends it should serve. In opening the way to reconsidering these questions, Bhutan has usefully highlighted the critical need for a more coherent moral response to expanding market destructiveness..

Fortunately for Bhutan, it has a living cultural framework that is more than capable of orienting itself with regard to these difficult challenges. In Mahayana Buddhism the basic principles could not be clearer—that true happiness comes from overcoming self-absorption and in learning to be appreciative and helpful to the greater wellbeing. Buddhism has long taught that any individual or culture dominated by greed, ignorance, and lack of care will spread and ultimately reap a miserable harvest. To date, the limited intrusions of marketed media have only had some effect on Bhutanese sensibilities, in part because much of the country remains unplugged from television. Buddhist institutions continue to thrive, emphasising the need to overcome selfishness through the cultivation of morally considerate thought, speech, and action. For Bhutan then, the primary issue is one of cultural containment. Of how the country can most effectively derive genuine benefit in granting some specific freedoms while avoiding the disastrous collapse into moral oblivion unrestrained consumerism normally breeds. To manage this will require strict control of the market and its influence on public culture. The Royal Government has enacted a number of policies in this direction, limiting the spread of television, banning tobacco products, removing stationary advertising, forcing land reform, and so forth, but much more needs to be done in order to contain the expansionary pressures of the private sector.

Accompanying these initiatives are continuing moves to ensure that the moral underpinnings of the existing culture continue to authoritatively guide the collective away from an isolated individualism. The collective consciousness is still pervaded by a fundamental conviction that happiness lies along the path of doing good with and for others. The mechanisms of the market, the dynamics of greed, the temptations of ethical avoidance, the futility of materialism—all of these can be contained easily within the Mahayana tradition. The real battle is to retain its relevance as an overarching framework amidst an increasingly clamorous cacophony of distraction.

In taking a stand on Gross National Happiness then, the Bhutanese have created the opportunity for alternative priorities and policies to emerge. The happiness that anchors national policy represents no simple policy choice. It involves a national commitment to building and maintaining the structures that facilitate growth towards maturity and responsibility. It requires that wisdom be constantly cultivated through a mindful appreciation of the complex inter-dependencies of society and nature. It must employ techniques aimed at expanding the capacity for material moderation and for a corresponding willingness to share. Above all, Bhutan's national agenda must retain the sovereignty of moral development in any real advance towards collective happiness. It is thus a courageous course for any elected government to set itself in an era of overwhelming consumer temptation.

Still, the task before Bhutan's politicians pales compared with the difficulties faced by the leaders of the so-called "free world." Not only must similar policies of economic containment be brought to bear in order to the reduce the demand for shared resources here, but this must be done against a backdrop of intensive commercial socialisation and a long-standing acceptance of the basic right to reject moralising authority. That freedom should reign is now an accepted principle; that it must be married to responsibility is its neglected counterpart. To try and bring the latter back to prominence is to challenge the very foundations of commercial modernity. Governments in market-driven societies have been singularly reluctant to challenge the unwise indulgences of the modern consumer. Commercial interests fight tooth and nail to continue feeding off the moral myopia that is materialism. The challenge to grow up and take responsibility for the impacts of the modern lifestyle will not go down well with the average motorist, airline passenger, or taxpayer. Against a backdrop of the right to choose, policies aimed at containing the economy within a broadened consideration must be persuasive enough to force the *willing* inclusion of global interests in the individual's search for happiness. Such policies seek

353

no less than a moral reconstruction of culture and demand that we challenge the problems of greed, ignorance and lack of concern head on and in these terms. Free market culture attempts a grand lie when it claims that moral disengagement can secure a genuinely happy advance as the parlous state of the contemporary world more than adequately demonstrates. Yet it still remains an untruthful convenience for governments and individuals alike.

We can then understand the dilemma not only of Bhutan, but of the whole global community in these relatively simple terms. The expansion of the global economy represents the spread of a collapsing morality and its effects are disastrous for the non-material ends it tries to render invisible. We now need to rapidly correct the ideological naiveté that has allowed us to accommodate such a slide into unmonitored over-indulgence. In a world rapidly approaching its ecological limits, aiming to maximise GNP (and so the rate and extent of resource use) is madness. The deeper challenge faced by all nations at this point in history is how to rein in the moral liberties that have been granted but which now require strict qualification. This will be no easy task.

There is one major factor that offers help in this regard though, that being the sheer urgency of containing our rates of consumption under current conditions. If one attends to the latest science on climate change, it promises to deliver intergenerational misery on a monumental scale. The need to reduce our load on the planet's regenerative capacities is now so pressing that it pushing against even the narrowest interests of the most detached consumer. Humanity currently faces a massive challenge that is fundamentally moral in form. It calls upon us all to begin seeking our happiness in ways that are considered and restrained.

All in all then, Bhutan's experiments with increasing national happiness expose deep cultural differences over the meaning, means, and ends of social development. In the space its formulations create, a non-hegemonic market can be judged by its contributions to a variety of more integrative and adaptive ends. When justice, sustainability, and happiness are conjoined as co-existent ends, the moral dimension so lacking in consumer society re-appears along with its potential to guide us towards a sustainable and just happiness. The Bhutanese search for GNH then offers a timely opportunity to reconsider the wisdom of separating a desire to feel good from the larger goal of becoming good.

That we should take advantage of this opportunity is obvious upon sober reflection, but the problem we face is one of resuscitating sober reflection per se in a culture drunk on its own fun-filled freedoms. To return to the start of this essay, I mentioned that many I encountered on return from Bhutan were delighted by the good sense of a focus on Gross National Happiness. However, in the minds of most, this no doubt implied a enhanced capacity for exactly the type of irresponsible happiness Bhutanese policy strongly opposes. Our misreading of the deeper implications of Bhutanese intent is testimony to the collapse in meaning happiness has endured at the hands of modern individualism. For a Western audience, then, Bhutan's focus on maximising happiness should be translated into less convenient yet more constructive terms. The Bhutanese are in reality seeking to find happiness in a material moderation that allows others, both human and non-human to thrive and find their own way to happiness. As friends in Bhutan constantly remind me, in Mahayana there is no prayer for a strictly personal outcome as all are dedicated to the "happiness of all sentient beings." This is ultimately the level of moral connection we all need to aspire to if we are to have any chance of securing a genuinely happy world.

BUSINESS, PHILOSOPHY, AND LAW IN THE AGE OF GLOBALISATION

THE DILEMMA OF HUDUD AND INTERNATIONAL HUMAN RIGHTS: PROPOSING A BENEVOLENT MECHANISM

Shahrul Mizan Ismail

Ever since the emergence of the international regime of human rights, the irresolvable dilemma has always been to draw an effective reconciliation between the theocentric essentials of Islamic law and the demands of International Human Rights Law. This problem is further exacerbated in the case of Islamic criminal punishments, especially Hudud,[1] because unlike Ta'zir,[2] where the offences are not prescribed and the punishments

---

[1] Hudud or Hadd penalties are unambiguously specified and prescribed-for criminal actions which have been explicitly stated by the primary sources of Islamic Jurisprudence, namely the Quran and Sunnah of the Prophet Muhammad, as offences against the right of God. Muslim jurists explained that the term "right of God" implies the betterment of the society (See Anwarullah, *Criminal Law of Islam* (Brunei: Islamic Da'wah Centre, 1995). Ibn Abdin states that "the cause of describing Hudud as rights belonging to God is because they are promulgated for the protection of the whole society." (See Muhammad Amin, Ibn Abdin, *Hashiat Radd Al Mukhtar* (in Arabic) (Bairut: Dar al-Fikr, [n.d.]), vol. 4. p. 3. The kind and quantum of implementation for these punishments are clearly defined and fixed by the aforesaid sources of Islamic law, and cannot be increased or decreased unnecessarily. (See Abdul Qadir Audah, *Al-Tashri'a Al-Jinai Al-Islami*, 2 vols (Bairut: Dar al-Kitab, [n.d.]), p. 343, and Mohammad Shabbir, *Outlines of Criminal Law and Justice in Islam* (Petaling Jaya: International Law Book Services, 2002), p. 11) Since, they are clearly enshrined in the holiest and most supreme source of Islamic law i.e. the Quran and Sunnah, many Muslims also unequivocally believe that they are utterly divine, unchangeable, eternal and immutable. (See "A Call for International Moratorium On corporal Punishment, Stoning and the Death Penalty in The Islamic World," www.IslamOnline.net) There are basically seven specific offences classified under Hudud, namely Zina (fornication and adultery), Qadhaf (false accusation of Zina), Sariqah (Theft), Hirabah (Robbery), Al-Baghy (Rebellion), Riddah (Apostasy) and Al-Khamr (Consuming Liquor).
[2] The third form of Islamic punishment is Ta'zir, denoting offences which neither the Quran nor Sunnah prescribe a penalty. See Matthew Lipman, Sean McConville, and Mordechai Yerushalmi, *Islamic Criminal Law and Procedure: An Introduction* (New York: Praeger, 1988), p. 50. These offences are neither covered by Hudud nor Qisas, but the commission of such acts threatens one of the five goals of Shari'a stated above (See Osman abd-el-Malak al-Saleh, "The Right of the Individual to Personal Security in Islam," in *The Islamic Criminal Justice System*, ed. C. Bassiouni (New York: Oceana Publications, 1982), p. 60. Numerous offences are classified under this category, but in normal circumstances, Ta'zir punishments are

are neither fixed nor quantified by the *Quran* and Sunna, the Hudud punishments are clearly laid down for offences which have been explicitly stated by the two highest sources of Islamic criminal law, namely the *Quran* and Sunna.[3] And differently from Qisas,[4] where punishments,

---

frequently inflicted in the following instances: (1) When the act does not fulfill all the technical requirements of Hudud or Qisas, therefore neither Hudud nor Qisas punishments could be inflicted on the offender. For example the theft of an item that is not of sufficient value to qualify as a Hudud offense, or attempted adultery or assault. (2) When the acts amount to Hudud or Qisas, but these punishments could not be imposed upon the offender due to extenuating circumstances (such as theft among relatives) or doubt (a failure of proof at trial, such as insufficient witnesses). In these kinds of situations, the offence will fall into the realm of Ta'zir. This is because theoretically a judge in Hudud or Qisas cases must either convict the accused after being satisfied that the offence was performed exactly according to the description, legal conditions and evidentiary requirements of the offences or else, acquit him from those charges. (3) When the acts do not qualify as Hudud or Qisas but are condemned in the Quran and Sunnah or are contrary to public welfare. When the acts do not qualify as Hudud or Qisas, but violate prominent Islamic norms. Since the punishments for these offences are not clearly prescribed by the Quran and Sunnah, the ruler of Islamic states and judges (qazi) are endowed with the discretionary authority to inflict the suitable punishment of Ta'zir on the culprit in accordance with the circumstances of each particular case, after careful consideration of the public welfare.

[3] Since the focus of this paper is to specifically discuss the nature of approaches taken by advocates of International Human Rights law in dealing with violations of Human Rights relating to the implementation of Hudud punishments, the writer will not be providing a detailed explanation as to the nature and types of Hudud offences. For a useful survey, see Shabbir, p. 11.

[4] The second type of criminal punishment, which is also specifically prescribed and described in the primary sources of Islamic law, is Qisas. Crimes under this category can be divided into two i.e. offences against the person (murder) and body (bodily injury). In the first category, the offenders of these crimes are usually subjected to either the punishment of retaliation (Qisas), or the payment of blood money (Diyat). With regards to bodily injury, the infliction of any act which causes bodily harm is subjected to retaliation if it results in serious, permanent injury or disfigurement to the victim. (See Lipman et al., p. 50) These punishments were designed merely to secure the rights of individuals in the society. Hence when a Qisas or Ta'zir has been committed, its punishments though clearly provided for by the Quran, may be altered or remitted by the victims or their legal heirs. They may for example, forgive the offender, waive their rights to retaliation and ask for the payment of blood money instead, as compensation to the harm that they have suffered. Qisas crimes include intentional murder, quasi-intentional murder, unintentional murder, intentionally causing physical injury or maiming, or unintentionally causing physical

although clearly prescribed, aim purely to secure the rights of man (which consequently allows the victim or his legal heirs to alter or remit the punishments), Hudud penalties were formulated to secure the rights of God. Hence it is often argued that no one but God himself may "forgive the crime or change the law." The fact that it involves the right of God signifies that it is meant to be mandatory punishment, a demand from God that requires fulfilment, and no one, including the victim, judge, or the head of state has authority to alter or modify, to pardon or suspend it. For these reasons, Muslim countries are usually of the view that the enforcement of such punishments is a non-negotiable religious obligation. Human rights activists on the other hand, have argued that the implementation of the Hudud laws contravenes multiple norms and values of international human rights law. Ever since then, there have been many attempts to stop the aforesaid violations by stopping altogether the implementation of Hudud punishments in numerous Muslim countries.

The writer contends that the current typical approaches adopted in international human rights law in attempting to prevent further violations of human rights in this respect are ineffective, insensitive, and have contributed even further to worsening the problem of human rights violations in relation to the implementation of Hudud punishments in Muslim countries. This paper aims to analyze critically the weaknesses inbuilt in the typical approaches adopted by human rights advocates in dealing with the issue of human rights violations relating to Hudud law.

HUDUD PUNISHMENTS AND VIOLATIONS
OF INTERNATIONAL HUMAN RIGHTS LAW

Before moving further into the crux of the discussion, we need to firstly understand the types of punishment prescribed under Hudud laws and how they are usually argued to be in violation of human rights by advocates of International Human Rights Law.

The Hudud punishments prescribed for the offence of Zina are one hundred lashes of whipping for unmarried offenders[5] and stoning to death

---

injury or maiming. See Abdurrahman I. Doi, *Shariah: The Islamic Law* (Kuala Lumpur: A.S. Nordeen, 1996), p. 233.

[5] This punishment is based on the Quranic verse, "The woman and the man guilty of adultery or fornication, flog each of them with a hundred stripes. Let not compassion move you in their case, in a matter prescribed by God, if you believe in God and the Last Day: And let a party of the believers witness their punishment." *The Holy Quran*, translated by Abdullah Yusuf Ali. www.islamicity.com/mosque/Surai.htm. 24:2.

for those who are married.[6] To ensure that innocent individuals will not abusively be inflicted with this harsh punishment, Islam prescribes the punishment of eighty lashes of whipping for the offence of Qadhaf, i.e. wrongfully accusing someone of Zina.[7] Sariqah on the other hand is punishable by amputation of the hand of the convict,[8] while the punishment for Hirabah is stated to be any one of the following methods: death, crucifixion, cross amputation of limbs, or banishment, depending on the severity of the crime committed.[9] The *Quran* did not specifically explain the exact punishment for the offence of al-Khamr. However, based on certain traditions of the prophet's companions, the Muslims jurists concur that the punishment for this type of offence is flogging. Apart from the Shafie school of law, other jurists agree that an offender may be flogged up to eighty strokes for this crime.[10] Finally, for the offence of al-Baghy the punishment is death,[11] and as for the offence of Riddah, the punishment is the death penalty for the Muslim offender who remains apostate after being given the opportunity to repent and return to Islam.

The above-mentioned punishments of Hudud violate the norms of international human rights in many ways. However, due to the limited scope of this paper, the writer will be discussing only the most obvious and

---

[6] This punishment is based on the hadith of the Prophet Muhammad, "Take from me, Allah has prescribed for them (those guilty of Zina) the way, unmarried will be punished with hundred stripes and expulsion of one year and married will be punished with hundred stripes and stoning to death," quoted by Anwarullah, p. 145.

[7] This punishment is based on the Quranic verse, "And those who accuse chaste women (of Zina) and produce not four witnesses (in support of their allegation), flog them with eighty stripes; and reject their evidence ever after; for such persons are wicked transgressors; unless they repent thereafter and mend (their conduct); for Allah is oft-forgiving most merciful." 24:4.

[8] This punishment is based on the Quranic verse, "And to the thief, male and female, cut off his or her hand." 5:38.

[9] "The Punishment of those who wage war against Allah and his messenger (in respect of endangering the security of the State established under the divine law) and strive with might and main for mischief through the land, is execution, or crucifixion, or the cutting of their hands and feet from the opposite sides, or exile from the land; that is their disgrace of this world, and a heavy punishments is theirs in the hereafter; except those who repent before they fall into your power; in that Allah is oft-Forgiving and Most Merciful." 5:33, 34.

[10] Anwarullah, p. 214.

[11] This punishment is derived by the Muslim jurists from the following verse of the Quran: "If two parties among the believers fall into a quarrel, make peace between them: but if one of them transgress until it complies with the command of God. But if it complies, then make peace between them with justice, and be fair; for God loves those who are fair (and just)." 49:9.

most quoted violations of Human Rights in relation to Hudud Punishments, and focus will be only on those violations that are relevant to the writer's analysis and proposal contained in this paper.

Firstly, international human rights law prohibits the implementation of torture and any forms of cruel, inhuman and degrading punishment upon any criminal convicts regardless of the offence that may have been committed.[12] Article 1 of *The Convention Against Torture and Other Cruel, Inhuman or Degrading Treatment or Punishment* (CAT), while defining the meaning of torture as "any act by which severe pain or suffering, whether physical or mental, is intentionally inflicted on a person for purposes (of) [...] punishing him for an act," has excluded from its definition "any pain or suffering arising from, inherent in or incidental to lawful sanctions." The Human Rights Committee (HRC) however noted in its General Comment 20 to Article 7 of the International Covenant on Civil and Political Rights (ICCPR) that the said prohibition extends to "corporal punishment, including excessive chastisement ordered for a crime."[13] This means that even though Hudud punishments implemented by Muslim states may not fall within the prohibition due to the exclusionary clause in CAT, they could still be declared by the HRC as amounting to "cruel, inhuman or degrading punishment" under the ICCPR, since Hudud punishments may still fall within the ambit of "corporal punishments and excessive chastisement" as stated in the said General Comment. While there have been disputes as to the actual scope and definition of the phrase "torture, cruel, inhuman, and degrading punishments" since it mainly depends on many sociological factors, the Hudud punishments of flogging, stoning, amputating limbs, cross amputating, crucifying, and death have been

---

[12] See Article 5 of the Universal Declaration of Human Rights (1948) http://www.un.org/Overview/rights.html; Article 7 of the International Covenant on Civil and Political Rights (1966), http://www.unhchr.ch/html/menu3/b/a_ccpr.htm; The Convention Against Torture and Other Cruel, Inhuman or Degrading Treatment or Punishment (1984) http://www.unhchr.ch/html/menu3/b/h_cat39.htm, art. 16. For a useful survey, See also P.R. Ghandi, "The Human Rights Committee and Articles 7 and 10 of the International Covenant on Civil and Political Rights, 1966," *Dalhousie Law Journal*, 13 (1990) 773–74 (p. 758); Peter Cumper, "Freedom of Thought, Conscience, and Religion," in *The International Covenant on Civil and Political Rights and UK Law*, ed. D. Harris and S. Joseph (Oxford: Clarendon, 1995), pp. 353, 355–89.

[13] "Compilation of General Comments and General Recommendations Adopted by Human Rights Treaty Bodies," HRI/GEN/1/Rev. 7, May 12, 2004.
http://www.unhchr.ch/tbs/doc.nsf/0/ca12c3a4ea8d6c53c1256d500056e56f/$FILE/G0441302.pdf.

repeatedly declared by Human Rights writers to fall within the domain of the said phrase.[14]

International Human Rights Law is of course silent on the question of fornication, however, the concept of "privacy" is inherent in much of international human rights.[15] The illegality of consensual relations between two unmarried people is hard to reconcile with the right to privacy guaranteed in the ICCPR. Neither flogging for fornication nor stoning to death for adultery can be countenanced.[16]

Another area of violation of human rights relates to the offence of apostasy and the freedom of religious belief. The ICCPR under Article 18 further provides that "no one shall be subject to coercion which would impair his freedom to have or to adopt a religion or belief of choice." Hence punishing a person for the act of converting to another religion and renouncing his or her former faith is not acceptable under human rights law.[17]

With regard to the death penalty punishment prescribed for the offences of adultery, robbery, rebellion, and apostasy, technically speaking International Human Rights law confines the implementation of death penalty to only the "most serious crimes." But it actually at the same time promotes abolition of the said punishment. For example, the UN Second Optional Protocol to ICCPR was expressly formulated with the purpose of abolishing the death penalty.[18]

---

[14] Edna Boyle-Lewicki, "Need Worlds Collide: The Hudud Crimes of Islamic Law and International Human Rights," *New York International Law Review*, 13:2 (2000), 43–86.

[15] Article 17 of the ICCPR states: "No one shall be subjected to arbitrary or unlawful interference with his privacy, family, home or correspondence, nor to unlawful attacks on his honour and reputation [...]. Everyone has the right to the protection of the law against such interference or attacks."

[16] Ibid.

[17] Ibid. See Moshe Hirsch, "The Freedom of Proselytism Under the Fundamental Agreement and International Law," *Catholic University Law Review*, 47 (1998), 407–27 (pp. 424–25); See also Larry Cata Backer, "Exposing the Perversions of Toleration: The Decriminalization of Private Sexual Conduct, the Model Penal Code, and the Oxymoron of Liberal Toleration," *Florida Law Review*, 45 (1993), 755–99; Makau wa Mutua, "Limitations on Religious Rights: Problematizing Religious Freedom in the African Context," *Buffalo Human Rights Law Review*, 5 (1999), 75–105.

[18] "Second Optional Protocol to the International Covenant on Civil and Political Rights, aiming at the abolition of the death penalty, Adopted and proclaimed by General Assembly resolution 44/128 of 15 December 1989." http://www.unhchr.ch/html/menu3/b/a_opt2.htm

Other forms of violation of Human Rights in relation to Hudud punishments mostly relate to issues unrelated to the nature and quantum of the punishments. For example, they centres on issues such as punishments which were recklessly inflicted upon the accused, violating his right to a defense, right against retroactive criminal law, right to appeal, and many more. These violations are not caused by the original nature and quantum of the punishments but are due to procedural abuses and errors in implementing the said punishments.

THE TYPICAL APPROACHES OF INTERNATIONAL HUMAN RIGHTS LAW "ENFORCERS"

In summary, the methodologies adopted by many human rights advocates in dealing with the issues of Hudud punishments are typically shadowed by the following pattern of actions. Firstly, there is public judging of the legitimacy of these punishments by the yardstick of international human rights law. Secondly, there is an excessive emphasis on the severity of the said punishments and denunciation of them as being in contravention of the universal norms of human rights.[19] Thirdly, there is a demand for obedience from states practicing Hudud by abolishing the punishments or repealing the laws which prescribe them, usually on the basis of the states' ratification of the international treaties which prohibit the implementation of the said punishments or customary international law.[20] The Sudan Human Rights Organization for example, in issuing its "Memorandum of Urgent Appeal to Stop the Killing of a Christian woman by Sharia law and Government Political Abuse," had demanded from the Chief Justice of Sudan, the Governor of Darfur and the Sudan Government in Khartoum to abolish altogether the Hudud penalties by repealing the Sudan Penal Code 1991:

> The Sudan Human Rights Organization has *repeatedly asked the Government of Sudan to abolish the Sudan Penal Code 1991* because it *contradicts international human rights standards and applicable norms*. For the majority Muslims of Sudan, the Sudan Penal Code 1991 is a primitive law [...].[21]

---

[19] Natana J. DeLong-Bas, "Review of *The Islamization of the Law in Pakistan* by Rubya Mehdi," *Journal of Law and Religion*, 15 (2000-20001), pp. 589–92 (p. 590).

[20] See Human Rights Watch, *International Reactions to Shari'a in Nigeria.* http://www.hrw.org/reports/2004/; See also Ann Elizabeth Mayer, *Reconsidering the Human Rights Framework for Applying Islamic Criminal Law.* http://lgst.wharton.upenn.edu/mayera/writings.htm

[21] http://www.hrw.org/reports/2004/nigeria0904/15.htm

Julie Chadbourne similarly makes an interesting point when commenting on the reaction of human rights organizations, activists, and women's groups in relation to the Pakistani Hudood Ordinance:

> [...] the majority of activists and writers on the topic of the Zina Ordinance *focus on either the severity or unjust "application" of Hadd* [...]. Consequently, almost twenty years after the inception of the Zina Ordinance, little has been said other than *"they are bad—repeal*, repeal, repeal."[22]

And usually, when these states predictably resist abiding by their treaty obligations to repeal the laws, human rights activists and organizations would exert pressure to compel them to comply, through multiple mechanisms such as lobbying with the media to provoke widespread international attention,[23] urging other states (especially influential Western states) to condemn the Hudud conviction of the offending state,[24] labelling the offending state as cruel, brutal, tyrant etc,[25] organizing a coalition or movement to demonstrate anger and outrage and stimulating debates, and public protests against the implementation of the punishments (Chadbourne, p. 185). The following report by the international non-governmental organization, the Human Rights Watch on Islamic Law in Northern Nigeria, best illustrates the aforementioned facts:

> At the international level, the introduction of Sharia in 2000 suddenly threw Nigeria into the spotlight. The sentences of death by stoning imposed on

---

[22] Julie Dror Chadbourne, *Never Wear Your Shoes After Midnight: Legal Trends Under The Pakistan Zina Ordinance*, Wisconsin International Law Journal, 17:2 (1999), 179–280 (p. 186).

[23] Denis J. Wiechman, Jerry D. Kendall, and Mohammad K. Azarian, *Islamic Law: Myths and Realities*. http://muslim-canada.org/Islam_myths.htm

[24] A good example would be the case of Amina Lawal, a Nigerian woman, convicted for the hudud offence of zina (adultery), where both Amnesty International and Human Rights Watch had issued urgent bulletins to American and European Governments, urging them to condemn the convictions and demand her release. Reza Aslan, "The Problem of Stoning in the Islamic Penal Code: An Argument for Reform," *UCLA Journal of Islamic and Near Eastern Law*, 3:1 (2004), 91–106 (p. 98).

[25] In 1990, Human Rights Watch / Africa, a non-governmental human rights group, branded Sudan's Islamic government, the most "brutal" to govern Sudan since independence. The report stated that the regime was guilty of human rights abuses "never seen before" in the country. See Judith Miller, *Islamic Laws As Violations Of Human Rights In The Sudan: God Has Ninety-Nine Names* (New York: Simon and Schuster, 1996).

Safiya Husseini and Amina Lawal were at the *centre of an unprecedented level of public attention and provoked reactions of outrage* among women's organizations, human rights organizations, parliamentarians, Christian organizations, and members of the general public in many countries. *Their cases were the object of massive public protests, appeals and petitions from around the world.* Some of these interventions focused specifically on the cases of Safiya Husseini and Amina Lawal, urging the government to ensure that their lives were spared. Others also called for an end to discrimination against women and *an abolition of the death penalty.* (Aslan, p. 91)

Similarly in Pakistan, it was reported that "in reaction to the Hudood Ordinance, human rights organizations as well as activists and women's groups from within Pakistan *gathered in revolt* to battle against the institution of the Pakistani Zina Ordinance" (ibid.).

Besides that, in pressuring these states to obey the international instruments, the human rights approach is constantly marked with the argument that "there is nothing in the human rights law which justifies the violation of human rights based on an alleged divine revelation" (ibid.). In other words, "cultural justification is not a sanction for disregarding basic human rights" and "making allowances for cultural pluralism will deny the universality of claims of all human beings to dignity" (ibid.). Human Rights Watch for instance, in its report with regards to international reactions to Sharia in Nigeria states that,

Whatever personal beliefs may prevail in different social and religious circles in Nigeria, the Nigerian government both at federal and state level, remains bound by international obligations and conventions. These are not conventions imposed by Western, Christian or secular countries, but international and regional instruments which have been willingly ratified by Nigeria as well as other countries with large Muslim populations.[26]

THE DRAWBACKS OF THE TYPICAL HUMAN RIGHTS APPROACH

The writer contends that the classical human rights approaches mentioned above are ineffective since they neglect, significantly, a number of decisive realities of Islam and Muslims in general.

To begin with, the very goal of the human rights—"to formulate a jurisprudence of rights valid for all of humanity"—has always been considered laudable by some,[27] and offensive to others."[28] While the

---

[26] http://www.hrw.org/reports/2004/nigeria0904/15.htm
[27] Henry J. Steiner and Philip Alston, *International Human Rights in Context: Law, Politics, Morals* (Oxford: Oxford University Press, 2000), p. 366.

human rights organizations and activists should be commended for the aforementioned efforts in bringing this issue into the public sphere and vigorously struggling to put an end to what is believed by them to be indisputably an egregious human rights violation, the writer maintains that, by ignoring the inherent realities attached to the customary lifestyle and way of thinking of the Muslims, these methodologies will not in the long term be useful in reconciling the gap between Islam and International Human Rights.

The most salient fact that may render the abovementioned efforts futile, relates to the divine weight of the Hudud punishments (Baderin, p. 76). Muslims perceive Hudud punishments as divine, evolved from Godly wisdom, which they believed to be beyond the mortal intelligence of the limited human mind. El-Awa pointed out that "while the considerations of social utility form the basis of the theories of punishment in Western penal system, in Islamic law, the theory of punishment is based on the belief in the divine revelation contained in the *Quran* and the Sunna of Prophet Muhammad" (ibid.). Robert Postawko further substantiates this point saying that "the Islamic community [...] insists that the essence of Islamic law is unchanging and knowable [...] to the extent that Islam was revealed in the *Qu'ran*, a 'communication from God to the Prophet Muhammad, conveyed by the angel Gabriel, in the very words of God,' and was exemplified in the life of the Prophet, hence its essence is by definition complete and unchanging."[29]

Based on the above reasons, Muslim jurists hold that the harshness of the Hadd penalties can never be questioned. Hence any attempt to abolish them directly, apart from being highly offensive, could easily be translated into trying to eliminate a part of the religion altogether. Heiner Bielefeldt explains that conservative Muslims always have the tendency to view the human rights movement as a new Western "crusade." They fear that human rights are part and parcel of an all-encompassing ideology or way of life that is intended to eventually replace Islamic faith and practice.[30]

Abdullahi Ahmed an-Naim correctly stated that "religion has a strong influence on human belief systems and behavior, regardless of the formal characterization of the relationship between religion and the state in any

---

[28] Jason Morgan Foster, "A New Perspective on the Universality Debate: Reverse Moderate Relativism in The Islamic Context," in *International Law and Islamic Law*, ed. Mashood A. Baderin (Aldershot: Ashgate, 2008), pp. 365–97 (p. 365).

[29] Robert Postawko, "Towards an Islamic Critique of Capital Punishment," *UCLA Journal of Islamic and Near Eastern Law*, 1:2 (2002), 269–95 (p. 277).

[30] Heiner Bielefeldt, "Muslim Voices in the Human Rights Debate." http://calliope.jhu.edu/journals/human_rights_quarterly/v017/17.4bielefeldt.html

society."[31] This is especially true with Islam, being a religion that governs almost every aspect of life of its followers. An-Naim further explained that while it is true that the behavior of believers is not always motivated by total fidelity to their faith, religious considerations have always been perceived as too important for the majority of people for human rights scholars and advocates to continue to dismiss them simply as irrelevant, insignificant, or problematic (ibid.). Thus, the idea that human judgment alone could determine the appropriateness or cruelty of a punishment decreed by God is simply out of the question. Questioning the Hudud punishments is considered as questioning the divine wisdom underlying them and impugning the divinity of the *Quran* and the theocentric nature of Islamic law (Baderin, p. 76). Abu-l Ala Mawdudi argued that, "where an explicit command of God or His Prophet already exists, not even all the Muslims of the world put together have any right to make the least alteration in it."[32] Thus, neither Islamic reinterpretation nor cross-cultural dialogue is likely to lead to their total abolition as a matter of Islamic law (Lipman et al.). The steadfastness of Muslims in adhering to this belief is especially reflected in the provisions of the Universal Islamic Declaration of Human Rights (UIDHR), which states that "the basis of all law is the Shari'a, and divine revelation has priority over human reason in determining human rights limitations in an Islamic state."[33]

Based on the above discussion, it is obvious that human rights advocates have a very limited prospect of success in "pressuring the governments of offending countries to put an end to the practice of Hudud laws, by solely relying on the so-called universal norms of International Human Rights Laws, which have little influence among the Muslims, especially in conservative Muslim countries where Hudud punishments are widely mostly practiced" (Aslan, p. 92). Reza Aslan is right when he says

Human rights organizations around the world have documented case after case in which Zina laws have been purposely and incorrectly applied for misogynistic ends. And while, as mentioned, these groups should be applauded for their tireless struggle to put an end to what is unquestionably an egregious human rights violation, *the very international human rights*

---

[31] Abdullahi Ahmed an-Naim, "Islam and Human Rights: Beyond the Universality Debate," *American Society of International Law Proceedings*, 94 (2000), 95–101 (p. 95).

[32] Aslan, p. 91. Abu-l 'Ala Mawdudi, *Islam: its Meaning and Message*, ed. Khurshid Ahmad, 2nd edn (London: Islamic Council of Europe, 1976), p.159.

[33] Ann Elizabeth Mayer, *Islam and Human Rights: Tradition and Politics*, 3rd edn (Colorado: Westview, 1998), pp. 54–55.

laws they employ to combat offending countries have often hindered their work. (p. 98)

Another reason why an approach purely based on international human rights law will fail is because Muslims have extremely high confidence in the deterrent impact of the Hudud punishments. They believe that although the punishments are harsh and violate the norms of international human rights, the implementation of such punishments is mainly necessary to deter future crimes from occurring (Baderin, p. 75). This contention is very much related to the first reason, i.e. the divine weight attached by the Muslims to Hudud punishments. The simple but unshakeable understanding that these punishments were originally derived from divine wisdom has cultivated a soaring faith among Muslims in the deterrent influence that the penalties may have on any potential perpetrator of the crime.

For example, during a Conference in Riyadh, Saudi Arabia in 1972 on "Moslem Doctrine and Human Rights," where the delegates were from Ministry of Justice of Saudi Arabia and the Council of Europe, a Saudi Arabian delegate by the name of Dr Dawalibi had confidently said

I have been in this country (Saudi Arabia) for seven years [...] and I have never seen or heard of any amputation of the hand for stealing. This is because crime is extremely rare. So, all that remains of that punishment is its harshness, which has made it possible for all to live in perfect security and tranquility, and for those who are tempted to steal, to keep their hands whole. Formerly, when these regions were ruled by the French inspired Penal Code, under the Ottoman Empire, pilgrims traveling between the two Holy Cities of Mecca and Medina could not feel secure for their purse or life, unless they had a strong escort. But when this country became the Saudi Kingdom, the Koranic law was enforced, crime immediately disappeared. A traveller then, could journey, not only between the Holy cities but even from Al Dahran on the Gulf of Jeddah on the Red Sea, and traverse a distance of more than one thousand and five hundred kilometers across the desert all alone in his private car, without harboring any fear or worry about his life or property, be it worth millions of dollars, and be he a complete stranger.

(Ibid.)

Another delegate was also reported to have said, "In this manner, in the Kingdom of Saudi Arabia, where Islamic law is enforced, state money is transferred from one town to another, from one bank to another, in an ordinary car, without any escort or protection, but the car driver. Tell me, Gentlemen: in any of your Western states, would you be ready to transfer money from one bank to another, in any of your capitals, without the protection of a strong police force and the necessary number of armored cars?" This confidence in the deterrent nature of the Hudud punishments is just one of its influencing factors within Muslim societies (ibid., p. 76). Postawko, in commenting on the high level of confidence among the Muslims in Islamic criminal punishments had said that when a society is so utterly and unreservedly sure of itself, as the Muslim society is, and has always been, it goes only to confirm the unshakable confidence that the Muslims have in pristine Islam. And in respect of Islamic criminal punishments, the general body of Muslim believers has not, even in its darkest hour, lost faith and confidence either in its general destiny or in the efficacy and unimpeachability of Islamic punishments (Postawko, p. 278, n. 38).

The third possible reason why the typical approach of human rights will be highly inappropriate and ineffective in dealing with violations of human rights that may have been caused by the implementation of Hudud laws arises from Muslims' basic perception of International Human Rights Law. This is because Muslims (especially conservative Muslims) always have the perception that the international instruments and movement of human rights are biased mechanisms employed by the Western countries to indirectly oppress and subjugate the Muslim states to Western domination. Thus, any attempt at trying to *directly* compel obedience to these international instruments are easily seen by the Muslim states as an indirect act of subjugation and oppression. It is argued that the problem with the human rights argument is that the appeal to the UDHR is so often viewed as biased and hypocritical that it has little hope of effecting permanent change in offending countries (Aslan, p. 98). In many instances, when Muslim states are declared to have violated norms of human rights and are called to comply with the international instruments prescribing the standard for such rights, most conservative Muslim countries will just as easily cite the relatively poor human rights record of the United States and European nations to argue that the west applies the UDHR selectively and only when it serves its own interests.[34]

---

[34] A good example would be the prohibition against the imposition of death penalty for minors as enshrined in article six of the ICCPR, where it is reported that at present, there are "six countries in the world that regularly impose capital punishment on minors," which include *inter alia*, the United States. The fact that the U.S being a signatory Nation of the UDHR and the most influential member of the U.N., is in violation of the ICCPR, a document that they themselves helped draft, cries hypocrisy in the eyes of many conservative Muslim governments. See Reza Aslan, ibid.

In fact, even certain Muslim writers who are in favor of human rights have been charged as being internationally biased. Foster gave the example of An-Na'im, whose approach is to try and "reach common ground with international norms on some issues by a plausible reading of local texts i.e. a theory based on international norms." Due to his slightly liberal approach in dealing with issues of Islamic law and human rights, he is at times claimed by many conservative Muslims to be offending local culture and labelled as a "dangerous neo-colonialist" (Forster, p. 46). This is because, according to Schooley, "although An-Na'im advocates a cross-cultural dialogue to define 'rights', he actually adopts as 'rights' those already considered the norm in international law and advocates that the Shari'a be reformed to meet these standards" (ibid.). If a distinguished Muslim writer such as An-Na'im can easily be labelled as a deviant Muslim and a neo-colonialist simply because he tries to fit Islam into the framework of human rights, imagine the conservative Muslims' reactions towards any human rights activists or organizations (especially the non-Muslim activists), directly advocating the abolition of the Hudud punishments simply because they contradict International Human Rights Law

Another reason why conservative Muslim countries would find the argument of human rights groups unpersuasive relates to the issue of universalism in international human rights law. By exclusively relying on *international* human rights law as the universal standards that offending Muslim countries have to abide by, human rights advocates unnecessarily provoke the problematical dispute of whether human rights are universal in the first place. This debate has for so long been one of the most obstructive barriers to any attempts at reconciling Islam (in general) and international human rights law.

As much as human rights advocates would like to think that the rights prescribed by international human instruments are the universal norms, unanimously recognized by the global community as a whole, regardless of the diverse origins and backgrounds of people, the reality is very much to the contrary. Muslims (especially conservative Muslims) are not entirely receptive to this philosophy. Instead, many Muslims, especially those living in the conservative Muslim states where Islamic criminal punishments are more inclined to be practiced, believe that the international human rights law today has sorely neglected a substantial portion of the Islamic perspectives on human rights when formulating the core ideals of International Human Rights law. Hence, Muslim states tend to view international human rights instruments as "unapologetically Western documents that reflect neither Islamic culture nor Islamic notions of human rights" (Aslan, pp. 99–100).

In fact, it is reported that the main reason why Saudi Arabia and a few other Muslim states abstained from voting for the UDHR when it was ratified by the UN was because they sensed a palpable lack of Islamic ingredients and aspirations in the "western legal traditions that permeated these international documents" (ibid.). Aziz Bari is right when he said that the "developing world has always been very critical of what they perceive as attempts by the West to impose their (Western) standards on them."[35] Abu'l-A'la Mawdudi, a well-known Pakistani author, for example, writes, "The people in the west have the habit of attributing every good thing to themselves and try to prove that it is because of them that the world got this blessing, otherwise the world was steeped in ignorance and completely unaware of all these benefits."[36] This sort of negative way of thinking in the mind of the Muslims will prevent genuine compliance towards the universal provisions of International Human Rights Law.

The majority of Muslim writers who subscribe to this premise argue that the very principle of human rights today was originally derived from the West, its legislative instruments "firmly rooted in Western fundamental principles, with its cradle in the early British and French philosophers like Locke and Rousseau" (Aslan, p. 99). It is argued that the concept of individual rights, which forms the root of the overall idea of human rights, had expanded most rapidly from the era of the European Renaissance where the initial emphasis had been on rationalism and humanism, to the Enlightenment, when these theories developed into the political arena, becoming the central theme of Western civilization (ibid.). Based on this belief, many leaders of conservative Muslims counties reject not only the notion of international human rights law, but any forms of Western influence which in their view run counter to the Islamic viewpoint on any particular issues.

Iran's Ayatollah Ali Khamenei for instance, asserted that "when we want to find out what is right and what is wrong, we do not go to the United Nations; we go to the Holy Koran [...]. For us the UDHR is nothing but a collection of mumbo-jumbo by disciples of Satan."[37]

In fact, the June 1992 assassination of Faraj Fouda, an Egyptian author who attempted to publicly propose an extreme adoption of secularist philosophy in Islam, demonstrates the harsher reality that even Muslim

---

[35] Abdul Aziz Bari, "Rethinking of Ideas and Content of Human Rights: A Response," *Current Law Journal* 1 (1997), xxxi–xxxii (p. xxxii).

[36] Abu'l-A'la Mawdudi, "Human Rights in Islam" (1976).
http://www.islam101.com/rights/hrM1.htm

[37] Cited in Mayer, *Islam and Human Rights*, p. 27.

reformers, who are somewhat liberal and outspoken in their approach, are not well accepted by other Muslims.[38]

Anthony Chase's observation is illuminative as this juncture:

> The real danger of the human rights movement's reliance on an ideology of universal rights is that it has a polarizing effect: *it raises mistrust and places local human rights activists in the politically uncomfortable position of siding with those "universal"* values popularly identified with outside powers, rather than working with "indigenous" local traditions. However clichéd and unfair the perception of such categories, it could well be that, tactically, universalizing language may have outlived its usefulness. At this point the universal vs. cultural particularities debate often obscures more than it illuminates.[39]

The fifth reason why the typical human rights approach will not work as expected relates to the frequent doubts in this area that would usually raise many "faith-related" questions such as, "Is it really a religious obligation upon all Muslims to implement these punishments?"; "Is it a sin not to implement these punishments? If it is, should it then be enforced regardless of whatever circumstances are prevailing in the community at present?"; "What are the actual rules for exercising these laws?"; and "Could the traditional rules be eliminated, altered, or modified to suit the current needs of the society?" In resolving these troubling thoughts in their minds, Muslims would definitely prefer the safer "more Islamic" option of implementing the divine punishments rather than abolishing them.

Bielefeldt makes an interesting observation on this point:

> One should take into account that *many Muslims still might feel insecure about the relationship between traditional religious norms on the one hand and modern legal standards on the other.* This is why many Muslims assert the validity of the traditional Islamic Sha'ria in principle and, at the same time, seems prepared to accommodate pragmatically some political and legal reforms. For instance, even those who defend the legitimacy of Hadd punishments in theory, frequently prefer to avoid the actual implementation of these punishments, invoking practical obstacles to their reintroduction.[40]

---

[38] See *Human Rights Watch World Report* (London: Human Rights Watch, 1993), p. 296.

[39] Anthony Chase, "Legal Guardians: Islamic Law, International Law, Human Rights Law, And the Salman Rushdie Affair." www.wcl.american.edu/journal/ilr

[40] See above, n. 30.

The aforesaid argument is very much related to another reason why the above approach of human rights will be unsuccessful in coercing change in the area of Islamic criminal law. Recent events seem to indicate a steady trend of many Muslim countries to undergo some sort of reform process to transform, fully or partially, their political, social, or economic structures towards a more Islamic system. The upholding of divinely ordained punishments would obviously be in line with this Islamization movement. Although voices within the Muslim world itself have been critical of Islamization as both a concept and a practice, it is difficult for Muslim politicians to ignore the rhetorical appeal of promoting the establishment of an "authentically" Islamic society.[41] Even if the leaders in control of a Muslim government may want to succumb to some values of international human rights, they might not want to do so since such will go against the desires of their own populace, if the said norms contravene Islamic law. For such a local constituency to emerge and be effective in its advocacy of human rights, these rights must be seen by the general public as consistent with its own religious beliefs (an-Naim, p. 96).

The following quotation from Chadbourne's analysis of the Pakistani Zina Ordinance may illustrate the above discussion:

> The Zina debate is now more or less at a standstill. Pakistan is sensing world pressure after the nuclear bomb contest with India. Its populace desires a move toward security. In the traditional pattern, Prime Minister Nawaz Sharif is promising to further Islamize Pakistan. Simultaneously, the Muslim world is invested in Pakistan surviving as an Islamic state. Removal of the Zina Ordinance, whether right or wrong, is highly unlikely to happen in the current political environment. (p. 87)

With the current (and rapid) resurrections and re-establishments of Islamic law in many Muslim states today, certain writers argued that perhaps a more feasible approach would be to seek for a subtle method of prevention, indirectly through legal procedural shields under Islamic law as is currently in the practice of some Muslim States that apply Islamic law as State law (Baderin, pp. 79–80).

---

[41] See Postawko, p. 271. See also Seyyed Hossein Nasr, "Present Tendencies, Future Trends," in *Islam: The Religious and Political Life of a World Community*, ed. Marjorie Kelly (New York: Praeger, 1984), pp. 275–92 (p. 280). See also Sarvenaz Bahar, "Khomeinism, the Islamic Republic of Iran, and International Law: The Relevance of Islamic Political Ideology," *Harvard International Law Journal*, 33 (1992), 145–90 (p. 159).

CONCLUSION

In their struggle to stop violations of human rights based on the cultural or religious practices of a certain community, human rights advocates tend to overemphasize the supreme status of International Human rights Law as the only universal set of value principles which transcend all boundaries and state sovereignties. This unintentional manoeuver frequently leads to inadvertently overstating the binding nature of these international instruments and how the international community must obey them, regardless of any differences in backgrounds and origins that may exist among the global population. Although *technically* speaking the aforesaid arguments are right and justified, this sort of approach suffers numerous disadvantages. By putting the emphasis on the universal and mandatory character of International Human Rights Law, human rights advocates complicate the issue by bringing into the picture the irresolvable debates of universalism against cultural relativism, the western values against eastern morals, and the foundation of theocentrism against athnopocentricism. As a result, the ultimate aim of human rights movement in this area is often diverted from upholding the values of human rights couched in these international instruments to just upholding the binding legal provisions, apparent in these instruments.

Looking back into the Universal Declaration of Human Rights (UDHR), the writer opines that the actual reason behind the establishment of the UDHR is none other than to have a definitive set of guiding norms, which could act as the mechanism that upholds the dignity of a human being and preserve his/her inherent rights and freedoms as a human person, in whatever circumstances that may prevail.

In finding the additional apparatus that could further strengthen the overall approach of human rights in handling these so-called human rights violations, the writer submits that it would be sufficient if the said mechanism, regardless of the label attached to it, upholds the same values and ideals of international human rights law. Perhaps the more effective approach would be to find an area of law where both Islamic and International Human Rights Law totally coincides. This area of similarity should not be one of those comparatively equivalent points of reconciliation between the two. It should be the rare spot where both Islamic and International Human Rights Law totally concur with each other. In other words, it is the area where labels such as Human Rights or Islam do not really matter since both systems of law share entirely the same set of value principles. Should this be possible, human rights activists may then uphold the values entrenched in the international human rights

374

instruments under the less threatening banner of Islamic law or a combination of Islamic and International Human Rights Law.

Based on the above, the writer therefore submits that the violations of human rights (in relation to Islamic law such as Hudud) should actually be dealt with by diverting our emphasis from discussing the severity of the punishments to exploring the various procedural safeguards provided by Islamic criminal law for the accused in Hudud trials. This is because by closer examination one would discover that some of them are basically the same as those enshrined in the international human rights instruments. In fact, it is safe to say that some of these procedural safeguards are even more protective towards the accused person in criminal trials. The typical approach of demanding conservative Muslim states to uncompromisingly stop the practice of Hudud punishments on the grounds of International Human Rights law must be diverted to demanding that the Muslim states adhere strictly to procedural rules and evidentiary requirements required by Islam before Hudud penalties can be imposed.

A SUSTAINABILITY AGENDA FOR INTELLECTUAL PROPERTY AND INDIGENOUS KNOWLEDGE

Dora Marinova

INTRODUCTION

One of the strong manifestations of globalisation is the power of the market to facilitate and guard innovation through the so-called intellectual property rights as represented by patents or copyright. The firmly entrenched patenting laws in the developed world provide recognition and economic monopoly to individual inventors, be it individuals or organisations. Consequently, large and small companies have been able to appropriate the economic benefits from the technological knowledge protected through patents on the presumption that they need to recover the investment in research and development projects through successfully commercialising the new products and reaping the benefits from a secured market.

The protection of intellectual property (IP) is claimed to be one of the pillars of capitalism and a sign of development through a globalising market economy. Once IP legislation is put in place, i.e. it exists, functions properly, is being observed and enforced, including through litigation, then no other interventions are needed as the market automatically assigns rewards.[1] The main argument in favour of IP is that it is perceived as a utilitarian and instrumentalist construct that encourages inventiveness and innovation through guaranteeing private ownership over the creations of the human mind.[2] The main underlying assumption of this scenario is that private ownership fuels innovation, progress and development, which deliver economic rewards.

The evidence, however, has been that this approach fails to take into consideration two important aspects in the context of this paper. Firstly, despite their power, western culture and western values, as represented by IP laws, often conflict with other values and traditions within society. Under the umbrella of the legal IP protection, many companies and

---

[1] Amitrajeet A. Batabyal, and Hamid Beladi, *The Economics of International Trade and the Environment* (Boca Raton: CRC Press, 2001), p. 107.

[2] For a historical analysis, see Kenneth Carlaw, Les Oxley, et al, "Beyond the Hype. Intellectual Property and the Knowledge Society/Knowledge Economy," *Journal of Economic Surveys*, 20:4 (2006), 633–690; For analysis of empirical evidence, see Dora Marinova, Michael McAleer, and Daniel Slottje, "Antitrust Environment and Innovation," *Scientometrics*, 64:3 (2005), 301–311.

individuals have exploited knowledge that has existed in traditional and indigenous cultures for thousands of years. The controversies surrounding the intellectual property type of protection for privately initiated inventiveness are most obvious when it comes to commonly generated and owned knowledge as represented by indigenous knowledge. Secondly, a meaningful development requires the right balance and integration of values that go beyond pure economic benefits to cover the full picture of human existence and activities. The climate change evidence convincingly shows that technological progress coupled with economic incentives has marginalised and neglected other essential aspects of the human presence on Earth which the sustainability agenda is currently trying to redress.[3]

The remainder of the paper is organised as follows. After outlining briefly the concept of sustainability, the paper examines the nature of indigenous knowledge for indigenous sustainability. It then outlines the incompatibility between the western IP model and the role and place of indigenous knowledge in society. A new model manifesting more ethical behaviour is outlined through case examples and its policy implications for a move towards sustainability are discussed.

SUSTAINABILITY AGENDA

The concept of "sustainability" is associated with a wide range of human activities related to the use of resources, including natural, human, and financial, and implies long-term continuity and the ability to carry on with these activities indefinitely.[4] Since the mid 1970s the term has also become laden with value judgments about justice in the distribution and use of these resources. This was started by the World Council of Churches during its 1975 Assembly in Nairobi,[5] followed by the publication of Our Common Future (or the Brundtand Report) by the World Commission on Environment and Development in 1987, the 1992 United Nations' Earth Summit in Rio de Janeiro (which adopted Agenda 21) and continued through the adoption of the Millennium Development Goals by the United Nations' General Assembly in 2000 and the 2002 World Summit in

---

[3] Intergovernmental Panel on Climate Change *Climate Change 2007: The Physical Science Basis. Summary for Policymakers* (Geneva: IPCC Secretariat, 2007). http://www.ipcc.ch/SPM2feb07.pdf

[4] Dora Marinova and Margaret Raven, "Indigenous Knowledge and Intellectual Property: A Sustainability Agenda," *Journal of Economic Surveys*, 20:4 (2006), 587–606.

[5] John B. Cobb, *Sustainability: Economics, Ecology, and Justice.* (Maryknoll, NY: Orbis, 1992).

Johannesburg.[6] As early as 1992, Pezzey published dozens of definitions of the term, including the most widely cited Brundlandt definition: "Sustainable development is development that meets the needs of the present without compromising the ability of future generations to meet their own needs" (WCED, p. 43).[7] Several years later Jacobs accepted that the concept would remain contested and politically fluid because of the different stances taken in relation to what can be considered "fair."[8] The Western Australian State Sustainability Strategy states, "sustainability is defined as meeting the needs of current and future generations through an integration of environmental protection, social advancement, and economic prosperity"[9] and this definition closely describes the thrust of the analysis in this paper. Anand and Sen claim that sustainability is analogous to the concept of usufruct rights (i.e. the right to use another's property without changing its substance) extended beyond the economic realm to cover social and environmental aspects of human activities.[10] This latter explanation is also of particular interest as it provides valuable insights into the use of indigenous knowledge.

INDIGENOUS KNOWLEDGE

Broadly speaking, indigenous knowledge is defined as the knowledge held by indigenous people. It is also described as local, folk, native, traditional, people's knowledge that is unique to a particular culture or society and is passed from generation to generation, usually by word of mouth and cultural rituals.[11] It is all-encompassing and has been the holistic basis for human survival throughout the centuries, including sustaining important aspects such as food preparation, health care, farming, education, nature

---

[6] World Commission on Environment and Development (WCED), *Our Common Future* (Oxford, New York: Oxford University Press, 1987).

[7] John Pezzey, *Sustainable Development Concepts: An Economic Analysis.* World Bank Environment Paper No. 2 (Washington, DC: The World Bank, 1992).

[8] Michael Jacobs, "Sustainable Development as a Contested Concept," in *Fairness and Futurity,* ed. Dobson (Oxford: Oxford University Press, 1999), 21–45.

[9] Peter Newman and Michael Rowe, *Hope for the Future: A Vision for Quality of Life in Western Australia (The State Sustainability Strategy)* (Perth: Western Australian Government, 2003), p. 24.

[10] Sudhir Anand and Amartya Sen, "Human Development and Economic Sustainability," *World Development,* 28:12 (2000), 2029–49.

[11] John Fien, Debbie Heck and Jo-Anne Ferreira *Learning for a Sustainable Environment: A Professional Development Guide for Teachers: Indigenous Knowledge–Module 5* (Brisbane: Griffith University, 1997). http://www.ens.gu.edu.au/ciree/LSE/MOD5.HTM#act1

conservation, and a wide range of cultural, spiritual, economic, and other activities. The existence of indigenous knowledge is conditioned on other introduced knowledge, such as during military conquests and colonisation in the past and globalisation more recently.

A crucial aspect of understanding indigenous knowledge is that it is maintained in social, economic, cultural, and political institutions retained by the local people irrespective of their legal status in the new introduced environment.[12] In other words this indigenous knowledge is resilient to the new culture but it is also a manifestation of the fact that the new institutions on the lands of indigenous peoples cannot serve the same purpose as the traditional ones. In the case of the patent system, this legal institution imposed by the West is not only in conflict with the traditional values within indigenous societies: it can also reflect conceptions and practices that are colonialist, racist, and usurpatory.[13]

Specifically in Australia, the term "indigenous" is used to link the politico-religious, social, environmental, and economic challenges faced by Aboriginal and Torres Strait Islander peoples to indigenous peoples around the world. Against the national governance structures,[14] it is an attempt to create an international agenda through connection to international institutions such as the World Trade Organisation (WTO), World Intellectual Property Organisation (WIPO) and the UN Convention on Biological Diversity (CBD).

Indigenous knowledge "encompasses the content or substance of traditional know-how, innovations, information, practices, skills and learning of traditional knowledge systems such as traditional agricultural, environmental or medicinal knowledge."[15] It can also be expressed in folklore, such as songs, chants, dances, narratives, motifs, and designs. According to a WIPO-UNEP report some indigenous knowledge "may be

---

[12] Caslon Analytics, *Intellectual Property Guide* (2005). www.caslon.com.au/ipguide13.htm

[13] Coordinating Body for the Indigenous Organisations of the Amazon Basin (COICA) (1994). *Statement of the Regional Meeting on Intellectual Property Rights and Biodiversity*, in Darrell A. Posey and Graham Dutfield, *Beyond Intellectual Property: Toward Traditional Resource Rights for Indigenous Peoples and Local Communities*, Appendix 9 (Ottawa: IDRC Books, 1996).

[14] See for example, Garth Nettheim, Gary D. Meyers and Donna Craig, *Indigenous Peoples and Governance Structures: A Comparative Analysis of Land and Resource Management Rights* (Canberra: Aboriginal Studies Press, 2002); Gary D. Meyers and Robyn Malcolm, "Native Title Rights and the Protection of Indigenous Cultural Knowledge," *Intellectual Property Forum*, 50 (2002), 12–25.

[15] World Intellectual Property Organization (WIPO) *Intellectual Property and Traditional Knowledge*, Booklet 2 (New York: WIPO, 2005), p. 4.

kept confidential to the originator(s) and their descendants and may be accessed only with restrictions, some may be disseminated locally, but may nonetheless, be restricted in scope or in terms of accessibility, and some of this knowledge may be shared widely within the community and with outsiders."[16] Because of the wide definition of indigenous knowledge, which is an attempt to define cultural forms and processes, the protection of intangible property extends copyright law, plant breeders' rights, patent law, geographic indicators, and trademark law (Marinova and Raven).

In relation to indigenous people and intellectual property rights, Brush and Stabinsky emphasise the richness of knowledge related to plants and their use. They distinguish between (1) crop germplasm and farmer knowledge of domesticated plants which have developed during the millennia in connection to human selection and (2) natural products derived from wild plants and knowledge about the plants and products.[17] On the other hand, we have witnessed the increased interest in the United States, the world's largest and technologically most advanced market, in protecting intellectual knowledge related to crop plants, particularly biotechnologically and genetically manipulated.[18] Another related booming area of patenting is the myriad of plant-based compounds, substances, composures, mixtures, and so on. In these circumstances, however, there is not a mechanism to protect the wild plants per se (Brush and Stabinsky). This leaves any indigenous knowledge associated with such plants open to the good (or bad) will of individuals, organisations, and the community. Moreover, a major aspect of the traditional in indigenous knowledge is the communal and intergenerational ownership which contradicts the notion of exclusive individual use espoused by patent laws and encouraged by the entrepreneurial West.

The sustainability concept is a valuable conceptual framework for understanding and promoting indigenous knowledge as it emphasises the integrated importance of social, environmental and economic values as well as the importance of relationships and partnerships to achieve a better future. Sustainability is not outside of economic theorising. However, it gives value to genetic and biological resources, and indigenous knowledge

---

[16] Anil K. Gupta, *WIPO-UNEP Study on the Role of Intellectual Property Rights in the Sharing of Benefits Arising from the Use of Biological Resources and Associated Ttraditional Knowledge* (Ahmedabad: WIPO/UNEP, 2002), p. 11.

[17] Stephen B. Brush and Doreen Stabinsky (eds), *Valuing Local Knowledge: Indigenous People and Intellectual Property Rights* (Washington DC: Centre for Resource Economics, Island Press, 1996).

[18] Dora Marinova, "Eastern European Patenting Activities in the USA," *Technovation*, 21:9 (2000), 571–84.

for what it represents, for how it is constructed and conserved. The "one-size-fits-all" models for protecting intellectual property do not work within the sustainability concept. On the contrary, sustainability requires respect for local knowledge and practices and argues for diversity to be allowed to flourish.

The need for alternatives that cater synergistically to economic, social, and environmental considerations and reflect the values of sustainability is in conflict with the increasing universality and globalisation of the patent system. The patent law fails to serve indigenous knowledge not only because of its complexity, intricate requirements, and prohibitive costs. Its very nature goes against the spirit of this type of knowledge. Firstly, the patent law recognises only economic or commercial value and does not cover non-market, purely spiritual, cultural, environmental, social, or political values. Secondly, even if legal protection is awarded to a group of individuals (e.g. an indigenous community), it will be offered only for a limited period of time, which contrasts with the long-term commitment, association and responsibility of indigenous people to their land as a source of habitat, resources, and knowledge. In other words, a different approach is needed which can provide a systematic all-encompassing framework that crosses the boundaries of institutions, regulations, research disciplines, and tradition. Sustainability as a practical philosophy can accommodate these requirements and provide ways of thinking and acting that look for positive solutions for complex situations.

Indigenous sustainability, in particular, as a new movement in the field of sustainability, is concerned with addressing the disadvantages experienced by indigenous people in all aspects of society, including the recognition of their knowledge and intellectual rights.[19] Under a sustainability framework, there is also a role for customary law in recognising value and giving value to indigenous knowledge. A new intellectual property protection should allow for maintaining the social, political, cultural, and physical environment where indigenous knowledge is created. According to McGrath et al., "indigenous people, whose spiritual practices connect with country and have the potential to provide a foundational ethic for sustainability generally have much to offer the Eurocentric rationalists who have separated themselves from ecological cycles between the earth, air and water and are thus disconnected from the

---

[19] Steve Kinnane, "Recurring Visions of Australindia," in *Country: Visions of Land and People in Western Australia*, ed. A. Gaynor, M. Trinca, and A. Haebich (Perth: Museum of Western Australia and the Centre for Studies in Western Australian History, University of Western Australia, 2002), pp. 21–31.

spiritual self."[20] This "offering" comes with certain obligations established through customary law that also need to be recognised through western legal regimes. Example of the latter is fiduciary, the legal term used to describe the relationships between a person who occupies a particular position of trust, power, or responsibility with respect to the rights, property, or interests of another trustee or the community (Hawley and Williams, for example, talk about the fiduciary corporation which represents the rights and interest of a large amount of shareholders).[21] Such relationships of trust need to be taken beyond the sphere of practical economic interests and need to become an essential block in building partnerships—an important mechanism for achieving a more sustainable development and way of living.

Alternative approaches to indigenous knowledge and indigenous sustainability ought to allow among others for caring for country, for preservation of languages programs, for improved health and living standards, for meaningful participation in employment and other culturally appropriate activities, and for political representation and participation. In other words they need to support a people-culture-country continuum and not treat indigenous knowledge as something which sits in isolation from present day reality.

DEFICIENCIES IN CURRENT PATENT LAW

The issue of a patent confers the patentee "the right to exclude others from making, using, offering for sale, or selling the invention throughout the United States or importing the invention into the United States" or any other territory covered by the patent law.[22] Although the exact role of a patent is the "right to exclude," in reality patents have a two-fold role: firstly, they recognise ingenuity and secondly, they allow for a monopoly over economic benefits. These two functions are potentially equally

---

[20] Natalie McGrath, Dora Marinova and Paul Flatau, "Institutionalising a Participatory Culture for Indigenous Sustainability in Western Australia," in *Proceedings of the International Conference on Engaging Communities, Brisbane, Australia* (2005). http://www.engagingcommunities2005.org/abstracts/Marinova-Dora-final.pdf

[21] James P. Hawley and Andrew T. Williams, *The Rise of Fiduciary Capitalism: How Institutional Investors Can Make Corporate America More Democratic* (Philadelphia: University of Pennsylvania Press, 2000).

[22] United States Patent and Trademark Office (US PTO) (2005), *General Information Concerning Patents.* www.uspto.gov/web/offices/pac/doc/general/index.html#patent

applicable to indigenous knowledge, i.e. it results from ingenuity and creativity and should generate economic benefits. However the current system for intellectual property protection has failed to deliver on both accounts. The use of patents in achieving access and benefit-sharing (ABS) of genetic and biological resources established through the Convention on Biological Resources in biodiversity conservation in particular was addressed by some authors in a special edition of the journal *Ecological Economics*.[23] Some further analysis and discussion are presented below in relation to recognition and economic benefits.

Recognition
There is a lot of controversy in relation to how traditional knowledge has been exploited by multinational companies. Biopiracy,[24] exploitation for the establishment of genetic banks,[25] and concentration of control over the world's essential food crops of maize, potato, soybean, and wheat[26] are just a few examples of the patent law being used to exclude rather than recognise the traditional owners and carriers of this knowledge. Some even argue that it can hardly contribute to modern technological advances.[27]

Indigenous knowledge has barely received official recognition in registered patents (or inventions). A keyword search with "indigenous knowledge" of patent texts (claims, abstracts, titles, and descriptions) at the world largest patenting institution, namely the US Patent and Trademark Office (US PTO) generates 0 hits between 1976 and 2006. This is not surprising given the prominence on the application of the public domain to indigenous knowledge, as something that has been disclosed and available in the public domain for longer than one year without having been patented during this time cannot be patented. Consequently the patent system cannot

---

[23] See Bernd Siebenhüner, Tom Dedeurwaerdere, and Eric Brousseau, "Introduction and Overview to the Special Issue on Biodiversity Conservation, Access and Benefit-Sharing and Traditional Knowledge," *Ecological Economics*, 53 (2005), 439–44.

[24] Alvaro Zerda-Sarmiento and Clemente Forero-Pineda, "Intellectual Property Rights over Ethnic Communities' Knowledge," *International Social Science Journal*, 54:171 (2002), 99–114.

[25] Michael Blakeney, "Intellectual Property in the Dreamtime–Protecting the Cultural Creativity of Indigenous Peoples," *Oxford Intellectual Property Research Centre* (1999). http://www.oiprc.ox.ac.uk/EJWP1199.pdf

[26] Martin Khor, "IPRs, Biodiversity, and the Theft of Indigenous Knowledge," *Interdisciplinary Science Reviews*, 28:1 (2003), 7–10.

[27] Ove Granstand (ed.), *Economics, Law and Intellectual Property: Seeking Strategies forResearch and Teaching in a Developing World* (Dordrecht: Kluwer Academic Publishers, 2004).

provide any recognition to the owners of indigenous knowledge for their creativity or ingenuity. If used, indigenous knowledge has been hidden or developed further under "scientific" terms making it unrecognisable and alienated from the people and the place where it originated.

For example, keyword searches for patent descriptions incorporating words such as "indigenous" or "Aboriginal" generate some hits, albeit a very small number—a total of 3,800 or 0.1% of all patents registered at the US PTO during 1976-2006 (see also Figures 1 and 2). A further search on the use of native species in the wording of patent attributes results in a total of 43,283 or 1.2% of all patents during the same period. Although the information provided in patent documents does not allow estimation of how much of the knowledge about these native species (plants, insects or animals) was newly discovered in scientific laboratories and how much was the contribution of native knowledge (held by or derived from indigenous people), there is a clear logical connection between the two. Case studies of particular patents related to the use of native species such as, for example, the neem tree, the tumeric herb (discussed below), or the medicinal kirar, habul, ber, almatash, and dhok bushes in India, show that the scientific and technical interest of inventors was backed up by publicly available indigenous knowledge.

It is also quite interesting that the late 1980s and the 1990s were the times when the world witnessed the greatest expansion in the scope of intellectual property rights.[28] This is also demonstrated in the number of successful US patent applications related to native species (see Figure 1). Starting from very low numbers in the 1970s, the number of these patents surged in the 1980s to reach a peak in mid 1990s followed by another all times high peak five years later. Another very important observation is that the rise was not only in absolute numbers, it was closely followed in the relative shares of patents related to native species compared to all patents issued in the USA (see Figure 2). The year 1995 was a big peak with 4,451 successful patent applications lodged which translated to a high of 2.8% of all US patents while the 2000 absolute peak of 4,465 still represented a relatively high share of 2.2%. The relative drop in 1996 is most likely due to the 1995 "draining" of the pool of technical knowledge. However later on, the patents issued on the base of 1997 to 2002 applications were very high and overall high for two or more consecutive years confirming that the interest in native species continued strongly.

---

[28] Keith E. Maskus, *Intellectual Property Rights in the Global Economy* (Washington DC: Institute for International Economics, 2000).

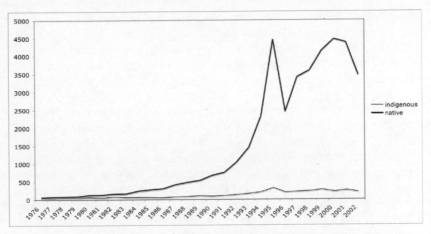

Figure 1. US patents related to indigenous topics and native species

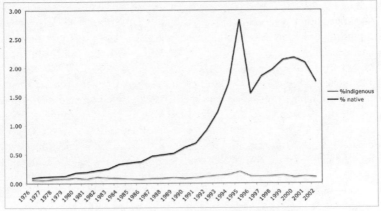

**Figure 2. Shares (%) of US patents related to
indigenous topics and native species[29]**

Let's take for example the neem tree. Its properties are mentioned in Indian texts written more than 2,000 years ago.[30] The US PTO has issued

---

[29] For Figs 1 and 2, the patent numbers are by date of patent application (as distinct from date of patent issue). The data were extracted from the US PTO on-line database at http://patft.uspto.gov/netahtml/search-adv.htm

[30] Philip Schuler, "Biopiracy and Commercialisation of Ethnobotanical Knowledge," in Finger and Schuler (eds), pp. 159–82.

280 patents (including to Australian inventors and companies) since 1976 for insect repellents, disinfectants, fungicides, gels and treatments of wrinkles, control of crawling insects, treatment of asthma and wood preservatives, to mention a few, based on the properties of the neem tree. Although 42 of these patents have been lodged by individual Indian inventors (with 37 assigned to Indian companies and organisations), the commercial benefits to the Indian farmers who have used extracts from the neem seeds for generations are only secondary, driven by the increased demand for (and consequently price of) neem seeds.

Similarly, the anti-oxidant, anti-inflammatory, anti-bacterial, anti-fungal properties, and other health benefits of the yellow spice tumeric, used extensively in traditional Indian cooking have been known for centuries. The number of US patents issued based on the scientifically and technologically proven properties of tumeric since 1976 is 584, and only two of them are to Indian inventors. The patents cover medical uses, such as treatment and prevention of skin disorders, osteoarthritis, rheumatoid arthritis and improved joint function; cooking products, such as coloured and flavoured frozen French fries, frozen dessert novelties and food additives and other products, such as paints, disposable wash-cloths, carpet yarn treatment to increase repellence. Again, there is only some economic benefit for Indian farmers derived from the increased demand for the large-leaved herb.

It is clear from the above examples that the patent system is not geared towards recognising the indigenous peoples' knowledge held collectively within the community. While the USA has been providing patent protection to individual inventors for more than two centuries (namely since 1790), it was only in the 1990s that the UN Commission on Human Rights' major study on the protection of indigenous intellectual property opened for the first time the debate about the use and recognition of indigenous knowledge. This coincided with the time of sharp increase in the number of patents based on native species which provided no recognition for indigenous knowledge.

Economic benefits

As patents provide exclusive use of the registered inventions, economic benefits are the major drive behind patenting.[31] These are collected through a myriad of different mechanisms and arrangements, including profits from

---

[31] See, for example Chris Freeman, *The Economics of Industrial Innovation*, 2nd edn (London: Frances Pinter, 1982); Gerhardt Rosegger, *The Economics of Production and Innovation: An Industrial Perspective*, 3rd edn (Oxford: Butterworth-Heinemann, 1996).

a temporary guaranteed market monopoly, royalty payments through licensing and patent pooling arrangements, income from patent sales or royalties from patent infringements. Economic benefits from patents can be very difficult to track down and separate from other business activities and generalised data are difficult to obtain.

The importance of economic benefits from protected intellectual property is particularly voiced within today's globalised world where countries such as China, Taiwan, Indonesia, India, Brazil, or the former Eastern Europe are often accused of breaching patent and copyright laws. The World Trade Organisation estimates that if developing countries were to pay their intellectual property royalties, this would generate about US$60 billion per year going towards the coffers of the developed world.[32] The infringement of patent laws is considered unethical. However, the grounds for this are purely economic and based on the western understanding of globalisation.

The aim of the WTO's Agreement on Trade-Related Aspects of Intellectual Property Rights (TRIPS), negotiated during the 1986–94 Uruguay Round, was to narrow the gaps between laws that govern intellectual property in various parts of the world, aligning them with the Western model which is believed to encourage technical innovation and economic development. In reality TRIPS enforces revenue collection from patent users to patent holders. Interestingly enough, however, there is still no agreement or negotiation as to using indigenous knowledge about plants, animals, other living species, organic and non-organic materials which would allow for the enforcement of the revenue collection mechanisms from developed countries going to the developing world, as the examples of the neem tree and tumeric show. If indigenous knowledge covers "all kinds of scientific, agricultural, technical and ecological knowledge, including cultigens, medicines and the rational use of flora and fauna," then surely the patent holders of the "new" neem and tumeric inventions are breaching ethical standards of indigenous ownership.[33]

Following Finger, the issue about indigenous knowledge is how to help these (poor) people benefit commercially using modern methods from their traditional wisdom.[34] In collaboration with another partner, and in

---

[32] J. Michael Finger, *The Doha Agenda and Development; A View from the Uruguay Round* (Manila: Asian Development Bank, 2002).
www.adb.org/Economics/pdf/doha/Finger_paper.pdf
[33] Erica-Irene Daes, *Discrimination against Indigenous Peoples: Protection of the Heritage of Indigenous People*, 1995, Final Report, United Nations Economic and Social Council, E/CN.4/Sub.2/1995/26, p. 10.
[34] J. Michael Finger, "Introduction and Overview," in Finger and Schuler (eds).

combination with scientific knowledge and methods, it may be possible for indigenous peoples to use patents to secure some rights over their knowledge while gaining economic benefits. In this instance, market-driven economic benefits can be derived by those individuals and communities that have the capacity, ability, and desire to both divulge their knowledge and to negotiate with other partners to create market-based economic values. Indigenous knowledge then becomes background intellectual property and through this process enters into the public domain, a route not without political, ethical and moral implications. However, through the formation of "new" intellectual property, indigenous peoples can albeit for a limited time, gain some recognition of their rights to knowledge, while creating opportunities for market-based value of their knowledge, and thus economic stability.

The majority of examples provided by Finger and Schuler demonstrate how indigenous people can successfully fight against the exploitation of their knowledge in newly issued patents and "fit" within the existing intellectual property system in order to gain economic outcomes. Although this may be one way of adjusting, it implies the superiority of the current institutional and social arrangements with little respect for traditional cultures. It also does not address concerns about reconciling economic rewards and moral obligations. Most importantly, it does not serve the tradition of community ownership, social justice, and responsibility for nature that exist in most indigenous cultures.

A NEW APPROACH TO INDIGENOUS KNOWLEDGE

In the absence of a widely accepted system that can properly serve indigenous people, the search for alternative practices is very important. Such a groundbreaking case is the indigenous plant accreditation protocol of the Songman Circle of Wisdom (representing the Kutkabubba Western Australian Aboriginal community) in partnership with the USA-based multinational cosmetics company, Aveda Corporation, and the exporter of Australian sandalwood oil, Mt Romance.

This first world event of global importance was launched in November 2004 in Perth, Western Australia. According to the indigenous plant accreditation protocol, both Aveda and Mt Romance donate $50,000 each to the Kutkabubba Aboriginal community for sourcing their products from Australia using the land and knowledge of the indigenous people. The money is then used by the community with no strings attached. The partnership under the accreditation protocol provides a new approach to protecting indigenous knowledge that is vastly different from the patenting law. Although as of May 25, 2007, there were 1,465 sandalwood patents issues by the US PTO between 1976 and 2005, none of them relates to the indigenous knowledge or usage by Aveda, Mt Romance, or the Kutkabubba community. The indigenous accreditation is a voluntary undertaking under a sustainability framework which allows for a holistic approach to indigenous knowledge. In a way, it is similar to environmental management systems accreditation under ISO 14001[35] which represents a voluntary recognition of the importance for business operations of sustaining the natural environment. However, while most ISO 14001 certified companies find direct economic benefits in accreditation due to the better monitoring and designing of their production processes,[36] the indigenous accreditation requires a substantial change in business ethics. It needs the companies to acknowledge that sustaining indigenous communities where indigenous knowledge is created is equally important to their business and can be achieved by working in partnerships. Indigenous people have long demanded not only recognition and protection of their knowledge but also the right to share equitably in benefits derived from its uses.[37]

These changing attitudes of the business community are an important component in an environment that is not legally regulated and where social and environmental responsibilities are as important as economic prosperity. The driver in the Western Australian case was Mt Romance, a company which almost went into liquidation in 1997 following the meltdown of the Asian import market where it was originally sourcing its products.[38] The third partner in the partnership, Aveda, is also renowned for its good environmental image and sustainable business practices. The company is committed to building sustainable business partnerships with indigenous

---

[35] See, for example, Dora Marinova and William Altham, "Environmental Management Systems and Adoption of New Technology," in *Technology Studies and Sustainable Development*, ed. A. Jamison and H. Rohracher (Munich: Profil, 2002), pp. 199–222.

[36] Dora Marinova and William Altham, "ISO 14001 and Adoption of New Technology: Evidence from Western Australian Companies," in *ISO 14001 Case Studies and Practical Experience*, ed. R. Hillary (Sheffield: Greenleaf, 2000), pp. 251–260).

[37] Michael Davis, *Biological Diversity and Indigenous Knowledge*, Research Paper 17 1997–98, Science, Technology, Environment and Resources Group (1998). http://www.aph.gov.au/library/pubs/rp/1997-98/98rp17.htm

[38] Fiona Sexton, "Masters of Reinvention Entrepreneur of the Year," *2004 Annual Review Magazine*, Ernst & Young, 2004.
www.ey.com/global/download.nsf/Ireland_EOY_E/thought-leadership-reinvention/$file/EOY_Masters_Of_Reinvention.pdf

people worldwide in the sourcing of its plant-derived ingredients. According to the company's president Dominique Conseil:

> At Aveda, we believe in beauty with a purpose [...]. Our ingredients must be not only high-quality, but high-integrity. We are dedicated to changing the way the world does business.[39]

The relationship established between Mt Romance, Aveda, and the Kutkabubba Aboriginal community through the protocol and through ongoing negotiations raises a number of challenges not necessarily unique to itself. For instance, how does one interpret the $50,000? This could be seen as a welfare handout. A critique could be levelled at the seeming lack of an adequate framework for access and benefit sharing. These agreements may be helpful in initially side stepping challenges associated with rewarding and recognising existing intellectual property, and giving it a financial value. However, how is this value determined and what percentage of this value should go to indigenous communities? Another issue includes the rewarding of any new intellectual property.

There are many unanswered aspects of this new approach. The most important point in this case study however is that a new value system is required for a change towards sustainability, where the integration of economics, environment, culture, spirituality, and society can occur simultaneously and in a balanced way. The pursuit of only economic benefits as the underlying motivation behind the patenting law not only creates disparities and insurmountable tensions but also has significantly contributed to the destruction of the foundations of life on Earth.

There have been other attempts at finding alternative models, including the popular case of Shaman Pharmaceuticals and the newly developing initiatives undertaken by the Australian Cooperative Research Centre Desert Knowledge.[40] In some cases, the courts have been successful in recognising common law, specifically in extending the interpretation of copyright law to accommodate indigenous cultural perspectives.[41] The usufruct rights of indigenous people in Brazil are protected by the

---

[39] Aveda, *"Taking Care of Business: A Dialogue on Environmentally Balanced Economics,"* (2005) aveda.aveda.com/about/press/wharton_conference.asp

[40] Roger A. Clapp, and Carolyn Crook, "Drowning in the Magic Well: Shaman Pharmaceuticals and the Elusive Value of Traditional Knowledge," *Journal of Environment and Development*, 11:1 (2002), 79–102.

[41] Michael Davis, *Biological Diversity and Indigenous Knowledge*, Research Paper 17 1997–98, Science, Technology, Environment and Resources Group (1998). http://www.aph.gov.au/library/pubs/rp/1997-98/98rp17.htm

country's Federal Constitution and such a legal environment is potentially much more encouraging to partnerships similar to the ones demonstrated in the Mt Romance, Aveda, and Kutkabubba Aboriginal people case study. Western countries, including Australia, however, are still looking for solutions that would have a bigger impact on how business is carried out, and often these delays are a disadvantage to the weakest people in society.

A widely accepted alternative to patent law is yet to emerge but it is clear that a more holistic approach is required in order to sustain the environment that has sustained indigenous knowledge and provides the basis for a substantial part of modern science, knowledge, and business. Such an approach also requires a change in ethics and the adoption of a culture of sustainability in order to maintain, generate, and look after the common good.

CONCLUSION

The inadequacy of the current intellectual property laws is well documented. The surge of patenting related to native species which started in the 1990s is going strong in the 2000s. The calls of globalisation for "ethical" behaviour in respecting patents, copyrights, and other IP are hypocritical against the continuing violation of indigenous people's rights. Shiva describes the patenting of indigenous knowledge as double theft—firstly, big companies acquire ownership over something that does not belong to them[42] and, secondly, the established patent rights prevent indigenous people from exploiting the economic opportunities linked to this indigenous knowledge. Plasencia argues that the USA, for example, has been "a major intellectual property pirate" for half of its existence.[43] Apart from the fact that this time was also the time when that country developed its economic prowess, there is also not a lot of evidence suggesting that the exploitation of the benefits from such piracy has actually stopped, at least not in the case of indigenous knowledge.

There is very little in the current patent laws that could have prevented Mt Romance (and consequently Aveda) as well as Shaman Pharmaceuticals or any research organisation from using the same approach and reaping economic benefits comparable to the world richest pharmaceutical or for that matter any "top ranking" businesses. What has made the change is the sustainability value system existing in these

---

[42] Vandana Shiva, "Poverty and Globalisation," BBC Reith Lectures 2000.
http://news.bbc.co.uk/hi/english/static/events/reith_2000/lecture5.stm
[43] Madeleine M. Plasencia (ed.), *Privacy and the Constitution* (New York: Garland Publishing, 1999), p. 288.

organisations, which has driven the search for an alternative approach. Economic recognition of the indigenous contribution is an important aspect of the sustainability triad that can help synergistically social and environmental sustainability.

The (paternalistic) encouragement of indigenous people to learn and use the "advantages" of the current patenting systems is not an appropriate policy. There should be policies in place to ensure that alternative approaches, such as indigenous partnerships with commercial companies and indigenous accreditation protocols, are applied to prevent the theft and exploitation of indigenous knowledge as well as deliver sustainable benefits to its traditional owners. The role of customary laws is increasingly seen as a powerful alternative for achieving a more sustainable development.[44] Siebenhüner et al., for example, state that the proper implementation of the Convention on Biological Diversity requires new intellectual property rights and new regimes that challenge the existing legal doctrines because of the complex interactions with pre-existing cultural frameworks.[45] Conserving the diversity of cultural knowledge of indigenous peoples is even harder as the only way to keep it alive is to keep it in use (Brush and Stabinsky) and to maintain in a sustainable way the social and natural environment that creates it.

ACKNOWLEDGEMENTS

The author acknowledges the financial support of the Australian Research Council (ARC) and is grateful to all indigenous peoples around the world for their wisdom and care for the planet Earth.

---

[44] Peter Ørebech, Fred Bosselman, et al. *The Role of Customary Law in Sustainable Development* (Cambridge: Cambridge University Press, 2006).

[45] Bernd Siebenhüner, Tom Dedeurwaerdere, Eric Brousseau, "Introduction and Overview to the Special Issue on Biodiversity Conservation, Access and Benefit-Sharing and Traditional Knowledge," *Ecological Economics*, 53 (2005), 439–44.

PHILOSOPHICAL, SPIRITUAL AND PSYCHOLOGICAL ASPECTS OF PEACE AND JUSTICE

REDISCOVERING THE SENSE AND ROLE OF COMMON GOOD IN THE GLOBALIZED SOCIETY

M. Lorenz Moisés J. Festín

INTRODUCTION

The main purpose of this paper is to investigate the relevance and significance of the concept of common good in contemporary society. As an essential element in any given social entity, common good constitutes an important subject matter that both invites and requires unremitting philosophical reflection as society progresses.

The paper has three parts. In the first part, I make a brief historical remark about the philosophical concept of common good. The concept could trace its origin to the ancient Greek philosophical understanding of society, namely as *polis*. Being the unique being that he is, the human being is thought to have an end that is not merely individual but also collective. He is not simply an individual, but also a social being. Thus, his *telos* is often seen as common with that of other human beings.

The second part discusses how societies have significantly changed over the years. They have become less isolated and more cosmopolitan. National borders and interests have given way to international collaboration and cooperation. The world we live in now has developed into a global village. In relation to this, I will argue that the current global order resembles the situation during the time of Alexander the Great, whose vision was to establish a *cosmopolis*, literally a global city.

Finally, in the third part, I consider whether the notion of common good in itself has lost its relevance in the face of manifold social changes. Is it really possible to conceptualize a notion of common good that would be applicable to the current global society or is the idea of common good, having originated from ancient Greek philosophy, a concept no longer relevant to present social life?

I bring my discussion to a close with a note on the universality and naturality of the common good of humankind.

A HISTORICAL NOTE: THE DISSOLUTION OF THE PLATONIC-ARISTOTELIAN POLITICAL THEORY IN A COSMOPOLITAN CONTEXT

Philosophy came to exist with man's constant quest for ultimate explanation. Confronted with the mystery that the world embodies, ancient Greek philosophers embarked on an enterprise that sought to answer the question, "Why?" The problem in itself could be understood and formulated in various ways and one usual way of approaching it is to inquire about the purpose of things. Accordingly, one of the earliest solutions is the teleological approach. Teleology envisions reality as purposive. Every being aims at its own *telos*, goal, or end and this goal or end of every being eventually came to be understood as its good.

In the *Nicomachean Ethics*, Aristotle states, "Every art and every inquiry, and similarly every action and choice, is thought to aim at some good; and for this reason the good has rightly been declared to be that at which all things aim."[1] The idea of common good stems from such a conceptualization of human good. Man is regarded as a being whose end can be achieved only in the context of a collectivity: that is, his society. He is thus not simply an individual, but also a social being. And he shares a common end with other human beings.

Ancient Greek philosophy sees the human individual always as part of a society. It identifies his end with that of his society. Hence, previously the study of man was just part of the study of his society and the treatment of his good is dissolved in the treatment of the common good, understood as the good of the society. It was only with Aristotle that an initial attempt to come up with a separate ethical science was made.

Our own concept of common good is closely connected with the ancient Greek notion of society. A look at history would show how St. Thomas Aquinas's employment of many of the ancient Greek philosophical thoughts has facilitated the adaptation and integration of the same into our thought paradigms today. One may thus wonder whether the notion of common good in itself is already an obsolete concept.

Certainly in the course of time ideas may lose their significance. In fact, much of Aristotle's political teachings became irrelevant—even during his own time—when society underwent significant changes. It may be recalled that Alexander the Great, who himself was a student of Aristotle, was instrumental in those changes. The success of his conquests from the year 334 until 323 BC resulted not only in the reshaping of the political map but also in the conceptualization of what a society should be. The conquests led to the integration of a multicultural and multi-tribal populace. It created a cosmopolitan society that diminished the importance and influence of the polis or city-state. And it enabled the individual to discover himself.

In the city-state the individual had a greater chance to take part in running the affairs of the state. After all, the size of such a society permitted that sort of involvement. A *polis* is "by definition a community of

---

[1] Aristotle, *Nicomachean Ethics*, I, 1, 1094a, 1–2.

individuals who participate in the government of the community." It is "the complete or perfect type of community." Its size hardly resembles that of present day states. Aristotle himself would describe a perfect city-state as neither too populated nor hardly populated. It has to be big enough to satisfy the needs of its citizens and small enough for each of its members to be given the chance to take part in its affairs.

Understandably a citizen was thus readily identified with "one who is able to participate in the deliberative and judicial areas of the government," whereas a slave was seen as "an instrument which precedes and conditions the other instruments."[2] Nevertheless, such a setup reduced the individual to a mere part of the society. His good was seen simply as integrated and dissolved in the public common good and when Alexander's cosmopolitan society supplanted the city-state community, people had great difficulty identifying society's good with theirs.

But that led to the individual's discovery of his own good. The individual saw his good as something not necessarily identified with that of the society. And the effect was the emergence of individualism among the citizens. Paradoxically then Alexander's conquests resulted in two phenomena: the movement toward greater integration and the movement toward individualism. And while they may seem to be opposed in direction, they are actually complementary movements.

The movement toward greater integration consists in the diffusion of the cosmopolitan ideal. This includes the conception of the entire world as one city. Peoples began to look at one another no longer as enemies but as possible partners in greater endeavors. Prejudice against the Barbarians started to diminish and intermarriage with them came to be accepted.

With the enlargement of the society, however, came the discovery of the individual. The human individual started to consider himself in isolation from his society. He began to see his good no longer as dissolved in the society's common good. And while such a view was still prevalent even after the revolution, people started to appreciate their individuality and differences.

THE GLOBAL VILLAGE

The current world order presents a situation quite reminiscent of Alexander's epoch. Movements toward greater integration can be discerned in the political and economic policies of many governments. Nations are learning to appreciate the importance and benefits of mutual cooperation

---

[2] See Jonathan Barnes, *The Cambridge Companion to Aristotle* (Cambridge: Cambridge University Press, 1995).

and the trend toward collaboration is beginning to penetrate every facet of social life, from economy to scientific research, from military development to ecological concerns.

Perhaps one concrete example of such a large-scale cooperation is the experience of the European Union. Organized in 1951, initially as an organization of six European countries for the purpose of drawing common guidelines in regard to coal and steel industries, the union has expanded not only in membership but also in areas of collaboration. The union no longer merely constitutes economic cooperation among trading partners. It has likewise adopted common policies and even established shared governing bodies concerned with issues such as legislation, defense, ecology, human rights, and the like. The success the union now enjoys has undoubtedly come to be a source of inspiration for neighboring countries to do the same.

The European experience of mutual cooperation is just one among the many attempts to achieve greater integration. Similar trends have also become quite visible in various parts of the globe, including the regional cooperation of ASEAN countries. International treaties and agreements have multiplied and the number of countries taking part in such agreements has swelled to new records.

Still, all these are just part of a much larger phenomenon that continues to baffle every human individual in the globe. The interdependence of countries beyond their respective regions attests to the fact that cooperation in matters not only economic transcends territorial proximity. The world itself has become a village. Thanks to globalization, this global village can even mimic in extra-larger scales the banalities of a rural community, where trade of goods and exchange of news, both factual and fictional, are a common occurrence. And just like in any typical village, where one is hard-pressed to conduct oneself in conformity to social norms, it seems that national governments can only afford to go with the flow of global trends.

One might thus wonder whether we as individuals are just part of an organic entity that has a life of its own. Are we simply a particular moment in this worldwide unfolding that globalization represents? Might this globalization be just an evidence of a global movement that is immune to any human intervention? Could Hegel be right in his claim that the world is nothing but a Spirit manifesting itself?

Perhaps it might be interesting to also ask how an individual feels about this global society. What is his outlook in regard to this colossal structure onto which he finds himself grafted? What does an ordinary citizen of a developing country, for example, think of his society that has come to be shaped in so many ways by globalization? Does he even have any idea of his place in the world right now?

I make this reference to the current world order to identify the context in which socio-political life in any given country is defined. My basic claim is that recent global developments and progress have created a situation in which countries like the Philippines, and, for that matter, the millions of ordinary Filipinos, are just some among the many constituent parts that compose the world community. I wonder, then, whether consequences similar to those of Alexander's conquests could be expected from all these recent global events.

Has globalization likewise instilled an individualistic outlook among the people of today? Is this recent progress toward greater worldwide integration just one side of the entire reality? Could there also be a parallel inward-bound movement toward individualism?

The occurrences at the dawn of the present millennium demonstrated the interconnectedness of the different parts of the world. Events at one side of the globe once again proved to have serious repercussions on the other. The effects of the terrorist attacks in the USA in 2001, for instance, could be felt even in the remotest regions of the least developed countries. Wars were started, governments were overthrown, and the global economy quivered.

And yet in all these, it is the individual who has to endure the consequences. The recurrent transport strikes in the Philippines, for example, are just an evidence of how helpless we have come to be in the face of a problem that traces its roots to an event that happened in a place very much distant from us. Could governments do something about it? Could people choose not to be affected by that event? Could transport groups modify the current global economic set-up by their clamor and protest? Could an ordinary citizen in any given country ever introduce a difference to the present state of things?

I guess our predicament is similar to the social condition after the conquests of Alexander the Great. Like the Greek city-states, countries and their governments are beginning to lose their relevance and importance. Their influence has significantly diminished. And like the human individuals during that time, we too are at a loss. We could hardly see how the common good that our state safeguards could embody our goods and aspirations. And the only alternative left to us is either to organize ourselves into smaller associations just like other interest groups or to withdraw ourselves entirely and simply embrace an attitude of indifference and individualism.

Is the notion of shared aspirations and goals then just a matter of human convention? Is there anything at all that binds us as a society and as human race? Is there really such a thing as common good?

REDISCOVERING THE SENSE AND ROLE OF COMMON GOOD

The relentless expansion of our society into a global village has made it hard for any human individual to see his good as embodied in society's goals and priorities. Understandably one could ask whether the notion of common good could ever find actuality in such a society. Does it still make sense to speak of common good when the number of people who will share in it has made a quantum leap?

Obviously if common good were to be understood simply as advantage or gain equally shared by all, it might be impossible to imagine billions of people taking benefit from it. But is that really what is meant by common good? Could common good, in the first place, be compared with a corporation's profit apportioned fairly to its shareholders? Is common good something that is voted upon by the citizens of a country?

There are many possible ways of approaching the question of common good. One familiar approach would be what we might call the Utilitarian approach. As a philosophical system, Utilitarianism identifies good with what is useful, beneficial, pleasurable, or advantageous. Central to its teaching is the principle that emphasizes the greatest advantage for the greatest number of people. Thus, the best choice for a Utilitarian is one that promotes the good of the majority. An act or a decision is valuable when, and only when, it is directed to the good of the greatest number.

And what constitutes this good of the majority? Utilitarianism would identify it simply with the totality of individual goods. The good of humanity thus is nothing but the "sum total of the good of its members."[3]

The Utilitarian approach, however, would make it all the more difficult for the notion of common good to make sense in a cosmopolitan society, for to understand common good as such is to conceive it as some commodity to be shared by every member of the society. Hence, just to define what would be beneficial to the majority or to the greatest number would already require some sort of election. But this is simply unrealistic if not absolutely impossible. Wouldn't that, in fact, imply that every time a policy affecting everyone in the society is introduced, a referendum would have to be called for?

St. Thomas Aquinas offers another way of understanding common good. According to him, common good is something that has a foundation on our nature as human beings. Aquinas argues that insofar as we share a common nature, we likewise have common aspirations and goals.

---

[3] Joseph de Finance, *An Ethical Inquiry* (Roma: Editrice Pontificia Università Gregoriana, 1991), p. 144.

The commonality of common good thus consists in the commonness not only of the ends that we pursue but also of the foundation that gives our pursuits justification. By virtue of our nature as human beings, we all pursue goals that evidence our humanity. Thus, common good is not something we vote upon. It is not something that is determined by the majority. It is rather something defined by the common nature we all share.

Understood in this sense, common good could no longer be conceived as a commodity or advantage that would have to be equally distributed among the citizens. Instead, common good consists in the goods that are proper to us as human beings. And these include the many rights we have by virtue of our humanity: e.g., the right to be treated and respected as a human being, the right to be given what is just and due to oneself, the right to realize one's person.

In view of this, the society does not lose its efficiency in promoting the common good, despite its relentless increase and expansion. For the common good that it safeguards is identified with the very goods that every single individual pursues as a human being. The common good of the society cannot then be alien to the good of the human individual, so that no individual can simply be sacrificed for the sake of the society.

That the central function of the society is the promotion of the common good means that it has to provide human individuals with the possibility of attaining the human goods. The common good of the society is not something that is isolated from the goods of individual persons, for there would be no such a thing as common good if in the first place there weren't goods that human individuals commonly pursue.

Of course, there are always disagreements among citizens in every society. Results of elections, referenda, plebiscites, and surveys, in fact, have never shown a unanimous opinion on any particular issue. There have been and there will always be dissenting voices. And in the context of the cosmopolitan society brought about by the current world order, the diversity of viewpoints becomes even more striking. The outcome of the last US elections, for instance, evidences a rift among Americans in regard to a host of issues—issues that have likewise divided the community of nations, such as the Iraqi War. (It must be recalled that the United Nations Security Council has never arrived at a unanimous decision prior to the invasion of Iraq, even if the serious repercussions of it affected everyone in the globe.)

Now, does that mean that the notion of common good is no longer realizable in the present-day social order? Is it still possible for a given society to arrive at a choice with which everyone agrees?

It's true, it has become extremely difficult and almost impossible for any society to attain consensus among its constituents. But then again, common good is not something that is arrived at through elections, surveys, or plebiscite. It is not to be understood as a result of consensus and compromise.

Common good is more fundamental than that. It refers to the more basic realities that evidence the commonalities we share by virtue of our nature as human beings. Common good therefore precedes society's every collective decision, expressed and arrived at in a variety of ways, including the electoral exercise.

Thus, although results of an electoral exercise may not be favorable to some sectors of the society, the presupposition should always be that the exercise itself constitutes an instantiation of common good, in that every citizen is given what is due to him—the possibility of expressing one's opinions, the opportunity to be heard on it, and so on.

The same applies to the task of legislation assigned to lawmakers. Although it could not be avoided that certain civil laws might be more beneficial to some members of the society than to others, basic to every form of legislation is that it should be directed to the common good. Aquinas thus defines law as "a certain order of reason for the common good, promulgated by him who takes care of the community."[4]

Common good, understood as more basic than every communal decision of the society, suggests that even beyond the specifically collective activities, like legislation and the electoral exercise, people have the duty and obligation to promote and seek the common good in all instances, even if they will not—either directly or in any way—benefit from it in each of those instances. For the pursuit of the common good should be motivated not by merely personal gain, but by the fact that the good one pursues forms part of the natural aspirations of every single human being. That is, insofar as human beings by virtue of their nature aim at certain goods, these human goods ought to be pursued whether these goods directly concern oneself or someone else in a given moment. Human goods form part of the common good insofar as they are shared goods commonly pursued by every human individual.

That is why, according to Thomas Aquinas, even to a stranger we ought to extend a hand when he is in need of help, especially if this help would be essential to his continued existence. Aquinas in *De Perfectione Spiritualis |Vitae* writes, "Because all human beings share in the nature of the species, every human being is naturally a friend to every human being; and this is

---

[4] Thomas Aquinas, *Summa Theologiae*, I-II, quaestio 90a, 4c.

openly shown in the fact that one human being guides, and aids, in misfortune, another who is taking the wrong road."[5]

Explaining Aquinas' argument, John Finnis states, "The only reasons we have for choice and action are the basic reasons, the goods and ends to which the first practical principles direct us. Those goods are human goods; the principles contain no proper names, no restrictions such as 'for me'. So it is not merely a fact about people's practical understanding, that they can be interested in the well-being of a stranger, whom they will never meet again but now see taking the wrong turning and heading over a cliff; for it is the same good(s) that the stranger can share in or lose and that I can: specifically human good(s)" (Finnis, p.111).

CONCLUSION: THE NATURAL FOUNDATION OF THE COMMON GOOD

That our world and the various societies therein have become inextricably tied up is a reality we can hardly deny. Our way of life and our daily concerns can readily attest to the fact that we live in a world that has become too small for anyone to escape the influence and impact of this interconnectedness. Such development has certainly been advantageous to humanity and to its progress. Every human individual in one way or another has felt the benefits it brings. And yet there is also a downside to it. For on account of the same interconnectedness, the significance of human individuality and the distinctiveness of every nation and state are at risk of being rendered relative to the totality that the emerging global society has come to represent.

Our concern thus is whether this social globalization has created a totalizing entity that simply defines the life and destiny of every human being. Would the human individual still be able to look at the goals and objectives of the global society as embodying his hopes and aspirations? Or would he instead find himself helpless in the face of such a gigantic entity that has become more evasive of human control and influence? And would it still be possible to regard the good that this global society aims at as common good, considering the multiplicity and diversity of the peoples and societies it embodies?

Again, it is important to go back to what the notion of society itself presupposes, for the existence of society is brought about by human being's fundamental need for fulfillment, which he cannot achieve except in the context of the society and in cooperation with his fellow human beings.

---

[5] Thomas Aquinas, *De Perfectione Spiritualis Vitae*, ch.15 [14], lines 27–31 [637], cited in John Finnis, *Aquinas: Moral, Political and Legal Theory* (Oxford: Oxford University Press, 1998), p. 111.

Thus the justification of society's existence can be made only with the recognition that human beings have common goals and ends. That is to say, a human being by nature aims at certain goods. And these goods are those that all human beings commonly pursue. Indeed, this is where the concept of common good is founded. Common good is not something decided and determined by human individuals' will and preferences. Rather, it is based on who they by nature are as human beings.

Hence, even if our society is becoming more cosmopolitan and interconnected with the rest of the world, common good remains an important consideration to be taken into account. For society, no matter how global it is, can achieve its purpose only when it serves the human beings' common good, which transcends space and time, history and territory, race and way of life.

FROM RAWLS TO A WORLDWIDE WELFARE SYSTEM: A PHILOSOPHICAL DRAFT OF ARITHMETICAL JUSTICE IN REDISTRIBUTION

Frank Tillmann

INTRODUCTION

One may intuitively say that the circumstances in the world are structurally unjust, though it may be impossible to specify the origins of this. The basic needs of a sizeable part of world population are not being fulfilled within the present social order. Thus, approximately one half of people all over the world live in precarious to horrible conditions. About 2.7 billion people do not have sanitation facilities; 1.3 billion do not have access to fresh water; the same number earns less than 1 USD a day; 800 Million people have no medical care and suffer from hunger.[1] Moreover, in the industrialised countries there is an obvious defect in the division of labour. A contingent of people is unemployed while there is an enormous amount of work severely lacking in remuneration. Furthermore, looking at the present global security situation, the current institutions are obviously not suited to providing a common system of protection from attacks—a fundamental purpose of social order.

The work of John Rawls still leaves one wondering what inferences could be drawn from it concerning the structures of the welfare state. This project assumes that the definition of a valid political framework can be evaluated and created by political theory. Therefore my reception of John Rawls' *Theory of Justice*[2] follows the notion of Condorcet's *Mathématique Sociale* which asks for anticipatory scientific coordination of individuals' actions.[3] According to Quines' ontological statement that "To be [...] is to be [...] the value of a variable,"[4] the social question deals with the problem of determining which conditions are to be established so that certain social variables do not reach a precarious value. Thereby a marginal utility as a

---

[1] Carl Haub, *Dynamik der Weltbevölkerung 2002* (Stuttgart: Balance-Verlag, 2002).
[2] John Rawls, *Eine Theorie der Gerechtigkeit* (Frankfurt am Main: Suhrkamp Taschenbuchverlag, 1975).
[3] Horst Dippel, *Individuum und Gesellschaft—Soziales Denken zwischen Tradition und Revolution: Smith—Condorcet—Franklin* (Göttingen: Verlag Vandenhoeck and Ruprecht, 1981), pp. 156ff.
[4] Wilfred Van Orman Quine, *From a Logical Point of View.* (Cambridge MA: Harvard University Press, 1953), p. 13.

just level of redistribution is to be identified. Finally, I seek to elaborate a conception of the notion of an *arithmetical justice* which could serve as a basic constitutional form to be approximated by positive law.

Among scientific disciplines it is the privilege of political philosophy to make a clean sweep and reconstruct the social world from the beginning without regard for the remains of former erroneous developments.

ADOPTING RAWLS' "THEORY OF JUSTICE"

To begin, it is necessary to restart with Rawls' concept of justice, considering to what extent the thoughts of the original position might be used to gain political rules out of it.

If we look for fair rules of social interaction, we always do it in the here and now. Some people live very comfortably in actual society, while others have to struggle hard just for their livelihood. How can we find just rules of co-existence then? Dworkin compared this situation with a round of card players who try to specify the rules of their game while they already hold their cards in hands. This is a most difficult venture and does not necessarily lead—even if majorities are to be found—to fair rules.[5] Now those who deliberate about a just society cannot abandon their social positions easily. Karl Mannheim referred to how obviously thinking is caught in social positions, whereby he also sees the possibility of making oneself aware of these social limitations on knowledge and ideas through intellectual abstraction and controlling them in that way.[6] Thus one can try to imagine for oneself which rules one would have voted for before the cards were distributed. This problem Rawls tries to illustrate with his thought experiment of the original position. In my opinion, the participants in the negotiation in this initial situation are enabled to state substantially more extensive definitions with practical consequences than the ones that were declared by Rawls. In Rawls' conception of justice there are statements of two different qualities to be derived, which refer to each other. In the long run the established rules are the results of a consideration process, which each rationally thinking human without knowledge of his or her actual identity would reconstruct by reasonable considerations. It is enough to know that there will be at least one further person, together with whom one has to find obligatory rules. From this result the formulation of first and second order declarations as quasi-objective human interests evolves—which exhibit only theoretical content—along with practical claims, each

---

[5] Ronald Dworkin, *Bürgerrechte ernst genommen* (Frankfurt am Main: Suhrkamp Taschenbuchverlag, 1990), p. 67.

[6] Karl Mannheim, *Ideologie und Utopie* (Frankfurt: Verlag Schulte-Bulmke, 1969).

asserted by political rules for its security. As Rawls suggested, these claims in later real situations cannot be put into question by national right, as long as their owners act according to the established rules.

The notional persons who meet in the original position wear a veil of ignorance, an imposed uncertainty about their later positions taken in the society, and ignorance of their characteristics as well. In view of the position of those involved in the original position, one can say there is a desire for certain basic goods that belongs to a state of being reasonable. These uncertain people would agree to rules which correspond to such interests, which they all share with each other equally. And because therein they agree in their interests, they will find a consent for certain basic rules easily. The participants in this situation of negotiation are conscious that the rules in which they agree henceforth are obligatory and final principles. They are established in consideration of possible consequences and serve to adjust later relations between people. With the lack of information about their own social position, each participant of a negotiation at the same time already attends to the interests of the other and vice versa. All agreements made there are fair, because they are impartial.

The rules that free and reasonable people in such a situation would decide on are plausible: First of all they would accept that they have common interests as well as conflicting. A clash of interest consists, for instance, in how the goods produced in co-operation are distributed. Under the described conditions of this thought experiment, reasonable persons without a defined identity would try to guarantee that even the worst position which results from the agreement for one is still acceptable. The two well known principles that Rawls expatiated everyone could agree to:

1. The principle of equal liberty, according to which all people are on an equal footing. Everyone has an equal requirement of the most extensive basic liberties, which are compatible with the interests of all others.
2. The difference principle, which means that an inequality is justified if even the least member of the society obtains an overall advantage out of it (Rawls, p. 336).

THE QUASI-OBJECTIVE INTERESTS OF PEOPLE

To transform these principles into a political agenda there first has to be added a systematisation of human interests. In contrast to the subsequent category of an agreement's quality, the first one just as a preliminary idea helps create awareness of one's own domain of interests. Practical impact on reality gives the next consideration the quality of second order. Rawls' idea of the original position refers to the notion that among anonymous participants certain interests are common, to which everyone would agree according to rational reasons. Here the objectivity of these interests is understood in the sense of impartiality. First of all it has to be accepted that the life goals of individuals can't be generalised, especially against the background of different values and life-styles. Thus needs simply cannot be universalised. The only statement which is generally applicable to such different subjects with certainty is the following: in the difference of their interests the single request they all have in common is to achieve *the most possible options*, so they can pursue their own subjective aspirations optimally. So, one could recognize this even as another primary principle that the people in the original position would agree to: All rules have to serve to impartially maximize individual options. This insight assumes that one—later in the real life—will possibly not need all the options which were granted by resolution in the initial situation. But it is much easier to refuse some of them than having to fight for them against the others laboriously. The hermit, who according to fair distributional rules is entitled to more income than he would like to have, can give it away easily. But someone disadvantaged by social inequity will hardly convince a court referring to the Rawls' concepts of justice to guarantee him benefits if this is not according to law. Of course one person's liberty is always limited by the liberty of another. But it is vague to assume that the ambitions of the individuals automatically aggregate to the common good. Instead there is a concentration of power and property arising, which can only serve the general interest of the society by a steady feedback. In situations of negotiation with those who possess less and are more dependent on co-operation therefore, more profit can be drawn out. Generally, inequality between people is inclined to strengthen. The creative effective principles of competition and co-operation must be shifted into a certain equilibrium so that the liberty of the individual does not result in contradictions regarding equality. To clarify this relation the term of *general and particular interests* is to be specified. General interests are defined by their relevance for everyone, being independent from the restrictive characteristics of the person, e.g. sex, nation or property. Such characteristics apply to particular interests, which prove themselves by the fact that theoretically one can conceive of a certain number of other persons pursuing directly contrary interests. Concerning this relation, the participants of negotiation in the original position would decide for an absolute priority of *general* over *particular interests*. So a *consensus* within the initial situation is only possible in view of the implementation of general interests, while particular interests are only to be found in the actual situations which have to be a subject for political negotiations in the instances where they occur.

GENERAL INTERESTS AND THEIR POLITICAL PROTECTION

The identification of practical claims in the original position precedes the insight that in the real future world the members of the society do not have the same preconditions (resources and talents) to struggle for their own interests themselves, even if the procedures for intermediation of interests are constituted fairly. That's why the participants in the negotiation would already in the initial situation insist on fixing general interests as much as possible to constitute inalienable fundamental rights. These have to be consistent with each other, so that they exhibit an objective quality, because they are shared intersubjectively as the participants of this mediative state will have granted them to themselves mutually. This constellation of interests corresponds to the idea of the Pareto-Optimum, a situation of distribution where nobody's position could be improved without worsening that of another.[7] Similarly, the task among the people in the initial situation is to concede options to each other until there are no more options that can be granted without curtailing others.

The resulting basic rights are to be awarded to everyone up from birth, because they are due to common impartiality and serve for the implementation of the five following options. So the declared rights are precious to each individual. They do not clash with other general interests, but maybe at worst only future particular interests. Therefore it is important to designate these interests, but they do not attain practical impact until they are each worded as political rules.

- The right to integral basic life resources would be agreed to among the participants in the initial situation. Because with the veil of ignorance none ultimately knows what time one would be born in, one would like to be sure that this fundamental option as a right to life is guaranteed.
- The claim for mobility in being at liberty to choose and to enter any place of residence in public space—this as a general interest would be decided too.
- The award of universal rights of integrity and sovereignty of the person, as well as freedom of opinion, religion and information likewise belong to the options, which all would include for themselves, as is already stated by Locke in his contributions.[8]

---

[7] Wulf Gaertner, *Pareto-Effizienz und normative Ökonomik* (Osnabrück: Universität Fachbereich Wirtschaftswissenschaften, 1993), pp. 18ff.

[8] David Boucher and Paul Kelly (eds), *The Social Contract from Hobbes to Rawls* (London: Routledge, 1997), p. 16; Jeremy Waldron, "John Locke: Social Contract

- The goal of maximum economic options includes the claim to property and a quota of participation in profits from any co-operation.
- The claim to be involved in the power which is exercised over one is also of interest to everyone. It would be put into effect by the political predefinition of majority democracy.

But some of the included rules, which do not refer to plausible liberty rights, need to be discussed in more detail.

PRACTICE RULES OF SOCIAL CO-EXISTENCE

The definition of these rules or procedures is necessary for a fair negotiation between particular interests. They are important to the persons in the initial situation because they do not yet know their later particular interests but they would like the intermediation of those interests to be based on fair principles.

- The participants of the initial situation would therefore arrive at the resolution that particular interests should be decided by majority vote, in case of a *consensus* becoming difficult due to increasing differences between the interests. Democratic models of intermediation between interests of global extent—as Hösle argued—surely would be specified.[9] Thus the principle of equality as well as the fundamental right to participation in political power would be taken into account.
- Because the veil of ignorance also hides the affiliation to a certain generation, the relation between generations is quite crucial and therefore regulation is needed. So there is—as already mentioned by Rawls—a demand on the principle of sustainability for justice between generations, i.e. only renewable resources. Thus, the accumulation of debts or the practice of leaving environmental costs or risks to subsequent generations is also to be prohibited.[10]

---

vs. Political Anthropology," in Boucher and Kelly (eds), pp. 52ff; Martin P. Tompson, "Locke's Contract in Context," in Boucher and Kelly (eds), pp. 85ff.

[9] Vittorio Hösle, *Moral und Politik—Grundlagen einer Politischen Ethik für das 21. Jahrhundert* (München: Verlag C. H. Beck, 1997).

[10] Andreas Suchanek, "Politischer Liberalismus und das Problem der intergenerationellen Gerechtigkeit," in *John Rawls' politischer Liberalismus* ed. I. Pies and M. Leschke (Tübingen: Verlag Mohr (Siebeck), 1995).

But the main challenge is to deal with the social question as an urgent task of the intermediation in the original position.

Just as with all the other aspects of co-existence already discussed, the individual in the initial situation has to calculate towards an equilibrium of costs and benefits and to balance the securities that are desired as necessities. Concerning financial income, the participants of negotiation would agree to a certain rule of distribution. Thus, if someone has the possibility of an income of any amount, this makes him unequal compared the others. In accordance with Rawls' second difference principle everybody would have to gain an advantage out of it. The question of the exact definition of the share's extent is subject to the consideration of those who don't know whether they will be the one benefiting from a share of other's income or vice versa. So the amount of share would be located somewhere between 0 and 100 percent of the income. If some had to deliver more than 50% of their income, then they would consider this amount of share as unfair, as all others together would get more from this income, than the earner, although he/she had invested efforts in it. That is why the one who has income may have an interest in letting the amount of share converge near 0%. But as the people involved in the original position are aware of the two different possible situations—either the dispensing or the benefiting—a rate of share at 50% would be chosen. In this ambivalent role of potentially being the beneficiary of the other's profits and keeper of one's own income at the same time, a probability of 1:1 would exist of finding oneself on one or the other side of the average income in the real life. In such prospects each rational individual would vote for the following code of distribution: "I am ready to divide half of any income I obtain among all others, if everybody does it in the same way." So everyone should share with everyone else, but would keep the main portion of his or her economic efforts. With such a manner of distribution the two principles of Rawls can be seen as fulfilled. However real people may regard this conception as strange, because any principle of efficiency and causation of the production of value seem to be ignored, as people suddenly participate in an income, they didn't made any contribution to—so where is the justice in this rule? All economic achievements, including income—afforded by many generations before—are not to be regarded as the product of a particular individual, but always as a result of co-operation with mankind as a whole.

Nevertheless the distribution of income is determined in such a way that the individual is incited to be economically active, which is to everybody's benefit. This leads to a justification of a relative basic income, unconditional but not as a social security at any costs. This suggested rule of redistribution thus is a consistent compromise between the justice principle

411

of achievement and the justice principle of equality as both are ranked equally which easily can be shown arithmetically.

If we assume that the income one earns (x_i)—because someone else is willing to pay—represents his or her produced results according to a principle of achievement the, distribution mode for the individual's outcome $(\hat{y})$ would be the following.

$$\mathrm{I}: \hat{y} = x_i$$

And if a distributive mode keeps to the justice principle of equality, one's outgoings would consist of the average income of all individuals $(\bar{x})$.

$$\mathrm{II}: \hat{y} = \bar{x}$$

Both modes in a synthesis would be a consistent compromise of the two equal rules in one equation.

$$\hat{y} = \frac{\mathrm{I} + \mathrm{II}}{2} = \frac{x_i + \bar{x}}{2} = \frac{x_i}{2} + \frac{\bar{x}}{2}$$

So one shares one's income and gets half of the average income back.

To visualize that a redistributive share of 50 percent of the average income was not found just intuitively or arbitrarily, the following model calculation may be helpful. There is the assumption that the redistributive rate can reach a value between 0 and 100 percent—0 percent by exclusive validity of the achievement principle and 100 percent by exclusive validity of the equality principle of justice. The Rawlsian attenuation of the notion of absolute equality by introducing the difference principle is due to the insight that a strict equal distribution of all profits of cooperation reduces the amount of goods to share because of decreasing economical incentives. So if one assumes that value creation decreases with increasing redistributive share, one could draw a curve of all hypothetically possible levels of a redistributive welfare state.

The dark part of the columns within the picture above represents the share of the average income, which accrues of the basic income. A general formula for the income to be expected in any welfare state with a redistributive rate $(1 \geq r \geq 0)$ and a basic income $(E_g = r\,\bar{x})$ is as follows:

$$\hat{y} = x_i(1 - r) + r\bar{x}$$

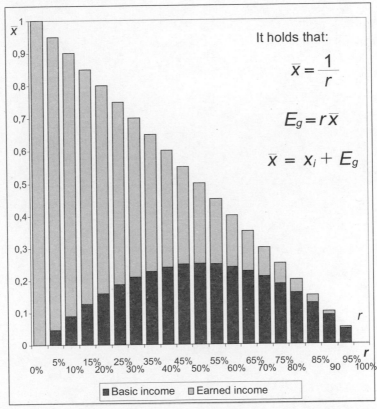

Graph 1: Amount of Basic and earned income by redistributive rate

So it is obvious that an optimum can be allocated at a rate of 50 percent where the "advantage of the least advantaged" (Rawls) is maximised—known as a so called "takehalf-solution." This leads to a substantiation of a relative basic income, which is unconditional but not existence-securing. For the final allocation of a just level of redistribution there is an empirical gap to fill. So the outlined ideal correlation between value creation and redistribution has to be analyzed by empirical macroeconomical data, because an optimum of basic income depends on it.

In an era of globalisation there is no way of thinking of the welfare state as anything other then global. A global welfare system which guarantees for every inhabitant of the world at least an unconditional basic income of

413

nowadays about two hundred US dollars per month minimum[11] would secure economical inclusion and satisfy the basic needs of everybody.

---

[11] Calculation based on data from the Berlin-Institute for World Population and Global Development (see Haub).

THE PSYCHOLOGICAL ASPECTS OF PEACE

Bahman Dadgostar and Ann Hallock

The Children of Humanity are each other's limbs
That shares an origin in their creator
When one limb passes its days in pain
The other limbs cannot remain easy
You who feel no pain at the suffering of others
It is not fitting you be called human
Saadi (1184-1283)
[Graces the Hall of Nations entrance to the
United Nations building in New York]

THE GROWTH OF HUMAN CONSCIOUSNESS

The heart of this discourse will primarily address the growth of human consciousness, the unity of all humankind, and the development of the choice to live in peace for the sake of all humanity. The challenges we face are essentially spiritual and moral. A vast change in human consciousness is underway—it is a process by which humanity's spiritual life evolves. We believe that there is no credible secular replacement for religious belief as a force capable of generating self-discipline and restoring a commitment to moral behavior. Everyone on the planet has been touched in some way by the breakdown of the religious and political institutions which traditionally have provided stability. We are currently faced with masses of people at odds with each other. These conflicts arise over diverse cultural, ethnic, and religious beliefs, as well as attitudes towards education and a great disparity in economic resources. Added to this are racial divisions and disparaging or dismissive attitudes towards disadvantaged groups such as women and children.

The search for justice and international peace yields new perceptions of the individual's role in society and the role of forgiveness, reconciliation, and intercultural relations. In addition, the sharing of resources and wealth must be addressed. There is also a need for the involvement of young people and the possibility of youth leadership to ease us into the twenty-first century.

Over the past century, as millions have fled their homelands to escape from persecution, there have been huge migrations of people as families and individuals sought refuge. There have been tidal waves of people sweeping across Europe, Asia, and Africa. Some have stayed in those places, while others moved on into Australasia and North and South America.

415

One result of this movement is the contact between races and cultures, which has exposed nearly everyone to norms and practices (foods, religions, histories, customs, languages, clothing, and music) about which our forefathers knew very little. This has caused a great deal of upheaval. Beneath all the dislocation and suffering, through shared discoveries and shared adjustments to losses, peoples of diverse cultures are being brought face to face with their common humanity. This process awakens a growth of consciousness, even as it is stubbornly opposed in some societies or welcomed as a release from meaningless and suffocating limitations inherited from the cultural past in other societies. As each learns that the earth's inhabitants are indeed like the leaves of one tree, they then can see that the earth can become one homeland and all humans are citizens, not of distinct countries, but of one planet—the Earth itself. Of course, it can also generate polarization.

Since the title of this discourse is "The Psychological Aspects of Peace," and it addresses the concept of choice regarding behavior, we note that the possibility of choice is inborn and comes from the inner adult ego state, which has a biological basis, yet needs to develop through a psycho-educational process. We will first address the use of aggression, violence, power, and anger and we will address the belief that anger is an emotion that needs release. We will show the developmental growth of consciousness and morality as a way of understanding why some people choose to solve their problems through aggression and violent behavior, while others utilize discussion, interaction, peaceful negotiation, and respect for others. We will also consider the role of family in creating the degree of organized consciousness, reason, rationality, and behavior (primarily aggression).

The psychological causes of violence have been categorized in *The Psychology of Peace*[1] with five sets of ideas:

- Disconnects—internal mental processes (conflict within the self);
- The Power of the Situation—external situations impacting mental processes;
- Beliefs;
- Personality—lifelong personality traits;
- Passions of War—society-wide psychological processes and emotions.

---

[1] Rachel M. MacNair, *The Psychology of Peace: An Introduction* (Westport: Praeger, 2003).

Disconnects

Researchers studying punitive behavior have found that moral disengagement is the psychological process that leads to the most inhumane behavior because it removes inhibitions to violence. This type of cognitive transformation changes reprehensible conduct into "good" conduct and can be done three ways:

- distorted moral justifications;
- comparison to worse conduct, making this conduct seem less consequential;
- use of euphemisms.

There are other effective ways to disengage:

- Scapegoating or deferring to authority—displacing or diffusing the responsibility or detrimental effects;
- Discounting the Effects—minimizing, ignoring, or distorting those detrimental effects;
- Discounting the Victim—dehumanizing or blaming the victim, labelling the victim in demeaning ways; i.e. as a "parasite, defective or deficient, diseased, non-human, non-person, animal, even as an inanimate object or waste product";
- Distancing—hand to hand combat is real and tough, but dropping bombs seems easier;
- Doubling—creating two identities—one who does the killing and one who is a good family man;
- Compartmentalizing—people put different parts of their lives into different compartments that they seal off from one another. Thus their beliefs can be different from their actions;
- Intellectualizing—involves a focus on reasoning that allows for violence without the accompanying negative emotions.

Therefore, through the use of disconnects, one may have more difficulty seeing that a choice of behavior exists.

The Power of the Situation

Throughout history, while most humans have had a strong aversion to killing other humans, many governing bodies have sent their citizens off to war. However, one can find many modern examples of men in combat attempting to avoid killing. Operant conditioning is a label used to describe behavioral modification techniques where a person can be taught through a series of stimulus-response activities to overcome their reluctance to be aggressive in stressful situations. This has been used by military organizations to overcome resistance to killing.

Many psychologists today warn about current video games because there are fears that many young people are being mindlessly taught in a sort of "murder simulation" by these games which could result in increased violence. Even violent media as a whole—movies and TV shows with graphic violence, watched while eating popcorn and other treats—can serve as a form of classic *operant conditioning*. This conditioning is called *desensitization*. This can lead to these viewers becoming inured to brutality and insensitive to the suffering of others and thus prone to the choice of aggression rather than the choice of peace to solve problems.

Beliefs
What people believe about situations affects their behaviour:

- The Just World View—a belief that the world is just—is a psychological mechanism that helps maintain the status quo even when a situation is clearly unjust. This creates a false sense of safety and also tends to blame the victim of injustice;
- Realpolitik—a belief that politics is about maximizing power as the safest course. If you are visibly strong, no one will dare attack you;
- Machismo—men should behave in a macho way, blustering and intolerant, which may lead to violent behavior;
- Violence is inevitable—human nature, it's in our genes;
- Retaliation—belief that justice demands a response in kind, vengeance;
- Violence as a Last Resort—the "Just War" doctrine—when injustice is great and therefore violence is justified and deemed necessary;
- Destructive Obedience to Authority—the authority defines reality and its meaning; therefore participants acquiesce to this authority, often a different experiential state from their own;
- Group Think—groups can make much more irrational decisions than individuals would do on their own due to the social pressure of the group;
- Technology—effectiveness can mobilize people to initiate violence.

These beliefs are examples of what can drive people to choose aggression and forget that they have other choices that may lead to peaceful negotiation.

Personality

According to this theory, some personality types may be more prone to certain actions than others. The highly authoritarian personality is more likely to provide political support for a dictator or violent social policies. The Machiavellian personality is more likely to supply technical support to a dictator by selling weapons. The narcissistic personality—grandiose, lacking empathy and compassion—can contribute to violent acts and as a leader can cause great problems. The antisocial personality is indifferent to the fate or feelings of other people, and comprises the cold-blooded killers and sadists.

Passions of War

According to Eric Berne, renowned psychiatrist and author of *Games People Play*[2] war is one of the games people play. It is a third degree game (meaning everyone gets hurt and can possibly die) so it is a very serious "game," but it is played much like children play to show who has a better toy than others and who has superiority over the other.

The attractions of war (what it is that makes people supportive of war):

- Pride—belonging, helping, a sense of aliveness;
- Meaning—gives meaning to a boring life;
- Target—projection of self-doubts or self-hatred onto someone else;
- Group cohesion—external threat gets everyone to pull together to defend their security;
- Virtues of discipline, courage and self-sacrifice for the greater good of the group or nation;
- War hysteria replaces the anxiety of uncertainty, everyone has a role;
- *War as pathology*: the universality of blood sacrifice. Religions have ended ritualized blood sacrifices, yet humanity has moved only slightly away from violence as the solution to problems. War may offer displacement of aggression onto an enemy, and it is now sanctioned and made sacred;

---

[2] Eric Berne, *Games People Play* (New York: Ballentine Books, 1964).

- Frustration—may lead to aggression;
- Catharsis—letting some anger out may actually lead to more aggression;
- Hatred—can lead to intractable feuds and difficult problems;
- Cognitive Dissonance and Effort Justification—if you have put effort, resources and energy into achieving a certain outcome, that outcome must be valuable;
- Conduct disorders, depression, substance abuse, personality disorders, bi-polar and schizophrenia.

There are other pathological pathways that lead to choosing violence in order to solve problems. When citizens are losing their belief in a leader or government, the leader may look for an outside scapegoat to focus the peoples' dissatisfaction on and rouse them to war against that group instead of against the leader himself. There are many scientific historical researchers who go into great detail about the use of scapegoating violence[3] and they have found evidence to illustrate that rituals of human sacrifice were used to bind a culture, to help focus the culture, and to increase social camaraderie. The sacrifice, human or other, was used to inspire awe, to deflect mob violence, and to bring people under control. The ritual was used primarily to restore order. These rulers were often aided and abetted by the religious leaders of the day. The end result was to keep or enhance the leaders' power and induce harmony among the people they controlled.

At the level of the family or individual, the excuse for war may be, "We love you so we have to attack with a war in order to help you and protect you." Or more destructively, "If you do not kill the enemy then you will be killed." Basically the idea is to create fear in a person or group (family) in order to get permission to behave aggressively. This is easiest to do with people who have grown up learning that there are no rights for others and whatever one needs must be gotten with aggression and violence:

> The motivations for today's warfare and violence can often be traced to deep psychological feelings of ethnic identity, animosity, and an acceptance of violence as an effective way for small groups or even individuals to confront what they see as aggressions. (MacNair)

Some present day government leaders use war instead of scapegoat violence. Power-hungry leaders provide the gravest example of this modern

---

[3] See, for instance, Gil Bailie, *Violence Unveiled: Humanity at the Crossroads* (New York: Crossroad Publishing, 1999); Rene Girard, *Violence and the Sacred*, trans. Patrick Gregory (Baltimore: Johns Hopkins University Press, 1979).

violence when they incite their citizens to war against another country by re-asserting nationalism, ethnicity, or religious zeal. Adding fear to this highly flammable emotional mixture of jealousy, envy, rivalry, and resentment triggers the values of loyalty and shared purpose to oppose the outside "other."

CONSCIOUSNESS, especially each individual's consciousness of the value of their inner convictions and their awareness that they can make the choice of peace, is the only way to avoid this conflagration of volatile emotions.

We live in an age where we are encouraged to manoeuver for social and economic advantage over and against others, even in petty rivalries.

What can we do? What must happen to bring about the consciousness that will allow us to find the reality of love and unity in all things and all people?

We need to look at the growth and psychodynamic development of human beings and the stages of consciousness. There are many theories of human growth and development and many studies on states of consciousness to support both scientifically and mathematically that everything is based on mathematics—technology, communications, the nervous system, thermodynamics—everything, every function. But mathematics itself is based on the non-material. Mathematics is based on spirituality: wholeness and integration are all based on mathematics. You can't quantify mathematics but mathematics quantifies everything. Everything must be balanced and the lack of balance creates problems.

We hope to tip the balance towards peace and understanding and a new way of life: to show some of the steps needed to create a world-embracing outlook and to foster a flowering of civilization based on choices made by individuals at the grassroots level. This transformation will come about gradually, which will make certain it endures. When people try to address everything at once, invariably what is seen as the solution becomes its undoing. Peace-building over the long term requires the transformation of society. This transformation must be based on justice, education for all, alleviation of poverty, and the abandonment of deeply rooted personal prejudices as a deliberate act of choice.

Real peace is individual peace. Individual peace includes freedom of choice. Without freedom of choice there is no rationality, because the lack of choice promotes war within the self. If a person is in conflict or at war within himself he cannot create external peace in the family or society. Even children of four to eight months of age have begun to realize that they have choices. Most children naturally look for fairness. When children are supported in fairness and given choices, they learn respect and justice.

Respect and justice create awareness; awareness leads to consciousness and reason, and from consciousness and reason comes the ability to choose.

Further we can choose to eliminate racial, ethnic, and religious prejudice and the oppression of women and children. There is only one race—the human race—but there is racism. The artificial racial categories that people have created to explain differences in facial features, pigmentation, and other distinctions have been proven scientifically to be incorrect. DNA studies have shown that with all our diversity, we are all very closely related to each other no matter where we live on the planet. Racism is a belief in biological superiority which is a contamination of our rational mind. Feelings of superiority are not feelings of hate, but they inspire hatred. We can choose to promote peace and reconciliation. Our consciousness can help us realize the oneness of humanity and thus uncover the unity of the world of humanity and of all elements of creation. All of this takes intention, confirmation, and action.

Such intention, confirmation, and action can only be achieved by people who have unity of conscience within themselves, from which flows integrity. This integrity inspires unstinting action on the part of the individual and inspires groups of people to work with one accord for the protection of all humanity. People who truly love themselves do not harm themselves or others. Freedom empowers both good and evil, but we believe that opening up the inner consciousness of each would, in turn, confer the values of freedom of choice, respect for justice, and respect for the choices of others.

Children can be liberated from the darkness of ignorance by opening up the concept of choice and helping them to use their choices. In this manner they can be guided to the light of true understanding. From that understanding will be laid the prerequisites of concord and understanding and enduring unity. In loving our children, we have to teach them to be responsible in their choices on behalf of themselves, the family, the community, and humankind.

In order to liberate humankind from the darkness of ignorance to a place where rights and responsibilities, justice and mercy, wisdom and compassion are balanced, we must understand human development and how humans learn. Of course, many people have studied this in great detail. There are many moral development theorists and most are basically in agreement, even on the stages addressed. For the purpose of this paper and the concept of choice, we will primarily focus on the work of Jean Piaget, but also draw on the contributions of Erik Erikson, Lawrence Kohlberg, and

Carol Gilligan and the Tantric traditions.[4] Ken Wilber's approach is another very comprehensive and inclusive approach. However, it is more complex than necessary for this paper.[5]

The levels or stages of development represent levels of organization or complexity which the individual has the capacity to attain. Each stage represents a higher capacity for care and compassion as the person integrates the principles and values of that stage and the tasks of the levels that came before. These become a part of the character of the person. The stages of moral development also follow cognitive development: each stage is a prerequisite for the one that follows. Piaget describes four major stages leading to the capacity for adult thought. The ability to advance morally in consciousness is predicated on advancing cognitive abilities, but it does not mean that a person will advance morally. Consciousness as well as cognitive ability can be blocked by family, society, and/or the circumstances to which the person is subjected.

LEVELS OF DEVELOPMENT

Level I.
Pre-conventional Morality parallels **Pre-operational Thought** in development. This is Piaget's sensory motor stage, Erikson's trust, autonomy, initiative, and industry stage, Kohlberg's egocentric stage and Gilligan's *Selfish* stage of development—in Tantric traditions, this is known as the first to third chakras corresponding to food, sex, power. Basically, this level is *me*; my body; survival drives; it resides in a person's own needs and wants, and is selfish and egocentric.

Stage 1 is characterized by an obedience and punishment orientation. There is a sense of good and bad but the person is unable to sort out moral dilemmas. There is a use of magical thinking, "this happened because I did something bad." The egocentricity of the stage renders the person unable to see another's point of view.

---

[4] See Jack Grebb, Harold I. Kaplan. and Benjamin J. Sadock (eds), *Synopsis of Psychiatry* (Baltimore: Williams and Wilkins, 1994); Karen Kirst-Ashman, *Understanding Human Behavior and Social Environment* (Belmont CA: Brooks Cole, 2007); John F. Longres, *Human Behavior in the Social Environment*, 2nd edn (Seattle: Peacock, 1995).
[5] See Ken Wilber, *Integral Psychology: Consciousness, Spirit, Psychology, Therapy* (Boston: Shambala, 2000); *Integral Spirituality: A Startling New Role for Religion in the Modern and Post-Modern World* (Boston and London: Integral Books, 2006).

Stage 2 is characterized by an instrumentalist-relativist orientation. The person is motivated by a need to satisfy his or her own desires. They may share or may hit back when hit.

Level II.

Conventional Morality parallels **Concrete Operations** in development. Piaget sees this stage as when egocentric thought is replaced by operational thought. Erikson sees this stage as one of forming an identity and the ability to share with and give to another person. Kohlberg sees this stage as one of pleasing others, performing good or right roles, and maintaining order. Gilligan calls this stage (the beginning of) *Care*. In Tantric traditions this corresponds to the fourth and fifth chakras relating to the heart and communication.

Stage 3 is characterized by the ability to follow rules, to reason, and to have a code of values. Kohlberg sees these values as shared values. It is the good boy/nice girl stage motivated by the need to avoid rejection or disapproval. Egocentrism gives way to ethnocentrism and leads to the exclusion of those not in one's group.

(*Note*: children who become overly invested in rules may show obsessive-compulsive behavior and children who resist a code of values are often seen as wilful and inactive. The most desirable developmental outcome is for the child to attain a healthy respect for rules and to understand there are legitimate exceptions to every rule)

Stage 4 is characterized by a law and order mentality. This level is *us*; the mind; and shared values and is motivated by a need to take action to keep from being criticized by a true authority figure.

Level III.

Post–conventional parallels **Formal Operations** in development. Piaget sees this stage as gaining the ability to think abstractly, to reason deductively; and more complicatedly, to reason inductively—from the general to the specific. Erikson sees this as the generativity and integrity stages. Kohlberg finds that moral values reside in principles separate from those who enforce them, and apart from a person's identification with the enforcing group. Gilligan calls this stage *Universal Care*. In Tantric traditions this is the sixth chakra, corresponding to the psyche.

Stage 5 is Legalistic Orientation; world centric; *all of us*; the level of the spirit; motivated by community respect for all, respecting the social order and living under legally determined laws.

Stage 6 is Universal, Ethical Orientation; individual moral judgment is motivated by one's own conscience.

Kohlberg gives the following points, which are relevant in helping us to understand the process of development (MacNair, p. 64):

- Stage development is invariant. One must progress through the stages in order;
- People do not understand moral reasoning more than one stage beyond their own;
- Individuals are attracted cognitively to reasoning one level beyond their own present level when it resolves more difficulties;
- Movement through stages happens when cognitive disequilibrium occurs;
- People look for solutions at the next level when their current outlook is not adequate to cope with a specific moral dilemma;
- It is quite possible for human beings to be physically mature but not morally mature.

Gilligan, while researching women's cognitive and moral development, postulated a fourth level of development for both men and women. She calls this level *Integrated*. This level relates very well to our theme of consciousness and the ability to make choices.

Level IV.
Integrated. This level corresponds to the Tantric traditional seventh and eighth charkas, which relate to the spiritual. Up until this level of development, men and women have a different voice and a different logic that rules their thinking and moral development. The male seeks autonomy while the female seeks relationship; the male looks for justice, the female seeks to give care and mercy; the male looks at rights, the female sees responsibilities; the male focuses on rules, the female on connections; the male hurts feelings to save rules, the female breaks rules to save feelings. But at the fourth level, the masculine and feminine meet and become one. A paradoxical union of autonomy and relationship, rights and responsibilities, agency and communion, wisdom and compassion, justice and mercy ensue from that unity of male and female. Their thinking is no longer dominated by the restrictions of gender.

Development of the capacity for care and compassion for the most part involves decreasing egocentrism and increasing consciousness—the ability to take other people, places, and things into account, and to increasingly extend care to each. For each step along the developmental path to a higher level, one includes more and more others with whom one shares a genuine concern and compassion, hopefully until humanity as a whole is included.

We must note that under conditions of stress and situations such as war or other catastrophes, people can and sometimes do regress to earlier levels, even to the earliest stages of survival mentality.

These are the theoretical building blocks of consciousness development. The remainder of this paper will explain the practical applications for individuals and families to assist them in the generative process of consciousness development to enable the concept of choosing peace to take root. It will also delve into the problems that interfere with that development.

The science of psychology is a foundation for healing some of the problems that individuals, families, and social groups are faced with. We already know that unbalanced leaders can cause grave problems for the world. For example, a leader suffering from bi-polar depression can, in a time of grandiosity from a mood swing, without constraints and aided by the support of opportunists and unscrupulous people, cause great and long lasting suffering for innumerable people in the world. Years of mortality, homelessness, hopelessness, and Post Traumatic Stress Disorder ensue for many people. Not only will those who are direct victims of this crime suffer. Media technologies such as television and internet connections make it not only possible but probable that the people who watch and hear about it are traumatized also.

One war may create hundreds of smaller wars. Some of those small wars occur within the unit of the family. The legacy of war is pain and suffering that goes on sometimes for generations, with broken families, broken people, wounded children, and psychological trauma. In psychology, we refer to "the wounded child," and this means the child who has been neglected, abused, or otherwise mistreated. Often parents who are traumatized are unable to attend to their children because of grief and depression and so neglect of the child ensues. Sometimes parents identify with the people who have traumatized them—this is called "identification with the aggressor"—and then they become aggressive with their own children, causing them harm. Another consequence is the problem of impulse control, leading to acting out behaviors and instability in the home, and the unpredictability of parental care and concern. The "wounded inner child ego state" stays with the person as they become an angry adolescent and continues (without the intervention of psychological treatment) to become an adult with a huge amount of smouldering and dangerous rage.

One of the worst consequences of violence and of war is the rape and sexual abuse of women and children. These assaults can result in both long-lasting physical trauma and emotional problems. Of the many consequences to women and children are shame, destruction of self-esteem, and deep anger at the injustice. Difficulties in being close to and caring for others can

426

be particularly disastrous for a woman's future, not to mention the burden of family shame and blame to which a woman is often subjected. For children, similar problems can occur. Boys especially, but girls also, can become angry, aggressive, and violent adults. Their targets are often people in authority. Often they become averse to taking direction or working for anyone because of the abuse they suffered. Sometimes, the whole of humanity becomes their target since their revenge is against the unjust and cruel world of mankind.

Violence perpetuates violence. Violence causes pathology and imbalance for the person, and from the imbalance revenge may result. The wounded inner child responds inappropriately to moral decisions. The ability to think things through objectively is blocked from the adult ego state and the response comes from a wounded rebellious child position or from a critical parent ego state.

These problems can seriously interfere with the individual's ability to make choices or to understand that they have a choice.

Advances in mental health care and advances in knowledge and understanding of brain chemistry and function has allowed professionals to give care and understanding that were not available to people as recently as forty years ago. Now that we know and understand that sexual crimes are about power abuses and not about sexuality, it is easier to help victims understand and come to terms with what has happened to them. Identifying post-traumatic stress disorder and being able to intervene and treat the disabling effects is helping many individuals and families to be able to carry on after a traumatic event. The recognition that people do have mental health issues has helped to allow many people, who in the past would never have been treated, to get help. Medication for many serious disorders is allowing people to stay with their families and to retain employment. There have been advances in the care and earlier diagnosis of bi-polar disorder. There is now the use of psychotropic medications to treat not only bi-polar disorder but other troubling conditions such as obsessive-compulsive disorder, impulse control disorders, anxiety, depression, and many others. A better understanding of brain electrical activity has kept many epileptics functional without seizures and has calmed many irritable and explosive individuals. More effective drugs for the treatment of psychosis has allowed continued functioning and stemmed the degenerative impact of schizophrenia.

However, anger and aggression can originate from what children learn in their families. Unresolved anger with parents contributes to acting-out behaviors. Constantly criticism and blaming of a child can lead to their experiencing a smouldering anger or a sense of inferiority, which may come bursting out in an explosion of rage. Punishing innocent others is another form of releasing pent-up anger—for example, beating up a younger sibling or kicking the family pet.

In psychology, we know that the other side of depression is anger. Some people believe that anger and depression are uncontrollable. However, we have learned that situational depression and anger can both be controlled by thoughts and actions. Changing how you think about a situation can change your reaction to it. Suppose you are in a crowd of people and someone bumps into you and steps hard on the back of your foot from behind. At first you are surprised and annoyed that this rude thing has happened, but you turn and discover the person who has hit you is blind. Your demeanor changes and now you are trying to assist this person to find his way amidst the crowd. The same thing has happened, but your reaction is totally different.

When our patients come to us with situational depression and anger, we teach them to change their thoughts and to control their actions and the situation improves. It should be noted that the biological inborn feelings (instinctual drives) of hunger, fear, anger, and libido are natural, and the energy that flows from these drives is a natural phenomenon. One does not control the flow or intensity of these drives. However, one does control the expression of the energy of the drive. For example: the expression of anger is a choice. So too is the expression of hunger: we control when, where, what, and how we eat. We make the same choices with sexuality: we choose when we will have sex, where, with whom, and how we will express our desire. Since fear plays such a big role in keeping us safe and secure, we have fewer controls about the expression of fear. Yet when fear is out of control, people generally seek help from others. Fear is contagious: it is easy to alarm others with our fears and for others to become uncomfortable when we are afraid. All of these drives carry a heavy amount of emotion along with them. People can learn that they can control their own emotions, that their emotions belong to them, that they are responsible for them, and they can have control over them. In order to make good choices, people must learn that feelings do not need to equal actions—in other words, if you feel angry with someone, you do *not* have to *do* something about it. You do have to decide what you are going to do to help yourself handle the feeling. You may decide to share the feeling with someone, but you don't need to demonstrate the feeling. Words can substitute for the action. This is actually revolutionary thinking and acting—a revolution in human development and consciousness.

All human beings develop a public self that they hide behind in social situations. Some people go too far or hide too deeply, creating a false self and actually losing a sense of their true self. Generally, this happens because within a family or social group people are not listening. They are too busy demanding certain behaviors from the vulnerable person who fears showing his or her real needs and feelings. A false self emerges. When people depend too much for too long on the false self, they find it easy to lie to others and deceive themselves about their true motives. They trick others into thinking they are good/successful/attractive, and so forth. Hollywood is all about image. When a person or a culture begins to rely too much on its image, its values become impersonal and the heart of the human being, which is such a rich source of love and spirituality, is deadened and the true values of love and care for others are lost. This type of problem is also called narcissism. As cultures and people wake from the deadening effects of pretending and image-making, they become more able to choose peaceful approaches. They then are able to listen, not just with their ears, but with their hearts and souls. First, they need to hear their own hurts and fears. This means someone has to listen empathically to them and help them hear themselves. Once they can hear their true feelings and acknowledge their real self, they will then be able to hear the cries of their neighbors.

We have the tools to help people wake up to themselves and to others. We know that families can raise a child to be a great source of support for human lives *or* to become an enemy of the people. The world of humanity needs to know it has choices and these choices can be made available to everyone once global priorities are focused on the welfare of all and on unity and equality. Prejudice is destructive because it interferes with hearing the voice and heart of another person. For example, "I have the answer before you talk. I know what you will say. I know what you want (and I don't like it!)" In reality, the truth comes from the conflict and clash of ideas exchanged in an environment of love and understanding. For example, "We see different things. We each have a different perspective. When we put them together we get a clearer picture of the reality of our situation. I can't see your side from over here: only you can see it. Even though we see different things, and say different things, we can still accept each other and love each other." When we can do this, we find acceptance and understanding, and with that understanding and acceptance we can experience empathy and from the empathy we can know love.

Love is felt in the heart, deeply within each person. Art in its various forms expresses this very well. Rumi describes it in his writings like this: love reaches deeply into the heart of any situation, any condition we encounter. Spirituality is what connects you to the source of love. From the source of love there flows forgiveness, justice, respect, generosity, and hope. If one were to think of designing a home built of love for a healthy human being, that beautiful home could be made of four walls. The foundation of this perfect home is hope, one wall is respect, one is justice, one is forgiveness, and the last is reason. The ceiling and solid roof is love. The door of the house is generosity, and the key to that house is spirituality.

There is so much potential for the development of higher levels of human consciousness that will empower the individual to think before acting and to make choices of peace rather than aggression. The growth of unity and concern for all peoples is within our reach, but the danger is that those with ulterior motives—many of them in positions of power because of their ability to keep in thrall their servile followers, followers who are still caught in unconsciousness and a penchant for violence—will fall back on the lowest levels of human interaction and lead us all into unending wars and strife.

The small percentage of humans who have been fortunate enough to develop a higher consciousness through experience, wisdom, and education must work tirelessly to achieve a dialogue with as many receptive and thirsty souls as can be reached. We must encourage each of them to grow to understand the concept of using their internal mental processes to develop the consciousness of the inner self, which in turn can lead to the utilization of fruitful discussion, negotiation, and choices to live in peace, encouraging them not to be too attached to what has been passed down to them, but to rise above their drive for survival and quests for retaliation into a universal vision of care and concern for all. This is our fervent hope for the future.

In hopelessness there is hope, walk the royal road of hopefulness.
In darkness turn toward the light, for many suns are shining.

                                                                Rumi

THE ISTANBUL DECLARATION

THE ISTANBUL DECLARATION

An Interfaith Perspective on Globalisation for the Common Good: The Sixth Annual International Conference

"A Non-Violent Path to Conflict Resolution and Peacebuilding"

Istanbul 2007 • Fatih University

"All roads lead to Istanbul." Meeting place of two continents and capital of two empires (the Byzantine and the Ottoman), Istanbul has been a crossroads of cultures for nearly 1800 years. The city offers a powerful metaphor for understanding and reconciliation between East and West. We gather here on the beautiful campus of Fatih University, grateful for their warm hospitality and support. We come together from many countries, six faiths, and countless areas of expertise to continue our exploration of pathways to Globalisation for the Common Good. In Turkey we experience the vital bio-diversity of the Earth and the rich cultural diversity of humankind. Our time here has been richly inspiring and profoundly motivating. It has yielded a very fruitful dialogue.

In this sixth international conference we affirm our shared commitment to non-violent conflict resolution and the building of cultures of peace around the world. The urgency of the challenge is particularly apparent in a region of the world that is so tragically afflicted by violence. The time has come for concrete new democratic and non-violent strategies that reflect global, regional, and local cultural and spiritual realities.

We recognize the deep-seated human desire for harmony in diversity, the source of our strength. We strongly acknowledge the interdependence of peace with justice and ecological sustainability. We recognize the urgent need for dialogue not only among the religions but also between religion and the sciences and between the religious and secular spheres. The strong engagement of these dimensions of human endeavor is vital if we are to address the critical issues that arise in the wake of globalisation.

We believe that education is the key that unlocks the door to globalisation for the common good. We call in particular for approaches to education that nurture interreligious and intercultural understanding, awareness of interdependence, moral values, and global citizenship. These essential elements shape personal decisions of social consequence, concern for the well being of others, and respect for other human beings and for the whole of the planetary community.

The movement from the myth of redemptive violence to the new story of restorative justice has informed our inquiry and inspired our deliberations. We urge the recognition of the spiritual dimension of the global dilemma in the early twenty-first century and of the spiritual component that must be present in the solutions we attempt.

We believe that enduring change emerges through the cooperative activity of men and women. Visionary activists must therefore work towards the evolutionary social transformation of fundamental values, especially those bearing on the empowerment of women.

We strongly acknowledge the vital importance of the following critical challenges for the twenty-first century. Each is a source of violence. But as we address each urgent issue, we open up a wellspring of peace. The path to that end leads through respectful encounter with the other, open dialogue, and cooperative common action to address the problems that face us all in the twenty-first century.

- Global poverty, hunger, disease, and unmet human life needs;
- International militarization and obscene levels of military spending;
- Unsustainable economic, political, cultural, and ecological structures of power;
- Social and economic injustice and the systematic violation of universal human rights;
- Worldwide gender inequity in the social, economic, political, legal, and religious spheres;
- Coercive violence against women and children, including the horror of children forced into combat;
- Rampant ecological degradation and disregard for the sacredness of all life;
- Intercultural and interreligious ignorance, mistrust, fear, and hatred.

We must strengthen the influence of the majority of humans that wish to live in peace. We strongly endorse efforts to combine our collective intelligence to build globalization from the bottom-up: creating a global consensus of commitment to the common good. In this way, we declare our global sovereignty and claim our global citizenship for the first time.

We urge the development of consensus for a common global action plan, beginning with a multi-stakeholder consultation process, and culminating in a common vision for ending poverty, reversing climate change, financing sustainable development, and creating structural reforms in global trade, finance, and energy policy.

As committed participants in the Globalisation for the Common Good Initiative [GCGI] we commit our individual and group support to the following:

- To create a network of organizations whose aims resonate with those of GCGI. This Internet-based network will facilitate the sharing of ideas, information, and courses of constructive action.

- To develop and maintain—on the GCGI web site and in the Journal of Globalization for the Common Good—a dynamic list of "what's working": initiatives, projects, and civil society organizations that are making a significant contribution to the common good.

- To explore ways to encourage young persons from around the world to become actively engaged with Globalisation for the Common Good. This will include participation in future conferences, international exchange programs, interreligious and intercultural study and dialogue, and other initiatives.

Globalization for the Common Good has come a long way over the past six years. Six successful conferences and an increasingly influential journal and web site mark our progress. We have cultivated a diverse group of scholars, leaders of civil society, religious and spiritual leaders, and global activists for intense explorations of a value-centered vision of globalisation and the common good. We invite all others who share our vision to join us on the path to a better global future.

**Globalisation for the Common Good, at Fatih University, Istanbul
8 July 2007**

www.globalisationforthecommongood.info

The 6th Annual International Conference on an Inter-Faith Perspective on Globalisation for the Common Good

"A Non-Violent Path to Conflict Resolution and Peacebuilding"

Istanbul, Turkey
The City of Understanding and Reconciliation
between East and West

5–9 July 2007